CW00552936

# CORBYNISM IN PERSPECTIVE

**Building Progressive Alternatives**

Series Editors: David Coates[†], Ben Rosamond and Matthew Watson

Bringing together economists, political economists and other social scientists, this series offers pathways to a coherent, credible and progressive economic growth strategy that, when accompanied by an associated set of wider public policies, can inspire and underpin the revival of a successful centre-left politics in advanced capitalist societies.

**Published**

*Corbynism in Perspective: The Labour Party under Jeremy Corbyn*
Edited by Andrew S. Roe-Crines

*Flawed Capitalism: The Anglo-American Condition and its Resolution*
David Coates

*The Political Economy of Industrial Strategy in the UK:*
*From Productivity Problems to Development Dilemmas*
Edited by Craig Berry, Julie Froud and Tom Barker

*Race and the Undeserving Poor: From Abolition to Brexit*
Robbie Shilliam

*Reflections on the Future of the Left*
Edited by David Coates

# CORBYNISM IN PERSPECTIVE

## The Labour Party under Jeremy Corbyn

EDITED BY

ANDREW S. ROE-CRINES

**agenda**
publishing

This volume is dedicated to Dr Judi Atkins, who was greatly loved by all who came into contact with her. She will be dearly missed.

© Editorial matter, introduction and selection 2021 Andrew S. Roe-Crines. Individual chapters: the contributors.

This book is in copyright under the Berne Convention.
No reproduction without permission.
All rights reserved.

First published in 2021 by Agenda Publishing

Agenda Publishing Limited
The Core
Bath Lane
Newcastle Helix
Newcastle upon Tyne
NE4 5TF
www.agendapub.com

ISBN 978-1-78821-291-5

**British Library Cataloguing-in-Publication Data**
A catalogue record for this book is available from the British Library

Typeset by Newgen Publishing UK
Printed and bound in the UK by TJ Books

# CONTENTS

# CONTRIBUTORS

**Phoenix C. S. Andrews** is a former fellow at the University of Leeds where they researched political fandom. They are also an activist for transgender rights.

**Andrew Barclay** is a research associate at the University of Sheffield on political campaigns, voting and religion.

**Mark Bennister** is Senior Lecturer in Politics at the University of Lincoln, where he researches political leadership, parliament and British politics.

**Lise Butler** is Lecturer in Modern History at City, University of London, where she researches left-wing politics. She is the author of *Michael Young, Social Science, and the British Left, 1945–1970* (2020).

**Steven Daniels** is a teaching associate at the University of Liverpool. He is currently in the process of turning his doctoral thesis on the miners into a monograph.

**Peter Dorey** is Professor of British Politics at Cardiff University and author (with Andrew S. Roe-Crines and Andrew Denham) of *Choosing Party Leaders: Britain's Conservatives and Labour Compared* (2020).

**Harry W. Fletcher** is a graduate of the University of Edinburgh where his work focused on politics and political psychology. He is now a professional humanitarian programmes officer for an INGO, working at the intersection of politics and public health.

**Mark Garnett** is Senior Lecturer in Politics at Lancaster University and author (with Robert Smith and Simon Mabon) of *British Foreign Policy Since 1945* (2017).

**Eunice Goes** is Professor of Politics at Richmond: The American International University in London and is the author of *The Labour Party under Ed Miliband: Trying but Failing to Renew Social Democracy* (2016).

**Emily Harmer** is Lecturer in Media and Communication at the University of Liverpool and has written a series of academic journal articles on the subject of gender in politics.

**Timothy Heppell** is Associate Professor of British Politics at the University of Leeds and the author of *Cameron: The Politics of Modernisation and Manipulation* (2019).

**David Jeffery** is Lecturer in British Politics at the University of Liverpool and co-editor (with Antony Mullen) of *Thatcherism Today: The Social and Cultural Legacy of Thatcherism in the 21st Century* (2020).

**Richard Johnson** is a Lecturer in the School of Politics and International Relations at Queen Mary University of London. He is the author of *Camaraderie: One Hundred Years of the Cambridge Labour Party* (2012, with Ashley Walsh), *The End of the Second Reconstruction* (2020) and *US Foreign Policy* (2021).

**Peter Kerr** is Senior Lecturer in Politics at the University of Birmingham and has written several articles on British politics.

**Thomas McMeeking** is a Teaching Fellow in British Politics at the University of Leeds. He is the author of *The Political Leadership of Prime Minister John Major* (2020).

**Glen O'Hara** is Professor of Modern and Contemporary History at Oxford Brookes University and is the author of *The Politics of Water in Post-War Britain* (2017).

**Andrew S. Roe-Crines** is Senior Lecturer in British Politics at the University of Liverpool and is the author/editor of several academic journal articles and books.

**Rosalynd Southern** is Lecturer in Political Communication at the University of Liverpool. Her research focuses on online political communication, particularly during election campaigns in the UK. She is also the author of a large number of academic journal articles.

**Bradley Ward** is a doctoral candidate at the University of Birmingham, where he is researching a thesis entitled "A Party Within A Party? An Ethnographic Account of Momentum".

**Ben Worthy** is Senior Lecturer in Politics at Birkbeck, University of London and is the author of *The Politics of Freedom of Information: How and Why Governments Pass Laws that Threaten their Power* (2017).

1

# INTRODUCTION: "OH, JEREMY CORBYN!" THE MISSION TO RENEW LABOUR

*Andrew S. Roe-Crines*

Jeremy Corbyn is likely to remain an important figure in Labour Party politics, even after his tenure as its leader. Partly because as a backbencher, he is still able to inform debates not just within the Labour Party but in British politics more broadly. He still attracts (virtual and live) audiences and media attention, for good or ill, not least as the ex-party leader, but also as a controversial figure within the labour movement. Moreover, Corbyn's time in office exposed the schisms within the party, provoking a debate at the heart of social democracy over its future and relevance in the twenty-first century. This volume presents a timely collection of essays on a range of issues relevant to understanding Corbyn as a politician and as a leader and Corbynism as a project and as a progressive alternative.

Following a damaging defeat in the general election under Ed Miliband, Labour's search for a new leader culminated in the surprise election of Jeremy Corbyn after an energetic, lively and optimistic leadership campaign in 2015. During the leadership election he:

> attacked the failures of capitalism for placing individualism ahead of the needs of the collective good; for creating a hugely unequal society; and for using war for the benefit of capitalistic goals. He also pledged to apologise for the Iraq War; argued Tony Blair should face legal action in the event that the delayed Chilcot inquiry places sufficient blame on the former Prime minister; and called for the removal of Trident.
>
> (Crines 2015)

This was a thoroughly left-leaning agenda, which chimed with some audiences across the country as authentic. At the start of the campaign, few expected Corbyn to win; by the end, many were surprised, especially those Labour MPs who had nominated Corbyn simply to expand the debate within the leadership election (Denham, Roe-Crines & Dorey 2020). As leader, he would have to defend his position from continual critique from his own backbenchers, including a formal leadership challenge by Owen Smith in 2016. Yet he remained in place and led the Labour Party into the 2017 general election, not only increasing the number of MPs but securing the largest vote share since the second Blair land-slide of 2001 and one of the best by any European social democratic party since the turn of the century. This was a significant achievement for a leader under considerable internal pressure.

There can be little doubt that Corbyn and his campaign team transformed the debate about what the Labour Party should stand for in the twenty-first century. Corbyn represented a break not just from a certain style of profession-alized Labour leader, but also from the ideological assumptions that had been consolidated within the party since Neil Kinnock's modernization agenda of the 1980s (Cronin 2004). These ideas embedded themselves at the top of the parlia-mentary Labour Party (hereafter PLP) throughout the 1990s, particularly under Tony Blair and Gordon Brown, who accepted the basic tenets of free-market capitalism as a means of funding limited redistributive policies as part of the Third Way approach. Granted, Ed Miliband's leadership drew a thin line under this embrace of free-market egalitarianism under the moniker of "One Nation Labour" (Crines & Hayton 2011), but the election of Jeremy Corbyn began the process of putting the state back at the heart of economic management and social policy. It was an exciting time for the Left in British politics, which was galvanized by the optimism of Corbyn's leadership campaign with the aim of changing the debate, not just within the Labour Party but in the country and across Europe more broadly.

The purpose of this book is to look at those ideas and to determine the extent to which Corbyn's time in office was successful in representing a wholesale re-evaluation of social democracy, socialism and left-wing politics in the United Kingdom. Corbyn's legacy is explored in more detail in the following chapters, in a systematic evaluation of Corbyn and Corbynism.

Before proceeding, however, it is worth remembering that Labour as a move-ment has always consisted of various groupings and factions (as well as the PLP). Indeed, as far back as its foundation, the Labour Representation Committee was a group with no single leader, relying simply on a chairperson (Ramsay MacDonald) to represent its groups (Thorpe 2008). From this, the Labour Party emerged with a wide range of different groups such as the Fabian Society, the Independent Labour Party and the Social Democratic Federation, who met with trade union leaders to create the new party to secure representation for the interests of their members in parliament. Throughout its subsequent history, the Labour Party retained connections with organizations and groups that repre-sented those Labour members within the movement both through the party con-ference and in the Commons. For example, Tony Benn's "Campaign for Labour

Party Democracy" was motivated by the desire to provide a stronger voice for the members in policy formulation through the conference (Kogan & Kogan 2018). Intellectual publications such as *Tribune* aimed to discuss ideas that could ultimately help inform the direction of the party in securing greater socialist change. Moreover, the "Rank and File Mobilizing Committee" sought to democratize the party to give members a voice in who represented them in parliament (Heppell & Crines 2011; for further antecedents to Corbynism see Seyd 1987). In the modern Labour Party, comparable groups such as Labour First, Labour for a Common Good, Progress, Left Futures, Labour Together, Saving Labour and Open Labour seek to follow a similar path in informing the ideological trajectory of the party to reflect the aims and ambitions of the membership(s). There is nothing unusual about various groups comprising the labour movement beyond the parliamentary party. Indeed, the Labour Party was comprised of similar groups throughout its history, including when it formed the welfare state under Clement Attlee's leadership, when it founded the Open University under Harold Wilson's leadership (Crines 2014) and when it ushered in the New Labour era under Blair and Brown, who introduced the minimum wage and devolution. Consequently, Corbyn's aims to connect the Labour leadership with the membership through groups such as Momentum is consistent not just with Labour history but also with the long-standing and current machinery of party governance.

## The Labour leadership of Jeremy Corbyn

So, why did Jeremy Corbyn stand for the leadership? Put simply, there has always been tradition of a left-wing candidate being fielded for leadership elections to offer a broad debate, and his nomination was initially intended to fulfil this purpose. The other candidates each represented (to varying degrees) an extension of the professionalized Labour leadership to follow Miliband, with no voice from the left of the party, which Corbyn believed still had a role to play in developing and growing the Labour Party (The World Tonight 2015). During the campaign, he sought to stand on a "clear anti-austerity platform" because "we are not doing celebrity, personality or abusive politics [because] this is about hope" for those impacted by government policy (Watt 2015). Indeed, he characterized Miliband's response to austerity during the 2015 general election as simply "austerity-lite". Fundamental to understanding his opposition to long-standing Labour attitudes towards the economy was his belief that "the economy is growing very unevenly on a regional basis, where wage levels are significantly lower in the east Midlands and the northeast compared to London and the southeast. In turn, it is growing unevenly because of unequal investments in infrastructure" (Corbyn 2015a).

3

For Corbyn, the purpose of the economy is to ensure equality of outcome, rather than simply equality of opportunity. To achieve this, the state needs to take not just a regulatory role but also an interventionist approach to shifting investment towards services and industries that provide a social function. By doing so, Corbyn believes these inequalities will be reversed. His candidature for the leadership represented something of an opportunity for Labour to retreat from the acceptance of free-market economics of *The Third Way* (Giddens 1998) and to embrace instead a more egalitarian approach to economic management and the creation of a fairer society.

He also argued that he would promise to re-examine Britain's role in the world more broadly by "seeking to withdraw from NATO" and review the Trident missile system (Corbyn 2015a). Simply promising to break with the acceptance of austerity by the other candidates and to commit Labour policy to peace was sufficient to galvanize the Left and shift support in his direction. Critics of Corbyn asked why it was necessary to change the relationship with NATO. Corbyn argued that "NATO was a Cold War institution. It has given itself quite extraordinary powers of insisting on 2% defence expenditure of all its member states" and that "there has got to be some serious discussions about de-escalating the military crisis in central Europe. NATO expansion and Russian expansion – one leads to the other, and one reflects the other" (Corbyn 2015).

Over the course of the leadership election, he continued to present himself as "just an ordinary person trying to do an ordinary job" (Corbyn 2015a). Corbyn's ideas attracted considerable support, with venues packed out across the UK in cities such as Liverpool (Crines 2015). Such was the surge of support for Corbyn relative to the other candidates for the Labour leadership (Andy Burnham, Yvette Cooper and Liz Kendall), that he reflected:

> it has grown a lot faster than anyone could have understood or predicted or expected. But it has shown that there is such latent good, such latent enthusiasm, such latent optimism in people. This is a positive process. It is not negative. We are looking to do things rather than stop others doing things.                    (Corbyn 2015a)

For Corbyn, his campaign was about presenting a hopeful vision of an alternative, new way of approaching how society functioned as a whole. This hopeful message inspired those seeking a better future together under the banner of Corbynism. This was evidenced in the surge in party membership during the campaign, as party-less groups and individuals flocked to the hope of the first opportunity for a left-wing leader of the Labour Party since Michael Foot.

So, why did it happen in 2015? Corbyn argues it was because "the mood is there and we happen to be in the middle of it" (Corbyn 2015a). For him, this was not simply a "blip" in Labour history or a response to domestic policy. Rather, the move towards the left was part of:

> equivalent movements across Europe, the USA and elsewhere. It's been bubbling for a long time. It is opposition to economic orthodoxy that leads us into austerity and cuts. But it is also a thirst for something more communal, more participative. That, to me, is what is interesting in this process. (Corbyn 2015a)

For Corbyn, his support was reflected by equivalent movements that had emerged in Europe with parties such as Syriza, the emergence of Bernie Sanders in the US and a general sense of disaffection with the free-market economic orthodoxy which had come to dominate policy formulation in the UK. Needless to say, others within the Labour Party disagreed with Corbyn's assessment, but for him, this was a debate in which he and other parties were on the winning side. Indeed, on those who disagreed with his arguments and beliefs, he argued that "there has to be an open debate in the party and so I have suggested we do a number of open conventions on the economy, the environment, the constitution, social and foreign policies" (Corbyn 2015a). By putting forward this suggestion, Corbyn was extending an invitation to long-standing mainstream Labour figures to challenge him on his positions in a respectful and dignified manner, while also highlighting the areas of prime concern to his transformative agenda, that is, the economy, environmental policy, constitutional reform, social and foreign policy. Such is the significance of these themes that many are discussed in this book.

## A labour movement for change: Corbynmania

Corbyn emerged during the leadership campaign and over the course of his leadership as an inspirational figurehead for the labour movement for change. His support was bolstered by an influx of new members and the emergence of the phenomenon known as "Corbynmania". It is also worth remembering that "popular leftism became less episodic and more consolidated, such that the years 2015–19 marked a reconstitution of left politics' status, impact and visibility within mainstream politics, culture and public life" (Dean 2020: 7). Indeed, a long-standing demonstration of support quickly emerged in the chanting of "Oh, Jeremy Corbyn!", which became something of an anthem for members to show their support at key events or moments of difficulty. This chant (drawn from "Seven Nation Army" by The White Stripes) was also heard during his famous address at the Glastonbury Festival in 2017. The crowd chanted his name as he waited for the moment to speak. Indeed, the chanting became louder and longer as Corbyn waited. He reflected on this to the Glastonbury founder (Michael Eavis) saying "Michael, you brought the spirit of music, of love, of ideas, and of great messages" (Corbyn 2017), after which he gave Eavis a copy of the Labour manifesto. Glastonbury represented a key moment in demonstrating Corbyn's appeal to younger audiences. This was, for Dean, a "testament to this apparent convergence of left politics and mainstream popular culture" (Dean 2020: 8). Much has also been made of the "Youthquake" at the 2017 general election (Cain 2017). Events such as Glastonbury helped demonstrate Corbyn's appeal to the potential new voters that Labour needed to secure office. When addressing the crowd, he argued "politics is actually about everyday life. It's about all of us: what we dream, what we want, what we achieve and what we want for everybody else" (Corbyn 2017a). The crowd again erupted into cheers. Moreover, it was an opportunity for him to articulate his ideas and motivations further, by arguing that "politics is about the lives of all of us. The wonderful campaign I was a part of and led, brought people back to politics because they believed there was something on offer for them" (Corbyn 2017a). There was also a sense that Labour had found a possible course to electoral "recovery" from 2015.

This was Corbyn at the top of his political game, particularly given that he had confounded the expectations of political commentators by increasing the number of Labour MPs during the 2017 general election, thereby solidifying his position further. When explaining how he had successfully motivated youthful audiences and deprived Theresa May of her majority, he reflected that "I do what I believe in, I try to promote what I believe in and change things in politics, and I'm happy to be a part of that change" (Corbyn 2017a). For him, Corbynism was a movement aimed at younger members of society who have the opportunity to forge new perspectives on how the country can be governed, with greater emphases on care, solidarity and fairness. When asked how this can be achieved, he concluded that it's "about changing the political atmosphere" (Corbyn 2017). This harks back to his original arguments for standing as the Labour leader in 2015 – put simply, to inspire hope of a change in direction, which by 2017 had begun to seem like a real possibility for British politics.

As a fundamental point, however, we need to ask where Corbynism (and Corbynmania) emanates from, and whether it represented a genuine change in attitudes. There is little doubting the authenticity of Corbyn as an individual who truly believes in radical socialist change, but who were his supporters?

Corbynmania was driven by those attending the large events and campaign rallies, who believe(d) the message Corbyn was delivering. Indeed, he argued that "all over the country we are getting these huge gatherings of people. The young, the old, black and white and many people that haven't been involved in politics before" (Corbyn 2015b). Also, it is important to acknowledge the importance of Corbyn's leadership team: John McDonnell, Diane Abbott, Rebecca Long-Bailey, Jonathan Ashworth, Richard Burgon and Dawn Butler, each fiercely loyal to Corbyn and his vision. McDonnell, in particular, was (and remains) a key ally of Corbyn and his ideas. As shadow chancellor, McDonnell spearheaded the key ideas and policies under the umbrella of "Corbynomics" to counter the austerity policies of the government (McDonnell 2007). Each member of the team fed into his communications strategy by making speeches in support of Corbynism, while contributing their own perspectives on what Corbynism stood for and why it was relevant. During his speech to the 2019 party conference, McDonnell, for example, reflected on the horrors of the Hillsborough disaster, how the working classes across the UK have been treated, and also the role Corbyn played:

> This election campaign began for me in Liverpool, the city of my birth. Only last week, the people of that city were forced to relive again the trauma of the Hillsborough Disaster. The memory of a previous Conservative government and how it treated the North, Midlands, Wales and Scotland – football fans, and the working class. I remember the Hillsborough Tragedy like it was yesterday. I remember the brave campaigners who have fought for justice ever since. And I remember how my best friend, Jeremy Corbyn, one of the bravest of politicians, stood up for them, fighting for justice for those denied it.
>
> (McDonnell 2019)

This reflection emphasizes Corbyn's long history as a campaigner for social justice and how his role within Labour politics has been about defending those on the receiving end of unjust government policies. Indeed, his opposition to the Poll Tax, to military action in the Middle East and to the exploitation of communities, and his support for the Campaign for Nuclear Disarmament (CND) represented significant ballasts of his rhetorical persona. A key objective of Corbynism (broadly defined as a set of ideas and beliefs around egalitarianism and social justice that inform left-leaning policy formulation/application) would be embedding changes to the nature of the state both in domestic and foreign policy. The question remained, however, whether he would be able to convince the voters to support the ideas he had campaigned for all his political life.

## Jeremy Corbyn: a prime minister in waiting?

The problem for Corbyn was the characterization of the "hard left" as a negative force, both in the UK and across Europe. Ideologically, both David Butler and Dennis Kavanagh (1997) had characterized Corbyn as hard left. When asked by Andrew Marr whether he was a hard-left Marxist, Corbyn responded by saying, "that is a very interesting question actually. I haven't thought about that for a long time. I haven't really read as much of Marx as we [*sic*] should have done. I have read quite a bit but not that much" (Corbyn 2015c). Here Corbyn eschews the label because it has taken on a negative definition relative to other political ideologies. This characterization of the hard left has been driven through years of political reform and changes to how ideas are articulated in British politics, with the underlying assumption that centrist policies denoted the optimum position to be in, and that deviation (to either the left or the right) would be a negative trajectory. This was because some parliamentarians may "not accept that the more leftist membership had chosen a leader that the PLP did not ideologically approve of" (Crines, Jeffery & Heppell 2017). Hence when he asked whether Corbyn was a Marxist, Marr was seeking to determine whether he sat inside or outside of that ideological orthodoxy. In the same interview, Corbyn went on to say he had also read Adam Smith and David Ricardo, yet it is the association with Marx that represented the perception of negativity.

This characterization, however, is based mostly on the fear of what Corbyn "might" have done, rather than the policies that he and the Labour Party sought to advance. It is to be noted that "For The Many, Not The Few" is a slogan devised during the Blair/Brown years (Labour Manifesto 1997), whereas much of the 2017 election manifesto (which also informed the 2019 manifesto) was ideologically consistent with the one presented by Miliband in 2015. For example, the proposed ban on zero-hour contracts (Labour Manifesto 2017: 27), reversal of the Conservatives' reforms of the NHS (Labour Manifesto 2017: 34) and greater emphasis to the point of parity on physical and mental health (Labour Manifesto 2017: 35) were all features of both manifestos. Moreover, each contained commitments to expanding social housing, alongside greater spending plans on infrastructure (Labour Manifesto 2015, 2017). These policies have much in common with traditional social democracy; indeed, a criticism could be that they did not fully deliver on the radicalism that some (even opponents) may have anticipated from a prospective Corbyn-led government. The Corbynism that was put to the voters cannot be described as "hard left". This does not mean to say it would not represent a significant departure from the free-market orthodoxy of the post-Thatcher, post-Blair Labour Party. However, it was a long way from the wholesale re-evaluation of society that had been predicted. Despite this, "the BBC, along with broadsheet newspapers, drew on the generally accepted judgement of the

Institute for Fiscal Studies, whose spokesman claimed that Labour's plans were 'simply not credible'" (Allen & Moon 2020), thereby characterizing the manifesto(s) to voters as being essentially unworkable.

An area of debate that is explored in later chapters is the extent to which Corbyn saw his leadership as an opportunity to convince others of his views, thereby inspiring a younger generation of socialists, or whether he sought the office of prime minister. To some extent the answer is that there is nothing mutually exclusive about putting forward big ideas about the country, while seeking prime-ministerial office. This point is noted by Rose's evaluation of the purpose of a political party, saying, "British parties have many functions beside that of supporting competing teams of leaders at general election" and that "in the Labour Party, there have always been some who have rejected electoral success as an irrelevant standard by which to determine party actions" (Rose 1964). However, MPs tend towards the belief that the leader of the opposition should seek to deprive the government of office in favour of bringing their own party to political power. Indeed, as seen earlier in this introduction, Corbyn already had a degree of power over those he had inspired. Consequently, if his objective was to inspire a new generation of socialists then he broadly succeeded. This increases the chances of future political activists who share Corbyn's idealism successfully securing the leadership in the future, and potentially even the office of prime minister.

It is worth noting, however, that events still play a key role, and two in particular blocked Corbyn's path to power. Corbyn's style and idealism prevented him from exercising the necessary authority and leadership skills as he was driven to find consensus among his leadership team, whose differing perspectives could not be reconciled. Brexit gridlocked political debate to the point where it dominated the discourse, shutting down opportunities to raise any other issues on which Corbyn had views. Brexit became all-consuming, with both the Labour Party and the Conservative Party unable to produce a resolution (see Chapter 11). Furthermore, antisemitism quickly became a problem for Corbyn as an individual, because his response was seen at best as inadequate, if not making things much worse (see Chapter 14). In combination, these issues derailed the optimism and support that Corbyn inspired in 2015 and at the 2017 general election.

## The themes and prospects of Corbynism

The contributors to this volume each evaluate a different aspect of Jeremy Corbyn and his leadership to allow us to position him within the broader political context of the Labour Party and, in turn, British politics. Each chapter initiates a discussion on Corbyn and Corbynism with the aim of understanding his impact on left-wing politics in the UK and beyond. For example, his beliefs and ideology, his attitudes towards state management of the economy, foreign policy, social policy, gendered politics, antisemitism and his fandoms. Each chapter presents a series of academically informed arguments to interrogate Corbynism as an ideology and also Corbyn himself as a political leader.

Why are these important? They remain relevant to our understanding of Corbyn's time as leader and how Corbynism as a concept may continue as a force in British politics. Indeed, today Corbyn remains an important figure in Labour (and left-wing) politics because of the impact he made as leader and the policies and ideas that he brought into the political arena again. The unexpected Covid-19 crisis has also produced a set of political circumstances where voters have demanded and become accustomed to state intervention in the economy, social policy and even individual liberties in a way that seemed absurd during the period of Corbyn's leadership. This poses a few questions for the future of both the Labour Party and Corbynism as an ideology.

Following the immediacy of the crisis, the process of post-pandemic social and economic reconstruction will be informed by those who are able to present their ideas most clearly and credibly to voters and policy-makers. This is an opportunity for Corbynism as an ideology aimed at increasing the role of the state as an active actor to be re-invented and re-articulated as a cohesive package of measures for economic reconstruction. Indeed, as we have seen, the Conservatives have also embraced elements of state intervention in areas such as nationalization of rail franchises. Those who lead that debate will ultimately have the opportunity to reshape not just the UK economy but also assumptions about economic management across the West. With populations receptive to state management of the crisis, it is likely they would be receptive to state management of the recovery. The question remains, however, whether Corbynism as an ideology can inform those discussions through the next generation of left-wing leaders, because the issue remains of who will lead those arguments in the current Labour Party.

## Conclusions: the continuation of Corbynism?

Corbynism as an ideological perspective remains relevant despite Corbyn's return to the backbenches. This is because it textures the debates and arguments about how Labour can respond to the 2019 election defeat, Brexit and the Covid-19 pandemic. Each of these challenges pose opportunities for a left-wing revival if the ideals underscore the solutions in a way that addresses real-world concerns.

However, it is important not to forget that Corbyn inspired many in 2015, which led to a significant growth in membership. Many of those who joined after 2015 remained steadfast throughout Corbyn's leadership and remain loyal to his ideals even after Labour's defeat in 2019, despite some choosing to leave the party after the election. In spite of this upsurge in left-wing membership, the Labour Party entered the general election(s) under Corbyn's leadership with policies that were largely consistent with what had gone before. The radicalism that opponents argued made Corbynism was absent from the policies and proposals Labour put forward to voters. In 2017 they were sufficient to grow the number of MPs and secure one of the largest vote shares in Europe, whereas in 2019 the same policies led the Labour Party to defeat. The conclusion? That it was Corbyn who lost Labour the election, not the policies he and others advocated. The policies themselves were largely supported by voters, as seen in 2017, yet it was the broader context of the 2019 election (on issues such as Brexit and antisemitism) that harmed Labour's electoral performance. This is not to understate the challenge Labour faces today, but it does suggest that without Brexit framing political debates and with the antisemitism crisis in retreat, the Labour leadership may be able to convince voters to lend them their support once more.

Finally, the issue of Covid-19 and its economic impact has presented an opportunity for Labour politicians to argue that the hand of the state has a role in services beyond its current remit. Indeed, the Conservatives have not retreated from using the state to fund schemes such as furlough, so the Labour Party would be likely to use it for reconstruction. It is likely that by doing so Labour may address Dean's assertion that "there is considerable uncertainty as to the future of left politics in the United Kingdom" (Dean 2020: 2) by providing certainty. This is because vital services need to be protected in an economy that (at the time of writing) has ceased to function. The areas that are able to operate include the provision of food supply chains, broadband (given more people are likely to continue working from home post-Covid-19), the Royal Mail, utilities and public health. These represent key sectors that, the current and the next generation of left-wing advocates could argue, require state ownership (not simply management) because they are the foundation of the economy. As such, those who remain inspired by Corbyn have the opportunity to put Corbynism as an ideology in action if they are able to capture the momentum of the post-Covid-19 economic reconstruction debates. It is hoped that this volume may act as a starting point in debating Corbyn's legacy for Corbynism and the future of politics more broadly, both in the UK and beyond.

# References

Allen, P. & D. Moon 2020. "Predictions, pollification, and pol profs: the 'Corbyn problem' beyond Corbyn". *Political Quarterly* 91(1): 80–88.

Butler, D. & D. Kavanagh 1997. *The British General Election of 1997*. Basingstoke: Palgrave Macmillan.

Cain, S. 2017. "Youthquake named 2017 word of the year by Oxford Dictionaries". *The Guardian*, 15 December. https://www.theguardian.com/books/2017/dec/15/youthquake-named-2017-word-of-the-year-by-oxford-dictionaries (accessed 12 March 2021).

Corbyn, J. 2015a. "Interview with Jeremy Corbyn". *The Guardian*, 7 August. https://www.theguardian.com/politics/2015/aug/07/jeremy-corbyn-interview-we-are-not-doing-celebrity-personality-or-abusive-politics (accessed 12 March 2021).

Corbyn, J. 2015b. "Where is Labour's Jeremy Corbyn mania coming from?" *BBC News*, 13 August. https://www.bbc.co.uk/news/uk-politics-33881104 (accessed 12 March 2021).

Corbyn, J. 2015c. Interview, *The Andrew Marr Show*, BBC. 26 January.

Corbyn, J. 2017a. "Jeremy Corbyn calls for unity in Glastonbury speech". *The Guardian*, 24 June. Available at: https://www.theguardian.com/music/2017/jun/24/jeremy-corbyn-calls-for-unity-in-glastonbury-speech (accessed 12 March 2021).

Crines, A. 2014. "Revisiting the Wilsonian language of renewal". *Renewal: Journal of Social Democracy* 22: 128–34.

Crines, A. 2015. "Jeremy Corbyn's rhetoric is effective because his style of engagement contrasts so markedly with the other candidates". *Democratic Audit*, 6 August. https://www.democraticaudit.com/2015/08/06/jeremy-corbyns-rhetoric-is-effective-because-his-style-of-engagement-contrasts-so-markedly-with-the-other-candidates/ (accessed 12 March 2021).

Crines, A. & R. Hayton 2011. *Labour Orators from Bevan to Miliband*. Manchester: Manchester University Press.

Crines, A., D. Jeffery & T. Heppell 2017. "The British Labour Party and the leadership election mandate(s) of Jeremy Corbyn: patterns of opinion and opposition within the parliamentary Labour Party". *Journal of Elections, Public Opinion and Parties* 28(3): 361–79.

Cronin, J. 2004. *New Labour's Pasts: The Labour Party and Its Discontents*. Harlow: Pearson Longman.

Dean, J. 2020. "Left politics and popular culture in Britain: from left-wing populism to popular leftism". *Politics*, online. https://doi.org/10.1177/0263395720960661.

Denham, A., A. Roe-Crines & P. Dorey 2020. *Choosing Party Leaders*. Manchester: Manchester University Press.

Giddens, A. 1998. *The Third Way: The Renewal of Social Democracy*. Cambridge: Polity.

Heppell, T. & A. Crines 2011. "How Michael Foot won the Labour Party leadership". *Political Quarterly* 82(1): 81–94.

Kogan, D. & K. Kogan 2018. *The Battle for the Labour Party*. London: Bloomsbury.

Labour Manifesto 1997. *New Labour Because Britain Deserves Better*. http://www.labour-party.org.uk/manifestos/1997/1997-labour-manifesto.shtml (accessed 12 March 2021).

Labour Manifesto 2015. *The Labour Party Manifesto*. https://action.labour.org.uk/page/-/A4%20BIG%20_PRINT_ENG_LABOUR%20MANIFESTO_TEXT%20LAYOUT.pdf (accessed 12 March 2021).

Labour Manifesto 2017. *For the Many, Not the Few*. https://labour.org.uk/wp-content/uploads/2017/10/labour-manifesto-2017.pdf (accessed 12 March 2021).

McDonnell, J. 2007. *Another World is Possible: A Manifesto for 21st Century Socialism*. London: Labour Representation Committee.

McDonnell, J. 2019. "John McDonnell full speech: Labour – laying the foundations of a new economy – real change that works for the many". *The Labour Party*, 4 December. https://labour.org.uk/press/john-mcdonnell-full-speech-labour-laying-the-foundations-of-a-new-economy-real-change-that-works-for-the-many/ (accessed 12 March 2021).

Rose, R. 1964. "Parties, factions, and tendencies in Britain". *Political Studies* 12(1): 33–46.

Seyd, P. 1987. *The Rise and Fall of the Labour Left*. Basingstoke: Macmillan.

Thorpe, A. 2008. *A History of the British Labour Party*. Basingstoke: Palgrave Macmillan.

Watt, N. 2015. "Interview with Jeremy Corbyn". *The Guardian*, 7 August. https://www.theguardian.com/politics/2015/aug/07/jeremy-corbyn-interview-we-are-not-doing-celebrity-personality-or-abusive-politics (accessed 12 March 2021).

The World Tonight 2015. BBC Radio, 2 June.

## 2

# THE ELECTION AND RE-ELECTION OF JEREMY CORBYN AS LEADER OF THE LABOUR PARTY

*Timothy Heppell and Thomas McMeeking*

The position of leader of the Labour Party was formally established in 1922[1] and Jeremy Corbyn became the fourteenth individual, excluding temporary acting leaders, to hold that office when he won the leadership election of 2015. Of the previous 13 holders, six – Ramsay MacDonald (1922–31) Clement Attlee (1935–55), Harold Wilson (1963–76), James Callaghan (1976–80), Tony Blair (1994–2007) and Gordon Brown (2007–10) – would also serve as Labour prime ministers. Of the seven who led the Labour Party but failed to serve as prime minister, two – Hugh Gaitskell (1955–63) and John Smith (1992–94) – were Labour leaders of the opposition who held a lead in the opinion polls and seemed on course to become prime minister, only to pass away suddenly. The remaining five who failed to serve as prime minister were Arthur Henderson (1931–32), George Lansbury (1932–35), Michael Foot (1980–83), Neil Kinnock (1983–92) and Ed Miliband (2010–15).

Miliband joined the list of Labour Party leaders who failed to become prime minister because of the poor performance of the party in the general election of 2015, which prompted his resignation. When Miliband acquired the leadership in September 2010, the Labour Party had recently lost the general election of May 2010 on the back of securing 8,606,518 votes and a 29.0 per cent vote share, which resulted in them securing 258 parliamentary seats, leaving them in opposition to a Conservative–Liberal Democrat coalition (Kavanagh & Cowley 2010: 350–51). The failure of the Miliband opposition era was confirmed at the general election of 2015, when their parliamentary representation went down from 258 to 232 seats (-26), even if in terms of votes cast and vote share there

---

1. Between the general election of 1906, when the Labour Party first secured parliamentary representation, and the general election of 1922, the leadership of the Labour Party was granted to the chair of the parliamentary Labour Party. After the general election of 1922 the positions of the chair and the leader of the parliamentary Labour Party were officially combined (Stark 1996: 14).

was evidence of a limited recovery – they secured 9,347,273 votes on a 30.4 per cent vote share (Cowley & Kavanagh 2015: 433; on the Miliband opposition era, see Bale 2015, Goes 2016).

Miliband had won the leadership of the Labour Party via the Electoral College system of leadership selection. The Electoral College was a one-member-one-vote system, but it had a tripartite structure with one-third weight given to each of the following: (a) the PLP plus Labour members of the European Parliament; (b) individual Labour Party members from constituency associations; and (c) members of trade unions and affiliated societies. Relative to the old parliamentarians-only ballot system for selection that existed until 1981, it amounted to democratization, but it did nonetheless retain significant leverage for parliamentarians. They retained one-third of the overall vote; they determined the nomination process (and could screen out unacceptable candidates) and it was they who retained control over the challenger provision (Quinn 2012: 31–96).

One of the weaknesses of the Electoral College was that it created the possibility that they could select a leader with a disputed mandate, which was the case with Miliband. He was the first preference of the trade union and affiliated societies tranche of the Electoral College by a large enough margin (119,405 votes to 80,266 votes or 59.8 to 40.2 per cent) to provide him with an overall victory over his brother of 50.65 to 49.35 per cent, despite the fact that David Miliband was the first preference among MPs and MEPs (140 to 122 votes or 53.4 to 46.6 per cent) and among Labour Party members (66,814 votes to 55,992 votes or 54.4 to 45.6 per cent) (Dorey & Denham 2011). Conservatives argued that not only was Ed Miliband the second preference in all of the eliminative ballots until the final ballot, but that he was only selected at the behest of the trade union tranche, thus playing into the "Red Ed" lurch to the left narrative that they thought would be electorally helpful to them (Heppell & Hill 2012: 211–12).

The issue of a disputed mandate, and the perception that he was in the pocket of the unions, aligned to negative media coverage about excessive trade union influence in parliamentary candidate selection, resulted in Miliband deciding to re-examine the party–union link by initiating a review process to be headed by Ray Collins, the former Labour Party general secretary. His findings and recommendations, published as the Collins Report (2014), were endorsed by 68 to 32 per cent of delegates at a special conference held in March 2014 (Bale 2015: 218). This would result in a change to the rules for selecting the Labour Party leader. The tripartite Electoral College was removed and a new true one-person-one-vote system was created. Three types of voters would now exist: party members, affiliated trade unionists and registered supporters. The registered supporters' category allowed those who were not members or trade unionists, but were sympathetic to the aims of the Labour Party, to pay a small fee to permit their participation in the leadership election. Without the aforementioned weightings of the

Electoral College, it meant a new registered supporter held the same influence in the process as a Labour parliamentarian (Quinn 2018). A system that diluted the influence of parliamentarians was a system that would aid the chances of an outsider, although this was not immediately evident.

## Electing Corbyn: the Labour Party leadership election of 2015

When Corbyn stood for the leadership of the Labour Party in 2015, he was viewed as a 100–1 outsider with bookmakers (Cowley & Kavanagh 2018: 68–9). At the early stage of the leadership election, it was not even clear that he would be able to pass the nomination threshold that would enable him to participate in the leadership ballot; this was set at 15 per cent of the PLP, which had 232 members, so the threshold was 35 nominations. It initially looked as if he was to experience the same fate as his ally, John McDonnell, when he had stood for the leadership of the Labour Party in 2007 (Heppell 2010a: 188). Operating under the old nomination rules, which at that time required the support of 12.5 per cent of the PLP, McDonnell secured only 8.2 per cent and 29 votes, which was short of the 45 needed, and with Brown securing the backing of 313 of his fellow parliamentarians, Brown automatically became the new party leader as he was the only candidate to pass the nomination threshold (Heppell 2010a: 188). However, that the Electoral College was not activated was seen to be undemocratic, as he was not formally endorsed or legitimized by all tranches of the Electoral College (Quinn 2012: 57–97).

Ultimately, Corbyn only passed the threshold because he was *lent* nominations by parliamentarians who did not want him to become their new leader, but did want to provide an ideological choice to their new electorate (Quinn 2018: 478). This mattered to social democratic Labour parliamentarians because it was certain (so they thought) that Corbyn would be defeated, but by his participating and being defeated it would reaffirm their continued dominance over the Labour Party (Seymour 2016: 16–19). They assumed that the Corbyn candidature would mirror that of Diane Abbott in the Labour Party leadership election of 2010. Abbott was also lent votes by Labour parliamentarians who did not want her to win, but who wanted ideological choice (and diversity) within the Electoral College (Dorey & Denham 2011: 295). The nomination threshold in the Labour Party leadership election of 2010 was 33 (i.e. 12.5 per cent of the then 258-strong PLP) and Abbott secured exactly 33 nominations (as did Ed Balls and Andy Burnham), but she was way behind the Miliband brothers on 63 nominations (Ed) and 81 nominations (David) (Dorey & Denham 2011: 295). Once the Electoral College was activated Abbott was the first to be eliminated; she secured the support of 7.4 per cent of the Electoral College, which was broken down into 7.3 per cent of the constituency Labour Party (CLP) tranche, 12.3 per cent of the affiliated members but only 2.6 per cent of the PLP tranche (or just seven of her fellow parliamentarians) (Pemberton & Wickham-Jones 2013: 714–17).

The first stage of the Labour Party leadership election of 2015 resembled earlier leadership elections under the now defunct Electoral College system, that is, candidates had to secure the pre-requisite number of nominations (35) from within the PLP. Four candidates passed the nomination threshold – Andy Burnham (68), Yvette Cooper (59), Liz Kendall (41) and Corbyn (36)[2] – while 26 parliamentarians did not nominate any candidate (Quinn 2016: 763). The four candidates provided parliamentarians with a clear ideological choice and two of them – Burnham and Cooper – had significant ministerial experience from the Blair and Brown administrations and had held senior positions within the Miliband shadow cabinet. While both of them were identifiable with traditional social democratic tradition, or the "old right", Kendall was more aligned with the Blairite or "new right" faction. Unlike Burnham and Cooper, Kendall could not offer ministerial experience as she had only entered parliament in 2010, whereas Corbyn had no ministerial or shadow frontbench experience, despite having been a parliamentarian for 32 years (Dorey & Denham 2016: 268–71).

However, during the campaigning period Corbyn was able to turn this apparent outside status – supposedly a disadvantage – into an advantage. He was able to present himself as an anti-establishment candidate, who could challenge the so-called Westminster elite, and his long-standing disassociation from the two great failings of the New Labour era – the Iraq intervention and the deregulated banking sector, which contributed to the financial crash – worked to his advantage (McAnulla 2011; Heppell 2013; Dorey & Denham 2016; Quinn 2016). Corbyn also presented himself as the antithesis of how mainstream political elites did politics. As the campaign unfolded, he remained unfailingly polite to the other candidates and refused to engage in personal attacks and the negativity associated with traditional politics (Goes 2018: 61). By offering a genuine ideological choice and rejecting austerity, Corbyn, the conciliatory and polite outsider, came across as authentic as opposed to calculated. That is, he said what he believed because he believed it. Diamond would later argue that this was reflective of how Corbyn rejected the "politics of valence in favour of position", as he believed that "politicians should support policies and ethical causes beyond their impact on electoral performance and governing competence" (Diamond 2016: 17).

---

2. Margaret Beckett was one of those who lent their support to Corbyn in order to provide an ideological choice, although she would later describe herself as a "moron" for doing so (BBC 2015).

In an age of political cynicism, the fact that Corbyn had deeply held principles that he had not really altered over decades would lead to the emergence, after 2015, of what became known as "Corbynmania" (Seymour 2016: 14; and on Corbyn and notions of "fandom", see Dean 2017). That Corbyn was part of a social movement seeking the party leadership in a new form of bottom-up politics was becoming apparent as the campaign unfolded (Goes 2018: 61). When the Labour Party contested the general election of May 2015, their membership hovered at around 200,000. In the ballot to determine their successor to Miliband, the membership had increased to 294,000 and additionally 147,000 affiliated supporters and 115,000 registered supporters had signed up, swelling the participation base that would determine the contest in the direction of Corbyn (Quinn 2016: 764). With leading trade unions deciding to endorse his candidature – including the largest in the shape of UNISON and Unite as well as CWU, ASLEF and TSSA, and with him securing the endorsements of the highest number of CLP branches, momentum was swinging his way – 152 CLPs backed Corbyn as compared to 111 for Burnham, 109 for Cooper and 18 for Kendall (Seymour 2016: 26). Although Corbyn was also speaking to large and enthusiastic crowds (Richards 2017: 76–7), his candidature was further galvanized by the dissemination via social media of pro-Corbyn material (on the use of social media as a means of promoting the message, see Dean 2019).

That Corbyn secured a landslide first-round victory with 59.5 per cent of the vote dumbfounded those on the social democratic wing of the PLP (Dorey & Denham 2016: 274). His mandate and legitimacy seemed clear as the overall gap between himself and the second-placed candidate, Burnham, was 40 per cent.

**Table 2.1** The Labour Party leadership election of 2015

|  | Jeremy Corbyn | Andy Burnham | Yvette Cooper | Liz Kendall |
|---|---|---|---|---|
| *Party members* |  |  |  |  |
| Votes | 121,751 | 55,698 | 54,470 | 13,601 |
| Percentage | 49.6 | 22.7 | 22.2 | 5.5 |
| *Registered supporters* |  |  |  |  |
| Votes | 88,449 | 6,160 | 8,415 | 2,574 |
| Percentage | 83.8 | 5.8 | 8.0 | 2.4 |
| *Affiliated supporters* |  |  |  |  |
| Votes | 41,217 | 18,604 | 9,043 | 2,682 |
| Percentage | 57.6 | 26.0 | 12.6 | 3.8 |
| **Total** |  |  |  |  |
| **Votes** | **251,417** | **80,462** | **71,928** | **18,857** |
| **Percentage** | **59.5** | **19.0** | **17.0** | **4.5** |
| Turnout: 76.3 per cent |  |  |  |  |

*Source*: Quinn (2016): 765.

The gap between Corbyn and Burnham in the party members section was 26.9 per cent; it was 31.6 per cent among affiliated supporters, and a massive 75.8 per cent gap existed between him and Cooper, as the second-placed candidate, among the registered supporters (see Table 2.1). However, despite the strength of his mandate to lead among members and registered and affiliated supporters, the fact remained that he had been overwhelmingly rejected by his fellow parliamentarians, at both the nomination stage (with only 36 votes out of 232) and in the actual leadership ballot (15 out of 232) (Crines, Jeffery & Heppell 2018: 364).

For the governing Conservatives, the divergence between the parliamentarians and the membership was just one opportunity for them to exploit. They saw a myriad of other opportunities to undermine Labour, now that Corbyn had been elevated to the leadership. They could emphasize that he was a serial rebel and imply he was a hypocrite if he demanded loyalty from his parliamentary ranks (Heppell 2019: 53). They could rely on the right-wing press to castigate and undermine Corbyn for his views on issues such as nationalization, unilateralism and his supposed sympathy with Hamas and Iran in the Middle East (Diamond 2016: 15–24). The Conservatives could also benefit from the difficulties that Corbyn would have with adapting to the demands of leading the Labour Party (Goes 2018).

What was uncomfortable for the Labour Party was the suspicion that many Labour parliamentarians might agree with these assumptions. The extra-parliamentary party had imposed upon MPs a new party leader who they felt was totally ill-suited to the demands of contemporary political leadership (Diamond 2016). Parliamentarians struggled to reconcile themselves to Corbyn as their leader. They viewed him as an electoral liability and feared that he lacked the credibility to serve as prime minister (Goes 2018). Moreover, his agenda might well mobilize the radical left, but they feared that it was too ideological and too left-wing for the wider electorate. They feared that this was reminiscent of the early 1980s and they cited as evidence how their heaviest electoral defeat of the postwar era occurred when they presented an overtly leftish manifesto at the general election of 1983 (Seymour 2016: 179–80). The lesson they took from this was the importance of remaining inside what political scientists implied was the "zone of acquiescence", that is, the centre ground of British politics, in which the plurality of largely moderate voters would be willing to reward the party with their vote and thus allow Labour to access power (Norris & Lovenduski 2004).

To prevent a challenge emerging from the social-democrat-dominated parliamentary party, Corbyn needed to show sensitivity around issues of party management within his parliamentary ranks, which he struggled to do; and evidence that the opinion polling position of the Labour Party could improve under his leadership, not just in terms of the headline polling on voting projections, but also in terms of leadership competence and economic credibility, which he also struggled to do (for a discussion on what makes for an effective leader of the opposition, see Heppell, Theakston & Searight 2015, and on opposition leadership more generally, see Heppell 2012).

The next ten months in British politics would be remarkably unstable. The European Union referendum (see Clarke, Goodwin & Whiteley 2017a) would result in the resignation of David Cameron and the emergence of Theresa May as the new leader of the Conservative Party and prime minister (see Jeffery *et al.* 2018), and would culminate in a naive attempt by non-Corbynite forces within the PLP to unseat him.

## Re-electing Corbyn: the Labour Party leadership election of 2016

Corbyn's immediate task upon assuming the leadership in September 2015 was to construct a shadow cabinet and allocate frontbench responsibilities. Although his ability to select a balanced frontbench team was compromised by the unwillingness of many senior figures to serve (Goes 2018: 61), he nonetheless left himself open to criticism on two grounds. First, although he appointed Burnham as shadow home secretary and the widely respected Hilary Benn as shadow foreign secretary, his decision to promote his close ally, John McDonnell to the role of shadow chancellor, was viewed as a provocative and unnecessary move in the eyes of those on the social democratic wing of the PLP (Cowley & Kavanagh 2018: 74). Second, it was immediately noted that Corbyn, a supposed advocate of gender equality, had appointed three men to shadow the three great offices of state, which was aligned to the fact that Tom Watson had been elected as deputy leader of the Labour Party. This created an impression of a gender imbalance in terms of the prestige portfolios (although the first Corbyn shadow cabinet did have more women than men, and later in his tenure Diane Abbott replaced Burnham and Emily Thornberry replaced Benn) (Cowley & Kavanagh 2018: 75).

Questions about internal unity shortly became evident in the aftermath of the Paris attacks (November 2015) associated with so-called Islamic State. This led to Cameron seeking parliamentary approval for military intervention in Syria and created the unusual situation of Benn, as shadow foreign secretary, delivering a parliamentary speech that offered support to the government, while sitting next to him on the frontbenches was Corbyn, who spoke out against intervention (Cowley & Kavanagh 2018: 75). This occurred after Corbyn offered a free vote to fellow parliamentarians once it was evident that a large number of them would vote against any instruction to vote against. A total of 66 voted with the government (with Benn) and 163 voted against (with Corbyn) with the remaining three abstaining (Diamond 2016: 16–22). The Syria vote reflected the uneasy relationship that Corbyn had with the PLP and the shadow cabinet. As a consequence, throughout the early part of 2016 political journalists became increasingly fixated with the internal conflict between Corbyn and his own parliamentarians. This included the leaking of a supposed "loyalty list" from within the Corbyn inner sanctum. The *Guardian* printed a grid in which every member of the PLP was identified as being either loyal (n=74); neutral (n=68) and hostile (n=79) with a further nine not listed (Asthana & Stewart 2016).

The willingness of those on the social democratic wing to tolerate Corbyn was undermined further by the European Union referendum of June 2016. This was the issue that captured the biggest contradiction between Corbyn and the membership. The latter was overwhelmingly pro-European and Remain in terms of its outlook whereas Corbyn held a long-standing scepticism towards Europeanism (Cowley & Kavanagh 2018: 81). However, despite the fact that Corbyn campaigned for Remain, his critics claimed that he did so without real enthusiasm. He was accused of having a detached and fractious relationship with the official "Britain Stronger in Europe" cross-party campaign (Ford & Goodwin 2017: 24). The consequence of this was that opinion polling showed that of known Labour voters almost half did not realize that the Labour Party was campaigning for Remain (Ford & Goodwin 2017: 24). Given that leadership cues matter in terms of persuading voters, Corbyn's lack of enthusiasm "eroded the strength of cueing effects" on behalf of the Labour Party (Clarke, Goodwin & Whiteley 2017b: 447).

When the electorate voted to leave the EU, those Labour parliamentarians who had never really accepted that Corbyn should be leader of the party engaged in a series of manoeuvres designed to get him to resign. They rationalized that the performance of the Labour Party overrode the mandate that he had secured just ten months earlier. Placing his leadership within its historical context, Corbyn's critics concluded that a correlation existed between leadership competence (i.e. net satisfaction rating) and voting projections. When the Labour Party had been on course for election success, the personal satisfaction rating of their leader was strong. For example, in the lead up to the general election of 1997, Blair had a +50 leadership satisfaction rating and the Labour Party had a projected vote of around 45 per cent. Corbyn had a leadership satisfaction rating of -30 plus by mid-2016, while the party's projected vote was hovering around 25 per cent. These combined findings were worse than the findings that fed into the general election defeats of 2015, 2010, 1987 and even 1983 (Payne 2016). Unless they could find a mechanism to evict Corbyn from the leadership they feared that the Labour Party was heading to a heavy defeat at the next general election.

The first part of this process involved Benn asking Corbyn to step aside. When Corbyn sacked Benn for his intervention it resulted in mass resignations from the frontbench and plunged the Labour Party into a crisis. However, Corbyn rationalized that because his mandate came from the extra-parliamentary party and not from within the PLP he was justified in continuing. As a result, he set about replacing those who had departed, with the consequence that the shadow cabinet after June 2016 became more Corbynite than before (Cowley & Kavanagh 2018: 84–5).

After the mass resignations failed to prompt Corbyn to step aside, his critics then decided to initiate an alternative means to pressurize him into resignation. Although a confidence motion was not part of the formal procedures of the Labour Party for evicting the incumbent leader, the PLP decided to hold one as a means of showcasing the scale of the opposition to Corbyn (Crines, Jeffery & Heppell 2018). Given that he had secured virtually no support within the PLP in the nomination stage of the leadership election and the subsequent ballot, it was inevitable that Corbyn would perform badly in the subsequent confidence motion. It was no surprise when the ballot produced a result of 172 parliamentarians out of 232 with no confidence in Corbyn and wanting a change in the party leadership (Crines, Jeffery & Heppell 2018: 361). Determined to continue, Corbyn stated that the confidence motion had no constitutional legitimacy and therefore he was not bound by it (Cowley & Kavanagh 2018: 84–5).

Having ignored the mass resignations and the confidence motion, Corbyn left his critics only one option: to initiate a formal challenge. If a leadership election were initiated, the question would now be whether Corbyn could secure enough nominations to proceed to the actual ballot. It was clear that any challenger would need to gain the support of 20 per cent of the PLP, the challenger threshold being higher than the 15 per cent threshold for a vacant contest, as had been the case the previous year. What was less clear from the rules is whether the same threshold needed to be passed by the incumbent, or whether the incumbent should automatically be allowed onto the ballot. This procedural debate mattered as Corbyn needed to be automatically permitted to be on the ballot, as it was clear that he would not be able to secure nominations from 20 per cent of the PLP (46 MPs). How would the members, registered and affiliated supporters react if Corbyn was not available for them to vote for? To resolve this procedural impasse, the National Executive Committee (hereafter NEC) voted by 18 to 14 that Corbyn should automatically be allowed to proceed to the ballot (Cowley & Kavanagh 2018: 84–5).

That left the critics of Corbyn with only one dilemma. They knew that they did not want to split the anti-Corbyn vote, so they needed to agree on just one candidate. The most credible leadership figures on the non-Corbynite wing of the PLP – Cooper, Burnham or Benn, for example, were not willing to act as the challenger – perhaps indicating their awareness that whoever challenged now would probably fail to unseat Corbyn. Eventually they settled on Owen Smith as their candidate over Angela Eagle, and while Corbyn was not required to submit a list of nominees, Smith advanced to the ballot on the back of 172 nominations, comfortably surpassing the 20 per cent threshold for activating a challenge (Quinn 2018: 478–9). Although Smith sought to present the challenge as being driven by perceptions of competence and electability, as opposed to a challenge to the Corbynite agenda, opinion polling evidence from the campaigning period clearly showed how his challenge was failing to gain traction among those to whom he most needed to appeal. Whereas among the wider electorate more thought Smith would be a better leader of the Labour Party than Corbyn (by 58 to 42 per cent), when the pattern of support was isolated to known Labour voters Corbyn led by 52 to 48 per cent, and when isolated further to Labour Party activists only, Corbyn led by 66 to 34 per cent (Harris 2016).

Part of the reason why the Smith campaign struggled was that he was identifiable as the PLP candidate and, whereas many Labour members saw Corbyn as a principled politician, they also thought many parliamentarians were unprincipled careerists (Blakey 2016). Having voted for Corbyn only a year earlier, many Labour members thought the PLP was disloyal and rebellious and they viewed their tactics – mass resignations, the confidence motion and their implication that Corbyn could only stand if he secured enough nominations – as an attempt to subvert internal party democracy and reverse their earlier decision (Blakey 2016).

Whereas Corbyn secured 59.5 per cent on the back of 251,417 votes in his first leadership election victory, he achieved an even more impressive endorsement in his second leadership victory as 313,209 backed him (on 61.8 per cent) (see Table 2.2). Although his percentage share among registered supporters fell from 83.8 to 69.9 per cent, his returns among members increased from 49.6 to 59.0 per cent and among affiliated supporters from 57.6 to 60.2 per cent (Stewart & Mason 2016). Ultimately, the Smith challenge was a mistaken and naive enterprise for

**Table 2.2** The Labour Party leadership election of 2016

|  | Jeremy Corbyn | Owen Smith |
| --- | --- | --- |
| *Party members* | | |
| Votes | 168,216 | 116,960 |
| Percentage | 59.0 | 41.0 |
| *Registered supporters* | | |
| Votes | 84,918 | 36,599 |
| Percentage | 69.9 | 30.1 |
| *Affiliated supporters* | | |
| Votes | 60,075 | 39,670 |
| Percentage | 60.2 | 39.8 |
| **Total** | | |
| **Votes** | **313,209** | **193,229** |
| **Percentage** | **61.8** | **38.2** |
| Turnout: 77.6 per cent | | |

*Source*: Stewart & Mason (2016).

THE ELECTION AND RE-ELECTION OF JEREMY CORBYN

the anti-Corbyn faction to engage in. It showed a complete lack of strategic planning and failure to learn the lessons of the leadership election the previous year.
Although the opinion polling in the interim period between the two leadership
elections showed that non-Labour voters had significant doubts about Corbyn as
a potential prime minister, there was no evidence to suggest that there was a softening of support for Corbyn amongst Labour members or registered and affiliated supporters (Chambers 2016). By winning and winning comfortably, Corbyn
was strengthened as leader, solidifying his position much in the same way that
Tony Benn's challenge to Kinnock in 1988 actually strengthened the position of
the incumbent (Denham, Roe-Crines & Dorey 2020). This would ensure he was
in place to contest the next general election, expected in 2020. However, Corbyn
would run a significantly better than expected election campaign when May
engineered an earlier than expected general election in 2017. The Labour vote
increased by 9.6 per cent from 30.4 to 40 per cent as their overall vote went up
from 9,347,273 to 12,878,460 (Dorey 2017). Even though the Labour Party lost
the general election, the consequence of their significantly improved standing
was that it legitimized Corbyn as leader of the Labour Party and Corbynism as
a project, and it made it significantly harder for any Labour parliamentarian to
justify challenging him for the leadership (Denham, Roe-Crines & Dorey 2020).


## Analysis and conclusions

It is clear that the decision taken during the Miliband opposition era to amend
the leadership election procedures within the Labour Party did matter and did
help Corbyn to win the party leadership. The tripartite Electoral College was built
around the affiliated trade unions, CLP members, and the PLP and MEPs, giving
one-third weighting to each. As we have seen, the equal weightings between the
three sections were removed and the new leadership rules were based on one-
member-one-vote among three types of members: paid-up members, affiliated
members (trade union members who registered to participate) and registered
supporters (those who paid a nominal fee to participate and declared their support for the Labour Party) (Collins 2014: 23). Whereas the old electoral system
set aside one-third of the electoral process to the views of the PLP and MEPs,
their influence was diluted considerably under the new rules, and left them with
the same status as a newly paid-up registered supporter (Russell 2016: 20–2; see
also Quinn 2016; Dorey & Denham 2016).

With the PLP seeing their influence restricted to that of gatekeepers, who
determine who is presented to their wider leadership electorate, they needed to
screen out (not include) a candidate they found unacceptable. That they deliberately chose to allow Corbyn to proceed to the ballot showcased two things

about those who lent their votes to Corbyn: first, that they simply failed to understand how the inclusion of registered and affiliated membership created a new dynamic within the leadership process; and second, that they were out of touch with opinion within their own CLPs and the wider membership (Quinn 2016: 767–70). Moreover, whereas the old Electoral College restricted participation to long-standing party members, the new leadership election rules created through the registered supporters section broadened the electorate beyond the traditional confines of the Labour Party (Denham, Roe-Crines & Dorey 2020). Dorey and Denham have also speculated on whether those new registered supporters who participated had even voted for the Labour Party in the general election of 2015, leading to speculation about entryism: the incursion of hard-left-thinking "new" voters (Dorey & Denham 2016). However, entryism should not be presented as the explanation as to why Corbyn actually won the party leadership, as Corbyn secured very strong returns in both of the other sections – the membership section and the affiliated sections – in both of the 2015 and 2016 Labour Party leadership elections (on the myth of entryism, see Cockburn 2016).

There is clear evidence to suggest that ideology and attitudes towards Corbyn were drivers towards individuals deciding to become members of the Labour Party. Whiteley *et al.* have identified how those who were previously "apathetic" and "uninvolved" re-engaged with politics because of the "shift to the left associated with [Corbyn's] leadership" (Whiteley *et al.* 2019: 83). As for the reasons why, they conclude that:

Relative deprivation was plainly a significant factor that drove people, and particularly first-time joiners, to join Labour once a candidate with a clear radical profile was on the leadership ballot: those who might be labelled "left behind" flocked to Jeremy Corbyn's colours, including graduates earning less than the average income. Anti-capitalist values also appeared to be a feature of the new members, as was disenchantment with politics as usual and a yearning for a new style of politics. However, incentives like ideology mattered too. Post-2015 recruits who had previously belonged to the Labour Party and who re-joined it were more left wing. Demographic factors played only a limited part in understanding Labour's membership surge, although it looks as if those in lower social grades seemed to be more likely than others to be attracted to the party. First-time joiners were not, on the whole, university graduates or high-income middle-class radicals; rather, they looked a little more like the party's "traditional" grassroots, being less educated and in lower status occupations than existing members.

(Whiteley *et al.* 2019: 95)

When we place the election(s) of Corbyn within the context of wider academic debates on party leadership, we can see that his rise seems to disprove the assumptions that have underpinned the so-called Stark criteria on leadership selection (Stark 1996).[3] The Stark criteria stipulate that there is a hierarchy of factors that a party should consider when selecting their leader: first, ideological acceptability, meaning that parties should remove candidates who cannot unify the party; second, electability, meaning that parties should show some sensitivity to opinion polling on the respective candidates and consider which of the remaining candidates would be best positioned to expand the existing vote base of the party; and third, competence, meaning that parties that aspire to govern are selecting not just a party leader but a potential prime minister, so they should be selecting the candidate who seems the most politically competent and thus worthy of the highest office (Stark 1996). This fact, and the overwhelmingly critical interpretations of Corbyn's leadership within the media and academic circles, has been noted (and critiqued) by Allen (2020) but also Maiguashca and Dean (2020).

Academics were quick to argue that the Stark criteria had been overlooked in the selection of Corbyn (see Quinn 2016; Dorey & Denham 2016), and that ideological purity, as opposed to unifying capability, electability and competence, seemed to have been more important. How valid is this assertion? Using opinion polling data from the Labour Party leadership of 2015 provides us with an insight into what was driving the vote for Corbyn. Voters in that first leadership election were given a range of possible reasons for why they voted for a particular candidate and the findings were illuminating. Those who voted for Kendall prioritized the following reasons for backing her: she would provide effective opposition (59 per cent) and she would have the best chance of regaining power (73 per cent). Kendall supporters were not motivated by a desire to engineer a break from the influence of Blair or New Labour (8 per cent), but it is worth noting that her backers did not place a strong emphasis on her ability to unite the party (only 10 per cent who voted for her identified this as primary driver of their vote). Those that voted for Burnham and Cooper also placed a strong emphasis on their ability to effectively oppose the Conservatives (52 and 70 per cent, respectively) and they also scored highly in terms of voters backing them because they were perceived as able to regain power, by 49 per cent for Burnham and 58 per cent for Cooper. As for Kendall voters, repudiating the

---

3. The work of Stark looms large in the academic literature on leadership selection within British political parties, with the following, among others, using it as an analytical tool for explaining how and why respective leaders of the Labour and Conservative parties were selected: Heppell 2010a, 2010b; Heppell and Crines 2011; Heppell, Theakston and Seawright 2011; Dorey and Denham 2011, 2016; Quinn 2012, 2016; Denham 2017; Crines, Jeffery & Heppell 2018.

Blair era was not a dominant priority for Burnham and Cooper voters, but both were seen as better at unifying than Kendall – 48 per cent of Burnham backers supported him as they believed he could unify the party and 34 per cent voted for Cooper for the same reason (Quinn 2016: 767).

The motivations of Corbyn supporters differed. His backers placed the lowest priority on his ability to unify the party, with only 5 per cent of backers identifying his ability to unify as their reason for backing him. Moreover, only 5 per cent identified his ability to win a general election as a motivation for them to back him. The evidence of their ideological intent was clear as 65 per cent identified that they were motivated to back Corbyn because he would enable the Labour Party to disassociate itself from the policies and positioning of the New Labour era and of Blair (Quinn 2016: 767).

We can argue, then, that the rise of Corbyn was a rebellion against the core assumption of New Labour that ideological compromise and centrist thinking was necessary in order to be electorally successful. It was a rebellion against the social democratic forces within the PLP who continued to hold such a view but had seen the Labour Party share of the vote fall from 43.2 per cent in the general election of 1997 to 29 per cent in the general election of 2010, with only a marginal recovery being evident at the general election of 2015. If ideological compromises resulted in electoral rejection, then why not make the case for greater ideological radicalism? The ability of Corbyn to offer that ideological radicalism, but also to be elected, stemmed in part from the inability of Labour parliamentarians to understand that changing the rules changed the game.

## References

Allen, P. 2020. "Political science, punditry, and the Corbyn problem". *British Politics* 15(1): 69–87.

Asthana, A. & H. Stewart 2016. "Labour MPs hostile to Corbyn named in leaked party document". *The Guardian,* 23 March.

Bale, T. 2015. *Five Year Mission: The Labour Party under Ed Miliband.* Oxford: Oxford University Press.

BBC 2015. "Margaret Beckett: I was a moron to nominate Jeremy Corbyn". BBC News, 22 July. https://www.bbc.co.uk/news/uk-politics-33625612 (accessed 12 March 2021).

Blakey, H. 2016. "Corbyn-mania: cult of personality or political movement". *Open Democracy,* 3 August.

Chambers, L. 2016. "Jeremy Corbyn's support rises among party members". 19 July. https://yougov.co.uk/topics/politics/articles-reports/2016/07/19/jeremy-corbyn-support-rises-among-party-members (accessed 12 March 2021).

Clarke, H., M. Goodwin & P. Whiteley 2017a. *Brexit: Why Britain Voted to Leave the European Union.* Cambridge: Cambridge University Press.

Clarke, H., M. Goodwin & P. Whiteley 2017b. "Why Britain voted for Brexit: an individual-level analysis of the 2016 Referendum vote". *Parliamentary Affairs* 70(3): 439–64.

Cockburn, H. 2016. "Labour's leadership contest: the truth about £3 party supporters and Jeremy Corbyn". *The Independent,* 13 July.

Collins, R. 2014. *Building A One Nation Labour Party: The Collins Review into Labour Party Reform*. London: The Labour Party.

Cowley, P. & D. Kavanagh 2015. *The British General Election of 2015*. Basingstoke: Palgrave Macmillan.

Cowley, P. & D. Kavanagh 2018. *The British General Election of 2017*. Basingstoke: Palgrave Macmillan.

Crines, A., D. Jeffery & T. Heppell 2018. "The British Labour Party and leadership election mandate(s) of Jeremy Corbyn: patterns of opinion and opposition within the parliamentary Labour Party". *Journal of Elections, Public Opinion and Parties* 28(3): 361–79.

Dean, J. 2017. "Politicising fandom". *British Journal of Politics and International Relations* 19(2): 250–66.

Dean, J. 2019. "Sorted for memes and gifs: visual media and everyday digital politics". *Political Studies Review* 17(3): 255–66.

Denham, A. 2017. "Choosing party leaders: anglophone democracies, British parties and the limits of comparative politics". *British Politics* 12(2): 250–66.

Denham, A., A. Roe-Crines & P. Dorey 2020. *Choosing Party Leaders: Britain's Conservatives and Labour Compared*. Manchester: Manchester University Press.

Diamond, P. 2016. "Assessing the performance of UK opposition leaders: Jeremy Corbyn's straight talking, honest politics". *Politics and Governance* 4(2): 15–24.

Dorey, P. 2017. "Jeremy Corbyn confounds his critics: explaining the Labour Party's remarkable resurgence at the 2017 election". *British Politics* 12(3): 308–34.

Dorey, P. & A. Denham 2011. "'O, brother, where art thou?' the Labour Party leadership election of 2010". *British Politics* 6(3): 286–316.

Dorey, P. & A. Denham 2016. "'The longest suicide vote in history': the Labour Party leadership election of 2015". *British Politics* 11(3): 259–82.

Ford, R. & M. Goodman 2017. "Britain after Brexit: a nation divided". *Journal of Democracy* 28(1): 17–30.

Goes, E. 2016. *The Labour Party under Ed Miliband: Trying but Failing to Renew Social Democracy*. Manchester: Manchester University Press.

Goes, E. 2018. "'Jez, We Can!' Labour's campaign: a defeat with the taste of victory". *Parliamentary Affairs* 17(1): 59–71.

Harris, L. 2016. "BMG poll: majority of British public back Owen Smith as Labour leader and prime minister rather than Jeremy Corbyn". *Evening Standard*, 16 August.

Heppell, T. 2010a. *Choosing the Labour Leader: Labour Party Leadership Elections from Wilson to Brown*. London: I. B. Tauris.

Heppell, T. 2010b. "The Labour Party leadership election of 1963: explaining the unexpected election of Harold Wilson". *Contemporary British History* 24(2): 151–71.

Heppell, T. & A. Crines 2011. "How Michael Foot won the Labour leadership". *Political Quarterly* 82(1): 81–94.

Heppell, T. (ed.) 2012. *Leaders of the Opposition: From Winston Churchill to David Cameron*. Basingstoke: Palgrave Macmillan.

Heppell, T. 2013. "The fall of the Brown Government 2010". In T. Heppell & K. Theakston (eds), *How Labour Governments Fall: From Ramsay MacDonald to Gordon Brown*. Basingstoke: Palgrave Macmillan.

Heppell, T. 2019. *Cameronism: The Politics of Modernisation and Manipulation*. Manchester: Manchester University Press.

Heppell, T. & M. Hill 2012. "Labour in opposition". In T. Heppell & D. Seawright (eds), *Cameron and the Conservatives: The Transition to Coalition Government*. Basingstoke: Palgrave Macmillan.

Heppell, T., K. Theakston & D. Seawright 2015. *What Makes for an Effective Leader of the Opposition?* London: Centre for Opposition Studies.

Jeffery, D., R. Hayton, T. Heppell & A. Crines. 2018. "The Conservative Party leadership election of 2016: an analysis of the voting motivations of Conservative parliamentarians". *Parliamentary Affairs* 71(2): 263–82.

Kavanagh, D. & P. Cowley 2010. *The British General Election of 2010.* Basingstoke: Palgrave Macmillan.

Maiguashca, B. & J. Dean 2020. "'Lovely people but utterly deluded': British political science's trouble with Corbynism". *British Politics* 15(1): 48–68.

McAnulla, S. 2011. "Post-political poisons? evaluating the toxic dimensions of Tony Blair's leadership". *Representation* 47(3): 251–63.

Norris, P. & J. Lovenduski 2004. "Why parties fail to learn: electoral defeat, selection perception and British party politics". *Party Politics* 10(1): 83–102.

Quinn, T. 2012. *Electing and Ejecting Party Leaders in Britain.* Basingstoke: Palgrave Macmillan.

Quinn, T. 2016. "The British Labour Party's leadership election of 2015". *British Journal of Politics and International Relations* 18(4): 759–78.

Quinn, T. 2018. "From the Wembley Conference to the 'McDonnell Amendment': Labour's leadership nomination rules". *Political Quarterly* 89(3): 474–81.

Payne, A. 2016. "This chart proves that Jeremy Corbyn's awful approval ratings matter – a lot". *Business Insider,* 22 August.

Pemberton, H. & M. Wickham-Jones 2013. "Brothers all? The operation of the electoral college in the 2010 Labour leadership contest". *Parliamentary Affairs* 66(4): 708–31.

Richards, S. 2017. *The Rise of the Outsiders: How Mainstream Politics Lost Its Way.* London: Atlantic.

Russell, M. 2016. "Corbyn as an organisational phenomenon: a response to Steve Richards". *Political Quarterly* 87(1): 20–2.

Seymour, R. 2016. *Corbyn: The Strange Rebirth of Radical Politics.* London: Verso.

Stark, L. 1996. *Choosing a Leader: Party Leadership Contests in Britain from Macmillan to Blair.* Basingstoke: Macmillan.

Stewart, H. & R. Mason 2016. "Labour leadership: Jeremy Corbyn wins convincing victory over Owen Smith". *The Guardian,* 24 September.

Whiteley, P., M. Poletti, P. Webb & T. Bale 2019. "Oh, Jeremy Corbyn! Why did Labour Party membership soar after the 2015 general election?" *British Journal of Politics and International Relations* 21(1): 80–98.

# 3

# CORBYNISM: A COHERENT IDEOLOGY?

*Bradley Ward and Peter Kerr*

Few people would dispute the fact that Corbynism sought to bring about an ideological paradigm shift in British politics. In this respect, Corbynism represented a serious challenge to the neoliberal consensus that has developed in the UK since the 1980s. However, as this chapter will show, beyond this several ambiguities and disagreements remain over the type of ideology that Corbynism came to represent. What labels should we apply to best describe it? Did it represent something substantively new, or was it, as some commentators have suggested, merely harking back to an older style of Labour politics? Within this debate, Corbynism has been variously described as an instance of "left-populism", as "socialism in the twenty-first century", as "class-struggle social democracy", as "Social Democracy in a New Left Garb", as "democratic socialist", as "reformism" but "transformative", and, as "anti-modernizing" by some and a "concrete utopia" by others. Moreover, it has been denounced by some critics as being too radical in its aims and, by others, as not radical enough.

In our attempt here to unpack the character of Corbynite ideology, we begin by highlighting the multiple ways it has been interpreted by both its supporters and its opponents. In doing so, we tease out some key areas of disagreement between commentators. These include debates over the extent of its radicalism, how it relates to the wider family of left ideologies that emerged after the global financial crisis, whether it should be considered part of the contemporary "populist moment" (Mouffe 2018), and how this relates to its democratic socialism. We then use Freeden's (1996, 2003) popular understanding of ideologies to map the character of Corbynism. In doing so, we argue that, although it is possible to identify core elements of Corbynism as a political project, there remained a sufficient amount of ideological ambiguity to give it a "catch-all" appeal within the broad family of left politics. This "leftist catch-allism", as we refer to it here, meant that Corbynism was able to mobilize a plurality of activists drawn from different leftist traditions. It also goes some way towards explaining the plurality of interpretations that have emerged within the existing literature.

## What was Corbynism?

As we will see, Corbynism came to represent different things to different people. However, despite this, few would dispute that Corbynism represented a challenge to the neoliberal consensus, which has dominated British politics since the time of the Thatcher governments. Although a number of debates have emerged over the extent to which various governments – not least the New Labour governments of Tony Blair and Gordon Brown (Hay 1999; Heffernan 2001) – have followed a neoliberal path, few would dispute that since the late twentieth century a relative degree of party consensus has developed, broadly underpinned by neoliberal ideas. This consensus, however, has come under increasing strain following the global financial crisis of 2008 and the subsequent implementation of a decade of austerity measures, intended to tackle the UK's public debt problems and financial deficit. The depth and breadth of these austerity measures prompted widespread criticism that they were unnecessarily harsh, and disproportionately affected women, Black, Asian and minority ethnic (BAME) communities and other vulnerable groups (Hall *et al.* 2017). In light of this, from 2010, an "anti-austerity" movement emerged around the world, which various commentators interpreted as a direct confrontation with neoliberal capitalism (see Gerbaudo 2017). Importantly for our concerns here, the anti-austerity movement provided a formative experience for many of the emerging "Generation Left" (Milburn 2019), who would go on to become an essential component of the Corbyn project.

It was only on Jeremy Corbyn's entry into the Labour leadership contest in June 2015 that the anti-austerity movement found itself with a prominent voice in a mainstream political party. His candidacy brought "Generation Left" together with two other tributaries in the labour movement, which together formed the bedrock of Corbynism. As Nunns explains: "the largest ran through the party itself, where the members had turned sharply against New Labour. The second flowed in from the trade unions and was the culmination of a 15-year shift to the left" (Nunns 2018: 8). Corbynism is probably best understood as a merging of these three tributaries, within the context of an ongoing crisis of neoliberalism. Yet, beyond these foundations, what Corbynism meant to its supporters remains ambiguous. As Bolton and Pitts (2018) point out, the Corbyn coalition drew in diverse actors from essentially different traditions, including Bennite "economic nationalists", "techno-utopian" post-capitalists, various assortments of Trotskyists and Marxist-socialists, and even middle-of-the-road social democrats.

In a similar vein, Gilbert (2017) also points out that Corbynism was the product of an interaction between the politics of labourism and the politics of movementism. As such, its roots in the protest coalitions that formed the anti-austerity movement and the broad church of competing traditions within the Labour Party perhaps explains why it was constituted by such a diversity of leftist traditions. The anti-austerity movement was itself a diverse movement made up of a wide range of actors, from "hard-left" socialists who saw this as a rare opportunity for radical change, to Conservative students who were involved because they opposed tuition fees (Myers 2017). The Labour Party, meanwhile, at different times in its history, has incorporated various traditions ranging from Third Way centrists, to traditional social democrats, to democratic socialists. Some of these groups supported Corbynism on the principle that it provided the space to push for what they saw as socialist reforms, whereas others supported it because of Corbyn's promise to challenge austerity, democratize the party, and promote a fairly moderate brand of social democracy (see Nunns 2018).

The diverse character of Corbynism is reflected in the ambiguity and debate that exist over the extent of its radicalism; at different times Corbynism has either been described as too radical in its aims or not radical enough. Byrne sums this ambiguity up well when he states that, while "read in isolation" Corbynism's policy commitments in the 2017 election can be seen as little more than a "social democratic offering", to many of its adherents it offered a "concrete utopia" based on a "far-reaching conceptualisation of a different type of society, invested with substantial emotional energy, presented as a realistic alternative to the status quo that could be built through practical and immediate political action" (Byrne 2019: 252).

Thus, for example, the "Generation Left" that made up an important element of the Corbyn project often view themselves as anti-capitalist, seeking out new forms of participation built around horizontalism and communal decision-making as a challenge to the oligarchy of mainstream representative democracy. Many of this generation have formed part of the "techno-utopian" wing of the project identified by Bolton and Pitts (2018), with their views being encapsulated by Aaron Bastani's (2019) *Fully Automated Luxury Communism* and Srnicek and Williams' (2015) *Inventing the Future*. Both of these texts viewed technology and automation as providing the potential space to achieve new and radical future possibilities.

Corbynism's challenge to neoliberalism led many to believe that it was the beginning of a revitalization of the Left within Britain (see Perryman 2017). Byrne, for his part, sees Corbynism as a "sustained repudiation of the market-based logic that has informed British (and international) policy-making of the past decades" (2019: 260) and points to policies such as the nationalization of key industries, the proposed National Investment Bank and the expansion of the cooperative sector as examples of such a challenge. This view is furthered by Guinan and O'Neill, who see the Alternative Models of Ownership Report, which formed the backbone of the Labour Party's economic policy during this period, as a bottom-up form of public ownership based around "the possibility of real democracy and participation, and providing the long-run institutional and policy support for a new politics dedicated to achieving genuine social change" (2018: 6). Corbyn (2016) himself described his politics as "socialism in the 21st century", a view supported by Panitch and Gindin (2018), who viewed Corbynism as a powerful ideology that restored credibility to the socialist challenge against a stagnant neoliberalism.

On the other hand, some within the Corbyn coalition saw it in less radical terms. Pitts and Dinerstein, for example, have identified a strand within the Corbynist coalition that focused less on "reinventing the wheel" and more on "grassroots initiatives rooted in local communities, with a programme of Syriza-style 'solidarity networks' in provincial towns across the United Kingdom" (2017: 424). This view presents Corbynism in less utopian terms as a grassroots project that was more concerned with developing community-based support systems to combat inequality at the grassroots level. This type of perspective is furthered by Bolton and Pitts (2018) who reject the claim – made by the more radical groups that coalesced around Corbynism – that it represents a potential break with capitalism. In a later article, Bolton argues that despite the radical ideological tendencies within Corbynism, it is hopelessly naive to think that democratic socialism is capable of transcending the relations between capital and labour. Even if a Corbyn government was able to bring large swathes of private capital into public ownership it would not be able to "escape the necessity to keep up with the socially determined rate of production" on the global market (Bolton 2020: 341).

Moreover, Bale, Poletti & Wenn (2016), in a survey of party supporters, showed that many Labour Party supporters did not think that the party was particularly radical at this point in time. While Byrne sees it as a utopian version of social democracy, others see it as a return to "Old" Labour, although as Batrouni (2020) notes, the leadership were eager to distance themselves from this type of link. Undoubtedly, many within the trade union movement and the Labour Party did view Corbynism as a route to overturning the direction taken during its New Labour years. This desire to return the party back to its former "roots" led some commentators to view Corbynism as part of a traditionalist backlash against some of the "modernizing" tendencies of New Labour (Kerr *et al.* 2018). Seymour (2016), moreover, argues that Corbynism represented a traditional "labourist" – rather than socialist – challenge to neoliberalism. Here, Corbynism is viewed as a revival of a labourism that was in decline, defined by Ralph Miliband as an ideology of "modest social reform in a capitalist system within which confines it is ever more firmly and now irrevocably rooted" (1972: 376). Seymour is critical of some on the radical left for overestimating Labour's radical potential and becoming "transfixed by an idea of Labour that has never been close to reality" (2016: 90). Indeed, Seymour concludes, contrary to Byrne, that "nothing is so utopian as to expect the party to be about radical transformation" (*ibid.*: 98).

There can be little doubt that Corbyn and many of his closest allies sat firmly in the Bennite tradition of the Labour Party, a tradition which has since the 1970s demanded the democratization of the party and the introduction of socialist demands as part of "a radical reorganisation of the relationship between state and party, and between party and people" (Panitch & Leys 2020: 8). This has led many to label it as "hard left", but this label arguably overlooks the internal plurality of the Corbyn movement and ignores the important lines of continuity that existed between Corbyn's Labour Party and more mainstream Labour traditions of the past (see Maiguashca & Dean 2019). Bassett (2019) captures these influences when he describes Corbynism as "social democracy in a New Left Garb". In this respect, the Corbyn project can be said to combine anti-racist, feminist and environmentalist politics with the more traditional "labourist" demands of fighting to win power in a parliamentary system. This combination of old and new elements is encapsulated by Bassett's use of the term "new labourism". Similarly, Dean argues that the anti-austerity movement has been characterized by an intellectual reorientation of the Left – which he defines as a "popular leftism" – that has involved the predominance of "post-colonial and de-colonial theory, environmentalism and radical green theory, and new strands of feminist thinking" (Dean 2020: 11). For Dean, this formed one part of the Corbynist coalition, representing a challenge to the more traditional demands of democratic socialism.

## Corbynism, class and populism

On one level, Corbyn's rise to the Labour leadership appeared to be part of a broader wave of popularity for radical left parties throughout the global North following the global financial crisis. Some notable examples include Bernie Sanders' presidential campaigns in 2016 and 2019, Syriza's period in government between 2015 and 2019, Podemos' rise to coalition government in 2019 and Jean-Luc Mélenchon's La France Insoumise, set up in 2011. This family of parties have often been described by commentators as examples of left-populism (Kioupkiolis 2016; Katsambekis & Kioupkiolis 2019; Damiani 2020). Podemos and La France Insoumise, for example, were founded with the specific intent of mobilizing a populist frontier predicated on a discourse of the "people" versus the "elite", and commentators have noted the common deployment of typically populist discourse by leaders such as Sanders and Alexis Tsipras.

In this context, some commentators have argued that Corbynism was similarly populist in its appeal, particularly following the leadership's reported "populist rebranding" in 2016, which looked to take advantage of the supposed rise of populism seen in the previous years (Stewart & Elgot 2016). Mouffe (2018a), for example, has written about her support for Corbynism because she saw it as an attempt to open a left-populist frontier by uniting a plurality of political demands against different forms of domination, although one that is divided between its more popular-democratic grassroots and traditional labourism. Extending this argument, Smith (2019) saw Corbynism as a popular frontier created through the "productively adversarial" construction of a people versus an elite, but with the caveat that this is a people that is not homogenous but plural and fluid. Corbynism was able to construct a fluid definition of the "people" to make "an economic and democratic offer that would be simultaneously enabling to the demands of all these individual groups, even as it makes no claim to insist on their being reconciled" (Smith 2019: 143). In a more critical view, meanwhile, Bolton and Pitts (2018) criticize Corbynism for embracing a simplistic Manichean worldview, which easily slips into what they describe as "populist nativism". This, for example, manifested itself in an anti-austerity populism whereby Corbynites treated the 99 per cent and the 1 per cent as mutually exclusive groups, complained conspiratorially of a "rigged system" and saw Corbyn as a "morally exceptional" character who stood against the establishment (Bolton & Pitts 2018). Thus, Corbynism had all the hallmarks of a populist political project representing the authentic voice of working-class "people" who are seen as "inherently moral and naturally good beings, and [...] as a whole a unified, self-sufficient, organic community" (*ibid.*: 198). According to Bolton and Pitts, this is how Corbynism cultivated what became a monolithic community out of its formerly disaggregated grassroots. Moreover, Corbynism's moral crusade filtered into internal party management whereby the basic litmus test for any candidate was whether they fell in line with the leadership, a form of populist management that closes rather than opens up debate. This point is echoed from within a different perspective by Watts and Bale (2018), who argue that Corbyn exalted the membership to legitimize his position against the PLP in a way that resonates with a populist leader's virtuous appeal to the "people".

Contrary to these accounts, Maiguashca and Dean (2017, 2019a) have argued that Corbyn's supporters did not construct a systematic notion of the "people", but instead saw Corbynism as a "movement" encompassing a diverse community of members, trade unions and extra-parliamentary groups on the left. Momentum, an organization of Corbyn's supporters, has been constituted by these plural strands and has deployed the language of "movementism" to create a sense of community (see Dennis 2020). The diversity resulted in the adoption of particular political positions and values – Dean and Maiguashca cite the examples of "anti-austerity", "equality", "fairness" and "hope" – which can be populistic but are not populist *per se*. Corbyn certainly made references to the "people" in some of his speeches, but they question whether this amounted to a fully articulated populism (Dean & Maiguashca 2020). It is argued that Corbyn's ideology, in line with the community of activists drawn towards it, was amorphous enough to defy any easy definition, representing a wide range of traditions on the popular left, including environmentalism, feminism and antiracism (Maiguashca & Dean 2019; Dean 2020). It is this "left catch-allism" that can arguably account for some of the contestation over what Corbynism stood for; a contestation that extended to its own followers.

Despite the amorphous character of the project, Corbynism evidently displayed a line of continuity with the democratic socialist traditions of the Labour Party, in particular the dormant Labour New Left, which has been one tenet of the party since the 1970s (see Panitch & Leys 2020). Indeed, Momentum (2017), set up to represent the supporters drawn in by Corbyn's leadership, self-identifies as a socialist organization. This has implications for how we should contextualize Corbynism within the wider family of left-wing parties that emerged following the financial crisis, and in particular for the view that it should be seen as an example of left-populism. Although the Corbyn project did display a lot of overlap with the broader wave of left-populism, especially in terms of its emphasis on popular-democracy, it was also strongly influenced by the long-standing democratic socialist tradition (see Panitch & Leys 2020). This socialist underpinning leads Panitch and Gindin to criticize those who describe the wave of radical left parties around 2015–20 as left-populist. For these authors, the socialist discourse from which today's radical left leaders draw is explicitly class-focused and aims to bring "fresh political attention to the dynamics, structures, inequalities, and contradictions of capitalism as the systemic core of neoliberal globalisation and ruling class privilege and power" (Panitch & Gindin 2018: 1–2).

## Freeden on ideology

As we have seen, then, the ideology of Corbynism defies any type of easy definition. However, before we attempt to approach a broad definition, it is perhaps useful to remind ourselves of what constitutes an ideology. Here, it is helpful to turn to the work of Freeden (1996, 2003), who is arguably the foremost contemporary scholar of ideology. Freeden sees ideology as a "set of ideas, beliefs, opinions, and values", "held by significant groups", who "exhibit a recurring pattern" and want to implement public policy with the "aim of justifying, contesting or changing the social and political arrangements and processes of a political community" (Freeden 2003: 32). From this starting point, Freeden provides a guide for researching ideology, which he calls a "morphological approach". Ideologies are seen as "clusters" of concepts – such as liberty, democracy and equality – which have an immanent and sustainable logic. The cluster has a three-tiered structure, comprised of core, adjacent and peripheral concepts. Any concept is "essentially contestable", but complete ideologies "decontest" their core concepts to the extent that they cannot be disputed (*ibid.*: 54). Core concepts must be present in all variants of an ideological family, whereas adjacent and peripheral concepts must accommodate core concepts without altering their central meaning. Freeden sees this as an inherent and necessary feature of ideologies, which enables them to make coherent collective decisions. For example, any one of the multiple variations of liberalism must have the core concept of liberty at its core. In addition to this, Freeden adds a temporal and spatial dimension to ideology, seeing them as fluid and shifting, and capable of adapting to prevailing circumstances. As such, they are a product of time, space and active political practice.

Freeden creates a distinction between "macro" (thick) and "micro" (thin) ideologies. Macro-ideologies are the grand ideologies of the twentieth century: socialism, conservatism, liberalism, fascism and communism. These ideologies seek "social and political dominance on both national and international levels" (*ibid.*: 78), whereas a micro-ideology, such as nationalism, does "not embrace the full range of questions that the macro-ideologies do, and is limited in its ambitions and scope" (*ibid.*: 98). He points out that mass parties are responsible for selling ideologies to the electorate but that these are at the long end of the production line, which inevitably leads to a dilution of the ideology. Thus, "ideologies *emerge* among groups within a party or outside of it. Those groups may consist of intellectuals or skilled rhetoricians, who themselves are frequently articulating more popular or inchoate beliefs or, conversely, watering down complex philosophical positions" (*ibid.*: 79; emphasis in original). Finally, Freeden paints a picture of twenty-first-century ideologies as an increasingly eclectic mix, which tends to be "more fragmented, more ephemeral, looser and less stable than the conventional model" of twentieth-century grand ideologies (Freeden 2017: 6).

Freeden's definition of ideology provides us with a useful starting point for understanding Corbynism. As we have touched on already, the ideological components of Corbynism are to some extent diverse, having been the product of some radical ideological tendencies working within the confines of a reasonably moderate, centre-left party. Inevitably, this means that we should expect Corbynism to be reflective of a series of compromises and mediations between the diverse range of groups that made up the Labour Party at that particular historical moment. Corbynism incorporated a diverse range of ideological inputs – including, among others, social democracy, democratic socialism, populism, feminism, antiracism and environmentalism – which perhaps goes some way to explain why it came to mean so many things to different people.

## Corbynism as an ideology

In order to try to reach a more concrete definition of the ideology of Corbynism, it is worth exploring Freeden's view of socialism, as this was the broad prism through which both Corbyn and many of his supporters viewed his leadership. According to Freeden (1996: 415–82; 2003: 83–6), socialists broadly believe that humans are social beings first and foremost; the pursuit of equality and the removal of hierarchy should be their central objective; work is a constitutive feature of human nature; the elimination of poverty is of the utmost importance; and history is broadly moving in a progressive direction. He argues that where socialism was originally concerned with the transcendence of existing social relations, it has gradually become more oriented to improving economic conditions for workers as well as their more effective participation in social and political life. In many cases this has led to a unification of socialism with more progressive liberalism to create a programme oriented around redistribution and an expanded welfare state, with the Attlee government being the most notable British example.

If we take Freeden's definition, it is not unreasonable to see Corbynism as a contemporary iteration of the long tradition of socialist ideas. At the core of Corbynism was a concern with rectifying inequality, and its supporters advocated, to varying degrees, some form of redistribution between capital and labour. This is reflected in various policies of the Labour Party under Corbyn, including the nationalization of rail, mail, water and electricity, the "inclusive ownership fund" and an increase in taxes for the wealthiest. Supporters were also critical of the hierarchical structure of past nationalizations under former Labour governments and demanded a more bottom-up form of public ownership based on "control, democracy, and participation" (Guinan & O'Neill 2018: 5). Corbyn also placed a commitment to ending poverty (in-work and out-of-work) at the centre of his agenda. And, as Byrne (2019) argues, there was a future-oriented element to the movement, and this was reflected in the work of Bastani (2019) and Srnicek and Williams (2015), both of whom played a formative role in shaping some of the ideas at the heart of Corbynism. There is also clearly a collectivist egalitarianism that runs through the Corbyn project, shaping its approach to issues of class, race, gender and sexuality.

Yet, all of this still leaves unanswered questions over the extent of its proposed radicalism. According to Freeden, although socialism aims to be transformative, over time it has gradually become less so. The accommodation that it seeks to make with capitalism and liberal democracy has led it towards social democracy, rather than socialism *per se* (see also March & Mudde 2005). As we discussed earlier, Corbynism has been labelled by some as a "social democratic" political project, and by others as an example of "democratic socialism". Whereas there is a significant degree of overlap between social democracy and democratic socialism, democratic socialism has come to distinguish itself by its more "radical commitment to systemic transformation, usually through a commitment to grassroots democracy and (especially) through a rejection of capitalism" (March & Mudde 2005: 34). Social democracy, on the other hand, tends to be more willing to leave management and control of firms in the hands of private ownership and retains a commitment to parliamentary democracy (Busky 2000; Bolton 2020). Given this, there remains some ambiguity over whether Corbynism deserves the label of social democracy or democratic socialism; in reality, it is probably best to view it as containing elements of both traditions.

In existing comparative accounts of Europe's radical left (for example, see contributions in March & Mudde 2016), neither the Labour Party nor Corbynism have thus far been analysed in any sort of depth. Bassett (2019) and Seymour (2016) have argued that Labour's programme under Corbyn's leadership showed strong lines of continuity with traditional social democratic offerings of the past and did not directly challenge capitalism. In fact, the Labour Party consistently argued that its policy package was supported by big business because of its commitment to investment and infrastructure (Walker & Weaver 2017). On the other hand, some agreed that Corbynism was not strictly socialist in and of itself, but that in the long run it was the first step towards a "radical shift in the balance of power, income and wealth, transforming the political, economic and social levels" (Schneider, quoted in Panitch & Leys 2020: 217). In terms of its commitment to grassroots democracy, Corbynism was ultimately wedded to parliamentary democracy, although the commitment to "members-led" democratization arguably represented a degree of normative commitment to a more direct style of democracy (see Ward 2021). As such, despite some social democratic leanings, Corbynism retained some elements of democratic socialist thinking.

As well as discussing the parameters of democratic socialism, March and Mudde also provide a definition of the label "radical left". According to these authors, the radical left is radical because it "rejects the underlying socio-economic structure of contemporary capitalism and its values and practices" and advocates "alternative economic and power structures involving a major redistribution of resources from the existing political elites" (March & Mudde 2005: 25). It is "Left" because it aims towards tackling economic inequality as a primary goal, and because "anti-capitalism is more consistently expressed than anti-democracy, although a radical subversion of liberal democracy may be implicit or explicit" (*ibid.*). Another feature of its politics, which defines it as leftist, is its commitment to internationalism.

Based on this definition, Corbynism was clearly left, but was not necessarily radical left. In terms of March and Mudde's definition of "radical", many support-ers of Corbynism perceived themselves to be anti-capitalist or post-capitalist, while others did not. While there was a future-oriented aspect to Corbynism, which attempted to conceive of alternative models of ownership as a challenge to capitalism, to some, this did not necessarily equate to a "rejection" of capitalism, rather than a rectification of its harsher injustices. What served as a further hin-drance to the radical potential of the Corbyn project is the fact that it was located within a relatively moderate, centre-left Labour Party (see Seymour 2016), which inevitably required it to make compromises. As such, although Corbynism may have been radical to some of its supporters, once it was passed through the medi-ating institutions of the Labour Party, it presented itself in a much more diluted form. As a result, while it does not squarely fit with the first part of March and Mudde's definition of "radical", it does fit with the second part, in its commitment to tackling inequality through redistributive measures.

Taking March and Mudde's definition of the "Left" in "Radical Left", equality is a core concept, whether on the basis of class, gender, race or sexuality. Various actors within the movement would probably give different levels of priority to these different equality struggles, but the overarching idea that inequality can-not be justified on the basis of individual difference lay at the core of Corbyn's ideology. Beyond that, anti-capitalism was not necessarily a central element of Corbynism, but it could be considered a common adjacent or peripheral concept to at least some of its supporters; some saw themselves as anti-capitalist, whereas others did not. Moreover, many Corbynites were sceptical of liberal democracy, instead preferring more participatory forms of direct decision-making, captured by the support for policies such as "open selection" and "member-led" democ-ratization, which envisage a wholesale redistribution of power away from the parliamentary elite towards party members (see Watts & Bale 2018). However, as we mentioned earlier, because Corbynism was an ideology rooted within a major parliamentary party, support for Corbynism required at least some implicit sup-port for the Westminster version of liberal democracy.

Finally, at face value, Corbynism appeared to be very internationalist or glo-balist in its outlook. Corbyn was one of the most pro-immigration Labour lead-ers in history, had always taken a keen interest in international relations and regularly employed the language of international solidarity, which was com-mon parlance among many activists. However, some argue that Corbyn's inter-nationalism was compromised after he took up his position as party leader. Hassan and Shaw (2019) contend that while there have been liberal and socialist internationalist traditions within the Labour Party, by far the biggest influence on its approach to foreign affairs has been a conservative form of traditional patriotism, and Corbyn proved to be no exception to this rule, despite his more radical domestic policy agenda. Bolton and Pitts root this "nativism" – which in their view informed the leader's "Lexit" position on Brexit – within the Bennite tradition that regards "the post-1945 international order as an [...] undemocratic, superficial cover for class, if not national, oppression" (2018: 68). However, as Panitch and Leys (2020) have argued, the critique of the EU and the broader "international order" by the Bennite left does not entail a rejection of internationalism so much as a rethinking of how it should be organized according to socialist credentials.

As has been stressed throughout this chapter, any interpretation of Corbynism as a collective ideology should consider the different strands within the broader community. Many supporters of Corbynism, including in Momentum, began their activism or participation in politics outside of the party. As Momentum's founders highlighted, this included people who had been members of other political parties, activists from pre-2008 social movements and the left of the trade union movement (Klug *et al.* 2016). Others, however, were drawn from the socialist tradition of the Labour Party or were perhaps discontented party members drawn to Corbyn's promise of party democracy and anti-austerity. Thus, the movement which began to spring up around Corbyn's leadership encompassed a diverse range of political actors and ideological inputs.

Adding to this complexity, Corbynism also involved an ongoing process of negotiation, at different decision-making levels, with the trade unions, who brought their own ideas and interests to the table. For example, at Labour's 2019 conference, the GMB union, which represents many workers in fossil fuel industries, opposed a motion setting the 2030 target for net zero fossil fuel emissions in the Green New Deal despite the overwhelming support of Labour members (O'Hagan 2019). During this episode, the environmentalist values of many grassroots activists found themselves in direct confrontation with the labourist values of the trade unions. In the end, the motion passed, although the 2030 target did not make its way into the 2019 election manifesto, which demonstrates why, to some, Corbynism was inevitably trapped within the confines of labourism (e.g. Seymour 2016). Although this is true to some extent, to others within the movement it nevertheless held the potential to be the first step towards radical progressive change (e.g. Smith 2019). While this footnote in Labour history highlights some prevailing ideological tensions, according to Freeden's definition of ideology it can be described as a contest over peripheral values, rather than core concepts. The final motions at the same conference included a commitment to maintaining unionized jobs as part of the green industrial revolution – demonstrating the combined influence of labourist and environmentalist values.

Returning to Freeden's work again, we might argue that, at its core, all supporters of Corbynism agreed that tackling inequality was a core aim that needed to be addressed, but what separated some of these supporters was the priority given to certain peripheral aims, such as the balance between protecting jobs and upholding environmental standards. Another area of contestation was the pace and depth of the changes that a Corbyn government should pursue. Some viewed change in a more gradualist sense, whereas others argued for more radical change. Yet all of its supporters agreed that "transformation" in some capacity or other was needed, even if this only came in the long term. There is also at its core a more critical view of contemporary capitalist social relations, coupled, among many of its supporters, with a keen desire for a more direct form of democracy than that offered by Labour's parliamentary traditions. From this then, although the extent of its potential radicalism might not be entirely clear, there remained a commitment to certain core concepts, regardless of whether or not these can all be considered "socialist" by March and Mudde's (2005) definition of the term. Very few people would doubt that Corbynism was "left", although there is a lack of clarity surrounding the extent to which it could be considered "radical left".

## Corbyn's leftist catch-allism?

From all of this then, we can see that, although Corbynism incorporated a diverse range of sometimes conflicting ideological inputs, it is nevertheless possible to identify a number of core elements that held the project together. These included commitments towards tackling inequality, redistribution, egalitarianism and a "transformative" ambition. Yet, beyond these core elements there still remained some level of ambiguity around whether Corbynism represented an example of social democracy or democratic socialism, and over the question of how radical its aims were. Additionally, there was still some uncertainty over the peripheral elements of its ideology: for example, in terms of the level of priority it gave to environmental issues, the nature and depth of its internationalism, the pace at which it would enact "transformative" change, its orientation in relation to capitalism, its commitment to liberal democracy, the relationship between its populist and class-oriented discourses, and over the priority it would give to certain groups' struggles for equality.

In many ways, this level of ambiguity was perhaps useful to the project. It arguably enabled it to appeal to and to mobilize a wide range of actors both on the left and the radical left. Thus, Corbynism became a focal point for a diverse group of activists, regardless of whether they prioritized environmental issues or traditional labourist issues, or whether they believed in prioritizing injustices relating to race, gender, class or disability, or saw themselves as socialists, social democrats, social liberals, anti-capitalists or post-capitalists. As a result, one way to capture the manifold character of the project, and its broad appeal across a wide spectrum of critical activists, would be to describe it as an example of "leftist catch-allism". Such a label could also, perhaps, help us to explain why Corbynism was able to grow Labour's membership, at its peak, to over 500,000, as it drew in a plurality of groups on the left and radical left, including socialists, environmentalists, feminists, social liberals and social democrats.

To explore this idea of Corbynism's catch-allism a little further, it is perhaps useful here to return to Freeden again and, in particular, to his attempt to introduce the concept of temporality, or time, into his conception of ideology. According to Freeden (2003: 75) ideologies contain different conceptions of time, and these play a critical role in shaping the way they interpret the social and political world and how they conceive of the need for collective political change. If we think about this point in relation to Corbynism, it is possible to identify at least four different conceptions of time that helped to animate the project in different ways and to enhance its catch-all appeal. On the one hand we can see within Corbynism an element of a forward-looking "utopian" vision, which aimed to bring the future into the present through its imagining of a "concrete utopia" (Byrne 2019). In contrast, Corbynism also retained a strong connection to the past and an attempt to rejuvenate some of the party's labourist traditions. Here, Corbynism could be seen as an attempt to return the party to its "traditional core values of social justice, redistribution, public ownership and state-led growth" (Kerr *et al.* 2018: 298). In terms of the pace of change, Corbynism contained both a social democratic commitment to a "gradualist" redistribution programme, which aimed to bring benefits to working people over time, and, at the same time, a more radical, socialist commitment to bringing about an accelerated transformation of capitalism and the introduction of an alternative model of economic growth.

While the concept of "leftist catch-allism" can provide some handle on why Corbynism was able to mobilize a plurality of actors, and why it has been described in such protean terms by different commentators, there still remain some unanswered questions. First, it still does not fully explain what united this diverse group of activists into one seemingly coherent community under the leadership of Corbyn. Some critics have even gone as far as to describe Corbynism as a "cult" (N. Cohen 2017), while other commentators have argued that the "moralization" that underpinned much of Corbynism's rhetoric was essential to its homogeneity (Bolton & Pitts 2018). In a more positive sense, Dean (2017) sees the relationship between Corbyn and his supporters as an example of a type of "politicising fandom" that he claims is reminiscent of pop stars' relationships with their fans. For Dean, this relationship can be a productive means for bringing to light a set of shared demands and grievances that the leader comes to embody. Yet, as it stands, the existing literature gives us few clues as to which particular sets of demands and grievances played a pivotal role in uniting so many activists and supporters behind the cause.

Second, there remain unanswered questions about the extent to which Corbynism can be described as a "populist" political project, and how it related to the broader family of left parties that emerged in the wake of the global financial crisis. It remains unclear whether these parties should be considered left-populist, "popular leftist", or whether they represent a renewal of the more traditional elements of democratic socialism. Is it the case that Corbynism could be considered to be part of the wider family of radical left parties? Or does it represent continuity with the lineage of traditions in the Labour Party?

Third, although some accounts of Corbynism have located its links to various ideological traditions, none of these provide a detailed account of the elements which made it a unique historical political project. What are the traits (for example the "fandom" surrounding Corbyn, or its combination of popular-democratic and socialist claims) that gave Corbynism its unique character and how do these compare to examples of radical left politics elsewhere in the world? In order to gain a fuller understanding of the significance of Corbynism as a unique period in British politics, further research is needed to explore where and how it represented divergence with its historical predecessors.

**Conclusion**

Returning to where we began this chapter, it seems reasonable to assert that Corbynism represented a serious challenge to the influence of neoliberalism on British politics. Not only did it provide a powerful ideological alternative, but it also captured a political party with a realistic chance of winning state power, as it came close to doing in the 2017 general election. Beyond this, however, while it is possible to identify several core concepts that brought a level of ideological coherence to Corbynism and enabled it to mobilize a diversity of political actors on the left, there are still a lot of ambiguities and unresolved questions about the precise character of its ideological make-up. This is in part due to the plurality of groups that helped to shape the Corbyn project and the different sets of priorities and types of emphasis each of these brought to the table. It is also due, as we have discussed, to the fact that Corbynism, as a political project that displayed a degree of radical potential, was located within a relatively moderate and divided Labour Party, which forced Corbyn and his supporters to make a number of ideological and policy compromises.

However, some of the unanswered questions around Corbynism also stem from the fact that there is still a relative dearth of detailed scholarly work on this period of Labour's history. As Maiguashca and Dean (2019) have noted, many of the existing studies fail, overall, to explain precisely why and how Corbynism incited such levels of passion among supporters and opponents alike. As Bolton and Pitts (2018) have highlighted, there is a tendency for commentators to take a relatively partial view of Corbynism, either to dismiss or conversely to glorify it, depending on the perspective of the commentator. The result is an often less than thorough understanding of the key dynamics that gave it both its dramatic rise between 2015 and 2017, and its abrupt decline between 2017 and 2019. More detailed empirical work is needed to give some firmer insights into the elements that allowed Corbynism to inspire such a dramatic increase in Labour's membership and put the Left in a historically unprecedented position in British politics. In addition, more detailed analysis is needed to provide some answers to how Corbynism unravelled to leave the Left once again in a position of disorientation and retreat.

## References

Bale, T., M. Poletti & P. Wenn 2016. "Ideology is in the eye of the beholder". LSE blog. https://blogs.lse.ac.uk/politicsandpolicy/ideology-is-in-the-eye-of-the-beholder/ (accessed 12 March 2021).

Bassett, L. 2019. "Corbynism: social democracy in a new left garb". *Political Quarterly* 90(4): 777–84.

Bastani, A. 2019. *Fully Automated Luxury Communism*. London: Verso.

Batrouni, D. 2020. *The Battle of Ideas in the Labour Party: From Attlee to Corbyn and Brexit*. Bristol: Bristol University Press.

Bolton, M. 2020. "Democratic socialism and the concept of (post)capitalism". *Political Quarterly* 91(2): 334–42.

Bolton, M. & H. Pitts 2018. *Corbynism: A Critical Approach*. Bingley: Emerald.

Busky, D. 2000. *Democratic Socialism: A Global Survey*. New York, NY: Praeger.

Byrne, L. 2019. "How Jeremy Corbyn brought Labour back to the future: visions of the future and concrete utopia in Labour's 2017 electoral campaign". *British Politics* 14(3): 250–68.

Cohen, N. 2017. "Labour conference? More like the Cult of St Jeremy". *The Guardian*. Available at: https://www.theguardian.com/commentisfree/2017/sep/30/labour-conference-more-like-the-cult-of-saint-jeremy (accessed 12 March 2021).

Corbyn, J. 2016. Jeremy Corbyn's speech to Annual Conference 2016. Available at: https://www.policyforum.labour.org.uk/news/jeremy-corbyn-s-speech-to-annual-conference-2016 (accessed 12 March 2021).

Damiani, M. 2020. *Populist Radical Left Parties in Western Europe: Equality and Sovereignty*. Abingdon: Routledge.

Dean, J. 2017. "Politicising fandom". *British Journal of Politics and International Relations* 19(2): 408–24.

Dean, J. 2020. "Left politics and popular culture in Britain: from left-wing populism to 'popular leftism'" *Politics*. https://doi.org/10.1177/0263395720960661.

Dean, J. & B. Maiguashca 2020. "Did somebody say populism? Towards a renewal and reorientation of populism studies". *Journal of Political Ideologies* 25(1): 11–27.

Dennis, J. 2020. "A party within a party posing as a movement? Momentum as a movement faction". *Journal of Information Technology and Politics* 17(2): 97–113.

Freeden, M. 1996. *Ideologies and Political Theory: A Conceptual Approach.* Oxford: Clarendon Press.

Freeden, M. 2003. *Ideology: A Very Short Introduction.* Oxford: Oxford University Press.

Freeden, M. 2017. "After the Brexit referendum: revisiting populism as an ideology". *Journal of Political Ideologies* 22(1): 1–11.

Gerbaudo, P. 2017. *The Mask and the Flag: Populism, Citizenism, and Global Protest.* Oxford: Oxford University Press.

Gilbert, J. 2017. "The absolute Corbyn". In M. Perryman (ed.), *The Corbyn Effect.* London: Lawrence & Wishart.

Guinan, J. & M. O'Neill 2018. "The institutional turn: New Labour's political economy". *Renewal* 26(2): 5–16.

Hall, S-M. *et al.* 2017. "Intersecting inequalities: the impact of austerity on black and ethnic minority women in the UK". London: Women's Budget Group, Runnymede Trust, Coventry Women's Voices and RECLAIM. https://wbg.org.uk/wp-content/uploads/2018/08/Intersecting-Inequalities-October-2017-Full-Report.pdf (accessed 12 March 2021).

Hassan, G. & E. Shaw 2019. *The People's Flag and the Union Jack: An Alternative History of Britain and the Labour Party.* London: Biteback.

Hay, C. 1999. *The Political Economy of New Labour – Labouring Under False Pretences?* Manchester: Manchester University Press.

Heffernan, R. 2001. "Beyond Euroscepticism: Exploring the Europeanisation of the Labour Party since 1983". *Political Quarterly* 72 (2): 180–90.

Katsambekis, G. & A. Kioupkiolis (eds) 2019. *The Populist Radical Left in Europe.* Abingdon: Routledge.

Kerr, P. *et al.* 2018. "Getting back in the Delorean: modernisation vs anti-modernisation in contemporary British politics". *Policy Studies* 39(18): 292–309.

Kioupkiolis, A. 2016. "Podemos: the ambiguous promises of left-wing populism in contemporary Spain". *Journal of Political Ideologies* 21(2): 99–120.

Klug, A., E. Rees & J. Schneider 2016. "Momentum: a new kind of politics". *Renewal* 24(2): 36–44.

Labour Party 2017. "Alternative Models of Ownership. Report to Shadow Chancellor of the Exchequer". http://www.labour.org.uk/page//PDFs/9472_Alternative%20Models%20of%20Ownership%20all_v4.pdf.

Maiguashca, B. & J. Dean 2017. "Corbyn's Labour and the populism question". *Renewal* 25(3/4): 56–65.

Maiguashca, B. & J. Dean 2019. "Corbynism, populism and the re-shaping of left politics in contemporary Britain". In G. Katsambekis & A. Kioupkiolis (eds), *The Populist Radical Left in Europe*, 73–92. Abingdon: Routledge.

Maiguashca, B. & J. Dean 2019a. "'Lovely people but utterly deluded?' British political science's trouble with Corbynism". *British Politics* 15: 48–68. https://doi.org/10.1057/s41293-019-00124-5.

March, K. & C. Mudde (eds) 2016. *Europe's Radical Left: From Marginality to the Mainstream.* New York, NY: Rowman & Littlefield.

March, L. & C. Mudde 2005. "What's Left of the Radical Left? the European Radical Left after 1989: decline *and* mutation". *Comparative European Politics* 3(1): 23–49.

Milburn, K. 2019. *Generation Left.* Cambridge: Polity.

Miliband, R. 1972. *Parliamentary Socialism: A Study in the Politics of Labour.* London: Merlin Press.

Mouffe, C. 2018. *For a Left-Populism.* London: Verso.

Mouffe, C. 2018a. "Jeremy Corbyn's Left Populism". https://www.versobooks.com/blogs/3743-jeremy-corbyn-s-left-populism(accessed 12 March 2021).

Myers, M. 2017. *Student Revolt: Voices of the Austerity Generation.* London: Pluto.

Nunns, A. 2018. *The Candidate: Jeremy Corbyn's Improbable Path to Power.* Second edition. London: OR Books.

O'Hagan, E. 2019. "Political highlight of the week? Actually, it was Labour's carbon game-changer". *The Guardian,* 25 September. https://www.theguardian.com/commentisfree/2019/sep/25/labour-green-new-deal (accessed 12 March 2021).

Momentum 2017. Constitution. https://peoplesmomentum.com/wp-content/uploads/2019/10/Amended-Constitution-2019-1.pdf (accessed 12 March 2021).

Panitch, L. & C. Leys 2020. *Searching for Socialism: The Project of the Labour New Left from Benn to Corbyn.* London: Verso.

Panitch, L. & S. Gindin 2018. *The Socialist Challenge Today: Syriza, Sanders, Corbyn.* Brecon: Merlin Press.

Perryman, M. (ed.) 2017. *The Corbyn Effect.* London: Lawrence & Wishart.

Pitts, F. & S. Dinerstein 2017. "Corbynism's conveyor belt of ideas: postcapitalism and the politics of social reproduction". *Capital and Class* 41(3): 423–34.

Seymour, R. 2016. *Corbyn: The Strange Rebirth of Radical Politics.* London: Verso.

Smith, J. 2019. *Other People's Politics: Populism to Corbynism.* Alresford: Zero Books.

Srnicek, N. & A. Williams 2015. *Inventing the Future: Postcapitalism and a World Without Work.* London: Verso.

Stewart, H. & J. Elgot 2016. "Labour plans Jeremy Corbyn relaunch to ride anti-establishment wave". *The Guardian,* 15 December. https://www.theguardian.com/politics/2016/dec/15/labour-plans-jeremy-corbyn-relaunch-as-a-leftwing-populist (accessed 12 March 2021).

Walker, P. & M. Weaver 2017. "McDonnell says government sees Labour as government in waiting". *The Guardian,* 16 November. https://www.theguardian.com/politics/2017/nov/16/end-austerity-public-services-john-mcdonnell-labour-budget (accessed 12 March 2021).

Ward, B. 2021. "Managing democracy in Corbyn's Labour Party: faction-fighting or movement-building?" *British Politics.* https://doi.org/10.1057/s41293-021-00158-8.

Watts, J. & T. Bale 2018. "Populism as an intra-party phenomenon: the British Labour Party under Jeremy Corbyn". *British Journal of Politics and International Relations* 21(1): 99–115.

# 4

# IS CORBYN A POPULIST?

*David Jeffery*

Populism is a difficult concept to pin down. This chapter follows the well-trodden path of opening with a statement highlighting that populism is an essentially contested concept, and that it has been conceptualized in a number of different – and often competing – ways.

The aim of this chapter is to analyse the nascent scholarship on Corbyn and Corbynism within the frameworks of four different understandings of populism. The first two notions – populism as an ideology and populism as a discourse – focus on populism as a substantive way of understanding the world. The third and fourth approaches focus on populism as a style, namely populism as a political strategy and populism as a socio-cultural approach to politics.

Naturally, the approach taken for this chapter involves covering a large theoretical landscape in a short space. Given the relative lack of academic attention given to the five years of Corbynism, this analysis only claims to be a starting point for a further unpacking of the relationship between Corbyn, the Corbynite movement, the Labour Party and populism.

This chapter argues that while Corbynism should not be labelled populist in a substantive understanding of the concept, elements of populism can be found in Corbyn's political style, with his emphasis on direct communication with supporters via rallies, his use of Momentum to reshape the Labour Party and to challenge the centrality of the PLP, and the importance of the moral and the authentic to Corbyn's own personal image, which holds the whole Corbynite experiment together. All of these contribute to a more populist style of politics, especially when considered within the context of the institutionalized British party-political system.

## What is Corbynism?

Before an analysis of whether Corbyn, or the broader Corbyn project, was indeed populist, we should briefly examine the core components of Corbynism (for more detail, see Chapter 3). Ideologically, Corbynism represents a marriage between traditional Bennite economics and a newer, more radical "'postcap-italist' techno-utopian wing", a worldview that sees technological advances, including automation and artificial intelligence, as providing an alternative to the current structure of work within a capitalist society (Bolton & Pitts 2018). The Corbynite project is based on a strong sense of economic nationalism, emerging from the Bennite legacy. Lexit (a portmanteau of left-wing Brexit) is the default position of Bennite economics, which sees the EU broadly, and the Single Market specifically, as imposing a neoliberal capitalist economic system on the state and removing its ability to protect its citizens from the ravages of the global financial system and the economic consequences of unrestricted migration. Benn himself portrayed "leaving the EU in anticolonial terms, describing it as a 'national liber-ation struggle', regarding it as a crucial part of the ongoing battle against 'inter-national capitalism'" (Bolton & Pitts 2018: 51). Thus, leaving the Single Market would allow the state to promote "Corbynism in one country" and enact a range of policies to "protect" the national economy from capitalist forces.

However, the rhetorical radicalism of Corbyn was not supported by radical manifestos, in either 2017 or 2019. As Goes has noted, Corbyn's 2017 election manifesto was "only marginally more radical than the 2015 Labour manifesto" issued under Ed Miliband (Miliband's own former chief adviser labelled it "Milibandism on speed") and it sought to balance the budget and reduce public debt (Goes 2018: 65). The rhetoric was notched up for the 2019 general election, with a series of promises that Corbyn proclaimed were a "once-in-a-generation chance to transform our country", as well as pledging to go after "the tax-dodgers, the landlords, the bad bosses, big polluters" (Goes 2020: 88). However, beyond some promises on free broadband, increased spending and some limited nationalization, the 2019 manifesto was also lacking in radicalism: corporation tax would be increased to a level *lower* than under New Labour, for instance. Thus, rather than representing a new radical economic model, Corbyn and his allies offered a social democratic left Keynesianism (Maiguashca & Dean 2019). To that end, it is somewhat ironic that Corbyn has donned "the mantle of the very social democracy he once decried as insufficient" (Stafford 2016).

In terms of foreign policy, nuclear disarmament was coupled with a strong anti-imperialist and anti-American streak running through Corbynism. This is rooted in two-campism, a hangover from the Cold War and epitomized by the Stop the War Coalition, of which Jeremy Corbyn was chair (and Tony Benn president). For the two-campists, the world is split into two camps (the clue is in the name): the "good" camp, and the "bad" camp. The "bad" camp comprises "imperialists" – the West, especially the US, the UK and Israel, and the EU when they are not opposing the first three – while the "good" camp comprises anyone who opposes states from the "bad". To this end, anyone who opposes "American imperialism" is lauded as a comrade, deserving of solidarity – and of forceful backing.

This leads Corbynites into morally dubious territory. The binary worldview removes room for nuance, especially when it comes to non-Western states. Corbynism, and two-campism more broadly, is unable to grapple with imperialist action undertaken by non-Western states – for example aggressive Chinese expansion or Iranian interference in Iraq and Syria. Furthermore, given their ontological privileging of the state, two-campists fail to grapple fully with internal state struggles, internal demands for independence, or abuses committed by non-Western states, in some cases leading to out-and-out denial of them, on the basis that that state is an anti-imperial ally; thus the Bennite/Corbynite denial of the genocide in Kosovo, the warm backing given to the terrorist group Hamas and Assad's use of chemical weapons on his own population (Bolton & Pitts 2018).

As Bolton and Pitts state, accepting this two-campist "binary worldview has long been the price of entry into Corbyn's milieu. Those who share in it must seemingly forego the capacity to be shocked by any action, however indiscriminately violent or even genocidal by those who are labelled 'anti-imperialist'" (Bolton & Pitts 2018: 80). Thus, all nuances are folded into the "anti-imperialist" label, which allows for a Manichean global divide between good and bad.

There is also a strongly moralistic element to Corbynism: he is perceived by his followers as having been on the "right side of history" on many of the big issues of the previous 40 or so years: apartheid in South Africa, Iraq, opposition to New Labour and to austerity. For Bolton and Pitts, this moral exceptionalism "has proven to be a vital political tool in overcoming the internal contradictions that run through the movement" (Bolton & Pitts 2018: 3). Unlike Tony Benn, who couched his socialism in spiritual references, Corbyn's ideology is more of a secular cosmopolitanism: "More rational dissent than old-time religion, he talks abstractly about justice and human rights, and struggles to invoke loyalty to anything that is historically rooted" (Stafford 2016).

Finally, outside of the party itself, Corbynism is sustained through Momentum, the grassroots organization born out of Corbyn's leadership campaign. Momentum "seeks to defend Corbyn and give voice to various shades of left politics in the UK", and often provided the most vocal support for Corbyn when faced with a hostile CLP (Maiguashca & Dean 2019: 149). To critics of Corbyn, Momentum was a party within a party, loyal not to the Labour Party as a whole but to Corbyn personally, who it saw as the embodiment of the labour movement. Momentum itself is "dual facing: internally, it strives to defend Corbyn's agenda and, in so doing, democratise the Labour Party and externally, to build a liberal-left social movement that can reach out to and engage with the wider public" (*ibid.*).

## Populism as an ideology

The first approach to populism considered is the ideational approach, which conceives of populism as "an ideology that considers society to be ultimately separated into two homogeneous and antagonistic groups, 'the pure people' versus 'the corrupt elite', and which argues that politics should be an expression of the *volonté générale* (general will) of the people" (Mudde 2004: 543). This bifurcation of the population into the pure people and the corrupt elite rests on a moral basis, not an ethnic, racial or class one, and sees the corrupt elite as having "willingly chosen to betray [the people], by putting the special interests and inauthentic morals of the elite over those of the people" (Mudde 2017: 30). This differs from socialism, say, where the people and elite are separated along class lines and class is the basis of their conflict within the political system.

Importantly, populism is a thin-centred ideology, rather than a full ideology. This means it does not possess a full and consistent worldview, nor a full range of solutions to questions of public life in the way that liberalism or socialism does. Instead, thin-centred ideologies like populism or nationalism have "a restricted core attached to a narrower range of political concepts" (Freeden 1998: 750). So, as Mudde notes:

> while populism speaks to the main division in society (between "the pure people" and "the corrupt elite"), and offers general advice for the best way to conduct politics (i.e. in line with "the general will of the people"), it offers few specific views on political institutional or socio-economic issues.                                         (Mudde 2017: 30)

This is important, because it means that populism typically needs a host ideology to which it attaches; it also explains why you can have right-wing populists such as UKIP alongside left-wing populists such as Respect or the Scottish Socialist Party, because the populist aspect of their ideology has attached to a different host ideology.

So, is Corbyn a populist? The media and commentariat seem to think so, as a quick online search will show. Bloom argues that Corbyn and his team had "given traditionally marginalized groups such as young people, non-whites and the poor a renewed voice for shaping the country's present and future. They have given us a positive version of populism" (Bloom 2017). Academic voices have also argued that Corbyn promoted a "variant of left-wing populism" (Dorey 2017: 309–10). Flinders has consistently argued that Corbyn "flirted with populist tendencies", or "offered a mutant or hybrid form of left-wing populism [...] it is difficult not to see Corbyn's success as synonymous with anything other than a distinctive brand of populism" (Flinders 2018: 228). He has also described Corbyn's populism as "populism wearing a cardigan" (Flinders 2019; see also Flinders 2020).

For Bolton and Pitts, both Corbyn and the broader Corbynism project are populist. From a Marxist perspective, they criticize the Corbynite project for having a truncated or personalized critique of capitalism, "one which regards the existence of economic crises, poverty, unemployment and inequality as the direct responsibility of identifiable people or institutions, rather than identifying them as the result of the abstract economic compulsions to which worker and capitalist alike are subject". If it were not for the moral failings of capitalists, "international finance, the 'wealth extractors', the market and the imperialist nations", and their manipulation of the economic system for nefarious ends – all at the expense of the hard-working, productive people – then a fairer system of "mediated labour and production" would follow. For example, in his leadership campaigns Corbyn spoke of "the barriers placed on workers' creativity by a parasitic 'elite'" (Bolton & Pitts 2018: 161). Thus, for Bolton and Pitts, there is a clear "us" and "them", with the moral failings of capitalists at the root of the failures of the current economic system.

However, these articulations are not generally supported by other scholars who classify populist parties or actors. Several expert surveys do not classify Labour under Corbyn as populist: the Popu-List (Rooduijn *et al.* 2019), and the Populism and Political Parties Expert Survey (Meijers & Zaslove 2020a, 2020b). The Chapel Hill Expert Survey ranks Labour's 2019 manifesto as the *least* populist (of the eight parties covered), measured by their position on whether elected office holders or "the people" should make the most important decisions (Bakker *et al.* 2020). The Global Party Survey 2019 finds Labour to be pretty much in the centre of its scale of populist rhetoric, as well as on sub-elements of populism such as how much the party emphasizes the will of the people, whether voters should decide important issues and whether they favour or oppose checks and balances on executive power (Norris 2020). So, in terms of expert surveys at least, Labour under Corbyn was not considered a populist party.

Perhaps the most useful tonic for the idea that Corbyn is a populist in the Muddean sense comes from March, who starts from the position that a party can only be populist if it meets all three conditions of seeing the world as structured in a Manichean binary centred on the notion of morality, seeing "the people" as a "homogenous and virtuous community" and "the elite" "as a corrupt and self-serving entity" (Hawkins & Rovira Kaltwasser 2019: 3). March operationalizes the core elements of Mudde's definition – people-centrism (the pure people), anti-elitism (the corrupt elite) and popular sovereignty (the will of the people) – and through an examination of quasi-sentences in party manifestos for general elections from 2001 to 2015, finds that "the populist Zeitgeist in the UK barely exists" (March 2019: 50).

Instead, both mainstream and non-mainstream political parties have high people-centric scores, relatively low popular sovereignty scores and even lower anti-elitism scores, the net effect of which is that, when combined, the average values make all parties look moderately populist, but when broken down it is clear that this is simply due to a party's people-centric positioning, rather than being populist *in toto* (March 2019: 54–5). For March, it is natural that all parties would want to appear close to "the people", however construed, and in and of itself that is not sufficient to be labelled populist – instead, we should use demotic/demoticism ("closeness to the people") as an alternative to populist/populism in these cases.

March's original analysis predated Corbyn's leadership. However, he later argues that "the 2017 Labour manifesto contains only a handful of invocations against the 'rigged system', and its central slogan ('For the Many not the Few') is authentically Blairite. So seeing Corbyn as a populist is, at best, a half-truth" (March 2017a). He also argues that Corbyn's ideology is too rooted in Bennite traditionalism to be populist (March 2017b), which ties back to Mudde's argument that at the core of populist thinking are moral concerns, rather than class-based concerns. This is a view shared by Martell, who argues that "Corbyn is a democratic socialist but his policies are social democratic, for political as much as ideological reasons" (Martell 2018: 5).

One area where Corbyn (and Corbynism) can be labelled populist, however, is in how they conceptualize the relationship between Labour membership and the PLP. Baggini argues that Corbynism is "populism in its purest form", "destroying the Labour party by pitting the membership against the PLP" (Baggini 2016). Although as leader of the party Corbyn is clearly part of the party's "elite", his long-term outsider status gives him an element of authenticity when he talks about reducing the distance between Labour members (who occupy the role of the "people", in this case) and the PLP (Atkins & Turnbull 2016).

Empowering the Labour membership is a core part of Corbynite ideology, with its roots in the Bennite programme of the 1980s. The Labour Party would be "democratized" and policy would be determined not by a negotiation between "the leadership, ministers, MPs, members, trade unions and affiliates", but rather by the members, who "would be given full control" (Bolton & Pitts 2018: 74). Watts and Bale argue that "the populism of Corbynism is, as it were, local rather than global – situated inside the party itself", thus making populism an intra-party phenomenon (Watts & Bale 2019: 101). In this understanding, the members represent the virtuous people and the elite are represented by the PLP, who are jealously guarding their power and influence within the party machinery. The party itself is viewed by Corbynites as "insufficiently responsive to its members and grassroots activists, who have long felt that the Labour Party under Blair had abandoned them as well as any semblance of left politics" (Maiguashca & Dean 2019: 147) – thus frustrating the translation of the general will of the members into policy.

Corbyn's (and Benn's) argument has long been that the membership is important far beyond its role in manning campaigns or party branches. The membership hold a special type of knowledge, rooted in their "ordinariness and a wisdom that put them in touch with an authentic moral plane" (Watts & Bale 2019: 102). The views of the members should be adhered to, especially when it comes to supporting their choice of leader. This is perhaps best summed up by Diane Abbott, a key Corbynite figure, around the time of the leadership challenge against Corbyn, who said "this is not the PLP versus Jeremy Corbyn – this is the PLP versus the membership. It is the inhabitants of the Westminster bubble versus the ordinary men and women who make up the party in the country" (quoted in Watts & Bale 2019: 106).

As Bolton and Pitts note, however, there are inherent contradictions within the Corbynite strategy of empowering members; when push comes to shove, on the big issues of the day – Brexit, immigration/freedom of movement and the party manifestos for instance – the membership were broadly observers. Policy "is in the last instance determined by the leadership itself, with the membership's role ultimately reduced to defending post hoc decisions taken elsewhere" (Bolton & Pitts 2018: 202).

Overall, then, using the ideational approach of populism we find that Corbyn, and the Corbynite movement in general, are not populist in the traditional sense. The language used by Corbyn is more focused towards people-centrism than it is populism as a whole, and thus does not suggest an element of ideological populism running through the Corbynite project. Instead, populist elements emerge when analysing the intra-party power relations during Corbyn's leadership, and the reification of the membership (even if this is often more pronounced in rhetoric than reality).

## Populism as a discourse

The second approach considered comes from the work of Laclau, who argues that populism is a discourse. Unlike the ideational approach, the Laclauian approach takes a normative stance – populism is good – and a poststructuralist approach, arguing that political identities, such as populism, are created through discursive practices (Hawkins & Rovira Kaltwasser 2019: 4) In this understanding, populism is an attempt to create a new political hegemony which places at its centre the conflict between the people and the elites (Laclau 2005).

A Laclauian understanding of populism sees it as a "political logic", rather than an ideology or movement (Laclau 2005: 117). The political logic of populism is rooted in a series of unmet demands, which are articulated together into a "chain of equivalence" that challenge the existing political hegemony; for example, in Eastern Europe after 1989, "the 'market' signified [...] much more than a purely economic arrangement: it embraced, through equivalential links, contents such as the end of bureaucratic rule, civil freedoms, catching up with the West, and so forth" (Laclau 2005: 95).

For Laclau, this chain of equivalence – various counter-hegemonic demands – is embodied in an "empty signifier", a concept, name, identity and so on, that can unite individuals and can be used to represent the demands articulated in the chain of equivalence (e.g. the Solidarność movement in Poland, or the market in the prior example) (Laclau 2005: 81). This populist logic of articulation thus has at its core the construction of *a* people, even if the empty signifier used is not *the* people. Indeed, an "ensemble of equivalential demands articulated by an empty signifier is what constitutes a people" (Laclau 2005: 171). This notion of the people is only kept together by the idea of a common enemy, the other, which must also represent a rival chain of equivalences: in the absence of an opposition figure, "the populist conception of the people would immediately dissolve into its constituent parts" (Bickerton & Accetti 2017: 193).

Populism is thus a politics of opposition and antagonism, one that challenges the established political hegemony. For Laclau, this is not problematic, but rather the basis "of that exhilarating game that we call politics" (Laclau 2005: 49). Populism stands in opposition to the institutional logic of liberal democracy, which seeks to deal with demands not as a chain of equivalence, but individually, through institutions: parties, parliament, the public sphere are all seen as depoliticizing tools (Peruzzotti 2018), which thus rob those demands of their potentially transformative potentials.

To what extent does Corbynism reflect a Laclauian understanding of populist politics? Laclau, alongside his long-time collaborator Chantal Mouffe, argued that a populist identity of "the people" could be used instead of the working class to provide "a unifying identity in opposition to capitalist elite, especially when built around the figure of a charismatic leader" (Hawkins & Rovira Kaltwasser 2019: 12–13). Mouffe herself argued that Corbyn's success in June 2017 (in so far as coming second in a general election, not being in government, and not being prime minister constitutes success) was due to Corbyn's adoption of a "left-populism", which created a chain of equivalence rooted in demands from "the different democratic struggles running through British society" (Mouffe 2018b). Mouffe argues that "they used the Blairite slogan 'For the many, not the few', but re-signified it in an agonistic way as constructing a political frontier between 'we' and 'they'" (Mouffe 2018a: 38).

Airas points to the populist potential within Corbynism: in arguing for "a fundamental change in the approach to politics in our society", a rejection of "top-down" policy-making and of the privileging of parliament as a site for decision-making, alongside other demands, Corbyn actively worked to create a chain of equivalence, making "populist demands", and could himself act as an empty signifier, "the symbolic leader of this subversive movement that portrays itself as 'the people', [and] opposes the hegemonic ideological consensus, neo-liberalism" (Airas 2019: 447).

Bolton and Pitts point to the post-capitalist wing of the Corbynite movement, directly inspired by Laclau and Mouffe, who strive for "new political subjects constituted beyond the traditional 'working class', and based in the latter's aboli-tion by means of new technological conditions pertaining to an automated end of work" (Bolton & Pitts 2018: 161). This is a prime example of attempting to build a "people" that goes beyond the traditional Marxist/socialist conception of the working class, through uniting various social demands into a chain of equiva-lence. Furthermore, the working class in Corbynism is seen as "a subjective force synonymous with the people", at the risk of – in Bolton and Pitts' critique – removing the urgency of a specific class struggle. Instead, the post-capitalist remedy is to technologically innovate one's way out of capitalist relations, rather than directly challenging or unpicking capitalist social forms (Bolton & Pitts 2018: 196).

However, there are numerous reasons to be doubtful of the claim that Corbyn represents a Laclauian populist movement. First, as with other left-wing parties such as Syriza in Greece and Podemos in Spain, Peruzzotti argues that these organizations "remain tied both to an organizational party structure and a par-liamentary system", even if they "might draw some inspiration from the con-ceptual model of Laclau" (Peruzzotti 2018: 43). Involvement in, or use of, the liberal democratic hegemonic tools of party, for example, undermines the chain of equivalence articulated by the Corbynite "people", given that supporters of other parties, by definition, do not buy into those demands or are making similar demands through rival parties, rather than in a single chain of equivalence. Hence these demands become simply one of many competing demands, either against the dominant hegemony, in support of it, or orthogonal to it: pluralism, not populism.

Second, as Bolton and Pitts argue, Corbynism does not articulate a Laclauian populism because his articulation of "the people" is not without internal demarcation: that "is impossible in a society criss-crossed with class relations" (Bolton & Pitts 2018: 168). Instead, they argue that the Corbynite rhetoric "easily comes to assume a nationalist dimension", rooted in Bennite ideas of "socialism as the protection of a nationally-defined people by a nation-state" (*ibid.*). Beyond class relations, in the Corbynite view society is also demarcated around other lines – gender, ethnicity, religion and sexuality are the obvious ones – with the Labour Party providing individual fora for group representation within the party framework, and prioritizing unique lived experiences over collective identity building. Corbynism does not seek to subsume these individual identities into "the people" – in fact, it seeks to represent individuals via their sub-group membership.

Third, Maiguashca and Dean argue that from the Laclauian perspective "Corbynism can only accurately be described as 'populist' if one were to stretch the meaning of populism so far as to render it meaningless" (Maiguashca & Dean 2019: 145). In presenting populism as an oppositional political logic, Laclau actually robs populism of all its descriptive use – at best it is stating the obvious: politics being about disagreement – but at worst this conception of populism "tell us very little about the specificity of either Corbynism as a movement or populism as a distinct mode of politics", beyond how all political movement seeking radical change can be described (Maiguashca & Dean 2019: 153). Because Laclau's understanding of populism "deals with the creation of political divisions, it becomes indistinct from virtually any other kind of political discourse" (Barr 2018: 153). Indeed, rhetoric around conflict from the Labour elite is centred on the "enemy" Conservative Party – a normal element of party politics! (Maiguashca & Dean 2019).

Thus, Corbynism works within established institutional political frames (parties, elections, parliament), does not seek to unite all social or community movement demands into a "chain of equivalence" and recognizes difference based on demographics. While Corbynism as a project does provide a challenge to the established hegemonic regime – neoliberalism – it does not do so in a Laclauian way.

## Populism as a political strategy

The third approach to populism is as a political strategy. Unlike the ideational or discursive approaches outlined above, this understanding of populism differs due to its concern with behaviour and strategy, as "a means of building and/ or maintaining political power based on the mass mobilization of supporters" (Barr 2018: 44). Weyland identified three components of this approach: there is a leader who *appeals* to a heterogenous mass of followers, and does so in a *direct* manner, with political *organizing taking the form of personal vehicles* with low levels of institutionalization (Weyland 1996). He would later define populism as "a political strategy through which a personalistic leader seeks or exercises government power based on direct, unmediated, uninstitutionalized support from large numbers of mostly unorganized followers" (Weyland 2001: 14).

In this understanding of populism, the role of the leader is vital. The people, as a bloc, are too heterogenous to act alone, and thus the leader provides direction and mobilization, as well as being able to identify the will of the people. The leader aims to reach followers directly, and serves as the unifying bond of the movement, over time developing "a quasi-direct, seemingly personal character" (Weyland 2017: 50). It is important to note that, for Weyland, this understanding of populism is not synonymous with strong leadership – if an organization is strongly ideological (Weyland uses the example of fascism under Mussolini and Nazism under Hitler) then it cannot be classed as populist because the leader is constrained by ideology. Instead, populism "is fully personalistic and therefore, following the leader's whims, more pragmatic and opportunistic"; the leader, not the ideology, is "the very axis around which populism revolves" (Weyland 2017: 54).

Thus, unlike Laclauian discursive populism, where demands emerge from a bottom-up process of articulation and then are projected onto the "empty signifier" of a leader, for adherents of populism as a political strategy it "really rests on a top-down strategy through which a leader marshals plebiscitarian support for the goals that she determines on her own" (*ibid.*).

Populists also rely on sheer numerical force to win influence, power and sustain their authority, rather than relying on groups with special weight within society (e.g. the armed forces, the media or economic elites). Thus, those following a populist political strategy mobilize "the people", showing their strength through mass rallies or street protests, with the hope of the movement sweeping their leaders into office. The direct link between the leader and the people does not lend itself to institutionalized connections such as parties, and thus populist leaders find it easier to mobilize support based on personal commitment and loyalty to the leader. Thus, the populist leader works to harness personal charisma to establish personal loyalty, which can "reach quasi-religious fervor" (Zúquete 2007). The populist leader is able to add a moral element to the struggle by identifying threats to the movement or the "will of the people" as originating from "the enemies of the people", painting their enemies as morally flawed.

Thus, at its core, populism as a political strategy sees a personalistic leader seeking or exercising power based on direct support from unorganized followers. The will of the people is interpreted directly by the leader, rather than via intermediate institutions such as the party. Representation is understood as an identity, rather than a process: people are represented via the leader, who alone understands the will of the people. Thus, charisma is a key element of ensuring the success of the populist leader by binding followers together through bonds of loyalty. As these elements come together "populism forms a coherent political strategy that has often served for winning and maintaining political power" (Weyland 2017: 59).

To what extent does this measure of populism apply to the Corbyn phenomenon? As Bolton and Pitts note, the Corbynite project rests on the idea of Corbyn's own "personal moral exceptionalism" (Bolton & Pitts 2018: 11). This is rooted in a notion – often fictional – that Corbyn has been on the "right side of history" on the big issues (and thus the implication is that things would be better if only Labour had listened to him). Indeed, even when Corbyn has been *proven* to be on the wrong side – sharing platforms with Holocaust deniers and antisemites, terrorist organizations, people holding anti-LGBT values and so on – "actual evidence of his statements and his actions, both past and present, comes a poor second to whatever he is *presumed* to have meant" (Bolton & Pitts 2018: 72). Thus, a moral mythology has sprung up around Corbyn, a quasi-religious movement that sees him as free of sin and incapable of wrongdoing, and when incontrovertible proof of the reverse is presented, the debate shifts to intention or meaning. This quasi-religious dedication among supporters ties in perfectly with the concept of populism as a political strategy.

Furthermore, this concept of Corbyn as "the moral paragon: virtuous, righteous, incorruptible" explains that the reason why many Remain voters stuck by the party even when Labour's stance on Brexit was "virtually identical to the Conservatives, is that they instinctively trusted Corbyn in a way they did not other politicians. And this trust, this absolute faith in his ethical infallibility, is something very specific to Corbyn on a personal level" (Bolton & Pitts 2018: 61). Supporters trust Corbyn's morals, and thus trust him to understand and interpret the "will of the people". Even when the Labour Party's own internal mechanisms for democracy – for example, conference votes – run contrary to the leadership's policy, "Corbyn's imagined persona is the means by which the internal contradictions of the piecemeal theoretical construction of Corbynism are temporarily contained and concealed – a concord altogether impossible without the political cover that his symbolic status provides" (Bolton & Pitts 2018: 73).

Furthermore, even when Corbyn admits an error, many of his supporters do not accept the self-criticism: "Corbyn's symbolic representation thus takes precedence even over the words from his own mouth. This illustrates how Corbynism has relative autonomy from Corbyn, but all the same cannot exist or survive without his image at the centre, holding things together" (Bolton & Pitts 2018: 107). This quasi-religious fervour leads to, as Flinders notes, "an underlying and faintly sinister streak of intolerance towards anyone who criticised the Labour leadership", casting Corbyn as the leader who is authentically in touch with the will of the people, and the establishment PLP as the enemy attempting to thwart this (Flinders 2018: 232–3). So, we can see clear evidence of a personalistic leader who is given scope to interpret the will of the people.

The Labour Party's campaign under Corbyn was rooted in demands for a "new politics" which, according to Flinders, adopted such a strong outsider status that it almost "existed outside and beyond its own parliamentary party" (Flinders 2018: 232). As noted by Worth, Corbyn long faced resistance from within the party, and thus had to look for "bottom-up 'organic' support in order to contest the elitist and established orders within" the party (Worth 2020: 89). This came through Momentum, the organization formed from Corbyn's leadership campaign, which functioned as a direct and unmediated channel of communication with his supporters.

Momentum is fiercely loyal towards Corbyn and was viewed with distrust by most of the PLP – it is often portrayed as a "'fan club' or even a 'cult' [...] as messianic in nature", aiming to defend Corbyn, "democratize" the Labour Party and engage with the wider public (Maiguashca & Dean 2019: 149). Jon Lansman argues both Corbynism and Momentum are "evidentially populist" because they rely on mass rallies. Lansman points to the "ten thousand people in the streets of Liverpool" (although Labour doing well in Liverpool is hardly a surprise (Jeffery 2017)).

The Corbynite leadership used Momentum to circumvent internal Labour Party mechanisms. As Bolton and Pitts argue:

> For all the lip-service paid to "open debate" within the party, the one criterion that counts when it comes to selection for a parliamentary seat, or a place on a Momentum-backed "left slate" for internal elections – which is now itself a guarantee of victory in any internal election, regardless of the strengths or experience of any particular candidate – is the extent of a candidate's explicit support for Corbyn.
>
> (Bolton & Pitts 2018: 202)

Furthermore, despite the call for empowering the members, as Stafford notes, rally audiences "never really [get] to set the agenda. The leader's hallmark is his 'principled', stubborn consistency, rather than any particular willingness to engage in genuine dialogue [...] this was very much politics as we have known it, and it was done rather well" (Stafford 2016). As such, Momentum as an organization strengthens Corbyn: the leader sets the agenda, and the leader best knows the will of the people or movement. The role of the supporter is to follow, to leaflet and to vote for the leader's preferred slate in internal party elections.

Fundamentally, Corbynism holds a highly negative view of "mediating institutions which are not directly shaped or controlled by the movement", seeing
them as:

> [an] obstacle to the direct expression of the desires of the community
> of the good represented by the movement itself [...] anyone who stands
> in the way of that direct relationship – existing democratic structures,
> MPs, non-Corbynite factions in the membership or the electorate itself
> – are placed in the enemy camp.          (Bolton & Pitts 2018: 201)

So, we see strong elements of populism as a strategic approach within Corbynism.
It is clear that Corbynism meets all three criteria of populism as a political
strategy, especially when we consider the fact that political parties are highly
institutionalized in the British political context. We have in Corbyn a leader who
appeals to a heterogenous mass of followers, and who typically does so in a direct
manner, through rallies and protests. Although political organizing does not
solely take the form of personal vehicles with low levels of institutionalization, it
is undeniable that Momentum, born out of Corbyn's leadership campaign, was
used by Corbyn to reshape the Labour Party – ironically through the party's own
internal democratic structures. Not only did Momentum provide a vehicle for
the Corbynite leadership to campaign across the country, but it also provided
an (outsider) vehicle for the Corbynite leadership to campaign *within* the party.
Other elements of populism as a political strategy were present, including the
moral authority of the leader and the movement's trust in the leader to identify the will of the movement in a top-down manner, rather than bottom-up
demands being articulated via the leader as a mouthpiece of the movement.

## Populism as a socio-cultural approach

The final section of this analysis considers populism as a socio-cultural approach,
which considers it in terms of a "high–low dimension", orthogonal to the classic left–right dimension. Ostiguy defines populism as "the flaunting of the
low" and sees defence of the "high" as a core feature of anti-populist politics
(Ostiguy 2017). The high represents the "proper", which is variously demarcated
depending on the relevant civilizational project: for example, liberalism, multiculturalism, orthodox economics or European integration. The low represents
the "other": those who have not necessarily bought into these projects, or who
have views that provoke shame and embarrassment for those on the high axis.
The socio-cultural populist "is almost always transgressive: of the 'proper' way of
doing politics, of proper public behavior, or of what can or 'should' be publicly

said [...] When it has the wind in its sails, populism is the celebratory desecration of the 'high'" (Ostiguy 2017: 76).

The role of the populist, in this understanding, is to "insist quite 'inappropriately' and loudly on making themselves present in the public sphere", acting as an "ugly duckling [...] linked to the most profound, 'truest', authentic, and most deserving part of the homeland". Thus, "the populist politicians and parties claim, loudly, politically incorrectly and often vulgarly, to be that (truly) authentic people's 'fighting hero'" (Ostiguy 2017). To that end, the politics of the high is not representative of the people or the national self.

The high–low axis, for Ostiguy, consists of both the social-cultural and the political-cultural. The social-cultural "encompasses manners, demeanors, ways of speaking and dressing, vocabulary, and tastes displayed in public", with actors on the high presenting themselves as "as well behaved, proper, composed, and perhaps even bookish" (sometimes appearing "stiff, rigid, serious, colorless, somewhat distant, and boring") while on the low:

> people frequently use a language that includes slang or folksy expressions and metaphors, are more demonstrative in their bodily or facial expressions as well as in their demeanor, and display more raw, culturally popular tastes. Politicians on the low are capable of being more uninhibited in public and are also more apt to use coarse or popular language.                                                        (Ostiguy 2017: 78)

For the political-cultural aspect, we see areas of overlap with Weyland's populism as a political-strategic approach: on the high, "political appeals consist of claims to favor formal, impersonal, legalistic, institutionally mediated models of authority", compared to the low where "political appeals emphasize very personalistic, strong (often male) leadership" (Ostiguy 2017: 81). The high represents normal procedure while the low prioritizes closeness to the people – and will often make a point of flaunting procedure to do so.

This social-cultural/political-cultural divide presents a good starting point to analyse Corbyn and Corbynism more broadly. With the socio-cultural emphasis on displayed tastes and demeanours, we do see some elements of the flaunting of the "low" and a rejection of the high, especially with Corbyn's dress sense. As a lifelong backbencher, Corbyn typically rejected a proper suit and tie. In 1984, shortly after he was elected, when asked why he did not take pride in his appearance, he said "It's not a fashion parade. It's not a gentleman's club, it's not a banker's institute, it's a place where the people are represented" (quoted by Samuel Windsor n.d.). Indeed, he spent the intervening 30 or so years looking every inch the stereotypical Trot. In one heated Prime Minister's Questions,

David Cameron – the epitome of "high" – told him to "put on a proper suit, do up your tie and sing the national anthem" (quoted by Watt 2016).

However, by the 2017 general election even Vogue noted how Corbyn's stylist had transformed his "look from a freight train-jumping hobo into a vaguely credible-looking adult" and noted his new penchant for "wearing a red tie for the big moments" such as keynote speeches (Pithers 2017). Still, the tie-less look (and often ill-fitting jacket and shirt) sometimes alongside "the Leninist hat" remained for other duties as leader (and at protests, marches and so on). As one fashion blogger argued:

> for all his dishevelled, careless choices he is saying something striking and important. "I am authentic, I think for myself, I am a man of the people before I am an MP. I want to stay connected. My politics are principled and I will not conform to the 'traditions' which keep the ruling class in power, even if they are trivial like wearing a dark suit and a silk tie".                                                (Fabrickated 2015)

Corbyn's interests were not carefully calibrated to show a false connection to the people, unlike David Cameron, who once forgot which football team he professed to support (Boffey 2015). Corbyn made no secret of his hobbies of making jam and growing fruit on his allotment, and his interest in "the history and design of manhole covers" (Wheeler 2017). These interests were not designed to show a closeness with the average person, but rather show an "unpolished authenticity" which is lacking in those on the "high" side of the axis (Martell 2018). As previously mentioned, this was "populism wearing a cardigan" (Flinders 2019), Corbyn's own brand of authenticity, to show that he was a normal person, just like the voter, and not the extremist that, his supporters felt, he was portrayed as in the media.

In terms of the political-cultural element, we have seen above how Corbyn used large rallies to speak directly to people and how he used Momentum as an organization to optimize support for his project within the Labour Party (to his supporters) or used entryist tactics (to his detractors), both of which challenged the institutionalized and formal organizational method the Labour Party was used to. Furthermore, the Corbynite leadership took inspiration from the election of Trump in 2016 and his "aggression against mainstream TV networks and newspapers" in order to "whip up support among those already distrustful of the media". Team Corbyn would also challenge the status quo by making "greater use of Twitter and Facebook to attack the media rather than attempting to manage it [...] drawing attention to Corbyn's 40 years 'taking on the establishment'" (Bolton & Pitts 2018: 208).

Here, then, we see further rejection of "formal, impersonal [...] institutionally mediated models of authority" related to the high, instead preferring personalistic, direct, and mischievous methods of communication and behaviour rooted in the need to connect to, and represent, the people directly (Ostiguy 2017).

Thus, when it comes to populism as a socio-cultural approach, Corbyn's populism may not be as on-the-nose as say Berlusconi's or Chavez' (both of whom would qualify as populist using the socio-cultural approach), but Corbyn could certainly not be classified as on the "high" end of the axis. Instead, he positioned himself as the authentic outsider, who rejected the "relevant civilizational project" (Ostiguy's term) of Thatcherite neoliberalism – once again, he could be seen as a populist within the framework of the Labour Party, staying true to his socialist beliefs even during the "relevant civilizational project" of New Labour, espousing views that were seen as uncouth, backwards or harmful to the interest of the party. There are direct parallels between how Ostiguy argues populists act vis-à-vis the people, and how Corbyn acted vis-à-vis his own party: if New Labour occupied the high, then Corbyn was proud to be on the low.

This continued once Corbyn became leader, with his positioning himself as the voice of the people, articulating an opposition to 30 years of the dominance of Thatcherite ideology. As Bolton and Pitts note, the 2017 general election turbo-charged this view – Labour's performance showed how "a properly socialist leader had put forward a properly socialist manifesto, in the teeth of ferocious opposition both internal and external – and the result had been anything but calamitous" (Bolton & Pitts 2018: 32). It was a vindication of Corbyn's views and evidence that he was speaking for the people; it was only parts of the establishment – the PLP and the right-wing media – that held him back by attacking his authenticity and his character.

Thus, Corbyn certainly represented a transgressive way of doing politics: first in terms of his relationship the New Labour party elite, and then his time espousing his "common-sense" socialism to the public (Miller 2018). Using this measure of populism, then, Corbyn does seem to qualify.

## Conclusion

The four approaches to populism outlined above can be divided into substance (the Muddean notion of populism as an ideology, and the Laclauian notion of populism as a discourse) and style (Weyland's understanding of populism as a political strategy, and Ostiguy's concept of populism as a socio-cultural approach). There is, almost by necessity, overlap between all of these understandings, rooted in the essentially contested nature of populism as a concept.

From the analysis above we are able to conclude that although the Corbynite coalition does contain some who would like to adopt the substantial understandings of populism (e.g. the post-capitalists who have been clearly influenced by Laclau, like the left-wing academics who formed Podemos in Spain), there is insufficient evidence of a populist ideology or a truly populist discourse within the Corbynite project. When we understand populism as a style of politics, we can find it within Corbynism. Corbyn's natural home was, and the Corbynite movement's strength lay in, mass rallies, mobilizing campaigners and, in many respects, preaching directly to the converted. When the Corbynite leadership thought the PLP were being recalcitrant or the media were being unfair, Corbyn took to the streets, speaking directly to supporters, and eschewing traditional institutions such as the party.

Under Keir Starmer, the emphasis on populist movement politics has all but disappeared. Momentum seems to have lost its relevance in a post-Corbyn Labour Party, Starmer seems to be in the ascendancy vis-à-vis the Corbynite left when it comes to inter-party factional battles and the publication of the Equality and Human Rights Commission's report into antisemitism in the Labour Party (see Chapter 14) has given Starmer the political cover needed to root out the more conspiratorial and racist elements within the party membership.

The Corbynite populist turn – which was largely in terms of style, not substance – was a deviation from Labour's status quo and was made possible by the messianic quality Corbyn's followers attributed to him, alongside a notion of personal authenticity resulting from over 30 years on the backbenches. Given this, it would be very difficult for another left-wing Corbynite figure to recreate Corbyn's populist style.

## References

Airas, I. 2019. "Hotspots: the affective politics of hope and the 'Corbyn phenomenon'". *Area* 51(3): 443–50. https://doi.org/10.1111/area.12476.

Atkins, J. & N. Turnbull 2016. "Jeremy Corbyn's rhetorical dilemma: left-wing populism or mainstream convention?" LSE British Politics and Policy, 26 April. https://blogs.lse.ac.uk/politicsandpolicy/jeremy-corbyn-rhetorical-dilemma/ (accessed 15 March 2021).

Baggini, J. 2016. "Jeremy Corbyn is a great populist. But that's no good for our democracy" *The Guardian*, 25 July. https://www.theguardian.com/commentisfree/2016/jul/25/jeremy-corbyn-populist-democracy-mps/ (accessed 15 March 2021).

Bakker, R. *et al.* 2020. *2019 Chapel Hill Expert Survey.* CHESDATA. https://www.chesdata.eu/2019-chapel-hill-expert-survey (accessed 15 March 2021).

Barr, R. 2018. "Populism as a political strategy". In C. de la Torre (ed.), The *Routledge Handbook of Global Populism*, 44–56. Abingdon: Routledge.

Bickerton, C. & C. Accetti 2017. "Populism and technocracy: opposites or complements?" *Critical Review of International Social and Political Philosophy* 20(2): 186–206. https://doi.org/10.1080/13698230.2014.995504.

Bloom, P. 2017. "Thanks to Jeremy Corbyn, populism is no longer a dirty word". *The Independent*, 12 June. https://www.independent.co.uk/voices/jeremy-corbyn-labour-populism-not-dirty-word-a7785556.html (accessed 15 March 2021).

Boffey, D. 2015. "David Cameron blames 'brain fade' for getting his football team wrong". *The Guardian*, 25 April. https://www.theguardian.com/politics/2015/apr/25/david-cameron-blames-brain-fade-for-getting-his-football-team-wrong (accessed 15 March 2021).

Bolton, M. & F. Pitts 2018. *Corbynism: A Critical Approach*. Bradford: Emerald.

Dorey, P. 2017. "Jeremy Corbyn confounds his critics: explaining the Labour party's remarkable resurgence in the 2017 election". *British Politics* 12(3): 308–34. https://doi.org/10.1057/s41293-017-0058-4.

Fabrickated 2015. *Men's Style – Jeremy Corbyn*. Fabrickated. https://fabrickated.com/2015/09/18/mens-style-jeremy-corbyn/ (accessed 15 March 2021).

Flinders, M. 2018. "The (anti-)politics of the general election: funnelling frustration in a divided democracy". *Parliamentary Affairs* 71(1): 222–36. https://doi.org/10.1093/pa/gsx058.

Flinders, M. 2019. "UK election 2019: this is what populism looks like when done by the British". *The Conversation*, 12 November. https://theconversation.com/uk-election-2019-this-is-what-populism-looks-like-when-done-by-the-british-126733 (accessed 15 March 2021).

Flinders, M. 2020. "Not a Brexit election? Pessimism, promises and populism 'UK-style'". *Parliamentary Affairs* 73(1): 225–42. https://doi.org/10.1093/pa/gsaa030.

Freeden, M. 1998. "Is nationalism a distinct ideology?" *Political Studies* 46(4): 748–65. https://doi.org/10.1111/1467-9248.00165.

Goes, E. 2018. "'Jez, we can!' Labour's campaign: defeat with a taste of victory". *Parliamentary Affairs* 71(1): 59–71. https://doi.org/10.1093/pa/gsx062.

Goes, E. 2020. "Labour's 2019 campaign: a defeat of epic proportions". *Parliamentary Affairs* 73(1): 84–102. https://doi.org/10.1093/pa/gsaa023.

Hawkins, K. & C. Rovira Kaltwasser 2019. "Introduction: the ideational approach". In K. Hawkins *et al.* (eds), *The Ideational Approach to Populism: Concept, Theory, and Analysis*. Abingdon: Routledge.

Jeffery, D. 2017. "The strange death of Tory Liverpool: Conservative electoral decline in Liverpool, 1945–1996". *British Politics* 12(3): 386–407. https://doi.org/10.1057/s41293-016-0032-6.

Laclau, E. 2005. *On Populist Reason*. London: Verso.

Maiguashca, B. & J. Dean 2019. "Corbynism, populism and the re-shaping of left politics in contemporary Britain". In G. Katsambekis & A. Kioupkiolis (eds), *The Populist Radical Left in Europe*, 73–92. Abingdon: Routledge.

March, L. 2017a. "Contrary to popular opinion, there is no populist upsurge in Britain". LSE British Politics and Policy, 6 July. https://blogs.lse.ac.uk/politicsandpolicy/populisms-in-britain/ (accessed 15 March 2021).

March, L. 2017b. "Left and right populism compared: the British case". *British Journal of Politics and International Relations* 19(2): 282–303. https://doi.org/10.1177/1369148117701753.

March, L. 2019. "Textual analysis: the UK party system". In K. Hawkins *et al.* (eds), *The Ideational Approach to Populism: Concept, Theory, and Analysis* , 214–31. Abingdon: Routledge.

Martell, L. 2018. "Corbyn, populism and power". *Hard Times* 101: 1–11. http://sro.sussex.ac.uk/id/eprint/78669/1/corbynpopulismsro.pdf (accessed 15 March 2021).

Meijers, M. & A. Zaslove 2020a. *Populism and Political Parties Expert Survey 2018*. https://poppa.shinyapps.io/poppa/ (accessed 15 March 2021).

Meijers, M. & A. Zaslove 2020b. "Measuring populism in political parties: appraisal of a new approach". *Comparative Political Studies* 54(2): 372–407. https://doi.org/10.1177/0010414020938081.

Miller, N. 2018. "Green jobs, zero emissions and socialism is 'new common sense': Corbyn". *Sydney Morning Herald*, 27 September. https://www.smh.com.au/world/europe/green-jobs-zero-emissions-and-socialism-is-new-common-sense-corbyn-20180927-p5068e.html (accessed 15 March 2021).

Mouffe, C. 2018a. *For a Left Populism*. London: Verso.

Mouffe, C. 2018b. "Jeremy Corbyn's left populism". https://www.versobooks.com/blogs/3743-jeremy-corbyn-s-left-populism (accessed 15 March 2021).

Mudde, C. 2004. "The populist zeitgeist". *Government and Opposition* 39(4): 541–63. https://doi.org/10.1111/j.1477-7053.2004.00135.x.

Mudde, C. 2017. "Populism: an ideational approach". In C. Kaltwasser, P. Taggart, P. Ochoa Espejo & P. Ostiguy (eds), *The Oxford Handbook of Populism*. Oxford: Oxford University Press.

Norris, P. 2020. *The Global Party Survey 2019*. https://www.globalpartysurvey.org/ (accessed 15 March 2021).

Ostiguy, P. 2017. "Populism: a socio-cultural approach". In C. Kaltwasser *et al.* (eds), *The Oxford Handbook of Populism*. Oxford: Oxford University Press.

Peruzzotti, E. 2018. "Laclau's theory of populism: a critical review". In C. de la Torre (ed.), *The Routledge Handbook of Global Populism*. Abingdon: Routledge.

Pithers, E. 2017. "Why Jeremy Corbyn's look is very vetements". *Vogue*. https://www.vogue.co.uk/gallery/jeremy-corbyn-style-analysis. (accessed 15 March 2021).

Rooduijn, M. *et al.* 2019. *The Popu-List: An Overview of Populist, Far Right, Far Left and Eurosceptic Parties in Europe*. https://popu-list.org/ (accessed 15 March 2021).

Samuel Windsor n.d. "How Jeremy Corbyn could smarten up his act". https://blog.samuel-windsor.co.uk/jeremy-corbyn-smarten-up-act (accessed 15 March 2021).

Stafford, J. 2016. "The Corbyn experiment". *Dissent*. https://www.dissentmagazine.org/article/jeremy-corbyn-experiment-british-labour-party (accessed 8 April 2021).

Watt, N. 2016. "David Cameron launches personal attack on Jeremy Corbyn's appearance". *The Guardian*, 24 February. https://www.theguardian.com/politics/2016/feb/24/david-cameron-launches-personal-attack-on-jeremy-corbyns-appearance (accessed 15 March 2021).

Watts, J. & T. Bale 2019. "Populism as an intra-party phenomenon: the British Labour Party under Jeremy Corbyn". *British Journal of Politics and International Relations* 21(1): 99–115. https://doi.org/10.1177/1369148118806115.

Weyland, K. 1996. "Neo-populism and neo-liberalism in Latin America: unexpected affinities". *Studies in Comparative International Development* 32(3): 3–31.

Weyland, K. 2001. "Clarifying a contested concept: populism in the study of Latin American politics". *Comparative Politics* 34(1): 1–22.

Weyland, K. 2017. "Populism: a political-strategic approach". In C. Kaltwasser *et al.* (eds), *The Oxford Handbook of Populism*. Oxford: Oxford University Press.

Wheeler, B. 2017. "The Jeremy Corbyn story: profile of Labour leader". BBC News, 23 May. https://www.bbc.co.uk/news/election-2017-39807055 (accessed 15 March 2021).

Worth, O. 2020. "Corbyn, Sanders and the contestation of neoliberal hegemony". In G. Charalambous & G. Ioannou (eds), *Left Radicalism and Populism in Europe*, 88–105. Abingdon: Routledge.

Zúquete, J. 2007. *Missionary Politics in Contemporary Europe*. Syracuse, NY: Syracuse University Press.

# 5

# CORBYNISM AS IDENTITY POLITICS

*Harry W. Fletcher*

The starting assumption of this chapter is that Corbyn views society not as net-worked flows of sovereign individuals, but as demarcated societal segments defined by essentializing factors that include ethnicity, income, religion and socio-economic class, organized into a strictly hierarchical class-based system with "the people" at the bottom of the chain.[1] The segments that make up "the people" can coexist, but are ultimately separated by temporary, strategic identity markers. This view of society is deliberate and multipurpose: dividing society into several homogeneous groups allows for the construction of juxtapositions between the "in" group and the "out" group. Once the electorate is neatly divided into labelled sections, policy and narratives can then be crafted around the assumption that these divisions between people necessarily exist, and that each group is somehow threatened by the "out" group (primarily the Conservative Party). This manifests in the political mobilization of multiple groups of citizens, each under a banner identifying their group identity, which Corbyn then brings under the umbrella of the Labour Party and prepares ideologically for a never-ending war against their ideological opponents, who they frame as the actor attempting to undermine that particular group's central unifying characteristic. Corbyn's ideology therefore defines itself in opposition to the "other" (Eide 2010). Another reason to follow this "divide-and-conquer" political strategy is Corbyn's ability to craft narratives that create cohesion within his ranks and activate otherwise disenfranchised members of the polity, who subsequently coalesce around himself – giving him legitimacy, at least in his and their eyes. Corbyn's narrative devices, used to construct false memories of oppression (meaning

---

1. This is the way things stood in 2019–20. When first elected leader, Corbyn frequently brought props in the form of letters to the Commons, with complaints raised by individuals within his constituency. Once his support became steadfast, he no longer needed to prove legitimacy using this method. He became the ultimate anti-Conservative symbol. He exchanged one form of instrumental populism for another.

that Corbyn's words paint a historical picture that the recipient internalizes and comes to believe), the plight of the working classes and a common enemy in the Conservative Party are topics that I will explore later in this chapter.

One of the key foundations of Corbyn's "us against them" construct is strategic essentialism: the idea that it can serve strategic purposes to exaggerate the differences and similarities between groups of people (Danius & Jonsson 1993). Strategic essentialism supposes that there are, in reality, no essential identities, while concurrently realizing that people in practice act (whether by need or by choice) as if there *were* such essential identities (Barker 2004). One could, in the case of Corbynism, temporarily enact and portray the identity of the "working class" as a seemingly stable categorization for the primary purpose of inspiring and mobilizing other "workers" for a political end, namely electing a Corbyn-led government and empowering *our* people at the expense of the tyrannical *them*. Thomas Crisp elaborates on this concept, albeit in a different context: "temporary deployment of positivist essentialism by a marginalised population" is what facilitates Corbynism's functioning (Crisp 2011: 95). Class divides (among other divides) must be strategically theorized, brought to the forefront of the public's attention and artificially deepened to give Corbyn issue ownership over class as a stable marker of political identity, and also to increase its salience within public debate. Corbyn uses this technique to unify divergent groups of people under common labels; these labels consequently become lenses through which people's political identities are constructed and enacted (Voronka 2016).

Corbyn himself takes on temporary strategic identities: his "Bennite Euroscepticism" has been apparent ever since he became a parliamentarian (Moore 2018). He campaigned to leave the 1975 version of the European Union and even claimed, as *The Economist* (2016) quotes, that the club was "directly responsible" for "gross abuse of human rights and natural resources", and that its project "has always been to create a huge free-market Europe". As the Labour leader, it became essential to Corbyn's political survival that he position himself favourably as regards his party, but also at direct odds with the Conservative Party at all times, lest the dichotomous "us against the enemy" construct dissolve. The former was the most difficult for him to achieve. Becoming leader stole from Corbyn the ability to think as radically as he did on the backbenches, instead having to win over his more moderate mainstream parliamentarians to retain their confidence. His previous Eurosceptic comments would have certainly alienated most of his parliamentary party, so for his own longevity it proved strategically necessary to temporarily adopt a Europhilic, or at least a less Eurosceptic, stance. The personal difficulty created by this strategic identity marker was evident in Corbyn's inability to produce a clear Brexit position or strategy for the party to follow, resulting in a confused offer to electors in 2019, and the unusual promise to stay neutral on the issue. This whole debacle evidences the theory that political identity, as far as party leaders are concerned, is formed through negotiation between the self and immediate colleagues. For Corbyn, this meant reconciling both grassroots Euroscepticism and fervent Europhiles within his shadow cabinet. The outcome was an identity which at best can be termed "semi-strategically confused".

One direct effect of the lengthy delays and confusion around the Labour Brexit position has been Conservative (and to a lesser extent Brexit Party) ownership of Brexit as a political issue in its entirety. By failing to adopt the strong Remain or "people's vote" positions and instead delaying, even dithering on the issue in fear of losing both Leave and Remain voters, and wrestling with his own internal debate on Brexit, Corbyn cast Labour's stance into obscurity and allowed the Conservative Party to become relatively stronger, and more trusted to deliver Brexit than the Labour Party. With nowhere else to go, issue ownership over Leave defaulted to the Conservatives, with the purest "no-deal" position being owned by the Brexit Party until their decision to stand aside in Conservative seats in the 2019 election, where the Conservatives decisively reclaimed this. The Conservatives have framed themselves as the only competent party to conduct the UK's departure from the EU. In other words, the Conservatives were gifted a strategic advantage over Brexit. Labour's second referendum demand might have satisfied members and parliamentarians within Corbyn's own party, but it came after such delay, and so begrudgingly that for many it was "too little, too late" (Piper 2021). That is, Labour's confused position on Brexit had become too entrenched and confused to change; issue ownership over any part of Brexit was no longer up for grabs. Even with Theresa May's weak handling of the withdrawal negotiations, the Conservatives and the Brexit Party had ownership over Leave; the Liberal Democrats had the same over Remain, and even "revoke". The Independent Group for Change (originally Change UK and eventually disbanded in December 2019) tried to take a slice of the Remain pie, but fell by the wayside: the British electorate does not enjoy being told, in a patronizing tone, that they voted incorrectly.

Turning away from Brexit and switching to the individual level of analysis, we find that Labour *does* have issue ownership over other aspects of political life. As for the emotional aspect of identity politics, and concurrently in explaining why so many students opt for a strong Labour Party brand association, I suggest we turn to Charles Taylor's thesis that identity is inwardly generated and dialogical (Dick 2011: 37; citing Taylor & Gutmann 1997). From this theory follows the idea that the recognition of one's identity is a vital human need. Our identities are formed in a dialogical process with others, and never in isolation. Identity is negotiated with others through a mixture of dialogue and internal self-reflection on events; it is because of these interactions that so much of our identity is a reflection of the people and groups that we take to be significant.

As Caroline Dick puts it: "our dependence on others for affirmation is ongoing and continuous" (2011: 38). We *need* recognition. Identities are created in relation to others and within a particular social context and were similarly crafted before our modern notion of identity came to be. In societies that preceded ours, identities were assigned according to prevailing hierarchical social structures in an uncontroversial manner. Your identity was fixed according to your social position within this hierarchy, and individuals accepted the role that the hierarchy presumed for them, absent nuanced consideration of how personal identities could or should be generated internally. These identities were nevertheless defined in concert with peers; however, to be socially recognized according to these identities was a given. In modern times, as democracy has risen and evolved and hierarchical societies have declined, social recognition is *not* a given. And for humans this creates a state of nature characterized by chaos and a terrifying lack of recognition.

In the modern sociopolitical landscape, where social recognition is craved but not automatically assigned, groupism becomes more significant than ever. Incorporating yourself into an existing, popular grouping of people who espouse a particular identity is an antidote to the chaos of a life without recognition. The low barriers to entry, and clear prevalence of left-wing Labour groups especially, but not only, for students on university campuses, provide ready-made and recognized identities into which one can insert oneself. The extent to which one associates with those ideologies initially does not matter; their nuanced identity *within* the overall spectrum of the group's ideologies will be negotiated and tested over time. Through this negotiation between the self and others, identity evolves; the echo-chamber of the group ensures that identity rarely becomes *less* left-wing, but it has the propensity to become *more* left-wing as socialist policies are trivialized and what is considered "normal" politics is left-shifted.

To explain my focus on student Labour groups, I will take a step back to look at what I consider to be the archetypal student journey from being without identity to identifying politically, and how this all relates to Corbyn himself. To be clear, this does not apply to most students who come to university. Many go through their years of study without a moment's thought for politics, and certainly without caring about Jeremy Corbyn.[2] This section speaks of those politically engaged and active students who come to university open to, and often expecting to become involved in politics in some way. Even for these students, many who join Labour groups will at no point feel any affinity with Corbyn or Corbynism, or any pressure to feel as such. This chapter does not necessarily speak to those students' experiences, but instead to the many who *do* feel social pressures to conform.

---

2. A prospect this author imagines to be very peaceful.

When attending university for the first time, those first formative weeks often involve forming political identities, whether subconsciously or deliberately. Going away to university means tearing oneself from one's sociopolitical context (thereby abandoning important social networks of peers, colleagues, and academic and pastoral mentors who have come to be a permanent comfort blanket over many years) and placing yourself into an entirely new context, usually geographically and financially far from home.

The familiarity of surroundings and networks dissolves, along with any pre-existing group identities in which we may feel "at home". Absent these identity markers one might expect to revert to a blank canvas, but this is far from being the case. While one may be naked of identity and personality in so far as other people's perceptions are concerned at this time (a state that humans detest, preferring to be a secure member of a social grouping of similar, like-minded people), latent political identities exist within each of us, built throughout our younger years in a dialectical fashion and through lived experiences that are ultimately drawn out and built on by groups that we encounter on campuses or elsewhere. Campuses become places of political growth and realization, and the dominance of Labour-affiliated groups (not to mention their attractive and organized marketing and branding campaigns) creates myriad opportunities to associate or experiment with this worldview. Their dominance underpins, reinforces and perpetuates their social acceptability, whereas Conservative societies on campus remain obscure and mired in unpopular images of rich, private-schooled "male, pale, and stale" students, images that are often realized (Mintz 2018). This may not always have been the case, but the prevailing entrenchment of this campus dominance is self-reproducing or memetic. For today, and the foreseeable future, Labour's presence is the most relevant on campus. Echo-chambers are entered into, through which left-wing worldviews are mainstreamed and reinforced through a constant circulation within these like-minded student groups (Chandler & Munday 2016). These ideologies offer group members a reasoned and structured understanding of the sociopolitical world from the perspective of existing group members (Goode *et al.* 2017: 259). Ideologies therefore become instruction manuals that teach new group members that there *is* a structure and order to the world that can satisfy their craving to reduce the chaos of their situation. It is a brilliantly persuasive message.

As we separate from family and pre-existing social networks, we are preoccupied with issues of identity formation and searching for belonging. Peer-attachment fills those vacuums and combats those existential anxieties that we submit to when leaving home, leaving us dependent on peers for our self-recognition and comfort. In doing so we imbibe the identity of those peers; if you join a group who identify as Corbynite, you become a Corbynite; the same with more moderate Labour groups. The satisfaction derived from transcending social chaos through group assimilation generates an unwillingness to upset or endanger one's new position within the social world.

This effect is brilliantly codified by Goode *et al.* in their work on compensatory control theory, which proposes how an individual, seeking a degree of personal control that is being threatened by an out-group, can manage this fear by identifying defensively with an external group that provides a feeling or sense that the outside world is ordered meaningfully. Individuals can find an antidote to the loss of control they feel during times of great personal change, such as coming to university, by adhering to a certain group's ideologies and beliefs concerning the social world and taking on this group's values. As they put it: "when perceptions of personal control are threatened, people use external sources of order to compensate" (Goode *et al* 2017: 259). This arises from an overarching need, as I have already discussed, to feel that the world is ordered. Internalizing the norms and beliefs of a new group, especially enacting or performing traits that are archetypal to the group's identity helps one to fit in (for right or for wrong) and become a part of something bigger than the self. Through this internalization, the way that the individual thinks *becomes* consistent with the group's ideology over time and acceptance of identity becomes more entrenched. This personal investment becomes greater and greater over time, with one's time, identity and emotions being invested in the cause with hope of a good return.

Students are therefore the ideal subjects for Taylor's theory: the lust for recognition that plagues contemporary politics is often brought to the fore "on behalf of minority or 'subaltern' groups" (Taylor & Gutmann 1994: 25). For this reason, you will find identifying flags pinned on university halls of residence walls, or pin badges adorning rucksacks announcing to all who may see them that the owner is a member of a particular identity group, and mass turnouts for campus-based protests, a small reason for which will be "to be seen and understood". Students can enter into the dialogical process of identity formation, as Taylor posited, within the safety of a university echo-chamber; dialogical yes, but with unwritten limitations that rarely challenge the left-wing norm. Those who would seriously challenge prevailing ideologies are discouraged from doing so by the expected negative response of their peers. This peculiarly circular kind of dialogue reduces the scope for discourse to develop. Discourse is no longer particularly pluralist, especially not on campuses; it is the very death of discourse.[3]

---

3. I define "the death of discourse" as the deliberate movement away from a pluralist discourse and towards a fatal echo-chambering of discourse; removing obstacles to one ideology becoming dominant, rather than viewing it with a critical eye and negotiating policy both on personal and party levels. Perhaps an alternative phrase would be "the death of critical thinking and policy scrutiny". On this point, the dialogical process proposed here, that leads to identity formation, is not one of open debate, more one of persuasion. Debate itself is discouraged, since challenging the prevailing opinion is to invite criticism and delay one's acceptance into the group.

It is not just discourse that has taken on a toxic flavour within universities. Jannie Malan (2011) rightly argues that when a group becomes so preoccupied by "who we are", and who the "other" is, the gradual development of identity takes on a more poisonous flavour: we become tempted to view our group identity as fundamentally better than that of other groups. Pressures from our group's culture and strongest personalities create and harden feelings of superiority over other groups; it reinforces an image of the group's ideology as inherently correct, to the extent that the opposing viewpoint can be disregarded en masse as right-wing, authoritarian or otherwise labelled so as to essentialize it and bring it lazily into disrepute. Meanwhile Corbyn's leadership is infallible. It becomes unthinkable to associate with the Conservative Party, or right-wing ideologies. The fear of being instantly socially outcast in the court of student politics closes the door to right-of-centre student groups being seen as legitimate. Joining such groups carries social sanctions; it inevitably affects the social standing of those who associate.

This narrowing of discourse has been perpetuated and facilitated by Corbyn's leadership: his election held deeper significance than those of previous leaders. For his supporters, Corbyn's election heralded the beginning of a new movement in the Labour Party. Backed unreservedly by Momentum, Corbyn came to power clothed in the "mythology of collectivism" (Bennister *et al.* 2017: 102) as the figurehead on the prow of the "movement". The specific institutional changes that paved the way for his election are discussed eloquently by Bennister *et al.*, but are beyond the scope of the present chapter. Corbyn played on the anti-establishment, anti-austerity sentiments in the country to rouse his natural supporters, the disenfranchised far left who felt left behind by David Cameron's austerity programme and an increasingly Blairite Labour Party. The fact that this would alienate moderates and much of the body politic was irrelevant then, as it is now. His grassroots supporters were already so steadfast in their support for Corbyn that any future electoral challenge would be likely seen off by the left wing of the membership:[4] the opinions of his MPs became increasingly

---

4. Corbyn's leadership is peculiar in the context of the United Kingdom. His deep unpopularity with the public at large and myriad scandals, not least over his handling of antisemitism within the Party, would have driven most other leaders to resignation, but not Corbyn. He knew that his loyalist base would keep him in power, no matter what. These might be far from a majority of Labour supporters, but they were sufficient in number to hold a privileged position in Labour's bureaucracies. We can consider Corbyn's grassroots support as a "movement" that is excessively devoted to one leader or idea that will employ manipulative or socially deviant techniques to strengthen and promote their leader (Petherick 2017). Such "techniques" might take a number of shapes. Most common will be a powerful persuasive pressure, the suspension of critical thinking and judgement, as well as the renunciation of individuality in favour of attaching oneself to the leader's identity. The result is a group of people willing to overlook the deficiencies of their hero. Their best weapon against critique is their tribal group identity, dismissing evidence of wrong-doing or mistakes as smears designed by the "other" to discredit Corbyn.

irrelevant. I hesitate to label him as "populist" without lengthy elaboration, since the term has been overused *ad nauseam* in political literature in recent years and has lost its salience of meaning, but it must be noted that Corbyn's leadership marked a shift from Labour as a party to Labour as a campaign opposed to the political status quo.

What might this mean for ideology? Perhaps this: if an individual becomes associated with a given ideology, and invests in that idea, they may come to view the world through that ideology's filter. If an ideology, in this case Corbynism or socialism, is potent enough, one might come to filter all issues through the lens of ideology. It is a dangerous habit to form; one that inevitably leads to reductionism or social dissonance in one's thinking processes. By articulating all issues through the self-built filter of ideology, one's political conceptions become one's worldview. This is not to be confused with echo-chambers, which are dialogical. Conversely, this is the individual taking in some issue and passing it through the sociological "black box" of ideology. This will most likely not lead to a constructive political space that is open to debate and multiple voices. It might lead to critical voices being seen as fundamentally incompatible with one's scheme of reasoning: if it does not fit through the ideological filter, it must be wrong and can be attacked or disregarded.

A little earlier, I promised to link my foray into student politics with Corbyn himself. On this I will now seek to deliver by looking at what "identity" looks like through the Corbynite lens; I will also suggest reasons why Corbyn has become the facilitator of the prevailing student leftism discussed. Unsurprisingly in 2019–20, class, or perceived class, still acted as the predominant identity marker in Labour Party politics. It is a strategic badge of honour, a modern iteration of the Labour Party's honourable history of class consciousness. As Phil Cohen (2017) argues, the class consciousness model, still popular with successive generations of students, has tacitly shifted in meaning. With Corbynism, no longer does class consciousness require some great intervention to lift up the workers and create a "class-for-itself" rather than a "class-in-itself". In contemporary Britain, "class consciousness" describes the process of discovering oneself as an actor in a relational political system, whereby your "class" is dependent upon your success in life relative to the success of others, your financial situation is relational to that of others in society, or the type of work that other people do compared to your work. These categories are non-exhaustive but help us to analyse the relationship between identity and Corbynism: his parliamentary electoral success and indeed his grip on the party require his electors to truly feel that they are situated within a class, or other identity group. It is his "black box". Corbynist discourse surrounding class or identity issues activates this underlying feeling to mobilize support. As political and economic contexts have changed since the Labour Party's beginnings, the way that Labour talks about class had to be reconstructed to fit a new demographic: the closures of mines and the restructuring of the economy away from blue-collar enterprises created a void in traditional Labour support.

The Labour Party's traditional "for the workers" motif was eroded by the Conservatives in the 2010, 2015, 2017 and 2019 general elections by their delivery of record-breaking employment figures and a national living wage. The Conservatives were becoming the party of the workers and rebranding to take advantage of the country's disillusionment with Jeremy Corbyn. This realization was a grave threat to Labour's "For the Many, not the Few" branding, and required a rethink. The question for Corbyn's Labour Party therefore became one not of changing the narrative to fit the demographic, but of convincing new demographics that they were part of the existing traditional catchment narrative. With students searching for identities with pre-prepared mass appeal, associating yourself with the "working class" and then accepting Corbyn as the protector of that grouping (or recognizing that the Conservatives are the existential threat) is a salient option. As a direct result of this, student debates tend to involve class-based articulations of issues not directly relating to class, for example Brexit (P. Cohen 2017). The resulting discourse is not terribly helpful, since it is based on an artificial construction of class that takes inspiration from a nostalgic image of Britain's industrial heritage. Workers are not the politically solid grouping Corbyn remembers them to be (Howell 2012). It was an aspiration, perhaps an extrapolation of the socialist vision of "The People", rather than a focus on the actual people. This is not to say that the identity groups associated with former industry do not exist – they surely do in areas affected by Thatcherite economic policy for example. However, in these areas, where Labour is "in my DNA",[5] the constructed identity carries a more visceral and personal quality. For students, however, absent lived experience of traditional class-based experience, the identity is constructed and interwoven with a Labour Party identity to create an "imagined community" that we will turn to later with reference to Benedict Anderson's (1991) seminal work on the matter in the context of national identities.

The most obvious example of this is Labour's traditional "oppression of the workers" narrative. This follows that the Labour Party was formed *from* and *for* the working classes. This message lost its salience in 2010 when the party haemorrhaged five million voters, partly because of, as Watts (2018: 506) agrees, its commitment to globalization and its loss of touch with its rural, working-class roots (Rutherford 2011). Since this time, re-carving Labour's traditional niche has come to the forefront of Corbyn's agenda. When making grand claims

---

5. As a resident of a former mining town, now disillusioned by Labour's "neutral until a general election" Brexit stance, said to the BBC (24 September 2019).

such as "What I remain opposed to is the idea that David Cameron could go around and give up workers' rights" (BBC 2015), he knows that the statement itself has little basis in fact; indeed this comment, made during the run-up to the Brexit referendum, means very little. Corbyn cannot know what Cameron would have done in the event of a Leave vote, or a Remain vote for that matter. This is not even to mention the substantive workers' rights commitments in successive modern Conservative manifestos. Therefore this, and similar comments, can only be designed to reaffirm Corbyn's issue ownership over workers' rights, and to depict Cameron as the actor attempting to erode them. In fact, when Corbyn makes these comments, he confirms the pre-existing narrative that exists within the minds of his sympathizers and voters that the Conservative Party, and Cameron in particular, are out to hold back the working classes, and to lift up the wealthiest in society at their expense (Tolchard 2017).

Jake Watts argues that from the 1980s onwards the Labour modernizers eroded this class-based worldview within the Labour Party and paved the way for a more individualistic type of Labour leadership (2018: 506). These modernizers sought to break down the class barriers that infected identities within the party. This reconfiguration of the Labour ranks may well have been ongoing before and during the first months of Corbyn's leadership, but I argue that the party's executive took steps to reverse these ideological changes and return the party to its traditional class-concerned roots, which formed the very basis of Corbyn's politics. One key step in this process was the removal from the PLP of MPs who were not aligned with Corbyn's worldview. In the summer of 2019, Labour's general secretary, Jennie Formby, wrote to Labour MPs requesting their intentions in the event, or expectation, of a snap election being called. Would they want to stand again as a Labour MP? She gave them a pressurizing July deadline by which to make this decision. Many MPs saw this as a purging process by the hard-left party executive, and claimed that Corbyn and Formby were attempting to use the reselection procedure to remove MPs critical of Corbyn's leadership or ideology. A group of moderate Labour MPs, formed by Tom Watson to oppose the Corbynite wing of the party, went so far as to organize lessons on the most effective ways to challenge deselection attempts against them (Schofield 2019). Momentum, the Corbynite group, pushed for "open selections" at a snap election, which they hoped would lead to the deselection of moderates. This ultimately gained insufficient traction with the trade unions, but Momentum's claim that "posh men from expensive private schools" dominated politics revealed a sinister identity-driven homogenization of the Labour Party (Hossein-Pour 2019).

Labour's 2017 general election slogan, "For the Many, not the Few" (Labour Party 2017), was only the initial reignition of the dichotomy upon which Corbyn's support would eventually grow. Corbyn's rhetoric relied on voters believing that the existing system is rigged against the working classes and led by the wealthiest in society, who do all they can to keep the workers at bay. These "necessary illusions" are drawn from the theory of false consciousness, a Marxist idea that takes Gramsci's ideas about cultural hegemony and states that the working classes support the status quo in society, often acting counter to their own interests, because they have been tricked into toeing the line (Meyerson 1991). They have been sold the lie that what is good for the elite in society is also good for them (Apperley 2018). This theory deserves some reconsideration in light of the rise of Corbyn. Corbyn's own narrative lore was built to frame him as the victim of attack by an establishment that desires only to retain the status quo of austerity. For his political project to make sense, one has to accept his belief that British institutions are components of a larger cultural hegemony, which cannot be trusted and must ultimately be dismantled (Francis 2016). Supporters become locked into expected patterns of thinking, in an environment impenetrable to dissent, which disables critical thinking and trivializes what most outside the echo-chamber would consider dominant, even extreme ideas (Thompson 2015). Through such mechanisms, a specific and false view of the world is created and reproduced. Distinct cultural myths are sold to the electorate, and memories and traditions are resurrected to mobilize a collective anger that binds people together under symbolic flags and banners.

## Reshaping the Labour Party

In a great stroke of irony, Corbyn's Labour Party attempted to construct a similar system to the one that they wished to destroy: whereas Corbyn might well regard the UK's institutions as a part of some capitalist hegemony, his own ranks were systematically being reorganized in his own image. Room for disagreement was sparse on the Labour front benches, as shadow foreign secretary Emily Thornberry found out when she was replaced in her role of deputy to Corbyn at Prime Minister's Questions by Corbyn-ally Rebecca Long-Bailey. Her crimes involved not only outshining Corbyn himself at the dispatch box, but also appearing on television and subtly attempting to shift Labour's official Brexit policy towards remaining in the EU. David Liddington, deputizing for Prime Minister Theresa May, captured the moment articulately in the House:

> Well, can I first of all welcome the Honourable lady [Rebecca Long-Bailey] to these new responsibilities for her [...] I feel slightly sorry for the Right Honourable lady for Islington South [Emily Thornberry] who I am used to jousting with, who seems to have been dispatched to internal exile somewhere else [...] I think there's a lesson there that

anybody who at the dispatch box outshines the Dear Leader risks being airbrushed out of the politburo history at the earliest opportunity.

(*Hansard* 2019)

While of course a partisan jab, this speech highlighted a particular symptom of an identity-driven party with a strong leadership hierarchy: when Thornberry publicly strayed from the official party line, she was quietly relegated to an inferior position, to be replaced by an extremely loyal mouthpiece who would reliably justify Corbyn's actions. It suggests a great deal of paranoia within the leadership. Liddington's language, drawing on Soviet imagery of shady and cut-throat backroom tinkering, spoke loudly of a Labour Party that was then attempting to make Corbynism, under the "Dear Leader", the only game in town. The deliberate shrinking of ideological space to shut out dissent in this way became one of the defining characteristics of Corbyn's tenure. This tactic was not unexpected: widespread opposition to his leadership and policy platform existed within the Labour backbenches, and had persisted ever since Corbyn took power after Ed Miliband's resignation in 2015. This discontent was evidenced by the mass resignations of shadow ministers in the summer of 2016, which led to a no-confidence vote in which 172 out of 230 Labour MPs voted against their leader (Crines, Jeffery & Heppell 2018). Those who voted no confidence represented a wider constituency of voters than just the party membership, who tended to err to the hard left. The core groups, such as Momentum, who are described as "the entryist hard left" by Blakey (2016), used their considerable strength inside the NEC to ensure that Corbyn could not be unseated. Their toolbox prioritized intimidation, targeted to silence opposing viewpoints within the party, and shout down any anti-Corbynite voices. At Labour's 2019 conference in Brighton, Momentum founder Jon Lansman attempted to table a motion to abolish the position of deputy leader, a move tantamount to abolishing Tom Watson.[6] This found support within Momentum as a whole, but ultimately was dropped altogether. Momentum's attempt to simply remove those with whom they disagreed might be seen as a contribution to the death of discourse; eliminating ideological nonconformists from positions of power to reduce internal scrutiny of Corbyn, and removing the figurehead and leader of Labour centrists in a deconstruction of the broad church into the "Corbyn cult". The whole endeavour exposed the reality that for Corbyn's grassroots supporters, political identity was maintained by taking a maximalist (and expansionist) interpretation of what was considered a "threat to Corbyn", and then rallying

---

6. A man who was publicly at odds with Corbyn's policy positions and worldview and drew incredible criticism from the left of his party as a result.

around him in solidarity. It was adversarial indeed, and most sincerely paranoid. At the same conference, familiar "Oh, Jeremy Corbyn" chants in celebration of votes passing reminded us that votes on policy positions were more motivated by loyalty to the leadership than perceptions of the economic or social good, or at least that the social good was inextricably anchored to the leadership and was synonymous with it.

Labour's internal bureaucracy, the NEC allowed Momentum to wield this much power: candidates endorsed by the group tended to win elections, leading to a situation in which the 39-member NEC was commanded solidly by the Corbynites (*The Economist* 2018). For Labour moderates, and those to the right of the party, this was a terrifying prospect: mass deselections became an urgent threat as the hard-left-controlled NEC attempted to rebuild the Labour Party around Corbynism. This unique structure placed large Labour groups at odds with Labour's majority of moderate parliamentarians: the former knew that the latter wanted Jeremy Corbyn replaced, whereas the latter knew that the far left wanted to deselect them as quickly as possible (Cohen 2015). What Corbyn came to represent in the wider party and country was much more than just himself. He was gradually *becoming* the party. Although this might not manifest in followers overtly labelling their ideology as "Corbynism", it could lead to a mental reordering of one's political value hierarchy to place more emphasis on the issues made salient by Corbyn. Political concerns became anchored to his name, building a "Corbynism" that people could subscribe to.

## Projecting personality

Corbyn existed within a "cult of personality"; his followers had an intense devotion to him and his politics, and they put him on a pedestal as a figurehead above all other political actors, a font of political wisdom and the only possible agent of grassroots social change (Kent 2006). Nick Cohen (2017) wrote in *The Guardian* that the 2017 Labour conference was awash with "cultism", from Corbyn memorabilia on sale to chants of "Oh, Jeremy Corbyn", which were also a defining feature of Corbyn's bizarre Glastonbury Festival appearance. This is not a normal reception for a British politician. It represents groupthink at its loudest. It brought together the hive mind of the Labour grassroots movements, and the desire to "fit in" and be a part of the movement, wilfully surrendering individuality or critical analysis of Corbyn as a politician to blend into the homogeneous crowd (Chandler & Munday 2016). To not join in the chant suddenly imbued one's silence with great symbolic meaning: if you're not with us, you're against us (perhaps an interesting research area for political scientists interested in semiotics). The only socially acceptable option was to comply, even if solely to present the image of cooperation, with no true intention of believing in Corbyn's politics.

The effect of this was that dissent became deviance, fast-tracking Corbynism to the status of "the only acceptable game in town", and attaching labels including "poor-hating", "xenophobic", "bigoted", "racist", or even "Tory!" to any individual who actively or passively declined to take part in the group's show of support for Corbyn. The spectrum of acceptable ideologies switched to a minimalist, Corbynite range, where any other position was unacceptable.

The shrinking of ideological space that groups like Momentum, or groups on campus produced was not the sole reserve of the shadow cabinet: it became Corbyn's legacy, built to be followed by Labour and left-leaning activist groups throughout the country. It was not Jeremy Corbyn himself who jeered "Tory!" as an insult to those who disagreed with him on Twitter, or on university campuses; it was his network of supporters that produced and reproduced an image of Corbynism as a cult-like, activist movement.

If we take Corbyn's "identity" to be his political ideology plus his personality (a reductivist shortcut, but a potentially useful one), Corbyn's personal brand of identity politics was embedded within hundreds of nodes across the UK: activist groups, student Labour societies, trade unions and other groups espoused Corbyn's identity and projected it across geographical space, while Corbyn himself could run the party largely from Westminster, with minimal involvement in the process.

The psychological mechanism through which Corbyn was able to maintain such disparate groups of people (both ideologically and geographically separated) can be revealed by viewing Corbyn's Labour Party as one of Benedict Anderson's (1991) "imagined communities". These communities are so described since it is not possible that every citizen can know every single one of their fellow citizens (Kesebir 2012). Despite this reality, members of a political superorganism such as the Labour Party feel an allegiance to their party that transcends barriers of geography and of unfamiliarity with their peers in the party. Labour, like all political parties, binds disparate citizens into groups, and in turn it bound those groups to Jeremy Corbyn using nuanced and elaborate universally shared symbols imbued with layered and historically contextual meanings. One need look no further than September of 2019, when Johnson's prorogation of parliament left an empty government bench and a packed Labour bench singing "The Red Flag", a display that served the symbolic goal of reinforcing a shared identity and solidarity among the varied groups represented by Labour MPs. This reinforcement was particularly salient given that it was shared anger directed at Boris Johnson. Nothing reinforces group solidarity like a shared political enemy.

## Conclusion: Corbynites – patient investors?

Throughout this chapter I have attempted to answer one basic question: why did people continue to support Corbyn on a visceral, emotional level when he was never able to govern, and his grand election pledges of 2017 were mostly admitted to have been ambitions rather than deliverable policies? This is not even to mention his unpopularity with the public and myriad scandals including over antisemitism (not that these factors are unique to Corbyn). Why did we not see a flight of support away from him despite his multiple failures? For a political psychologist, cognitive consistency could be the key. Activists and members had invested in Corbyn. They might have invested their time or their money into his campaign. They might have invested socially, by announcing publicly on social media their intention to vote for Labour, or their belief in Corbyn; they invested their very intelligence in his ideology. Like all investments they expected a return. It would have been irrational for them to not stay within the fold until they received that return. People really do not want to lose on any of those investments when not only their money but their being proved right or wrong to their peers is at stake. No matter how they contributed to Corbyn's campaigns, they held on to a belief that his lack of success in general elections was someone else's fault, or that the system was somehow rigged against him – rather than admitting that their investment returned a loss because of the electability – or lack thereof – of the politician.

What Corbyn's followers received in return for their investment was a sense of belonging and of community, of doing and achieving something. The electoral success of Corbyn was merely a part of this, albeit a very salient part which might have convinced people to follow him in the first place. The reason people stayed with him, however, was because of the other benefits gained. For students this could have been a sense of belonging and an antidote to the chaos of their new life. Online, it might be the reasonable expectation of vocal support you could gain by publicly supporting Corbyn – and attacking other parties – on social media: it feels good to receive a large positive response, that of the perceived majority; it acts to reinforce your developing political beliefs by associating them with praise and "correctness", with membership of the "in" group. The alternative is admitting your investment has become worthless, or that you wrongly predicted the outcome of your investment endeavours. This could be applied to most activist movements, but is especially loud when applied to Corbyn's followers; few political parties demand such devotion. Besides, any failure to achieve a goal can be explained by the internal logic of Corbyn's identity politics. For example, a theoretical scandal might be disregarded by supporters as a right-wing political attack, triggering a defensive response and a deepening of loyalty to Corbyn and distrust of other leaders: a political positive feedback loop.

Throughout this chapter, I have attempted to demonstrate that Corbyn's party was not like the Labour Party of the recent past. Corbyn's leadership facilitated a deepening of artificial divides between people, many created through his speech acts and divisive class-based rhetoric. In expanding this reach outside of London, nodal networks of party activists voluntarily became memetic identity proxies, allowing Corbynism to project across geographical space.

Corbynism was the ideal vessel for identity politics. A once broad church was slowly normalizing the intolerance of alternative ideologies or visions. Political debate descended into personal attack; it became acceptable to disagree with someone purely based on their political affiliation, an identity marker which in itself came to encapsulate a constructed set of beliefs imagined to be identical in every individual who espoused a certain viewpoint, an imagined community. It was a politics in which left-leaning individuals could expect to receive a great deal of support and praise for bluntly berating Conservatives on social media; far from a politics of inclusion, we saw the facilitation of a politics of exclusion, of "in" and "out" groups who could never reconcile. To risk association with the "out" group was to make yourself available to remonstration.

There is an antidote to this, and it is two-pronged. The first prong is debate. I do not mean scripted television debate, for these by their very structure position leaders in direct opposition to prove the other wrong on the issues of the day. Instead, it needs to happen at universities, colleges, schools and wherever young people develop their political identities. If we can institutionalize tolerance in debating, and free ourselves from prejudiced expectations of others based on their political label, a more constructive paradigm will emerge. The second prong is to think critically about ideology, and avoid it altogether wherever possible. Adopting an ideology instantaneously reduces one's worldview to a lower resolution version; ideas are filtered through one's ideological lens, producing an output that is tainted with underlying bias. Ideology takes the truth of a situation and refuses to observe it from any perspective other than that which is consistent with itself. When ideologies meet in debate, therefore, common ground upon which to conduct productive discussion cannot be found. Ideology, no matter where on the political spectrum it exists, reduces debate to argument. Living in a world of rival political camps is inevitable: humans are groupish. There is no reason, however, why identity groups should not come together and negotiate, striving towards agreement, rather than indulging in the lazy mindset that "our group can never find common ground with your group", ask why that might be, discuss ideas and try to understand each other. Debate and understanding are an antidote to the chaos in our political culture. By understanding the other, we could remove our ideological filters and clearly see the distortive view of others that they create.

# References

Anderson, B. 1991. *Imagined Communities: Reflections on the Origin and Spread of Nationalism.* London: Verso.

Apperley, A. 2018. "False consciousness". In G. Brown, I. McLean and A. McMillan (eds), The *Concise Oxford Dictionary of Politics and International Relations.* Oxford: Oxford University Press.

Barker, C. 2004. "Strategic essentialism". In *The Sage Dictionary of Cultural Studies.* London: Sage Publications.

BBC 2015. "Jeremy Corbyn: Labour will not back EU exit". https://www.bbc.co.uk/news/uk-politics-34272334 (accessed 26 March 2021).

Bennister, M. *et al.* 2017. "Jeremy Corbyn and the limits of authentic rhetoric". In J. Atkins & J. Gaffney (eds), *Voices of the UK Left*, 101–22. Cham: Springer.

Blakey, H. 2016. "Corbyn-mania: cult of personality or political movement?". Open Democracy, 3 August. https://www.opendemocracy.net/en/opendemocracyuk/corbyn-mania-cult-of-personality-or-political-movement/ (accessed 15 March 2021).

Chandler, D. & R. Munday 2016. "Echo chamber". In *A Dictionary of Social Media.* Oxford: Oxford University Press.

Cohen, N. 2015. "Converting the Corbyn cult: before they can talk to the wider electorate, Labour MPs must win a life-or-death argument with their core supporters". *The Spectator* 329(9766): 22.

Cohen, N. 2017. "Labour conference? More like the cult of Saint Jeremy". *The Guardian*, 30 September. https://www.theguardian.com/commentisfree/2017/sep/30/labour-conference-more-like-the-cult-of-saint-jeremy (accessed 15 March 2021).

Cohen, N. 2019. "Corbyn's crack-up: The Labour leader's personality cult is on the verge of disintegrating". *The Spectator* 339(9938): 12.

Cohen, P. 2017. "Finding uncommon ground: working-class identity politics after Labourism". *Soundings: A Journal of Politics and Culture* 66: 113–28.

Crines, A., D. Jeffery & T. Heppell 2018. "The British Labour Party and leadership election mandate(s) of Jeremy Corbyn: patterns of opinion and opposition within the parliamentary Labour Party". *Journal of Elections, Public Opinion and Parties* 28(3): 361–79.

Crisp, T. 2011. "It's not the book, it's not the author, it's the award: the Lambda Literary Award and the case for strategic essentialism". *Children's Literature in Education* 42(2): 91–104.

Danius, S. & S. Jonsson 1993. "An interview with Gayatri Chakravorty Spivak". *Boundary 2*, 20(2): 24.

Dick, C. 2011. *The Perils of Identity: Group Rights and the Politics of Intragroup Difference.* Vancouver, BC: UBC Press.

Eide, E. 2010. "Strategic essentialism and ethnification: hand in glove?" *Nordicom Review: Nordic Research on Media & Communication* 31(2): 63–78.

Francis, R. 2016. "Corbyn's cultural hegemony". Medium, 18 August. https://medium.com/@rob_francis/corbyns-cultural-hegemony-1913ff9ffe93 (accessed 15 March 2021).

Goode, C. *et al.* 2017. "Group identity as a source of threat and means of compensation: establishing personal control through group identification and ideology". *European Journal of Social Psychology* 47(3): 259–72.

Hansard 2019. 661 Parl. Deb. H.C. (6th ser) col 135. https://hansard.parliament.uk/Commons/2019-06-12/debates/1233765F-C22F-40DE-8D34-0A03EEE70CBF/HouseOfCommons (accessed 26 March 2021).

Hossein-Pour, A. 2019. "Momentum launches bid to help Labour members deselect sitting MPs". PoliticsHome, 12 July. https://www.politicshome.com/news/uk/political-parties/labour-party/news/105252/momentum-launches-bid-help-labour-members (accessed 15 March 2021).

Howell, D. 2012. "Defiant dominoes: working miners and the 1984–5 strike". In B. Jackson & R. Saunders (eds), *Making Thatcher's Britain*, 148–64. Cambridge: Cambridge University Press.

Kent, M. 2006. "Cult-of-personality". In *The Oxford Dictionary of Sports Science and Medicine*. Oxford: Oxford University Press.

Kesebir, S. 2012. "The superorganism account of human sociality: how and when human groups are like beehives". *Personality and Social Psychology Review* 16(3): 233–61.

Labour Party 2017. *For the Many, Not the Few: The Labour Party Manifesto 2017*. London: The Labour Party.

Malan, J. 2011. "Being similar, different, and coexistent". *ACCORD Occasional Paper Series* 5(3): 1–71.

Meyerson, D. 1991. *False Consciousness*. Oxford: Clarendon Press.

Mintz, L. 2018. "Pale, male, and stale: are men really suffering from workplace discrimination?" *The Telegraph*, 14 November. https://www.telegraph.co.uk/women/business/pale-male-stale-men-really-suffering-workplace-discrimination/ (accessed 22 March 2021).

Moore, C. 2018. "Don't let Jeremy Corbyn gloss over his Eurosceptic past". Coffee House blog, *The Spectator*, 12 July. https://blogs.spectator.co.uk/2018/07/dont-let-jeremy-corbyn-gloss-over-his-eurosceptic-past/ (accessed 15 March 2021).

Petherick, W. 2017. "Cults". In W. Petherick & G. Sinnamon (eds), *The Psychology of Criminal and Antisocial Behaviour*, 565–87. Amsterdam: Elsevier.

Piper, E. 2021. "Jeremy Corbyn, UK's unlikely EU warrior, makes last stand on Brexit". Reuters. https://www.reuters.com/investigates/special-report/britain-eu-corbyn/ (accessed 6 April 2021).

Rutherford, J. 2011. "The future is Conservative". *Soundings* 47(47): 54–64.

Schofield, K. 2019. "EXCL Moderate Labour MPs to get lessons in how to avoid being purged by left-wingers". PoliticsHome, 20 June. https://www.politicshome.com/news/uk/political-parties/labour-party/news/104714/excl-moderate-labour-mps-get-lessons-how-avoid (accessed 15 March 2021).

Taylor, C. & A. Gutmann 1994. *Multiculturalism: Examining the Politics of Recognition*. Princeton, NJ: Princeton University Press.

Taylor, C. & A. Gutmann 1997. "The politics of recognition". *New Contexts of Canadian Criticism* 98: 25–73.

*The Economist* 2016. "The telling sincerity of Jeremy Corbyn's EU conversion". *The Economist*, 14 April. https://www.economist.com/bagehots-notebook/2016/04/14/the-telling-sincerity-of-jeremy-corbyns-eu-conversion (accessed 6 April 2021).

*The Economist* 2018. "Momentum gains momentum: the Labour Party". *The Economist* 426(9075): 27.

Thompson, M. 2014. "False consciousness reconsidered: a theory of defective social cognition". *Critical Sociology* 41(3): 449–61.

Tolchard, H. 2017. "The power in a political narrative". Berkeley Political Review, 5 December. https://bpr.berkeley.edu/2017/12/05/the-power-in-a-political-narrative/ (accessed 15 March 2021).

Voronka, J. 2016. "The politics of 'people with lived experience': experiential authority and the risks of strategic essentialism". *Philosophy, Psychiatry & Psychology* 23(3): 189–201.

Watts, J. 2018. "The lost world of the British Labour Party? community, infiltration and disunity". *British Politics* 13(4): 505–23.

# 6

# AN END TO MARKET MANIA AND MANAGERIALIST MADNESS: CORBYN(ISM) AND THE PUBLIC SECTOR

*Peter Dorey*

When Jeremy Corbyn became Labour leader, his party faced a public sector that had endured two particular problems, one relatively recent, the other longer-term and thus deeper-rooted. The more recent problem had been the decade of stringent financial constraints imposed as part of the austerity programme implemented by the Conservatives since 2010, to tackle the economic problems accruing from the 2008 financial crash. As the public sector consumed the vast majority of government expenditure, it naturally bore the brunt of cuts intended to reduce the fiscal deficit and borrowing. Of course, the Conservatives could have raised taxes in order to pay off some of the deficit and/or sustain public services, but this option – apart from increasing VAT (a regressive tax) from 18 to 20 per cent – was largely rejected on ideological grounds. Indeed, the post-2010 Conservative governments actually cut the top rate of income tax from 50 to 45 per cent and reduced corporation tax, suggesting by their actions, rather than their words, that "we were most certainly *not* all in it together".

The longer-term and deeper-rooted problem endured by the public sector since the late 1980s has been the dual processes of "marketization" and "managerialism" introduced by the Thatcher and Major governments, but zealously continued and extended by the Blair and Brown governments, and then consolidated, under the auspices of austerity, by the post-2010 Conservative-led governments. Marketization compelled public services either to incorporate private sector principles and practices – through the adoption of "business models", "internal markets" and enforced competition, both within and between, public sector institutions, with funding often linked to success in competing against "rival" institutions (and thus imitating the profit motive) – or to "contract-out" some of their activities to the private sector. The latter reflected the neoliberal–Thatcherite premise that the private sector was inherently superior to the public sector because of competition driving up standards, and the need to make a profit in order to survive, which could only be achieved by attracting and retaining enough customers, rather than relying on guaranteed annual taxpayers' subsidies to monopolistic services which were deemed to lack incentives to improve their performance.

The process of marketization also entailed a significant change in the governance of the public sector via the phenomenon of "managerialism", or what some academics termed New Public Management. Indeed, from a neoliberal perspective, managerialism was necessary in order to enforce marketization and impose it on often recalcitrant or sceptical professionals in the public sector. For example, "internal markets" and "cost centres" within institutions yielded a burgeoning of accountants and financial managers, while the public sector in general witnessed a marked increase in managerial appointments, such as business managers, strategic co-ordinators, quality assurance officers and corporate compliance officers. In many public sector institutions, a Byzantine bureaucracy became established, with a behemoth of senior and middle managers exercising ever-increasing control over front-line professionals, to ensure compliance and conformity with institutional and political goals.

At the same time, former Personnel Departments were transformed into Human Resources Departments, which were less concerned with supporting staff, or acting as mediators between employees and management in the case of formal grievances, and more concerned with imposing increasingly stringent "performance management" targets and monitoring exercises on employees: core aspects of what Power (1999) characterizes as "the audit society", and various scholars – especially with regard to the education sector – refer to as "hyper-accountability" (e.g. Lodge 2005: 130; Mansell 2011; Millar 2016). Amann (2003) has highlighted significant similarities between the post-1980 governance of Britain's public sector and aspects of the thoroughly dysfunctional command-and-control regime of the former Soviet Union.

## Corbynism and the public sector

As other chapters have explained, Corbynism was committed to a recalibration and reform of the British (or Anglo-American) model of capitalism. Contrary to the alarmist and often paranoid warnings of the Right that Corbynism would herald draconian (and disastrous) state control of the economy, to the extent that Britain would soon resemble North Korea or Venezuela, what was actually proposed was rather less revolutionary, albeit still potentially transformative. That Corbynism was so readily denounced as dangerously Marxist and "hard left" was reflective of how far to the right the UK had drifted during four decades of neoliberal hegemony, with its Orwellian mantra of "private-sector good; public-sector bad", and the *a priori* assumption that the only viable policy solution to any economic or social problem was yet more privatization, deregulation or marketization.

In contrast, Corbynism sought to advance the intellectual and ideological case for an increased role for the state in the economic sphere, and an expanded, reinvigorated, public sector. This would restore a genuinely mixed economy, comprising a few nationalized industries and a more prominent public sector in policy spheres such as such as education, health, policing, prisons, probation and social services. Most of the economy, however, would remain privately owned, just as it had after the 1945–50 Attlee government had nationalized several major industries and utilities, and established a comprehensive welfare state, much of the latter having led to the creation or expansion of the public sector alongside a greatly enhanced role for local government in terms of service "delivery".

Labour's shadow chancellor and key "theorist" of Corbynism, John McDonnell explained that what was being proposed was a transformation that would entail breaking with neoliberalism and "changing the framework in which decisions are made" (2018a: ix, x). In effect, what Corbynism proposed was a rather different model of capitalism to the increasingly brutal and inherently dysfunctional Anglo-American version that had been installed since the 1980s. For example, he argued for a much clearer distinction and demarcation between the private sector and public services, with the latter to play a more extensive and active role after decades of denigration and evisceration.

The approach to the public sector adopted by the Labour Party under Corbyn's leadership thus explicitly aimed to reverse the post-1980 trends delineated above, namely "marketization" and "managerialism". In other words, it was intended to restate the political case for a genuinely *public* sector, ring-fence public services from incursions and encroachment by private companies – "to bring public services back under public control" (McDonnell 2018a: x) – and reform the governance of public services, in order to eradicate the hitherto relentless growth of top-down, target-obsessed, corporate management and the concomitant erosion of professional autonomy and expertise.

Corbynism also deemed it essential, as a matter of priority and urgency, to reverse the relentless "austerity" cuts in public sector funding that had been imposed by Conservative-led governments since 2010. As such, Corbyn's "priority [was] rescuing public services and combatting stagnation, poverty and inequality" (Blackburn 2018: 11).

## Increasing funding and staffing

Many of the Corbynite pledges that garnered most attention, and certainly the most critical headlines in the Tory press, were those pertaining to public sector funding, in the context of a more general commitment to ending a decade of austerity. The post-2010 Conservative-led governments had viewed most of the public sector as irresistible low-hanging fruit, which could deliver a veritable harvest of financial savings for the Treasury. Moreover, cutting expenditure on public services (and welfare) could readily be presented as an unfortunate and reluctant economic necessity, rather than a conscious political choice deriving from ideological hostility to the public sector – shared, to a considerable extent, by the "Orange Book" Liberal Democrats who had acquired strong influence in their party by this time – and a concomitant political determination to exploit the financial crisis by attacking the residual vestiges of collectivism and social democracy through further "rolling back the state" and yet more privatization (Eaton 2018; Klein 2007; McDonnell 2018; Mirowski 2013).

This section will focus specifically, but briefly, on the pledges concerning increased funding and staffing for public services. Labour's 2019 election manifesto explained that most of the additional monies pledged to the public sector would accrue from increasing income tax on salaries above £80,000, reversing recent cuts in corporate tax (by raising it from 18 to 26 per cent) and pursuing "the biggest ever crackdown on tax avoidance and evasion" (Labour Party 2019a: 30). Cognisant that the Conservatives, big business and Britain's rabidly pro-Conservative press would bitterly denounce Labour's planned tax increases, Corbyn emphasized that:

> our new spending commitments would be paid for by asking the top five per cent to pay a small amount extra in tax, still with a lower tax rate than under most of Mrs Thatcher's reign, and by asking big business to pay a little more but still a lower rate than any other country in the G7.
> (Corbyn 2017b)

Much of the additional revenue would then be spent on improving public sector infrastructure, staff pay and increasing recruitment of front-line workers. With regard to the former, a £150 billion "Social Transformation Fund" was pledged, which would be devoted to replacing or rebuilding dilapidated schools, hospitals, care homes and council houses, both to make them physically fit for the twenty-first century, and to ensure that they were environmentally friendly (in terms of tackling climate change). In terms of public sector pay, Corbyn's Labour Party pledged this would initially be increased by 5 per cent, and raised at a rate higher than inflation in each subsequent year, the medium-term objective being to restore public sector pay to its pre-2008 level (Labour Party 2019a: 30).

Meanwhile, in order to tackle staff shortages caused by a decade of austerity, Labour pledged to address the shortfall of 43,000 nurses by increasing the NHS's budget by £26 billion over the five-year lifetime of a parliament, to facilitate an average 4.3 per cent annual increase in NHS funding (compared to the 3.4 per cent pledged by the Conservatives). It was intended that the additional funding, and the restoration of bursaries for student nurses, would eventually enable 24,000 additional nurses to be recruited, while funding would also be provided to facilitate the training of 5,000 doctors. More doctors would mean more patients being seen and thus a reduction in waiting lists, and patients receiving surgery or other medical treatment earlier, before symptoms became more serious or protracted, and often more costly to treat (Labour Party 2019b). Elsewhere, Corbyn's Labour promised that enough teachers would be recruited to ensure that class sizes did not exceed 30.

It was also assumed that, in additional to the recruitment of new nurses and teachers, Labour's promised year-on-year, above-inflation, pay increases in the public sector would improve the retention of staff who would otherwise have left the NHS and education. It was also suggested that some front-line workers left these professions because of disillusionment and frustration with the mode of governance, in terms of constant monitoring, top-down targets, bureaucratic interference and general loss of autonomy and capacity to exercise professional judgement and discretion. These causes of "exit" would, it was assumed, be tackled by Labour's proposed reforms of public sector governance, which we outline below.

With regard to staffing in other parts of the public sector, Labour promised, in 2017, an increase of 10,000 (community) police officers, but when Boris Johnson pledged in 2019 that a re-elected Conservative government would increase police numbers by 20,000, Labour responded by pledging to "recruit 2,000 more front-line officers than have been planned for by the Conservatives" (Labour Party 2019a: 43). Meanwhile, whereas Labour had promised 3,000 additional fire-fighters, this figure had increased to 5,000 in 2019. Elsewhere, Labour pledged to restore the number of prison officers to 2010 levels; their numbers had declined from almost 20,000 in 2010 to just under 14,500 by the end of 2016,[1] despite a record number of prisoners in Britain's jails.

With regard to the funding of higher education, Labour contested both the 2017 and 2019 general elections with one of its most prominent commitments, pledging to abolish student fees and restore maintenance grants: in effect, reviving free university education for many students. This was part of Corbynism's more general commitment to ending the commercialization and marketization of higher education, whereby universities had been treated as businesses, students as consumers or customers and degrees as merely another

---

1. Data retrieved from Ministry of Justice, HMPPS workforce statistics bulletin: June 2017 tables. https://www.gov.uk/government/statistics/her-majestys-prison-and-probation-service-workforce-quarterly-june-2017 (accessed 17 March 2021).

commodity, albeit a commodity whose ultimate value was defined by the size of the graduate earnings they could be "exchanged" for. It was further intended that educational maintenance allowances would be restored for 16–18-year-olds in further education. However, there was little indication of whether a Corbyn-led government would also seek to increase staffing in Britain's universities, after a decade of redundancies, early retirements and casualization among academics.

Much of Labour's planned extra spending on education was to be funded by the £19.4 billion that would supposedly accrue from reversing post-2010 cuts to corporation tax, while a commitment to provide free school meals to all primary school pupils would be funded by charging VAT on private school fees (Labour Party 2017a).

## Replacing "outsourcing" with "insourcing"

Corbynism's long commitment to a genuine public sector naturally meant that it was instinctively and intrinsically hostile to the manner in which the private sector had been actively encouraged and enabled to "deliver" a growing number of public services since the 1980s – a trend enthusiastically promoted by Conservative and New Labour governments alike. According to Corbyn, a major consequence of this trend was that "corporate vested interests [...] have infiltrated our public services" (Corbyn 2017a).

This phenomenon, as an integral aspect of "marketization", had increasingly blurred the boundaries between the public and private sectors, as a growing number and range of public services were contracted out to private companies, with £200 billion annually spent by central and local government on procuring private sector delivery or management of public services (Labour Party 2017b: 14). Usually this was accompanied by claims that it would enhance competitiveness, increase cost-effectiveness, ensure value for money and improve quality, both for service users and taxpayers. Ironically, but also predictably, this blurring of boundaries between the public and private sectors rather undermined the "accountability" often cited as an additional justification for his shift, because it made it more difficult to attribute responsibility for subsequent policy failures; each "sector" could blame the other if and when errors or failings occurred. Moreover, the accountability of private providers was often concealed or obfuscated, because some companies claimed "commercial confidentiality" as a justification for withholding information that might reveal their culpability or incompetence.

Corbynism was ideologically opposed to marketization and contracting out of swathes of the public sector, adamant instead that public services such as education, health, the provision of school meals, refuse collection and road maintenance, should *not* ordinarily be delivered by private companies whose prime objective was maximizing profits and shareholder value. Whereas the default stance since the 1980s had been that as many public sector services as possible could and should be delivered by private companies – outsourced, contracted out or directly privatized – and only retained in-house if and when a strong case could be made for doing so, the Corbynite premise was the opposite: that public services should usually be provided in-house, whereupon contacting out would become the exception rather than the norm. This reversion to "insourcing" was deemed to offer seven advantages over the extant outsourcing regime:

- lower costs
- a public service ethos
- a longer time horizon
- greater scope for coordination and integration of services
- economies of scale
- greater accountability and transparency
- better management of risk (Labour Party 2018: 6, 16–20).

Corbyn's Labour thus intended that outsourced public services would steadily be brought back in-house, resulting in "a 'new normal' where insourcing is preferred, an 'insourcing-first' model", thus superseding the hitherto *a priori* preference for outsourcing public sector service delivery to private companies and consortia (Labour Party 2018: 21).

Furthermore, Corbyn's Labour proposed that the public sector should be subject to a 20:1 pay ratio, meaning that the annual salaries of the highest-paid staff would be no more than 20 times higher the earnings of the lowest-paid staff (Labour Party 2017b: 47; Labour Party 2019a: 30; for academic arguments in favour of a 20:1 pay ratio see Dorey 2020). Thus, if a full-time public sector worker received a salary of £15,000, the highest-paid employee in the same institution or sector would not be permitted to earn more than £300,000 annually. Labour's adoption of a pay ratio policy under Corbyn not only accorded with the party's commitment to fairness and greater equality but was also intended to make the public sector more affordable and facilitate the employment of more front-line staff.

This reflected another criticism of marketization in the public sector, namely that the salaries of some senior staff, such as the chief executives of NHS Trusts and university vice-chancellors, had enjoyed greatly increased remuneration packages because of the alleged need to ensure comparability with the private sector, and improve recruitment and retention of such high-fliers. How could a local health service or university attract successful businesspeople to manage them and provide corporate leadership, if they did not offer salaries commensurate with those paid in the private sector, where the pay ratio in some large companies or sectors is 160:1? Corbynism's response, in effect, was that the public sector should reject the Conservatives' obsession with appointing private sector business leaders to manage public sector services and organizations.

The fact that someone had successfully created or managed a company manufacturing toilet rolls or selling dog food, for example, did not in itself mean (as Conservatives often assumed) that they were qualified or suitable to manage a hospital or university. Besides, if someone's willingness to accept a senior post in the public sector was dependent on the size of the salary, then they were probably the wrong person for the job anyway, because they were evidently motivated more by pecuniary rewards than genuine commitment to public service.

However, promoting a principle or policy on normative or philosophical grounds is sometimes insufficient to garner much electoral support, even when the professed advantages are clearly or confidently delineated. What is also usually necessary, in order to imbue the principle or policy objective with greater salience, or render it more meaningful or "relatable", to voters, is to highlight specific problems or failures which would purportedly have been prevented by the new approach or would now be ameliorated by its adoption.

This is redolent of John Kingdon's "policy streams" model of policy change, whereby policies are often drafted or adopted because their advocates intellectually believe in them or favour them, and *then* seek to identify empirical examples of problems that the new policy would solve. In other words, rather than a linear or sequential "stagist" approach to the policy process, whereby a problem prompts the drafting of a policy, a policy is adopted on normative grounds (its advocates believe it is intrinsically or intellectually better) prior to searching for real-world problems to which it could be applied (Kingdon 1995). This tactic can furnish a policy proposal with practical relevance or legitimacy, and thereby potentially increase its popularity, while simultaneously discrediting both the extant policy and its adherents.

In this regard, Corbyn's Labour Party was able to draw critical attention to various recent policy failures and scandals accruing from private sector delivery of public services, the claim being made that: "Examples now abound of serious failings in contractual delivery, across a range of service areas and regions in the United Kingdom" (Labour Party 2018: 12). Corbyn himself was reputed to be an avid reader of the fortnightly exposés of Private Finance Initiative[2] failings and scandals published in *Private Eye* (Blackburn 2018: 11). One of the most

2. PFIs have been increasingly popular with British governments since the 1990s (but particularly the Blair governments) because they provided a means of funding new infrastructure and other capital projects without needing to raise direct taxes. Instead, repayments were made by the relevant institution, organisation or local public body, usually over a 25–30-year period. However, these PFIs have been subject to widespread and often trenchant criticism, not least from the House of Commons' Public Accounts Committee (House of Commons 2018).

egregious examples was the 2018 collapse of Carillion after the company had accrued debts totalling £1.5 billion, in spite of having been a major beneficiary of financially lucrative central and local government contracts to "deliver" a wide range of public sector services, often pertaining to infrastructure construction and facilities management (BBC 2018a).

Meanwhile, in 2017, Labour's shadow justice secretary, Imran Hussain, cited a National Audit Office report that was highly critical of the 2014 part-privatization of the Probation Service, both in terms of the costs and the subsequent failure to hit contractual targets. Initially, the total value of the eight-year contracts awarded by the Ministry of Justice was to be £3.7 billion, but this was subsequently reduced to £2.1 billion after it had transpired that by February 2017, the private companies had, on average, only achieved 33 per cent of their targets (National Audit Office 2017: 7–8). This led Hussain to deem this as "yet more evidence of how the Conservatives' part-privatization of probation has been a costly failure [...] hundreds of millions of pounds are being wasted [on] private probation companies which are not even meeting basic performance targets" (Hussain 2017).

Similar criticisms were levelled against the contracting out of prison management at some of Britain's largest jails, after investigations by HM Inspectorate of Prisons revealed appalling living conditions and/or serious mismanagement (see, e.g. Grierson 2019; Silvester 2019; Travis 2018). It was in this context that Hussain's successor as shadow justice secretary, Richard Burgon (2019), asserted that "the Tories' ideological obsession with running prisons for private profit is dangerously flawed", adding that such a policy was a "scandal" which the next Labour government would terminate.

Elsewhere, albeit on a smaller, much more local, scale, Labour's shadow communities secretary, Andrew Gwynne, cited an autumn 2018 audit report that strongly criticized serious financial irregularities totalling £2 million accruing from a contract between Barnet Council and Capita, the latter being one of the main private sector beneficiaries of contracts for delivering public services. Gwynne alleged that this was "a textbook example of why outsourcing fails our public services. This mass-outsourcing experiment with our public services has failed" (Gwynne 2018).

Not only was contracting out often followed by an inexorable decline in the quality of service provision, Corbynism argued, but also by a corresponding deterioration in employment conditions for the workers, as wages, jobs and pensions were often cut. In fact, the two trends were inextricably linked, because "cutting corners" in terms of service delivery to the public and driving down the wages and pensions of staff, were both a logical consequence of the corporate priority ascribed to maximizing profitability and "market value", and thus the dividends paid to shareholders. It appeared that the much-vaunted increased competition and consequent improved quality of service, which were supposed to accrue from contracting out swathes of the public sector, often failed to materialize.

On the contrary, Corbynite critics of contracting out were able to cite numerous cases (of which those just cited were just a small number) where relentless cost-cutting, to increase profits, had actually resulted in a worse standard of service to public sector users, and a notable lack of value for money for taxpayers, coupled with an absence of accountability. Shadow Chancellor John McDonnell encapsulated such criticisms when he asserted that: "It's time to end the outsourcing scandal which has seen private companies rip off the taxpayer, degrade our public services and put people at risk, while remaining wholly unaccountable to the people who rely on and fund these services" (McDonnell 2019).

Consequently, Corbyn's Labour Party was committed to ensuring that, as far as practicably possible, its default stance would be that public sector services should be "delivered" in-house, instead of being semi-privatized via compulsory competitive tendering and outsourcing. However, it was acknowledged that insourcing would need to be "phased", partly to prevent local authorities from suddenly being overwhelmed with new responsibilities for providing public services, but also because in some instances, it would often be necessary to wait for an outsourced contract to reach the end of its fixed term before being brought back in-house, in order to avoid litigation, on commercial grounds, from the current holder of the contract.

## How would unavoidable outsourcing be tackled?

Declaring that public sector services ought to be provided in-house was straightforward; a declaration of principle and purpose, coupled with a list of supposed advantages. However, Corbyn's Labour Party needed to answer the question of what it would do if a public service did need to be contracted out to a private company or consortium, because it absolutely could not be performed in-house, perhaps because of a lack of relevant expertise or other essential administrative or technical resources. The answer was that in such exceptional cases, contracts awarded to a private company would stipulate a range of additional conditions that would need to be met. These conditions were intended to ensure that the commissioned company would be required to fulfil several specified obligations towards their workers and the wider community, namely:

- fair wages and workers' rights
- compliance with the Freedom of Information Act 2000 and Human Rights Act 1998
- use of local labour and local products as far practicably possible

- gender pay audits
- maximum contractual periods
- provision for monitoring of performance
- community benefit contributions
- prohibition on involvement of parties who have been engaged with illegality, improper tax practices, or corruption (Labour Party 2018: 6, 27–33).

It was also claimed that where outsourcing was unavoidable, contracts would only be awarded to private firms who had adopted the 20:1 pay ratio that Labour intended to apply to the public sector.

In effect, a Corbyn-led Labour government would seek to compel private firms to accept a range of ethical and social responsibilities, rather than being solely concerned to maximize shareholder value. For example, Shadow Education Secretary Angela Rayner pledged that when a Labour government embarked upon a major school-building programme, "not one brick will be laid by a company that doesn't pay its taxes or a builder who is falsely self-employed" (Rayner 2018). Cognizant that some private firms would baulk at meeting the additional contractual requirements, Corbyn's Labour Party tartly suggested that those who were unable or unwilling "to comply with more stringent labour and community standards are perhaps not contractors that should be delivering key public functions" (Labour Party 2018: 48).

## Reforming public sector governance

In tandem with proposals to reverse the post-1980s pursuit of "marketization", Corbynism also aimed to roll back and dismantle the parallel phenomenon of "managerialism" in the public sector. It was a supreme irony of Conservative and New Labour reforms of the public sector that transforming hospitals, probation services, schools and universities into quasi-businesses, partly on the grounds that this would facilitate greater dynamism and innovative practices as well as slash red tape, actually spawned a sprawling, Soviet-style, command-and-control bureaucracy determined to micro-manage front-line professionals, and relentlessly measure and monitor every aspect of their "performance"; not just measuring *what* they did, but stipulating *how* they did it, in order to render it bureaucratically measurable.

In stark contrast, Corbynism promoted an alternative mode of public sector governance, one couched in a discourse of "democratization", for it was deemed axiomatic that by returning most public services in-house, elected local authorities would often regain the control – financial and political – that had been forcibly relinquished by contracting out to the private sector. Moreover, the

Corbynite proposals for transforming public sector governance envisaged that front-line professionals and service users would both play a much more influential and participatory role in decision-taking and problem-solving. Or, as John McDonnell promised: "The next Labour government will put democratically owned and managed public services irreversibly in the hands of workers, and of those who rely on their work" (BBC 2018b).

In this regard, Corbyn's perspective on the democratization and devolution of decision-taking in the public sector logically reflected his stance towards (re-) nationalization of key utilities. He had asserted that "I believe in public ownership, but I have never favoured the remote nationalized model that prevailed in the post-war era [...] public control should mean just that, not simply state control", entailing service employees and users, in partnership with elected politicians "co-operatively running" public sector services "to ensure they are run in our interests and not for private profit" (quoted in Morris 2015; see also John McDonnell quoted in Maher, Gindin & Panitch 2019: 10).

For example, in education, it was pledged that teachers would be granted "more direct involvement in the curriculum" while simultaneously "reducing monitoring and bureaucracy" (Labour Party 2017b: 38). Similarly, it was pledged that by reversing the privatization of the NHS, the next Labour government would "return our health service into expert public control". As part of this proposed democratization and devolution, it was pledged that the party would "ask local people to participate in the redrawing of plans to reform the governance of the NHS" (Labour Party 2017b: 69), and thereafter, "ensure the voices of local people and NHS staff are heard in future developments of the health system" (Labour Party 2019a: 33). There remained, however, a lack of specificity about how, when and where these "voices" would be heard, or how divergent views would be reconciled if front-line staff, service users and/or a local authority, senior management or central government had markedly different or irreconcilable preferences.

One of the most notable proposals with regard to reforming public sector governance, and, among other things, paying more heed to the concerns of front-line professionals, was with regard to schools, where Corbyn's Labour pledged to abolish the Office for Standards in Education (Ofsted), whose inspections had long been a cause of considerable complaint from the teaching profession. This resentment derived not only from the amount of time and paperwork that each Ofsted inspection entailed for the school being visited, but the perception that the subsequent decisions could be rather arbitrary or subjective, in spite of the purportedly objective criteria deployed by its inspectors. The verdict accruing from the Ofsted inspection determined the school's "rating" and, potentially, its future pupil intake; a less than "excellent" rating might mean fewer parents choosing that school for their child(ren) and, ultimately, closures and/or redundancies, because marketization meant that funding was linked to intake ("customers").

Under a Corbyn-led Labour government, Ofsted inspections would be replaced by a dual system entailing two forms of inspection. The first would a "light touch" audit undertaken by local authorities – who would enjoy a revived, and much more active, role in education provision and school management after decades of marginalization – while the second would be a more in-depth inspection conducted by Her Majesty's Inspectors (HMIs), which would itself operate under the auspices of a new National Education Service. However, unlike Ofsted inspections, the HMI visits would be mostly conducted in response to problems identified by the local authority checks, or if concerns were expressed by parents, teachers and/or school governors. This was portrayed by Corbyn's Labour as a means of democratizing the governance of education, both because of the greatly enhanced role ascribed to local authorities, and because of the manner in which key stakeholders at the school level could call on the HMI if they had concerns.

A further envisaged benefit of the proposed abolition of Ofsted was a marked improvement in teachers' morale, and a concomitant reduction in the stress that regular inspections were alleged to have cause hitherto. Indeed, Angela Rayner suggested that these reforms would significantly improve the retention of teachers, because the abolition of Ofsted would herald an end to "a system that hounds teachers from the classroom" (Rayner 2019).

Again, however, there was rather less clarity about how governance would be reformed, and democratic control implemented, in other parts of the public sector, such as the NHS, policing, probation and universities. The implication seemed to be that restoring the former role of elected local authorities, and other community-based institutions, would facilitate the democratization of most public services, and render them more accountable.

## Conclusion

It would be claiming too much to argue that there was a distinctly "Corbynite" policy on the public sector, although there was clearly an ideological commitment to expanding this realm after decades of "market mania". There were, however, some interesting and well-considered proposals on some aspects of public service delivery and governance, most notably with regard to the crucial sphere of funding and staffing after a decade of ideologically motivated cuts, and the objective of replacing outsourcing by "insourcing". Two particularly innovative and noteworthy policies were, first, the proposals for a pay ratio (of 20:1) in the public sector, which could be justified both in terms of curbing excessive pay among senior public servants, and in reducing inequality (and thus actively pursuing Labour's egalitarian principles), and second, the list of conditions that would have to be met in the few residual cases where contracting out would still be necessary, whereupon the recipients of contracts would be required to ensure that they accepted a wider range of responsibilities than solely maximizing shareholder value.

Where Corbynism's stance towards the public sector needed more firmness or fleshing out was in terms of the third dimension discussed in this chapter, namely democratization and reforms of governance to supersede managerialism. Here, the most advanced proposals were in the realm of school-level education, with teachers and parents to be granted a greater "voice", and Ofsted to be replaced by a more participatory and "bottom-up" mode of inspection, and one which would be a lot less bureaucratic (and thus less stressful for teachers). Yet even here, there was opacity about aspects of secondary education such as the future of the National Curriculum and curriculum content, as well as whether a Labour government would tolerate the continued existence of the different types of schools (Free Schools and Academies) that had been encouraged since the 1990s, in the context of choice and competition (coupled with political antipathy towards supposedly "bog-standard comprehensives"), or seek to abolish them?

There was even less clarity over Corbynism's plans for higher education, apart from the much-vaunted abolition of student fees and restoration of student grants. Similarly, beyond the welcome – indeed essential – increases in funding and staffing, it was not quite clear how Corbyn's Labour intended to democratize, or otherwise reform, the governance of the NHS, policing or probation, including the manner in which they were inspected and held accountable.

Ultimately, Corbynism's "policy" towards the public sector was somewhat patchy and seemingly incomplete; a work-in-progress it seems. The often intelligent and innovative thinking which had evidently been devoted to aspects of education policy (albeit still incomplete) was seemingly not matched by comparable reflexivity or creativity in other spheres of (proposed) public sector reform, beyond increased funding. As such, if Corbynism's proposals for the public sector had been submitted as an undergraduate essay, they would have been a borderline C+/B- ("very promising in parts, but more care and consistency needed"), and had they been submitted as a journal article, they would undoubtedly have been designated "revise and resubmit".

## References

Amann, R. 2003. "A Sovietological view of modern Britain". *Political Quarterly* 74(4): 468–80.
BBC 2018a. "Where did it go wrong for Carillion?". BBC News, 15 January. https://www.bbc.co.uk/news/business-42666275 (accessed 17 March 2021).
BBC 2018b. "John McDonnell: Labour public ownership plan will cost nothing". BBC News, 10 February. https://www.bbc.co.uk/news/uk-politics-43014861 (accessed 17 March 2021).

Blackburn, R. 2018. "The Corbyn project: public capital and Labour's new deal". *New Left Review* 111 (May–June): 5–32.

Burgon, R. 2019. "Running prisons for private profit is dangerously flawed". https://labour.org. uk/press/running-prisons-private-profit-dangerously-flawed-richard-burgon/ (accessed 17 March 2021).

Corbyn, J. 2017a. "Speech at Labour's South East Regional Conference, 18 February". https:// web.archive.org/web/20200125093042/https://www.jeremycorbyn.org.uk/articles/ jeremy-corbyn-my-speech-at-labours-south-east-regional-conference/index.html (accessed 8 April 2021).

Corbyn, J. 2017b. "Speech at UNISON annual conference, 23 June". https://labour.org.uk/ press/jeremy-corbyn-speech-to-unison-annual-conference/ (accessed 17 March 2021).

Dorey, P. 2020. "A 'middle way' between 'equality' and 'the market': a pay ratio". In A. Örtenblad (ed.), *Debating Equal Pay for All: Economy, Practicability and Ethics*, 117–34. Basingstoke: Palgrave Macmillan.

Eaton, G. 2018. "Austerity: how an ideological project failed on its own terms". *New Statesman*, 10 October. https://www.newstatesman.com/politics/economy/2018/10/austerity-how-ideological-project-failed-its-own-terms (accessed 17 March 2021).

Grierson, J. 2019. "G4S stripped of contract to run Birmingham prison". *The Guardian*, 1 April. https://www.theguardian.com/society/2019/apr/01/g4s-stripped-contract-run-hmp-birmingham-prison (accessed 17 March 2021).

Gwynne, A. 2018. "This case in Barnet is a textbook example of why outsourcing fails our public services". Press release, 21 September. https://labour.org.uk/press/case-barnet-textbook-example-outsourcing-fails-public-services-gwynne/ (accessed 17 March 2021).

House of Commons 2018. Committee of Public Accounts; Private Finance Initiatives, Forty-Sixth Report of Session 2017–19, H.C. 894, 13 June. https://old.parliament.uk/business/ committees/committees-a-z/commons-select/public-accounts-committee/inquiries/ parliament-2017/private-finance-initiatives-17-19/ (accessed 17 March 2021).

Hussain, I. 2017. "The Conservatives' part-privatisation of probation has been a costly failure". Press release, 19 December. https://labour.org.uk/press/the-conservatives-part-privatisation-of-probation/ (accessed 17 March 2021).

Kingdon, J. 1995. *Agendas, Alternatives, and Public Policies*. Second edition. New York, NY: HarperCollins.

Klein, N. 2007. *The Shock Doctrine: The Rise of Disaster Capitalism*. London: Allen Lane.

Labour Party 2017a. "Labour will transform education for the many not the few". Press release, 9 May. https://labour.org.uk/press/labour-will-transform-education-for-the-many-not/ (accessed 17 March 2021).

Labour Party 2017b. *For the Many, Not the Few: The Labour Party Manifesto 2017*. London: The Labour Party.

Labour Party 2018. *Democratising Local Public Services: A Plan for Twenty-First Century Insourcing*. London: Labour Party Community Wealth Building Unit.

Labour Party 2019a. *It's Time for Real Change: The Labour Party Manifesto 2019*. London: The Labour Party.

Labour Party 2019b. *Labour's NHS Rescue Plan*. 12 November. https://web.archive.org/ web/20191213040928/https://labour.org.uk/page/labours-nhs-rescue-plan/ (accessed 8 April 2021).

Lodge, M. 2005. "Accountability and transparency in regulation: critiques, doctrines and instruments". In J. Jordana & D. Levi-Faur (eds), *The Politics of Regulation*, 124–44. Cheltenham: Elgar.

Maher, S., S. Gindin & L. Panitch 2019. "Class politics, socialist policies and capitalist constraints". In L. Panitch & G. Albo (eds), *Beyond Market Dystopia: New Ways of Living: Socialist Register 2020*, 1–29. London: Merlin Press. https://socialistregister.com/index.php/srv/ article/view/33126/25453 (accessed 8 April 2021).

Mansell, W. 2011. "Improving exam results, but to what end? The limitations of New Labour's control mechanism for schools: assessment-based accountability". *Journal of Educational Administration and History* 43(4): 291–308.

McDonnell, J. (ed.). 2018. *Economics for the Many*. London: Verso.

Millar, F. 2016. "Forty years after the Ruskin speech, education needs another moment". *The Guardian*, 13 December. https://www.theguardian.com/education/2016/dec/13/ruskin-speech-education-jim-callaghan-reforms (accessed 17 March 2021).

Mirowski, P. 2013. *Never Let a Serious Crisis Go to Waste: How Neoliberalism Survived the Financial Meltdown*. London: Verso.

Morris, N. 2015. "Labour leadership race: rivals turn on Jeremy Corbyn in row over Clause IV". *The Independent*, 10 August. https://www.independent.co.uk/news/uk/politics/labour-leadership-rivals-turn-on-jeremy-corbyn-in-row-over-clause-iv-10447690.html (accessed 17 March 2021).

National Audit Office 2017. Investigation into changes to Community Rehabilitation Company contracts, H.C. 676, Session 2017–2019, 19 December. https://www.nao.org.uk/wp-content/uploads/2017/12/Investigation-into-changes-to-Community-Rehabilitation-Company-contracts.pdf (accessed 17 March 2021).

Power, M. 1999. *The Audit Society*. Oxford: Oxford University Press.

Rayner, A. 2018. "Labour Party Conference 2018 speech". 24 September. https://schoolsweek.co.uk/labour-party-conference-angela-rayners-speech/ (accessed 17 March 2021).

Rayner, A. 2019. "Labour Party Conference 2019 speech", 22 September. https://labour.org.uk/press/angela-rayner-speaking-labour-party-conference/ (accessed 17 March 2021).

Silvester, N. 2019. "Crisis-hit private prisons to return to public ownership in Scotland". *The Daily Record*, 17 November. https://www.dailyrecord.co.uk/news/scottish-news/crisis-hit-private-scottish-prisons-20895824 (accessed 17 March 2021).

Travis, A. 2018. "Liverpool prison has 'worst conditions inspectors have seen'". *The Guardian*, 19 January. https://www.theguardian.com/society/2018/jan/19/liverpool-prison-worst-conditions-inspectors-report (accessed 17 March 2021).

7

# JEREMY CORBYN AND DILEMMAS
# OF LEADERSHIP

*Mark Bennister and Ben Worthy*

Traditionally, the Labour Party has been hesitant to acknowledge the power and authority of the leader (McKenzie 1963: 297). After an often painful modernization process, the party now accepts that "leaders do matter" for the party (James & Buller 2015). Leadership of Labour has always been a "complicated phenomenon" (Morgan 1987: 4). Attempts to evaluate party leadership have tended rather predictably to focus on the leadership's ability to win elections. Across the 28 general elections held since 1918, Labour have won 11, and only eight with majorities. Of Labour's 14 leaders, just three have won elections outright: Attlee, Wilson and Blair (Gamble 2017). Only rarely – in 1945, 1966 and 1997 – has Labour built a large winning coalition. Gamble characterized Labour as a party with several cycles of victory, defeat and rebuilding, as between 1931 and 1951, 1951 and 1979, 1979 and 2010, made up of an arc including defeat and major victory, then loss and a process of rebuilding (Gamble 2017). The problem, famously labelled the "progressive dilemma", is one of uniting the anti-Conservative coalition while still remaining wedded to Labour values (Marquand 1999; Gamble 2017). Added to this has been the inability of Labour to renew itself in power; as Harold Wilson put it: "If you rattle along at great speed, everybody is too exhilarated or too seasick to cause any trouble. But if you stop, everybody gets out and argues about where to go next" (quoted in Smith 1964: 193).

Labour, as McKenzie pointed out, only gradually came to recognize that the original chairman of the party was indeed a potential prime minister, sowing the seeds for the "reluctant leadership" narrative as a key part of the Labour discourse (Gaffney 2017). For a centre-left collectivist party, Labour holds a paradoxical attitude to its leaders (Diamond 2016: 21). Labour "venerated the collective idea" and was uncomfortable with personalized leadership, and yet it has at times perpetuated an individualized "cult of personality", supported by the "evocation of former heroes", so that the collective story of Labour becomes one of the "triumphs and defeats of individuals", interwoven with an occasional theme of betrayal (Morgan 1987: 1; James 2015). Morgan argued that Labour had a tendency to look to a past "rich in symbolism" (1987: 1–2). In such a party "assertive leaders have invariably been at odds with their party and at worst are portrayed as betraying socialism" (Gaffney 2017: 23).

So how should we judge and evaluate Labour leaders? Leonard Stark set three aims for party leaders in opposition: to "maintain *party unity*, to make the party *electable*, and [to] project an image of *competence*" (Diamond 2016: 18). A "continuing problem" has been to find a "leader with the capacity to combine both the realism of the pragmatists and charisma of the prophets" that can achieve these three aims (Morgan 1987: 11). Labour leaders have traditionally been caught between conscience and cunning, or idealism and pragmatism (Buller & James 2015). Labour leaders of "conscience" push an ethical or moral approach, while those with "cunning" focus on electioneering, strategy and appeal. Any leader must square the "constant tug and pull between those who claim to be 'pragmatic' and those who 'stick to principle'" (Pike & Hindmoor 2020: 154).

The most successful Labour leaders have been the "pragmatic operators" such as Attlee, Wilson and Blair, who managed not only to win elections, but also to coexist "with prophets and apostles of the old faith" within the party (Morgan 1987: 11). The varied mixture of autodidacts, technocrats and "machine politicians" who led at other times have fared less well (Morgan 1987). Attlee is widely regarded as Labour's most successful leader, combining moral conscience and political cunning, although he exemplifies the paradoxes in perhaps being the least "leader-like", as a "self-effacing egoist" (Morgan 1987: 4).

## Jeremy Corbyn, 2015–20

Any analysis of a leader faces the problems of subjective views, the exact nature of their responsibility and the problem of determining whether the context was difficult or favourable (James & Buller 2015; Diamond 2016). Corbyn was a perceived outsider who was an "agitator and protester" and an "anti-careerist" who had been "monumentally unsuccessful in constructing a career path" (Seymour 2017). His victory in the leadership election of 2015 was "unexpected", as he possessed "few conventional attributes" of a leader, having never held office and seemingly being inexperienced in everything from dealing with the media to running an organization (Diamond 2016: 15–16). It was also an unexpected victory for the Left, which had habitually lost out in factional battles (Hannah 2018).

Corbyn's five-year leadership was marked by a constant churn of controversy and contradiction, embodying both unexpected electoral gains and widely predicted electoral failure. Corbyn's time in office between 2015 and 2020 was tumultuous, even by Labour Party standards. He fought two general elections and a nationwide referendum, as well as two leadership elections. His tenure was marked by deep division and splits, with factional fighting and controversy over policies and personalities generating a toxic atmosphere within the party and a slump in trust and electability outside. One way to understand the many contradictions of Corbyn's leadership, is that he was an effective campaigner, but a poor party manager. Throughout his time as leader his reluctance to respond with any decisiveness or urgency to party issues, especially around antisemitism, undermined his personal leadership.

In terms of electoral success, he defied all expectations in the 2017 general election to deprive Theresa May of a majority, only to then lead the party two years later to its greatest defeat (in terms of seats) since 1935. Corbyn's leadership created a significant schism within the party. On the one hand, he was beloved by his grassroots supporters, and during his early time as leader he reversed a decade-long decline in party membership, to establish the Labour Party as one of the largest supported parties in Western Europe. On the other hand, his leadership set him deeply at odds with his own parliamentary party: over 80 per cent of his MPs expressed no confidence in his leadership in June 2016 and although he avoided a formal split, several MPs and prominent supporters left the party. Supporters argued that Corbyn was uprooting and challenging convention and past practice, while critics claim Corbyn proved either unable or unwilling to appeal beyond the narrow constituency that propelled him to the leadership and sustained him there (Bennister, Keith & Worthy 2017).

Corbyn was lauded by his many supporters as a "conscience" leader, following a lineage of rebels who had led the party, such as Arthur Henderson, George Lansbury and Michael Foot (Morgan 1987; James & Buller 2015). As a backbench MP Corbyn had been a serial rebel; under New Labour he was the MP with the second largest number of rebellions against his party whip (with his shadow chancellor the most rebellious). Corbyn was seen as moral and principled, with the lowest MPs' expenses claim of £8.59 for a print cartridge (Seymour 2017). His rhetorical purism and stance on touchstone foreign policy issues such as the Middle East and Northern Ireland set him outside of the mainstream views of his colleagues and his party (*ibid.*). It also meant he was swiftly presented as a national threat for his past association with radical figures with links to terrorism. Being an outsider allows a leader to offer radical change, while "flouting or ignoring convention" and challenging the "inner club" (King 2002: 441). For outsiders, perceptions matter, as "ethical" leaders are subjected to praise for their virtues, but also criticism for their ineffectiveness (Iszatt-White *et al.* 2019).

As an outsider, Corbyn pitched himself as a collective leader, promising he would not be "an all seeing, all-knowing leader who decides things" (Corbyn 2015 in Watts & Bale 2019). Critics saw this as a renunciation of former party leaders and "characterised him as a *protest politician* [...] warning of the dangers of his leadership turning the Labour Party into a *party of permanent protest*"

(Iszatt-White *et al.* 2019: 542; emphasis added). After the 2019 election Tony Blair pointedly emphasized this, describing Labour under Corbyn as a "glorified protest group with cult trimmings" (ITV 2019).

Yet Corbyn's leadership was also a product of a particular time and place, and the uncertain position of the Labour Party in 2015 (Gaffney 2017: 69). He succeeded the "flawed leadership" of Ed Miliband and inherited an "electoral project in decline" (Seymour 2017). With a falling vote share and hollowing out electoral heartlands, Corbyn's entire leadership masked "the longer term, chronic symptoms of a restructuring of the Labour vote" (Sturridge 2020: 19). After June 2016, Brexit also exacerbated many of the fault lines in the party and created new ones. The referendum set the majority of the PLP against Corbyn, with the grassroots (with the membership surge concentrated in the South East), generally pro-European, supporting Corbyn and Remain, encapsulated in the "love Corbyn, hate Brexit" slogan. Corbyn failed to gain any traction in Remain-supporting Scotland and was haemorrhaging its traditional vote in Brexit-supporting regions. The referendum and subsequent general elections left the UK "polarised in terms of public opinion, destabilized in terms of its territorial politics" (Jennings & Stoker 2018: 1).

Despite this, Corbyn assembled an electoral coalition that was nearly able to gain power and confounded expectations in 2017. The close result was, according to Mellon *et al.*, driven by "a general rise in support for Labour resulting from Corbyn's appeal" (2018: 719). Just as Corbyn's leadership – relative to May's – was partly responsible for his near-victory in 2017, so it appeared to have been responsible for the calamitous defeat of 2019. Corbyn went into the 2019 election with the lowest poll rating of any opposition party leader since 1977 and far greater suspicion of the party's Brexit position than in 2017. The two years between 2017 and 2019 had further reshaped traditional Labour voter attitudes, just as the Scottish independence referendum had reshaped traditional Labour voters in Scotland (Fieldhouse & Prosser 2016). The blame for this electoral disaster was presented as obvious. Opinion polling in the aftermath of the December 2019 general election identified "leadership" as the defining factor for the loss (YouGov 2019). Lord Ashcroft's poll concurred, finding that "not wanting Jeremy Corbyn to be Prime Minister" was the single biggest motivation for Labour defectors (Ashcroft 2020).

Corbyn was, however, operating in his own hostile leadership environment and any assessment of his leadership must acknowledge that his five years at the helm were "characterised by relentless criticism [...] about his left-wing stance and associated policies, and his apparent lack of competence and credibility as Party leader" (Dorey 2017: 309). Academic and media views have been "overwhelmingly critical" with an "underlying hostility to the Corbyn project and its supporters" (see Crines, Jeffery & Heppell 2018; Allen & Moon 2020: 80). One academic analysis concluded that the attacks were "well beyond the normal limits of fair debate" (Cammaerts *et al.* 2016: 2). This discussion was "reflective of a dismissive underlying attitude towards [...] his candidacy and subsequent leadership" from commentators, broadcasters and academics alike, across the political spectrum (Allen 2019: 1; Allen & Moon 2020: 80).

Corbyn was casually labelled as a "far left" or "hard left", an "extremist" and "terrorist sympathizer". The party under his leadership was accused, on slender evidence, as being taken over by "Stalinists and Trotskyites" (Maiguashca & Dean 2019). Personally, Corbyn faced continual attacks on his credibility, intelligence, patriotism, style of campaigning and ability to lead the party in a way that, for example, Boris Johnson did not (Allen 2019).

## Corbyn's leadership capital

Opposition leadership has a particularly institutionalized role in British politics. For Heppell, "effective Opposition leadership involves a complex interaction between the need to strategically reposition the party to broaden appeal by demonstrating that the party is adaptable and ensuring that the leader is visible, charismatic, likeable and competent" (2012: 249). With scope to make an impact limited by political context, effective opposition party leadership depends very much on perception and the contemporary role of leaders as the embodiment of the party itself. It is this authority, or lack of it, that could enable or prevent a leader from creating the unity, electability and image of competence needed (Diamond 2016: 18). The concept of leadership capital offers a tool to understand the extent to which leaders are able to establish and shape positive perceptions of themselves and the party they lead. It represents the "aggregate of authority" that grants or limits a leader's "room for manoeuvre" or a "warrant to lead" in a particular context (Bennister, Keith & Worthy 2017: 3). As the "credit granted to leaders", it allows us to trace how authority is "accumulated, diminished and depleted" over time (*ibid.*: 4). Decline and diminishing returns are the normal trajectory for leaders, as their capital is naturally depleted by defeats, mistakes and scandals. They may be constrained by context, but they can learn in the role. Indeed, some politicians can rebuild their capital through electoral (or factional) victories and policy successes (*ibid.*: 3).

In Corbyn's case, as opposition leader and not in elected office, we consider the ebb and flow of his leadership capital based on the three core elements of leadership capital: skills, relations and reputation. Contradictions run through each of these areas for Corbyn. His political skills were lauded as authentic, but inadequate for party leadership. His relations built strong party support and loyalty for many, but alienated and divided others. His reputation for policy purity was tarnished by his vacillation on Brexit and inability to rid the party of antisemitic elements.

The trajectory of Corbyn's authority is unusual. After rising to a rather unexpected peak, it fell dramatically. Low expectations at the outset were then overturned by the 2017 general election when he came close to winning power. Between 2017 and 2019, despite having a far stronger influence over May's minority government, his "bounce" or uptick of authority failed to hold, heading downwards towards the 2019 election.

## Political skill: an effective campaigner, but a poor manager

Political skills that build or shrink capital include the projection of a vision and communicative and performance abilities. You may have a political vision, but you need to articulate it to accumulate valuable capital. For Corbyn, his leadership was based on a clear vision of a "new politics", an authenticity and an appeal based on the "politics of conscience" (Diamond 2016; Watts & Bale 2019). He followed the principles he had pursued throughout his life, as an outsider and backbencher. His vision was that of the "prophet leader", harking back to the ethical, moral socialism of Foot or Lansbury, and the Labour Party as, in Wilson's words, a "moral crusade" (Morgan 1987). In 2017 the policies that emerged from this new approach, on student fees or nationalization, also proved popular. Byrne argues that "Labour's unanticipated surge in the 2017 British election [...] was the result of its construction of a vivid and compelling vision of a possible alternative future" (2019: 250).

Corbyn's vision helped redefine Labour's policy platform and where the party stood, with a rejection of the supposed centrism of the past and an embrace of anti-austerity. Tony Benn was a major influence in shaping Corbyn's approach to politics, although any ideological link is overstated (Bennister, Keith & Worthy 2017). His rejection of free-market approaches appeared popular with voters in 2017, when he argued that the politics of 2016 had caught up with the economics of 2008. As leader he challenged long-established policies over immigration, Europe and foreign policy. Yet closer analysis of the 123-page 2017 manifesto by Manwaring and Smith (2020: 44) found that "The media claims about Corbyn offering a 'hard left', 'socialist', or 'left-wing' agenda are simplistic, and generally underestimate the extent to which the programme consolidates a new approach set out by Ed Miliband at the 2015 general election". Similarly, Labour's 2019 manifesto was the first ever to open with a new green deal on climate change, which was tied to a deep programme of social and economic reform. Little noticed, Corbyn also bought a series of explicitly anti-racist and feminist policies centre stage (Maiguashca & Dean 2019). Bassett (2020) concluded that "Corbyn's appeals to voters also had a distinctly social democratic, rather than 'hard left', flavour" and "in practice, Corbynism resembled a democratized and regionalized version of postwar welfare capitalism, far more than state socialism".

Corbyn's vision and approach managed to both divide and unite the party he led. It helped create "an ideological disjuncture between Corbyn and his grassroots supporters on the one hand, and most of the parliamentary Labour Party on the other" (Dorey 2017: 310). Opponents continued to attack Corbyn as a "far-left extremist" or even a "Marxist", although "Corbyn's putative extremism comes into sharp relief only when compared to [...] New Labour [and] the hegemonic neoliberal consensus of the day" (Maiguashca & Dean 2019: 58). This disjuncture continually undermined Corbyn's leadership (Watt & Bale 2019). His past statements and poor answers, over issues from antisemitism to Brexit and the royal family, were used to prove his unsuitability for high office and demonstrate his "extreme" politics (Maiguashca & Dean 2019).

Yet it was exactly this vision that also helped the Labour Party become the largest left-wing party in Western Europe, in stark contrast to the decline elsewhere, a success that was in part built around Corbyn's anti-establishment credentials (Watt & Bale 2019). His leadership attracted returning activist party members, left-behind voters and idealists (Whiteley *et al.* 2019; Watts & Bale 2019). Whiteley *et al.* (2019) found that it was Corbyn's radical appeal (anti-elitist, anti-corporate) that helped draw in disaffected and left-wing re-joiners.

Corbyn's communication was, paradoxically, poor but effective. His communicative skills compared unfavourably with previous Labour leaders, such as Blair or even Kinnock. He was regarded as a poor performer in the Commons, but an effective campaigner and stump speaker: his comfort zone was the mass rally, the impromptu protest, the supportive crowd requiring reaffirmation. In the softer broadcast settings, he was a poor and sometimes irritable interviewee, exemplified during the 2019 election campaign by a disastrous BBC interview with Andrew Neil on 26 November.

But perhaps this is the point; Corbyn's success in winning the leadership election was in part rooted in the different kind of communication that he was able to utilize (Crines 2015). His old fashioned "mass rallies" existed in parallel to sophisticated use of social media, where his outsider status (albeit manufactured) helped the guerrilla-style social media campaigns (see Margetts 2017). In 2017, "Corbyn's public appearances, both at rallies and on television, won him and Labour new sources of support, as many voters warmed to him" (Dorey 2017: 332). Most importantly, his different approach was portrayed as a sign of his authenticity, integrity and difference, most evident during his visit in the aftermath of the Grenfell Tower fire in 2017.

On the one hand, Corbyn's consistent anti-austerity message, and folksy, authentic demeanour, had potential to be enticing, especially at the mass rallies where he was most comfortable. On the other hand, critics highlighted Corbyn's lack of basic communication skills in a variety of other settings, which was exposed in his vacillation over Brexit and inability to address antisemitism. Such a focus on the messenger opened up a chasm between the PLP, the electorate in general and his sizeable supporter base. He was unable (or lacked the necessary skills) to bridge this chasm.

## Relations: loyal supporters and divided MPs

Few leaders of the Labour Party have possessed Corbyn's party leadership mandate. He began the 2015 campaign as the outsider and "token" left-wing candidate but, helped by the changes to membership voting rules and procedures of his predecessor, won a resounding victory. He was elected leader with 59 per cent of the vote and re-elected a year later in 2016, with 61.8 per cent, a slightly increased share. His party leadership wins gave him a mandate that he used continuously to justify his actions, while his position was protected by support from grassroots members. Yet his leadership clearly divided the party from the outset:

> When Corbyn rose to deliver his acceptance speech at the QEII Centre in Westminster on 12 September 2015, he was greeted with roars and whoops by those who had elected him. Two days later, when he entered Commons Committee Room 14 to address the parliamentary Labour Party (PLP) for the first time, he was met with silence.
>
> (Eaton 2018)

After Owen Smith's failed leadership challenge in 2016, Corbyn faced no major leadership challenge, and party procedures left him secure as leader, a security then subsequently reinforced by his near-victory in 2017. Yet his security in post did not lead to party unity, and his legitimacy and fitness to lead were constantly challenged. The habits of factionalism and internal fighting seemed deep-rooted, and he appeared reliant (as did Blair and leaders before him) on a small faction of advisers around him. He chose to appoint stalwarts of the Labour left in the PLP to key posts, such as John McDonnell and Diane Abbott, who both served throughout his tenure. His advisory team proved equally divisive, with former *Guardian* journalist Seumas Milne as his key media adviser, the formidable Karie Murphy – a close confidant of Len McCluskey – as his chief of staff, former communist and Unite chief of staff Andrew Murray as his policy advisor, and Andrew Fisher as head of policy and manifesto writer. The appointment of such outsiders, with established direct links to left-wing trade unions (particularly Unite), was added to the powerful new extra-party organization Momentum, led by Jon

Lansman, which entrenched Corbyn's supporter base and created a very different leadership network from the past. When the Labour General Secretary Ian McNicol was eventually ousted in early 2018, it seems the Left had truly taken hold of the party. There was talk of implementing a series of changes to Labour Party organization, including greater democratization and grassroots influence, symbolized by the introduction of mandatory reselection of MPs.

Despite his mandate and apparent party control, Corbyn faced continual criticism and factional fighting. The exact nature of the internal opposition was more fluid and a more "complex pattern emerges in terms of opinion and opposition to Corbyn within the PLP" than simple left–right narratives (Crines, Jeffery & Heppell 2018: 376). Throughout his leadership there were rumours of defections, and in 2019 eventually several MPs (most prominently Chuka Umunna) left the party, some to the short-lived, new centrist, Change UK party, which folded into the Liberal Democrats. Ex-leaders publicly criticized him, with Tony Blair seemingly publicly doubting the wisdom of voting Labour. As Corbyn stepped down, the extent of the intra-party division was laid bare in a leaked report that detailed the deep and bitter conflict between Labour Party headquarters and the leadership itself, with claims of racism, factionalism and withholding of funds for candidates.

By 2020, many of the symbolic organizational changes Corbyn's supporters had championed, from greater democracy to mandatory reselection of candidates, did not become sufficiently entrenched to ensure a legacy of Corbynism. Battles over the NEC and the issues of reselection, which led to a series of trigger ballots in 2019, fizzled out. After five years of seemingly endless internal warfare, Corbyn "left the Labour Party in a similar [organizational] state to how he found it" (Bassett 2020).

## Reputation: policy purity, but vacillation

Corbyn could not establish a coherent and consistent reputation as a party leader in charge of his party's own policy platform (on Brexit) and party discipline (antisemitism). The policy platform of Corbynism created a series of controversies that split the party and caused continual conflict. Although his anti-austerity policies marked consistency, his Brexit policy (partly a result of his own equivocation on Europe and his party's Remain stance) was uncertain and fluid. Corbyn's triangulation on Brexit had him caught between pro-Leave Labour MPs, who feared challenging the "will of the majority", against the pro-Remain grassroots. Corbyn, by inclination opposed to the EEC and EU since the 1980s, was pushed towards a broader, less clear compromise that, eventually, resulted in a second referendum promise. Rather than policy purity, here Corbyn and his colleagues' shifts and opaqueness resembled the triangulations of Blair or the "muddy, messy middle" compromises of Harold Wilson. Into the vacuum came others such Hillary Benn, Yvette Cooper and Tory rebels such as Dominic Grieve, who became the parliamentary opposition, spearheading government defeats. However, Corbyn could still claim that, with him as leader, the Labour Party, in the Commons and the Lords, forced the government into a series of damaging U-turns and defeats that helped end May's premiership. The consequent slow march to opposing a "Tory" Brexit, and towards a possible second referendum, worked as compromise in 2017, but was undone by 2019.

On foreign policy more generally there was continual trouble. Corbyn's pacifist tendencies led him to express lukewarm support for the police in dealing with terrorism and to scepticism over the role of Russia in the Salisbury poisoning. His past support for groups and figures in Palestine and Northern Ireland generated controversy and criticism, suggesting to his internal and external critics that he was an unreconstructed extremist, unpatriotic and unfit to hold the highest office. This perception was exacerbated by his poor performance in set-piece events, and opponents (inside and outside the party) often upstaged him, as Hillary Benn did on Syria in 2015.

One general measure of leadership success or failure is whether a leader outpolls their own party, acting as a net vote winner or loser. However, the direction or even existence of causality between leader and party is unclear (Bartle & Crewe 2002). Party and leader evaluations interact, but for "party leaders approval ratings fluctuate much more dramatically than parties" (Mughan 2015: 30. The more the electorate saw of Corbyn the less they trusted him, and this appeared to damage the party in the polls.

Corbyn's leadership ratings reflected the bell curve of authority, and the contradictions and dilemmas of his leadership. His ratings began low in 2015 and fell deeper still until 2017, when they unexpectedly revived. In June 2017, amid widespread predictions of disaster, Corbyn transformed public opinion of his leadership. However, his poll improvement failed to hold. By the middle of 2019 "voters like him less, think he is less competent and has less integrity than they did in late 2016" (Sturridge 2020). He had been unable to build a credible reputation leveraging the unexpected 2017 bounce. In fact, the expectation generated proved counterproductive.

Corbyn was praised for authenticity and consistency, but also criticized for being outdated. He was "characterised as someone who would enact his deeply held principles however unpopular or uncomfortable this may be, connecting to the idiom of 'practicing what you preach'" (Iszatt-White *et al.* 2019: 541). Polls throughout his leadership showed that the public saw him as "honest" and even as late as 2019 they broadly viewed him as authentic (YouGov 2019a). Corbyn's image as a "normal" person, with his allotment and jam-making, reinforced this claim. It was in the area of trust in his competence, rather than "morals", where

Corbyn's leadership was weak. By 2019 he was viewed particularly poorly on decisiveness, strength and competency: 69 per cent of Britons believed him to be indecisive, 64 per cent thought him weak and 63 per cent saw him as incompetent (YouGov 2019a).

Successful leadership is about timing, context and relative appraisals. For a leader in opposition, Heppell (2012: 246) speculates that "the ideal time to be Leader [...] is against a long serving administration engulfed with economic difficulties and against an uncharismatic Prime Minister". Corbyn faced three prime ministers: David Cameron, Theresa May and Boris Johnson, facing the latter two in general election campaigns. Corbyn was fortunate from 2016 to 2019 in facing Theresa May, whose communication skills, vision and increasingly desperate political situation after 2017 gave Corbyn a series of opportunities (Bennister & Worthy 2020). Corbyn was less fortunate in facing Boris Johnson after 2019, a more effective communicator, who had shifted the terms of the Brexit debate. By 2019, fully 70 per cent of the British public had a negative opinion of Corbyn and only 20 per cent thought he would make a better prime minister than Boris Johnson (YouGov 2019a). By the time of the election his personal reputation had slumped back to pre-2017 levels.

## Conclusion

Corbyn failed the most basic test of opposition party leadership, that of winning power (James 2015). In this sense, he joined a long list of Labour leaders who failed to gain the highest office. Like apparent outsiders, Foot in the 1980s or Lansbury in the 1930s, he led the party to a large defeat. He was unable (or unwilling) to build and hold together the diverse electoral coalition of Blair or Attlee, although Corbyn's two predecessors similarly failed to resolve this progressive dilemma.

Navigating the complex dilemmas of political leadership will challenge any party leader, but Jeremy Corbyn presented a perhaps unique set of contradictions and paradoxes. His authority was both strong (in terms of his supporters) and weak (with the wider public), and created an unusual arc of failure, near-success and then catastrophic defeat. His staunch left-wing vision was undermined on Brexit, where he offered uncertainty and vacillation. His authenticity earned him trust, but many questioned his competence. He mobilized the grassroots of the party, boosting membership levels to an unprecedented high, but divided the party in parliament.

Dividing our analysis into the core components of leadership capital we see that Corbyn's skills, relations and reputation were all flawed. On skills, Corbyn was evidently not up to the formal, managerial aspects of the job: he did not possess or learn in office the necessary political skills to create a coherent vision for governing in key policy areas and communicate it successfully. On relations, he failed to reach beyond a narrow base to build a broader political coalition likely to win an election, relying on a narrow and divisive set of confidants whom he was unable or unwilling to control. On reputation, he failed to deliver the perception of competent leadership that demonstrated that he could "get things done". Harry S. Truman famously kept a wooden plaque on his desk in the White House that read: "The buck stops here." Truman is describing the very core of what political leaders do: they make decisions and determine policy (Laing 2020). Corbyn, on Brexit or on rooting out anti-semitism within the party, never gave the impression that he was the one in charge, making decisions and determining policy direction. In fact Corbyn's leadership capital rose from nowhere, peaked in 2017, could not be sustained, then swiftly ebbed away under intense scrutiny.

However, agency failings can only take us so far; of course he was the product of a particular political context that propelled him into the leadership position. Once there, he had to operate within a context dominated by the post-referendum wreckage of British politics after 2016. Yet some leaders find the "skill in context". Corbyn failed to find the right policy approach to "solve" the issue of Brexit for the party and the wider electorate. On the central issue facing his party Corbyn opted for a Harold Wilson-style compromise that suited no one. However, it is not apparent that any other leader could have found the right balance, or that one even existed. Brexit divided the main political parties, and the Conservatives lost two prime ministers to Brexit while Corbyn was opposition leader.

For all his individual faults and obvious failures as a leader, Corbyn did reshape the party and its ideology, mobilizing it in a way few predicted. Future leaders will hold to his anti-austerity and public sector message (particularly relevant in a post-Covid-19 UK). His campaigning techniques and grassroots activists will remain part of his legacy. If future party leaders can overcome the toxic intra-party feuding left behind, they may seek to emulate some elements of his "anti-establishment" approach and policy positions, and not see his leadership tenure as a total aberration for the party.

## References

Allen, P. 2019. "Political science, punditry, and the Corbyn problem". *British Politics* 15: 1–19.
Allen, P. & D. Moon 2020. "Predictions, pollification, and pol profs: the 'Corbyn problem' beyond Corbyn". *Political Quarterly* 91(1): 80–88.
Ashcroft, M. 2020. "Diagnosis of defeat: Labour's turn to the smell the coffee". Lord Ashcroft Polls, February. https://lordashcroftpolls.com/wp-content/uploads/2020/02/DIAGNOSIS-OF-DEFEAT-LORD-ASHCROFT-POLLS-1.pdf (accessed 19 March 2021).

Bartle, J. & I. Crewe 2002. "The impact of party leaders in Britain: strong assumptions, weak evidence". In A. King (ed.), *Leaders' Personalities and the Outcomes of Democratic Elections*, 70–95. Oxford: Oxford University Press.

Bassett, L. 2020. "Constitutionally, Corbyn will leave the Labour Party in a similar state to how he found it". LSE blog, 20 February. https://blogs.lse.ac.uk/politicsandpolicy/corbyn-reforms/ (accessed 17 March 2021).

Bennister, M., D. Keith & B. Worthy 2017. "Jeremy Corbyn and the limits of authentic rhetoric". In J. Atkins & J. Gaffney (eds), *Voices of the UK Left: Rhetoric, Ideology and the Performance of Politics*, 101–21. Basingstoke: Palgrave Macmillan.

Bennister, M., P. 't Hart & B. Worthy (eds) 2017. *The Leadership Capital Index: New Perspectives on Political Leadership*. Oxford: Oxford University Press.

Bennister, M. & B. Worthy 2020. "'Dominance, defence and diminishing returns'? Theresa May's leadership capital July 2016 to July 2018". *British Politics.* https://doi.org/10.1057/s41293-020-00133-9.

Byrne, L. 2019. "How Jeremy Corbyn brought labour back to the future: visions of the future and concrete utopia in Labour's 2017 electoral campaign". *British Politics* 14(3): 250–68.

Cammaerts, B. *et al.* 2016. "Journalistic representations of Jeremy Corbyn in the British press: from watchdog to attackdog". http://www.lse.ac.uk/media-and-communications/assets/documents/research/projects/corbyn/Cobyn-Report.pdf (accessed 17 March 2021).

Crines, A. 2015. "Jeremy Corbyn's rhetoric is effective because his style of engagement contrasts so markedly with the other candidates". Democratic Audit UK, 6 August. https://www.democraticaudit.com/2015/08/06/jeremy-corbyns-rhetoric-is-effective-because-his-style-of-engagement-contrasts-so-markedly-with-the-other-candidates/ (accessed 17 March 2021).

Crines, A., D. Jeffery & T. Heppell 2018. "The British Labour Party and leadership election mandate(s) of Jeremy Corbyn: patterns of opinion and opposition within the parliamentary Labour Party". *Journal of Elections, Public Opinion and Parties* 28(3): 361–79.

Diamond, P. 2016. "Assessing the performance of UK opposition leaders: Jeremy Corbyn's 'straight talking, honest politics'". *Politics and Governance* 4(2): 15–24.

Dorey, P. 2017. "Jeremy Corbyn confounds his critics: explaining the Labour Party's remarkable resurgence in the 2017 election". *British Politics* 12(3): 308–34.

Eaton, G. 2018. "The meaning of Corbynism". *New Statesman*, 5 March. https://www.newstatesman.com/politics/uk/2018/03/meaning-corbynism (accessed 22 March 2021).

Fieldhouse, E. & C. Prosser 2016. "When attitudes and behaviour collide: how the Scottish Independence Referendum cost Labour". SSRN, 27 April. http://dx.doi.org/10.2139/ssrn.2770996.

Gaffney, G. 2017. *Leadership and the Labour Party: Narrative and Performance.* Basingstoke: Palgrave Macmillan.

Gamble, A. 2017. "The progressive dilemma revisited". *Political Quarterly* 88(1): 136–43.

Hannah, S. 2018. *A Party with Socialists in it: A History of the Labour Left.* London: Pluto.

Heppell, T. (ed.) 2012. *Leaders of the Opposition: From Churchill to Cameron.* Basingstoke: Palgrave Macmillan.

Iszatt-White, M. *et al.* 2019. "The 'Corbyn phenomenon': media representations of authentic leadership and the discourse of ethics versus effectiveness". *Journal of Business Ethics* 159(2): 535–49.

ITV 2019. "Blair attacks Corbyn for turning Labour into 'glorified protest movement' and says it is 'marooned on fantasy island'". ITV News, 18 December. https://www.itv.com/news/2019-12-18/tony-blair-warns-labour-must-renew-itself-as-progressive-or-face-slow-demise (accessed 6 April 2021).

James, T. & J. Buller 2015. "Statecraft: a framework for assessing Labour Party leaders". In C. Clarke & T. James (eds), *British Labour Leaders*. London: Biteback.

Jennings, W. & G. Stoker 2018. "The divergent dynamics of cities and towns: geographical polarisation after Brexit". *Political Quarterly* 90(S2): 155–66.

King, A. 2002. *Leaders' Personalities and the Outcomes of Democratic Elections*. Oxford: Oxford University Press.

Laing, M. 2020. *Political Leadership: An Introduction*. London: Red Globe Press.

Maiguashca, B. & J. Dean 2019. "'Lovely people but utterly deluded': British political science's trouble with Corbynism". *British Politics* 15(1): 48–68.

Manwaring, R. & E. Smith 2020. "Corbyn, British labour and policy change". *British Politics* 15: 25–47. https://doi.org/10.1057/s41293-019-00112-9.

Margetts, H. 2017. "Why social media may have won the 2017 general election". *Political Quarterly* 88(3): 386–90.

Marquand, D. 1999. *The Progressive Dilemma: From Lloyd George to Tony Blair*. London: Weidenfeld & Nicholson.

McKenzie, R. 1963. *British Political Parties*. Second edition. Oxford: Heinemann.

Mellon, J. *et al.* 2018. "Brexit or Corbyn? Campaign and inter-election vote switching in the 2017 UK general election". *Parliamentary Affairs* 71(4): 719–37.

Morgan, K. 1987. *Labour People: Leaders and Lieutenants, Hardie to Kinnock*. Oxford: Oxford University Press.

Mughan, A. 2015. "Parties, conditionality and leader effects in parliamentary elections". *Party Politics* 21(1): 28–39.

Pike, K. & A. Hindmoor 2020. "Do as I did not as I say: Blair, New Labour and party traditions". *Political Quarterly* 91(1): 148–55.

Sampson, A. 1982. *The Changing Anatomy of Britain*. London: Random House.

Seymour, R. 2017. *Corbyn: The Strange Rebirth of Radical Politics*. Second edition. London: Verso.

Smith, L. 1964. *Harold Wilson, the Authentic Portrait*. London: Hodder & Stoughton.

Sturridge, P. 2020. "Beyond Brexit: Labour's structural problems". *Political Insight* 7(1): 16–19.

YouGov 2019. "Labour economic policies are popular, so why aren't Labour?" 12 November. https://yougov.co.uk/topics/politics/articles-reports/2019/11/12/labour-economic-policies-are-popular-so-why-arent- (accessed 17 March 2021).

YouGov 2019a. "Boris Johnson fans now outweigh his detractors". 8 November. https://yougov.co.uk/topics/politics/articles-reports/2019/11/08/boris-johnson-fans-now-outweigh-his-detractors (accessed 17 March 2021).

Watts, J. & T. Bale 2019. "Populism as an intra-party phenomenon: the British Labour Party under Jeremy Corbyn". *British Journal of Politics and International Relations* 21(1): 99–115.

Whiteley, P., M. Poletti, P. Webb & T. Bale 2019. "Oh Jeremy Corbyn! Why did Labour Party membership soar after the 2015 general election?" *Journal of Politics and International Relations* 21(1): 80–98.

8

# THE ABSOLUTE BOY VERSUS MAGIC GRANDPA: JEREMY CORBYN AND GENDER POLITICS

*Rosalynd Southern and Emily Harmer*

The relationship between politics and gender has been extensively studied in the UK context but, for obvious historical reasons, tends to focus primarily on how political institutions and processes work to exclude or marginalize women as well as on proposing mechanisms to correct these forms of discrimination. In this chapter, we take a broader view of the gendered nature of politics in order to discuss Jeremy Corbyn and his leadership via a gendered lens. Therefore, as well as assessing the extent to which Corbyn and his politics are compatible with increased gender equality, we will also consider Corbyn as a gendered figure. We will furthermore discuss how his supporters and detractors recognized and made use of his gendered performances to both champion and vilify his leadership.

Factors that impact on women's recruitment into politics include systematic factors (such as the legal, electoral and party systems and structures that set the broad context for women's representation), how parties are organized (their rules and ideological positions) and individual factors, such as the resources and motivations of aspiring candidates and the attitudes of party selectors (Norris & Lovenduski 1995). Women have also been found to suffer from direct discrimination from party selectors where negative judgements are made based on perceived characteristics of their group, or indirect discrimination that occurs when ideas of what constitutes a "good" representative count against women (Childs 2008). Since the 1980s, the Labour Party has led other mainstream political parties in recruiting and promoting women politicians. The introduction of all-women shortlists in the 1997 election resulted in a record number of women MPs being elected to parliament (Childs 2008). Since then, they have consistently returned more women candidates than other parties at all subsequent general elections. The Labour Party, however, has (at the time of writing) failed to elect a female leader, which is a matter of concern for many within the party.

Recent scholarship has emphasized the importance of performing masculinity for effective political leadership (Conroy 2015; Katz 2016; Harmer, Savigny & Ward 2017). Conroy (2015: 75) argues that the perception of manliness is important when voting for a politician. This tendency to emphasize the masculine credentials of political leaders has been critiqued and debated most often in relation to presidential political systems (see Conroy 2015; Campus 2013), but masculinity clearly underpins ideas about political leadership in the UK as well. Harmer, Savigny and Ward (2017) assess the extent to which press coverage of the 2015 leadership debates constructed politics as a masculine space where male political opponents were portrayed as weak and emasculated in contrast to those whom the press supported. Although media coverage is not the best way of measuring the importance of gendered performances for voters, research has shown that traditionally masculine traits (including being perceived as confident, macho, single-minded and strong) are assumed to be essential for political leadership. Traditionally feminine traits, such as being caring, passive, empathetic and apologetic may be interpreted more negatively (Campus 2013; Conroy 2015). Scholars have argued that political leaders need to distance themselves from femininity and display hegemonically masculine ideals such as strength, independence and determination (Parry-Giles & Parry-Giles 1996; Coe *et al.* 2007).

Here we will discuss these concepts in the context of Corbynism. First, we will discuss Corbyn's treatment of women, from his appointment of female cabinet members to his citing of female political influences. Second, we will outline what Corbynism means in reality from a gender perspective by assessing policy. Third, we will discuss how Corbyn himself has been subject to gendered media coverage, which often ridiculed his non-traditional brand of masculinity before contrasting this with the more traditional masculinity his supporters often exhibit.

## Corbyn and women

During the Labour leadership election in 2015, gender arose as a concern. Many high-profile politicians declared that it was "time the Labour Party elected a woman leader" (Smart 2015) because, apart from Margaret Beckett and Harriet Harman's stints as interim leaders, the party had never had a formally elected female leader, which is seemingly in tension with its progressive values. Similarly, when Corbyn began his tenure as leader, debates about gender arose again. His first shadow cabinet was hailed as the first potential cabinet in the UK's history to contain more women than men (Goddard 2015). Criticisms crept in, however, even when some questioned the appointment of John McDonnell as shadow chancellor, citing the fact that Angela Eagle, whom McDonnell had supported in the previous weeks for deputy leader, was more qualified as a former shadow Chief Secretary to the Treasury (Wintour, Mason & Syal 2015). In an interview with *The Observer*, however, McDonnell rejected accusations of being appointed via "jobs for the boys". He insisted that although Eagle had been seriously considered for the role, Corbyn had wanted to avoid a situation where the leader and chancellor had differences of opinion on economic policy which he felt (not unfairly) had been problematic during the Blair–Brown and the Miliband–Balls years (Rawnsley & Helm 2015).

Corbyn has never openly described himself as a feminist, in contrast to the previous leader, Ed Miliband, who famously got into hot water over wearing a "this is what a feminist looks like" t-shirt, which it later transpired had been made by women in an Indonesian sweatshop (*The Guardian* 2014). However, throughout his leadership, Corbyn consistently recognized the contribution of women in left politics and supported feminist causes. For example, in a blog on the LabourList website just after he became leader, he wrote of the importance of education as a collective good. He highlighted the work of Jennie Lee in establishing the Open University and called hers "one of the most underrated achievements of a Labour government" (LabourList 2015). While he does not explicitly state that this is underrated because Lee was female, there is a long-standing history of women's political achievements being overlooked. Highlighting it shows that he is mindful that women have often been marginalized in the movement. This was followed up in the 2019 manifesto where a new cultural strategy, the Charter for the Arts, was outlined and Corbyn wrote that "A Labour government elected in 2019 will proudly embrace Jennie Lee's legacy to renew the cause of arts for all" (Labour Party 2019). On the centenary of some women's suffrage, his office released a video of Corbyn recalling how he and close friend Tony Benn had smuggled a toolbox into the Palace of Westminster, in order to affix a plaque dedicated to Suffragist Emily Wilding Davison in a broom cupboard. This was the same broom cupboard where Davison had hidden herself during the 1911 census so that she was able to record her address as "The House of Commons", thus making a powerful political statement that women should be afforded the same political rights as men. In the video, he praises her "bravery" and speaks of how the plaque was condemned by some other representatives at the time for "defacing" parliament but has now become a key tourist attraction (ITV 2018). Corbyn also centred "Red" Ellen Wilkinson in his first speech as leader at the Durham Miners Gala. He read extracts from her 1939 book *The Town That Was Murdered* and spoke of her strong leadership role in the Jarrow Marches (BBC 2016).

Corbyn has also publicly recognized the work of contemporary female colleagues, even when they do not necessarily share his politics. In his victory speech he paid tribute to Harriett Harman, saying "her absolute commitment and passion for decency, equality and the rights of women in our society is something that we will honour her for, thank her for and we have legislation that is being brought about by her determination. Harriet, thank you so much for all you have done and the way in which you have led the party since the tragedy of the election result in May" (BBC 2015). In several conference speeches he also spoke highly of her work on all-women shortlists and the 2010 Equality Act, and urged action on her long-standing suggestion that the Labour Women's conference have policy-making powers (Corbyn 2016). More broadly, he has been a consistent supporter of the so-called WASPI (Women Against State Pension Inequality) women. These women have lost significant pension benefits by, they claim, not being given sufficient time to prepare for the raising of the retirement age. Corbyn described their losses as an "historic injustice" (Aldrick 2019) and praised their strength and perseverance in their campaign. A pledge to right this injustice was included in the 2019 manifesto. Despite these claims of support for women, some critics were not convinced, suggesting that Corbyn's leadership had resulted in the entrenching of a politics where class inequality is positioned as more important than other forms of oppression and accused him of lacking an understanding of issues affecting women (see Bergman 2017). Although Corbyn's vocal support for women's achievements is not in doubt, it is also essential to consider the extent to which Corbyn's leadership is concerned with the advancement of gender equality in real terms. In order to do this, we will now consider how this translates into actual policies.

## Corbyn's gendered policy priorities

Policies that appear in party manifestos are perhaps the clearest indicator of the priorities of values being advanced by a party under specific leaders. Corbyn led the Labour Party into two successive general elections, and despite both of these campaigns being called in somewhat unusual circumstances, it is reasonable to assume that the manifestos these campaigns produced can tell us something about the relationship between Corbyn and gender. In 2017, the Labour manifesto offered the most extensive range of gendered policy pledges of all the main parties. Key pledges focused heavily on social security, whereby they promised to address pension inequality, the so-called "Tampon Tax" and childcare provision; the latter by funding it directly rather than passing subsidies to parents. The manifesto also included a range of pledges to support women in the workplace, increase support to tackle employment and maternity discrimination, and increase paid paternity leave (Harmer & Southern 2018).

The 2019 manifesto was billed as the most radical since 1945 (Blakely 2019), and therefore we can perhaps assume that this is the most explicit expression of the direction of travel for Corbynism. When it comes to specific gender-based policies, there was a good deal carried over from the previous manifesto. The 2019 manifesto, however, proposed several structural changes. First, it contained a pledge to create a new Department for Women and Equalities with a full-time secretary of state, with the role of this department being to make sure all policies and laws would be equality-impact assessed. Second, there is a pledge to establish a modernized Women's Commission as an independent body working with the government. Third, the manifesto also promised to increase the representation of women in parliament and to implement Section 106 of the Equality Act to ensure political parties publish diversity data (Labour Party 2019).

The manifesto importantly also emphasized Labour's commitment to tackling gender-based violence, pledging to ratify the Istanbul Convention on Domestic Abuse. The party also promised to prioritize domestic abuse as a health issue, to ensure funding for refuges and to make misogyny and violence against women and girls specific hate crimes. Employment-related policies included pledging to take action to close the gender pay gap by 2030, by making the state responsible for enforcement of the Equal Pay Act for the first time, among other measures. The manifesto also promised to increase paid maternity leave from 9 to 12 months and to double paternity leave to 4 weeks, as well as to increase provision for flexible working more generally. Perhaps more radically, the manifesto also promised to enforce the need for larger employers to have a formal menopause policy in order to recognize the strains that it places on older women in the workplace, and furthermore pledged to enable positive action in recruitment under certain circumstances. The manifesto also pledged to extend 30 hours free childcare or preschool education to all two-, three- and four-year-olds within the next five years, and to increase provision for one-year-olds.

There were also specific promises to fully implement the law ensuring women in Northern Ireland have access to safe abortions, and to abolish the controversial "rape clause" in child benefit payments where women wishing to claim for more than two children must disclose that they have been victims of sexual violence to qualify. The party also agreed to work with the WASPI women.

This brief overview of the manifestos demonstrates that Corbyn's Labour Party had a lot to offer women voters. Although we have focused specifically on those policies that overtly refer to women, they would obviously also benefit from the broader policies such as the pledge to reform universal credit, given that research shows women have been more negatively impacted by recent austerity policies (Hall *et al.* 2017). So far, our analysis suggests that Corbyn's politics does recognize the importance of gender inequality concerning women in the political realm as well as in society more generally. In many ways, the Labour Party continued to lead other parties in this area under his leadership. In the remainder of the chapter, we will now turn to Corbyn's performance of masculinity and how Corbyn was understood as a gendered figure by his supporters and detractors.

## Corbyn and masculinities

Corbyn's persona does not involve a straightforwardly masculine leadership style. He was somewhat older than the previous few Labour leaders when elected, a keen cyclist who also enjoys working on his allotment and "collects" manhole covers (*The Guardian* 2017). He also did not insist on making use of his family or spouse in his campaign communications. His personality and performance of masculinity, then, did not conform to the stereotypically macho leadership observed in other leaders (see Campus 2013; Conroy 2015). This contributed to his negative treatment by sections of the British press, and online by his detractors, for example in the way that his sartorial choices and appearance were repeatedly criticized. The press often focuses on female politicians' clothes and appearance (Harmer & Wring 2013; O'Neill, Savigny & Cann 2016); therefore, using the same approach to describe Corbyn can be perceived as a means of emasculating him. Previous scholarship shows that the press can often play on appearances of politicians, and focusing on their dress and appearance can be a means to attack male politicians by feminizing them (Harmer, Savigny & Ward 2017). For Corbyn's predecessor Ed Miliband, the press paid far more attention to his image than that of other male leaders at the 2015 election, referring to his "lucky tie" and his being "dressed for a wedding" (*ibid.*: 972), demonstrating once again the role of media imagery in feminizing political opponents. This serves to reinforce politics as a space for traditionally masculine men and further undermines them by suggesting they do not "look" or "act" prime-ministerial (i.e. traditionally "male").

One example of how this operates is the way that Corbyn's choice of clothing and appearance were reported. Early on in his leadership, there was a fascination with his dress when not "on duty". A few weeks in, he was pictured coming out of his Islington North home in a grey and red tracksuit to go cycling with his wife. An article in the *Daily Mail* captioned the pictures in a similar style to their paparazzi images of film stars and models, describing the tracksuit and its fit in detail, right down to the material it was made from. As his wife also had a tracksuit on for their ride, their look was described as "his 'n' hers" (Charlton 2015). Another early example ridiculed his choice of shorts, well-worn trainers and a polo shirt to pick up his post in the morning. He was referred to as "showing some leg" (Chorley 2015) a phrase usually reserved for female figures in this publication (Mason 2014).

Importantly, Corbyn's style of dress was also linked more explicitly to his political beliefs and were used to bolster negative suggestions about him. There was uproar, again by the *Daily Mail* but also *The Sun*, over his choice of coat to attend a Remembrance Sunday event at the Cenotaph (O'Brien 2018). This inevitably led him to being compared to former leader Michael Foot, whose wearing of a "donkey jacket" to the Cenotaph was derided as scruffy, inappropriate and offensive to those who had died in conflict, in order to construct him as unfit for the office of prime minister. The *Mail Online* published several articles of Corbyn in his Marks & Spencer waterproof jacket, which he chose instead of the more traditional long wool coat that male leaders often wear. One article (*ibid*.) was mostly a list of tweets on the subject, referring to Corbyn as, for example, a "scruffy geography teacher". Beyond this, the coat was used to make insinuations about his broader political beliefs, suggesting he wore it to signal support for his "anti-War chums". Similarly, his often worn fisherman's cap has been described variously as a "Bolshevik cap" (Vine 2018) and a "commie hat" (Culbertson 2019), suggesting that the media use Corbyn's clothes to exaggerate certain aspects of his politics. The same cap was at the centre of a BBC bias row after it appeared that they had darkened the cap in a segment on *Newsnight*. Some supporters suggested this had been done to make it look like a Russian Cossack hat, and therefore exaggerate Corbyn's left-wing reputation (BBC 2018a). These incidents suggest that stereotypical reporting techniques that have been used to trivialize and "other" female politicians were to some degree applied to Corbyn (and other Labour leaders before him), which reinforced political leadership as a masculine enterprise and attempted to place Corbyn outside of it.

The feminization of Corbyn also appears to have been used by his detractors online. One of the most common images in anti-Corbyn memes and his opponents' attack advertisements was a slightly manipulated picture of him making an overly "hench" (an online slang term for "strong" or "hard") stance with a slightly camp look on his face. This served a dual purpose of underlining that he was a political hardliner but also trivializing him by attempting to make him a figure of fun in part because of his non-traditional masculinity. Gendered media representations of Corbyn were problematic from this perspective, but also because they reinforced gender stereotypes about who is, and who is not, fit for party leadership.

Although Corbyn himself did not display an overtly masculinized form of political leadership, some of his close political allies did tend to conform to a more robust and at times aggressive style. Figures such as John McDonnell and Len McCluskey, the general secretary of Unite, adopted a much more combative style. Some of Corbyn's most vocal supporters online have also been accused of taking an aggressive approach. Importantly, however, even though Corbyn did not attempt to convey a traditionally masculine performance, this became central to how his supporters and detractors discussed him in online spaces.

Corbyn's detractors frequently referred to him as the "magic grandpa" in social media posts, which implies that there was considerable surprise that this seemingly incompetent leader (from their point of view) had captured the imagination of many people on the campaign trail, particularly younger voters. This invocation of masculinity is far from positive, casting Corbyn as an old and incapable man living in a fantasy world rather than operating in the political reality that those who use this nickname inhabit. In contrast, supporters of Corbyn's leadership, particularly his younger proponents, quickly dubbed him "the absolute boy" (thought to have been coined by Novara Media's Aaron Bastani, one of Corbyn's most vocal supporters, in a YouTube video released just after Corbyn's election) (Chakelian 2017). This is a tongue-in-cheek way of juxtaposing his age and demeanour with the laddishness implied by this nickname. Throughout the 2017 election, Corbyn's supporters on social media repeatedly referred to him in this way. This assertion was playful, and yet it continued to reinforce the idea that ideal political leadership is associated with masculine behaviour (Campus 2013). While referring to Corbyn in a way that jokingly emphasizes his masculinity might not be particularly harmful in itself, it does reveal something interesting about the gendered culture that has been developed by his supporters in online spaces.

## Corbyn supporters online

Corbyn's most vocal online supporters tend to be younger and male – and have seemingly, in contrast to Corbyn's gentler brand of masculinity, adopted a more traditional or "laddish" form, which they explicitly link to their support of him. As discussed above, parlance such as the "absolute boy" underscores this culture in his supporters. Although there are several examples on Twitter of a female Corbyn acolyte (usually Emily Thornberry) being called the "absolute girl", this has never quite taken hold in the Corbyn-supporter vernacular in the same way "absolute boy" did. Corbyn's detractors come in for similarly laddish treatment, being dubbed "melts", "slugs" and "gammons". Although the origin of such terminology is unclear, "melt" evokes softness and is often aimed at proponents of a more soft-left tradition compared to the more hard-left stance of those who use it. "Slug", as well as being a straightforward insult, suggests sliminess, and as this has often been a term levelled at Tony Blair for his over-polished persona (Booth 2003), it may be that this is an alternative means of calling an opponent a Blairite. "Gammon" emerged as an insult in response to a meme created by children's author Ben Davis when he tweeted a composite image of several members of a *Question Time Election Special* studio audience who were angry at Corbyn's reluctance to state that he would launch a nuclear attack. He dubbed them the "Great Wall of Gammon". The tweet received some backlash, and the author later distanced himself from the tweet, and the term in general, stating that he felt it only added to the coarsening of political discourse. However, he insisted that the term was meant to target a person's opinions, not their appearance or other physical characteristics (Davis 2017).

Matt Zarb-Cousins, a high-profile online Corbyn supporter and former Corbyn aide, echoed this when he explained the term as "a condition that once manifested itself as an affinity to UKIP but now more so to high blood pressure and a red meat complexion. Baldness is optional" (BBC 2018b). In the aftermath of the term becoming mainstream, there was much debate over whether there were classist (because of gammon being a traditionally cheap cut of meat) or even racial elements to the term, as it seemingly refers to skin colour (BBC 2018c). This has been rejected by proponents of its use, who point out that it is often used to describe upper-class figures such as Nigel Farage and Boris Johnson, and that it has also been levelled at Black men like James Cleverly (the Conservative Party chairman). What is clear, however, is that there is a gendered element to the term. It appears only ever to be applied to men. This is an interesting element of the laddish language of Corbyn supporters. Most of their insults seem designed to be aimed at men, or are at the very least gender-neutral in application. There have, however, been accusations from several female Labour MPs that the laddish culture that seemed to permeate through certain elements of Corbyn's support base made them "bro-cialists"; that is, a certain strain of left-wing men who centre men and reinforce politics as a male space. Jess Phillips even suggested that much of the abuse and incivility that had been directed at her online was down to her supposed disloyalty to the "bro-cialists that run Labour nowadays" (Hattersley 2020).

Corbyn's online supporters are seemingly keen to project more traditional masculinity onto him in other ways too. During the 2017 election, several internet memes featuring Corbyn circulated on social media (McLoughlin & Southern 2020). Many of them contrasted Corbyn's supposed "fun" and "naughty" persona against his opponent Theresa May's more reserved and staid one. Among the most popular were those that portrayed Corbyn as a laddish character. In the most shared meme of the whole election, a short video was uploaded of Corbyn briskly walking down some stairs. He looks to be in a buoyant mood and claps his hands saying "Hi, how you doing? We're back and we're ready for it all over again", before proffering an enthusiastic thumbs-up to the camera. This video was uploaded with the caption "when you walk back into the sesh after throwing up". The original tweet by @bagelpicbot got over 105,000 retweets and 236,000 likes. The assertion here is that Corbyn is in "the club" and has had to vomit after drinking too much, but is now ready to continue binge drinking. Binge drinking and "the sesh" (short for a session, with the slang meaning of a long period of drinking) are vital components of UK lad culture (Day, Gough & McFadden 2004). In reality, Corbyn is a clean-living vegetarian who barely drinks (Peck 2017) and so clearly some of the humour here derives from the incongruity between this and his true lifestyle. Nonetheless, it is interesting from a gender perspective that his supporters framed his image in these memes in this way.

Other memes also foisted a more masculine image onto him. The most viewed viral video of the whole 2017 campaign, produced by social news site Joe.co.uk, portrayed Corbyn as the Grime artist Stormzy, with Corbyn's head photoshopped onto Stormzy's body in his famous "Shut Up" video (Joe.co.uk 2017). Instead of the original lyrics, the video was a mash-up of the song with excerpts of Corbyn's speeches added. This riffs on the Grime4Corbyn movement, which sprang up at the 2017 election and was active again at the 2019 election (Clifton 2019). However, Grime music is undoubtedly a masculine art form, and the video that was chosen is confrontational, with him directly addressing the camera with a group of men behind him also squaring up to the audience. Again, Corbyn is cast in a more masculine role via memes from his online supporters than his real-life persona.

These memes were all mostly good-natured. However, it is interesting to consider that many of his supporters were seemingly eager to reshape him in a more masculine light, perhaps having absorbed the message that in politics performing a traditional form of masculinity is something "winners do", as previously discussed (Harmer, Savigny & Ward 2017). Undoubtedly, however, some of his online supporters often tipped over into sexism or outright misogyny, which we will now discuss in more detail.

## Online othering of women political figures and journalists

As mentioned above, one female Labour MP (Jess Phillips) in particular felt some of the online misogyny that had been sent to her on social media had come from a specific section of Corbyn's supporters. To examine this phenomenon, we conducted a thematic analysis of tweets including the #jc4pm hashtag that were sent over the second full week of the 2019 election campaign (between 14–20 November). We analysed 741 tweets containing the hashtag, following the principles of thematic analysis set out by Braun and Clarke (2006). First, sexist or misogynistic tweets were identified. These tweets were then divided into themes based on the most common types of sexism present in the data. The handles of those who sent them were removed in line with ethical guidelines.

All original spellings and grammatical errors have been preserved in full here, although occasional minor edits have been made for clarity of meaning.

It is important to note that most tweets on this hashtag were not in any way sexist; instead, they either made a case for Jeremy Corbyn as their idea of the best prime minister, or criticized his political opponents, notably Boris Johnson. Many tweets were supportive of Corbyn's female shadow cabinet, many pushing back against criticism levelled at Diane Abbott in particular. This is perhaps to be expected from proponents of Corbynism, which styles itself as progressive. There were, however, some tweets that were clearly misogynistic or sexist in more subtle ways that demonstrate that although Corbyn himself may not have been problematic in terms of his gender politics, some of his supporters could be. We observed three categories of sexist tweets, all of which were aimed at female opponents or female journalists who had been critical of Corbyn: (1) infantilization and demonization; (2) questioning the professionalism of women MPs; and (3) focus on appearance and sexualization of female critics of Corbyn.

### Infantilization and demonization

Some of those using the hashtag were openly critical of BBC Political Editor Laura Kuenssberg, because of her perceived bias against the Labour Party and Corbyn specifically. She was described as:

> lightweight & amateurish. But here her raw, childish rage, just below the surface, is an absolute delight! She's almost screaming "It's not fair!" & bursting into tears. Going well for the Tories, eh? #toriesout #jc4pm

Liberal Democrat leader Jo Swinson was similarly dismissed as:

> Dispicable. Wetting her knickers over the thought of vapourising thousands of people! *JC4PM* [in response to a tweet about her saying she would press the Trident nuclear button].

These tweets both contain infantilizing elements, suggesting that an adult woman would burst into tears at not getting their (perceived) own way, or would lose control of their bladder with excitement. The infantilization of women MPs is problematic because it suggests that they are too immature to be able to participate in public life, presumably in contrast to the emotionally mature and controlled characteristics of Corbyn and other male political actors. During the campaign, Swinson was repeatedly referred to as a "head girl", another infantilizing refrain (*Mail Online* 2019). The further implication here is that she is officious, bossy and self-important. This is, again, a common stereotype aimed at women who assert themselves (Ross 2002). Tweeters on this hashtag also made use of this stereotype when referring to Swinson:

> Jolyon Swinson's head girl act is grating as fuck. Fuck off. #JC4PM

> Anyone else think of the girls who grassed the poor kids up for smoking? #JC4PM

There were also tweets that demonized the women in question, some using sexist slurs. The below tweets all referred directly to Jo Swinson:

> She'd press the button [again referring to Trident] Murderous hag. @jeremycorbyn would be negotiating a peace deal, I know which I would prefer for this world. #JC4PM

And:

> Decietful, decieving woman. We see you crave for the ministers car NO MORALS #JC4PM

Swinson is heavily demonized in specifically gendered ways. The implication here is that her stance on the use of the Trident nuclear deterrent and ambition to be a minister is somehow illegitimate and transgressive for a female politician. In the second tweet, ambition is directly elided with having no morals, which is a long-standing sexist trope and one regularly levelled at female politicians (Ross 2002). The tweets found here play on and reinforce this underlying stereotype.

## Questioning professionalism

Another common technique for undermining female politicians is the questioning of their position as representatives. Previous work on gendered othering on Twitter has shown that female representatives were more likely than male representatives to have their roles and suitability as politicians questioned (Southern & Harmer 2019). This also featured in tweets using the #jc4pm hashtag. Along with the tweet above describing Laura Kuenssberg as "lightweight and amateurish", there were several others:

> You [Jo Swinson] can't wait to be a subordinate lapdog to Boris can you? You have nothing to offer and can't be trusted #JC4PM

The leader @joswinson voted for the accelerated raising of the #Pension age for women, along with 4 other female Fibdem MPs. Jo is a tory, her voting record speaks for itself. #JC4PM

Here Swinson is depicted as untrustworthy and untruthful ("Fibdem"), which presents her as an unsuitable choice for prime minister. In the second example Swinson is held particularly accountable for letting down women because she voted to increase the pension age. While criticizing a politician's political record is a legitimate activity for voters to engage in, suggesting it is worse to let woman voters down because Swinson is herself a woman is a common double standard applied to women in politics (Ross 2002).

Focus on appearance and sexualization

Finally, there were several tweets which focused on the female subject's appearance and which, in some instances, sexualized them. Again, this is not uncommon for female politicians and other women in the public eye, holding them to higher standards of appearance and using appearance-based insults in online discussions (Southern & Harmer 2019). One tweet suggests Jo Swinson is jealous of another female MP because she is more conventionally attractive, and adds to this by attaching an unflattering picture of Swinson:

Laura (Pidcock) is gorgeous. Swindleson looks like this... jealousy #JC4PM

Another example refers to Laura Kuenssberg as having a "crooked mouth". This has a clear double meaning, suggesting that she lies and denigrating her appearance:

Tory love dripping out of her crooked mouth again. Not a gaffe! #JC4PM [in reference to Jacob Rees-Mogg's offensive comments on Grenfell].

There were also two tweets which suggested that Laura Kuenssberg was having an affair with Boris Johnson in return for favourable coverage:

We know why she (Kuenssberg) gives BJ an "easy ride" hahah #JC4PM

And, in reply to the above tweet:

Yes she's had her (AHEM!) gagging orders.

This sexist suggestion not only sexualizes Kuenssberg but also undermines her professionalism, by suggesting she is not doing her job correctly by applying less scrutiny to Johnson. The objectification of women is a long-standing problem in the mediated representation of women in politics (Ross 2002) and, as this analysis demonstrates, these problematic forms of representation are readily taken up by Corbyn supporters (and doubtless others) in online spaces. Although most tweets that appeared on this hashtag were not sexist and many were supportive of women, there was evidence of the use of established sexist tropes that make the job of female politicians and other women connected to politics (such as political journalists) more challenging.

## Conclusion

Our analysis has shown that the gendered politics of Corbyn and his leadership was very complex and at times contradictory. While the party's gendered policy agenda remained the most progressive offering of the mainstream parties and Corbyn publicly advocated for the recognition of women, the culture adopted by some of his supporters was problematic in various ways. This could reflect the historical tensions of the Labour Party's roots in the workers' movement, which was built to guarantee fair treatment and good working conditions for the working class. However, some elements of this movement tended to conceive of workers in gendered terms whereby male breadwinners took precedence, leading to tensions with feminists who have traditionally been drawn to the Labour Party's ethos of equality. It may well also reflect the nature of his supporters who largely communicated online, which often encouraged a more "knock-about" and antagonistic style of communication which often tipped over into laddishness. It is furthermore interesting to note that Corbyn himself has borne the brunt of gendered media coverage and attacks on his masculinity by his opponents.

The future of Corbynism from a gender perspective is also a potentially interesting one. When Rebecca Long-Bailey announced she was running for Labour leader in the wake of Labour's crushing defeat in 2019, she was immediately dubbed the "Corbyn continuity" candidate and referred to as "John McDonnell's protégé" (*Financial Times* 2020). This led some to suggest that the narrative around her was sexist, suggesting she did not have her own mind or her own political views and that she was controlled by men. Long-Bailey herself addressed these narratives, insisting that she had her own vision for the future of the Labour Party and joking "I'm from Salford, no-one tells me what to do" (Crerar 2019). It is also notable that detractors of Corbyn seemingly coalesced around a male candidate for leadership (Keir Starmer, who went on to win), rather than a female candidate with similar experience, background and politics (Emily Thornberry). With Labour once again having chosen a man as leader, it seems as though debate will continue about why the "party of equality" cannot seem to elect a female leader.

# References

Aldrick, P. 2019. "Election 2019: Corbyn pension giveaway will benefit richest women". *The Times*, 28 November. https://www.thetimes.co.uk/article/election-2019-corbyn-s-pensions-giveaway-will-benefit-richest-women-k0f3cgfcl (accessed 17 March 2021).

BBC 2015. "Jeremy Corbyn: full victory speech". BBC News, 12 September. https://www.bbc.co.uk/news/av/uk-politics-34233529/labour-leadership-jeremy-corbyn-full-victory-speech (accessed 17 March 2021).

BBC 2016. "Jeremy Corbyn remembers Jarrow crusades 80 years on". BBC News, 1 October. https://www.bbc.co.uk/news/uk-england-tyne-37530067 (accessed 17 March 2021).

BBC 2018a. "BBC rejects complaints over Jeremy Corbyn's 'Russian hat'". BBC News, 19 March. https://www.bbc.co.uk/news/entertainment-arts-43463496 (accessed 17 March 2021).

BBC 2018b. "Left-wing internet phrases: gammon, melts and slugs". BBC News, 15 May. https://www.bbc.co.uk/news/av/uk-politics-44129228 (accessed 17 March 2021).

BBC 2018c. "Are slug, gammon and melt offensive terms?" *Daily Politics*, 15 May. https://www.bbc.co.uk/programmes/p0678328 (accessed 17 March 2021).

Bergman, S. 2017. "Calling Jeremy Corbyn 'the absolute boy' isn't funny, it's a reminder of how little he understands women". *The Independent*, 1 July. https://www.independent.co.uk/voices/jeremy-corbyn-absolute-boy-meme-sexism-womens-rights-labour-party-a7818431.html (accessed 17 March 2021).

Blakely, G. 2019. "Labour's economic programme isn't just radical, it's credible too". *New Statesman*, 22 November. https://www.newstatesman.com/politics/economy/2019/11/labour-s-economic-programme-isn-t-just-radical-it-s-credible-too (accessed 17 March 2021).

Booth, L. 2003. "Lauren Booth insists Blair wasn't always so slimy". *New Statesman*, 6 October. https://www.newstatesman.com/node/158470 (accessed 17 March 2021).

Braun, V. & V. Clarke 2006. "Using thematic analysis in psychology". *Qualitative Research in Psychology* 3(2): 77–101.

Campus, D. 2013. *Women Political Leaders and the Media*. London: Palgrave Macmillan.

Chakelian, A. 2017. "The absolute boy and the melts: how Corbynism created a new political language". *New Statesman*, 5 October. https://www.newstatesman.com/politics/uk/2017/10/absolute-boy-and-melts-how-corbynism-created-new-political-language (accessed 17 March 2021).

Charlton, C. 2015. "Pedal power couple: Corbyn and his wife spotted in 1980-style his 'n' hers grey tracksuits". *Daily Mail*, 4 October. https://www.dailymail.co.uk/news/article-3259393/Labour-leader-Jeremy-Corbyn-wife-spotted-cycling-n-1980s-style-grey-tracksuits.html (accessed 17 March 2021).

Childs, S. 2008. *Women and British Party Politics: Descriptive, Substantive and Symbolic Representation*. London: Routledge.

Chorley, M. 2015. "Corbyn shows some leg: leftwinger plots first days of leadership (and let's hope it includes a new wardrobe)". *Daily Mail*, 11 September. https://www.dailymail.co.uk/news/article-3230435/Corbyn-poses-threat-national-security-Cameron-attacks-socialist-economy-Tories-plan-paint-weak-terror.html (accessed 17 March 2021).

Clifton, K. 2019. "Stormzy urges fans to vote for Labour and Jeremy Corbyn in impassioned video". *Evening Standard*, 12 December. https://www.standard.co.uk/news/politics/general-election-stormzy-labour-jeremy-corbyn-polls-vote-a4312271.html (accessed 17 March 2021).

Coe, K. *et al.* 2007. "Masculinity as political strategy: George W. Bush, the 'war on terrorism', and an echoing press". *Journal of Women, Politics & Policy* 29(1): 31–55.

Conroy, M. 2015. *Masculinity, Media and the American Presidency*. London: Palgrave Macmillan.

Corbyn, J. 2016. "My speech at the Labour Women's Conference 2016". 28 September. https://web.archive.org/web/20201029224246/https://jeremycorbyn.org.uk/articles/jeremy-corbyn-my-speech-at-the-labours-womens-conference/index.html (accessed 8 April 2021).

Crerar, P. 2019. "Labour's Rebecca Long-Bailey says 'I'm from Salford – no-one messes with me'". *The Mirror*, 22 January. https://www.mirror.co.uk/news/politics/labours-rebecca-long-bailey-says-21330820 (accessed 17 March 2021).

Culbertson, A. 2019. "General election: a *Love Actually* spoof and some mean tweets. Leaders try to go viral". *Sky News*, 12 December. https://news.sky.com/story/general-election-johnson-and-corbyn-star-in-love-actually-and-mean-tweets-clips-to-sway-voters-11882737 (accessed 17 March 2021).

Davis, B. 2017. "I'm the one who coined the term 'Gammon': now I deeply regret it". *The Independent*, 15 May. https://www.independent.co.uk/voices/gammon-brexiteers-angry-white-men-middle-age-immigration-a8352141.html (accessed 17 March 2021).

Day, K., B. Gough & M. McFadden 2004. "'Warning! Alcohol can seriously damage your feminine health': a discourse analysis of recent British newspaper coverage of women and drinking". *Feminist Media Studies* 4(2): 165–83.

Financial Times 2020. "Corbyn loyalist determined to keep Labour on the far left". *Financial Times* Editorial, 12 January. https://www.ft.com/content/4bee9b10-3300-11ea-a329-0bcf87a328f2 (accessed 17 March 2021).

Goddard, D. 2015. "Who holds the power in Corbyn's majority-female shadow cabinet?". *The Conversation*, 15 September. https://theconversation.com/who-holds-the-power-in-corbyns-majority-female-shadow-cabinet-47516 (accessed 17 March 2021).

*Guardian* 2014. "Feminist t-shirts worn by politicians allegedly made in sweatshop conditions". *The Guardian*, 2 November. https://www.theguardian.com/world/2014/nov/02/fawcett-society-feminist-t-shirts-allegedly-sweatshop-conditions (accessed 17 March 2021).

*Guardian* 2017. "Manhole covers, jam and allotments: Jeremy Corbyn on the One Show – video". *The Guardian*, 30 May. https://www.theguardian.com/politics/video/2017/may/30/manhole-covers-jam-allotments-corbyn-bbc-one-show-video (accessed 17 March 2021).

Hall, S.-M. *et al.* 2017. *Intersecting Inequalities: The Impact of Austerity on Black and Minority Ethnic Women in the UK*. Report by Women's Budget Group and the Runnymede Trust with RECLAIM and Coventry Women's Voices. http://wbg.org.uk/wp-content/uploads/2018/08/Intersecting-Inequalities-October-2017-Full-Report.pdf (accessed 17 March 2021).

Harmer, E., H. Savigny & O. Ward 2017. "Are you tough enough? Performing gender in the UK 2015 leader debates". *Media, Culture and Society* 39(7): 960–75.

Harmer, E. & R. Southern 2018. "More stable than strong: women's representation, voters and issues". *Parliamentary Affairs*, 71(1): 237–54.

Harmer, E. & D. Wring 2013. "Julie and the cybermums: marketing and women voters in the 2010 election". *Journal of Political Marketing* 12(2/3): 262–73.

Hattersley, G. 2020. "I'm just trying to constantly remind people, 'don't forget women' – Labour MP Jess Phillips". 4 January. https://www.vogue.co.uk/article/jess-phillips-labour-mp-vogue-interview (accessed 17 March 2021).

ITV 2018. "Jeremy Corbyn reveals how he sneaked into parliament to put suffragette plaque up". *ITV News*, 7 February. https://www.itv.com/news/2018-02-07/jeremy-corbyn-put-secret-suffragette-plaque-up-in-parliament/ (accessed 17 March 2021).

Joe.co.uk 2017. "No-one spits like Jeremy Corbzy". Facebook post, 30 May. https://www.facebook.com/watch/?v=902260309938036 (accessed 17 March 2021).

Katz, J. 2016. *Man Enough? Donald Trump, Hillary Clinton, and the Politics of Presidential Masculinity*. Northampton, MA: Interlink Books.

LabourList 2015. "Jeremy Corbyn – education is a collective good – it's time for a national education service". *LabourList*, 9 July. https://jeremycorbyn.org.uk/education-is-a-collective-good-its-time-for-a-national-education-service-labourlist/ (accessed 17 March 2021).

Labour Party 2019. "Manifesto 2019: Charter for the Arts". 21 November. https://labour.org.uk/manifesto-2019/charter-for-the-arts/ (accessed 17 March 2021).

*Mail Online* 2019. "Jo Swinson says being a woman won't stop her toppling Boris". 17 September. https://www.dailymail.co.uk/video/news/video-2007578/Jo-Swinson-says-woman-not-stop-toppling-Boris.html (accessed 8 April 2021).

Mason, R. 2014. "*Daily Mail* 'Downing Street catwalk' condemned by MPs". *The Guardian*, 16 July. https://www.theguardian.com/media/2014/jul/16/daily-mail-downing-street-catwalk-female-ministers-outrage (accessed 17 March 2021).

McLoughlin, L. & R. Southern 2020. "By any memes necessary? Small political acts, incidental exposure and memes during the 2017 UK general election". *British Journal of Politics and International Relations* 23(1): 60–84. http://doi.org/10.1177/1369148120930594.

Norris, P. & J. Lovenduski 1995. *Political Recruitment*. Cambridge: Cambridge University Press.

O'Brien, Z. 2018. "Scruffy and disrespectful: Corby slammed for his appearance at the Cenotaph". *Daily Mail*, 11 November. https://www.dailymail.co.uk/news/article-6377075/Scruffy-disrespectful-Corbyn-slammed-looking-like-tramp-Cenotaph-service.html (accessed 17 March 2021).

O'Neill, D., H. Savigny & V. Cann 2016. "Women politicians in the UK press: not seen and not heard?". *Feminist Media Studies* 16(2): 293–307.

Parry-Giles, S. & T. Parry-Giles 1996. "Gendered politics and presidential image construction: a reassessment of the 'feminine style'". *Communications Monographs* 63(4): 337–53.

Peck, T. 2017. "Jeremy Corbyn on alcohol: I don't drink any: my secret is coconut water". *The Independent*, 6 June. https://www.independent.co.uk/news/uk/politics/jeremy-corbyn-alcohol-no-drink-unilad-coconut-water-apple-juice-labour-leader-a7775461.html (accessed 17 March 2021).

Rawnsley, A. & T. Helm 2015. "John McDonnell: it was a difficult appointment ... we knew we were going to be hit by a tsunami". *The Observer*, 19 September. https://www.theguardian.com/politics/2015/sep/19/john-mcdonnell-interview (accessed 17 March 2021).

Ross, K. 2002. *Women, Politics, Media: Uneasy Relations in Comparative Perspective*. Cresskill, NJ: Hampton Press.

Smart, A. 2015. "Why it's time the Labour Party elected a woman leader". *LabourList*, 20 May. https://labourlist.org/2015/05/why-its-time-the-labour-party-elected-a-woman-leader/ (accessed 17 March 2021).

Southern, R. & E. Harmer 2019. "Twitter, incivility and 'everyday' gendered othering: an analysis of tweets sent to UK Members of Parliament". *Social Science Computer Review*. https://doi.org/10.1177/0894439319865519.

Vine, S. 2018. "Why the lessons of Jeremy Corbyn's cap scare me to death". *Mail Online*, 21 March. https://www.dailymail.co.uk/debate/article-5525343/SARAH-VINE-lesson-Jeremy-Corbyns-cap-scares-death.html (accessed 17 March 2021).

Wintour, P., R. Mason & R. Syal 2015. "Jeremy Corbyn appoints ally John McDonnell as shadow chancellor". *The Guardian*, 14 September. https://www.theguardian.com/politics/2015/sep/13/jeremy-corbyn-shadow-cabinet-andy-burnham-labour (accessed 17 March 2021).

## 9

# WHO ARE THE CORBYNITES?

*Glen O'Hara*

It would be very easy to caricature the new members Labour has gathered up since 2015. Many traditional commentators – such as writers for *The Economist* – have continuously portrayed the surge of enthusiasm for Jeremy Corbyn among Labour members as something from beyond politics' normal bounds, contrasting "energized" young Corbynites with the "dark" and depressed mood of MPs (*The Economist* 2016). Part fringe pressure group, part student activism and part political suicide mission, the fervour and emotional commitment of many of Corbyn's supporters has been displayed in so many unflattering ways that it is hard to winnow the reality from the fantasy. Labour's deputy leader, Tom Watson, talked of the left-wing pressure group Momentum as if it was formed of far-left infiltrators leading on young people who lacked the experience to see what was really happening (Stewart 2016). Momentum's own internal battles, fought out between insurgents stressing their participatory politics and more established leftists, have helped to reinforce the impression of forces entering Labour from "outside" in an attempt to take it over, while the angry and often unpleasant rhetoric deployed by a small number of Corbynites on social media has also poisoned the atmosphere (Murray 2016). All in all, the general public has been treated to analysis that characterizes the average Corbyn supporter in three ways: young, very left-wing and extremely angry.

But is this picture the right one? It seems, from what evidence we have, that it is somewhat wide of the mark. Although students, young people and (now ex-) members of small parties such as the Socialist Party have all indeed helped shape the story, the reality of Labour's new membership is somewhat more prosaic. Older, better educated and more politically experienced than they have been painted, Corbynites are just as likely to be Labour returnees who left during the years since Neil Kinnock became leader and the party made its move towards the political centre; Peter Mandelson rather derisively termed them "retreaded Old Labourites" in a memorandum circulated to Labour centrists soon after Corbyn's leadership victory in 2015 (Mandelson 2015). Their worldview is very different from that of most of the electorate, but they are not noticeably more left-wing than the party membership was in the 1980s, before the burst of "moderniza-tion" under leaders from Kinnock to Gordon Brown. In this sense, the claim of many Corbyn supporters that their leader is taking the party back to its roots has at least some justification. Corbyn himself was an utterly unexpected leader, and most of his own personal views are as far from those of Clement Attlee, Ernest Bevin and even Aneurin Bevan as it is possible to be and still remain in the same party. The advent of his particular post-1968 form of left-radicalism was a break with Labour's past, especially in the realm of foreign policy (O'Hara 2015). However, his supporters, at least, can claim some continuity with earlier years, if not from the era before the 1970s, when more Labour members and activists were drawn from among a much more highly unionized, blue-collar working class.

We actually have good comparative data on party members' views going back to the early 1990s, from the work of the academics Patrick Seyd and Paul Whiteley, who surveyed Labour members in 1989–90 and again at the high point of New Labour's electoral success in 1997 and 1999. In order to look at change over time, we can compare their work with surveys commissioned by the polling expert Ian Warren during 2016. Two issues can be taken to illustrate some of the relative stability, rather than change, that we see. Sixty-eight per cent of Labour members opposed renewing the Trident nuclear weapons system in 2016, while the party under Blair was evenly split, with 45 per cent thinking that the UK should keep Trident, and 44 per cent opposing that decision. But if we go back to 1989–90, 72 per cent of Labour members thought that Britain should renounce nuclear weapons, a very similar figure to that returned in the 2016 data. If we turn to the Conservatives' restrictive trade union laws from the 1980s, even in 1997, 74 per cent of Labour members thought that they should go no further, and the same proportion disagreed with the view that "it is better for Britain when trade unions have little power". It is far from clear that this is very different to the 64 per cent of 2016 Labour members who think that trade unions today should have more power (Seyd & Whiteley 1992: 52–3, 2002: 54–5; YouGov 2016a).

As part of their Research Council-funded party members' project, Monica Poletti, Tim Bale and Paul Webb further analysed the post-2015 new members' true character towards the end of 2016. At that point at least, the influence of young people and students appears to have been wildly overdone. Their findings are instructive, and an antidote to journalistic exaggeration. The average age of *both* new and old members in May 2016 was 51, with newer members being only very slightly younger: there had been no significant change in this field at all. Nor was Momentum the key factor in their new loyalty: only one in ten of the new members was involved with the grassroots campaigning group (Poletti, Bale & Webb 2016b). By 2017, the single largest group among them lived in the

South of England outside London, and the average age of Labour members had gone *up*, not down – to 53 on average (Poletti, Bale & Webb 2018: tables 1–2, 8).

The justifications usually given for Labour's new direction are also much simpler than any Machiavellian wish to take over the Labour Party. The Labour activist Phil Burton-Cartledge, no uncritical Corbynite but still sympathetic to the leadership's aims, cast the appeal of Corbyn's policies in the following manner:

> Can we talk of Corbynism as a body of ideas? Contrary to the sneers, people are attracted to Corbyn's person on this basis. He's against cuts. He's against war. He stands up for the poor and vulnerable, defends social security and the NHS, attacks the scapegoating of immigrants and refugees, opposes privatisation and blind faith in markets, and rejects a system loaded in favour of the rich.
>
> (Burton-Cartledge 2017)

Labour's membership has definitely moved sharply to the left since its members – rather than its trade union affiliates, who opted for Ed Miliband – voted for David Miliband to be leader in 2010. Surveys of party members do not, however, indicate that they shifted rapidly or hugely leftwards either in their self-image or across a range of policy areas between 2015 and 2017, although they did become more socially liberal (Bale, Webb & Poletti 2020: tables 4.1–4.2, 54–6). But the moves since 2010 are conceptualized by many new members as just a return to pre-Blair "common sense", and a reaction against the New Labour project that is itself thought of as disruptive and alien to Labour's traditions. Adopting this mindset brings with it some practical advantages. First and most importantly, Labour has not been outflanked to the left, as Pasok in Greece and to some extent the German Social Democrats have been. There will be no equivalent of Spain's populist Podemos siphoning votes away among more socialist voters (Bush 2016). Labour, of course, managed to poll 41 per cent of the vote in the 2017 general election, and 32 per cent even as it was humbled in December 2019 (Cowley & Kavanagh 2018: table 16.3, 420–21; BBC News 2019).

Another possibility much mooted among Labour's new mass membership was that they might be able to engage with grassroots politics and community organizing in a way that the Conservatives, with a shrunken and ageing membership, simply could not. Corbyn's 2017 "relaunch", during which his team attempted to cast him as a man who spoke his mind without fear or favour, is a case in point here, and appeared to work well in that year's election at least. In an era when inconsistent – even incoherent – but emotional and apparently "genuine" communication seems more powerful than analytical reasoning, presenting Corbyn as a principled "outsider" was one coherent choice, however fraught with difficulties that course remained given the Labour leader's long political career (Pedley 2017). That idea came to grief during the 2017–19 parliament, during which Corbyn's ratings as leader of the opposition fell to an all-time low with Ipsos-Mori (Ipsos-Mori 2019). That collapse of his appeal, however, was caused by the sheen of honesty and outspokenness wearing off amidst a welter of allegations of antisemitism, favouritism and factionalism: one poll conducted in May 2018 found that only 18 per cent of voters trusted Corbyn to be "honest and transparent" about the antisemitism crisis engulfing his party (Welch 2019a). His extreme unpopularity by the end of 2019 did not make the idea of an honourable fresh voice a particularly bad political strategy *per se*.

The dangers involved in this project were, however, always very high, as the disaster of the 2019 general election in the end demonstrated. Many new Labour members' views were very far indeed from those of the average voter: so far, indeed, that it is with hindsight hard to see Labour ever bridging the gap. Take foreign policy for instance, admittedly the area in which Corbynite views differed most extensively from the general public's, but a policy sphere that was only going to become more important in the era of Brexit. Here new Labour members differed markedly in their attitudes. One survey taken by Opinium in September 2015 showed that Corbyn supporters overall had only a narrowly "positive" view of the United States, by a net figure of 8 points, as against a net positive of 24 per cent among voters as a whole. Forty-four per cent of Corbyn supporters placed the USA as one of the top three "dangers to world peace": only 23 per cent of the wider sample did so. Pro-Corbyn responders were also much more likely to believe that the US had brought the 9/11 terrorist attacks upon itself, and that the main motivation of US foreign policy was to secure control over oil supplies (Drummond 2015). Although the onset of the Trump administration may well have pushed many voters closer to the Corbynite view, the difference in *attitude* and overall *outlook* is instructive: Corbyn supporters' emphasis on Palestinian rights, scepticism about Western intervention in Syria and constant evocation of the Second Iraq War as justification for their stance all emanate to some extent from this deep-seated distrust of the United States.

A similar picture emerges if we look at domestic issues: Warren's polling shows that 78 per cent of the 2016 Labour selectorate think immigration "good for Britain's economy", whereas only 41 per cent of Labour voters, and 29 per cent of the electorate as a whole, agree. Eighty-eight per cent of those with a vote in the Labour leadership contest of that year thought "it's more important to create a more equal society than to create a more prosperous society"; although a small majority of the public concur with this proposition (52 per cent), that figure is still much lower than inside the Labour Party. The Labour selectorate strongly opposed the proposition "it is possible to achieve better public services such as health, education and the police by running them more efficiently, without spending more on them": only 23 per cent thought this view correct, as against 57 per cent of the general public (YouGov 2016a). Overall, it is hard to avoid the conclusion that Labour members, now overwhelmingly new to the party, would always have found themselves on a collision course with voters at a general election.

It is true that individual parts of Labour's programme, such as rail nationalization and the idea of a minimum-to-maximum wage ratio floated early in 2017, were indeed popular. In September 2016 ICM found that 47 per cent of the public favoured rail nationalization, as against only 25 per cent who did not. One Scottish poll carried out late the same year showed support for nationalization even higher, at 58 per cent. The recent troubled history of franchises such as Southern and ScotRail helped to convince many voters that the experiment with private ownership and management had failed (ICM 2016; *The Scotsman* 2016). Although YouGov found that a hard wage "cap" or limit was not favoured by the public, Corbyn's more nuanced policy of encouraging a maximum pay ratio within companies, encouraged by public sector commissioning practices, did meet with majority support in research undertaken by ComRes (Smith 2017a; ComRes 2017). The programme that Labour took into the 2019 election was full of popular policies. YouGov found at the time that voters backed increasing income tax for those earning more than £80,000 by a net score of 37 points; nationalizing the railways, again, by 34 points; taking the water industry into public ownership, by 25 points (Smith 2019b).

But these are only episodic, isolated instances of a retail offer, satirized by the American political strategist David Axelrod in his comments on Ed Miliband's 2015 election campaign as amounting to little more than saying "vote Labour and win a microwave" (Wintour 2015). Miliband's own relatively popular efforts in this respect, for instance the concept of a cap on energy prices raised at the 2013 party conference, did not in the end prove to be a recipe for victory – not the only way in which Corbyn's leadership came to resemble Miliband's. Wider problems of credibility, and the desirability of plans in a wider context as well as in detail, are likely to stand in the way of any wider appeal based on these single-issue campaigns (Kellner 2015). Labour partisans' strategic vision and overall view of the world did not in the end chime with the wider public. As one Labour canvasser found during the 2019 election in the North West of England: "our broad scope [...] backfired. It felt to many like too much, causing the plan and its funding to feel unrealistic and risky. 'How are you going to pay for all that?' and 'You will never be able to achieve so much' were common responses" (*Will to Truth* 2019).

The appeal of particular emotional or evocative issues, often based on redistributive appeals to absolute or relative "fairness", was not an accident. It was a fundamental and structural part of the new Labour selectorate's thinking, partly emanating from their origins in the party system. Corbyn supporters were quite likely to have come from other parties, especially the Green Party: 17 per cent of them voted Green in the 2015 general election. They were much less tribal than more long-standing members, could indeed be kaleidoscopic in their loyalties, and often saw Labour as only one campaigning group among many which might achieve some of their individual aims. One new member from London told *The Guardian* that meetings were "quite boring", "bureaucratic and hierarchical", and that he would only campaign for Labour if it changed its approach: "pounding the streets is only appealing if you feel you own the policies" (MacAskill 2016). This message was also obscured by the messengers. Corbyn, along with John McDonnell and Diane Abbott – the key figures in the new Labour Party that emerged between 2015 and 2019 – were very imperfect vessels for the idealism clearly felt by many new Labour members. Corbyn's own ratings always lagged far below those even of Ed Miliband at the same stage in the parliamentary cycle: they were only competitive over the very brief period before and after the general election of 2017 (Cowley & Kavanagh 2018: table 16.2, 413).

Corbyn himself appears to have consistently dragged down Labour's polling scores on almost every measure. In January 2017, YouGov found 28 per cent of the electorate willing to give Labour their vote, but only 17 per cent of Britons thought that Corbyn himself would be the "best Prime Minister" (45 per cent preferred Theresa May) (Smith 2017b). Even more worrying for Labour, a ComRes poll taken at the same time showed that 43 per cent of the public trusted May with the NHS, versus only 31 per cent thinking that Corbyn would be more suited to look after the health service. At a time when YouGov was reporting an 11-point lead for Labour as a whole on this issue, Corbyn was clearly reducing Labour's advantage by some way (ComRes 2017). During the 2019 election campaign, some polls showed that Boris Johnson was ahead of Corbyn on stewardship of the NHS, albeit much more narrowly (Survation 2019).

Corbyn's rise was not inevitable. It is all too easy, when confronted with such a significant and unexpected change at the head of a party, to conclude that it must have long-standing and deep-seated causes: the rise of the anti-war movement since the Second Iraq War, for instance, or the emergence of the anti-globalization movement since the 1990s, or the disengagement of Labour's working-class electoral base even as Labour became more entrenched in liberal, outward-looking, youthful and racially-mixed cities (Eatwell & Goodwin 2018: 254–6; Gest 2016: 53–66, 120–26). All of those developments are important reasons for the Corbynite moment. But future historians would be wise to avoid the error of attributing far-reaching change to large-scale causes. Leaders can secure victory against their rivals by small margins and for highly contingent reasons, and *then* go on to change the party in their image – just as Miliband had done between 2010 and 2015 (Bale 2015: 7–29).

It remains the case that, had Corbyn not secured two last-minute nominations from MPs who had no intention of voting for him, he would not have made it onto the ballot in the summer of 2015 (for a discussion on Corbyn and the parliamentary party, see Crines, Jeffery & Heppell 2018). MPs nominated Corbyn for a range of reasons: his affability in person, pressure from local members and most of all because they wanted a "wide debate" at a time when the arguments as to why Labour lost in 2015 was dominated by the party's right. Only a handful thought he had even a chance of winning, an impression that helped circumvent the checks and balances deliberately inserted in Labour's new one-member-one-vote system of electing its leaders. Corbyn would not have been nominated had his subsequent victory looked at all possible (Nunns 2016: 113–20). In that situation Andy Burnham would very likely have been elected leader. He would have set out a soft-left agenda, which owed much to Miliband's ideas, with a distinctive emphasis on meeting the threat to Labour posed by the United Kingdom Independence Party in the North of England. MPs would have been much happier with this situation than the Corbyn leadership, although undoubtedly there would have been discontent on both the party's left and right at the lack of any really new agenda.

The elements of chance and happenstance that helped to remake Labour were matched, in their shifting and shapeless way, by the new party's protean and fluid nature. The data makes it clear that most new members were not ideologues, still less Trotskyites or Leninists. In fact, they had little in the way of a structured, programmatic view of the world. As the philosopher John Gray has written:

> The party Corbyn has created is not easily defined [...] it has no coherent ideology. The legacy of Marxism is notable for its absence. There is no analysis of changing class structures or any systematic critique of the present condition of capitalism. Such policies as have been floated have been plucked from a blue sky, without any attempt to connect them with earthbound facts. The consensus-seeking values of core Labour voters are dismissed as symptoms of backwardness. As for the concerns about job security and immigration that produced large majorities in favour of Brexit in what used to be safe Labour areas, the Corbynite view seems to be that these are retrograde attitudes that only show how badly working people need re-education [...] But far from being a debilitating weakness – as it would be if Labour were still a conventional political party – this rejection of realistic thinking is the principal source of his strength in the new kind of party he has created. From being a broad-based institution that defended the interests of working people, Labour has morphed into a vehicle for an alienated fringe of the

middle class that finds psychological comfort in belonging in an anti-capitalist protest movement.                                  (Gray 2016)

Other critiques of Corbynism have reinforced this impression of a reaction against prevailing ideas and practices of austerity (Bolton & Pitts 2018: 96–8), dependent in large part on negative myths about the wickedness of the political right and the supposed hidden persuaders (rather than structures) that govern the global capitalist order (Clarke 2019: 31–6).

There is, once more, some psephological support for this link between inchoate protest and Labour's new membership. One key group within Labour's new selectorate was younger graduates who, despite their high levels of education and articulate, assertive personalities, were paid much less than they would have been in their parents' generation: a key part of the "low productivity, low profit" business model that Corbynite thinkers such as Paul Mason took aim at (Mason 2015). A majority of Labour's new members in the spring of 2016 (albeit a bare majority of 51 per cent) were graduates who earned less than the average salary of £25,000; of more long-standing members, 41 per cent earned below average wages (Poletti, Bale & Webb 2016b). Nor, as wealth was shifting from earning to owning, from income to property and from younger to older, did they have much hope of owning their home or investing in a stable pension. Little wonder that they turned to a party that promised, however vaguely, to cap rents and to build more houses. Articulating this sense of injustice, even outrage, can be more important to members than winning power: in one 2016 survey, only a third of them thought that appealing to the average voter should be one of their leader's priorities, an idea to which members who joined before 2015 were more attracted (Poletti, Bale & Webb 2016a). Many Labour members were quite explicit: they did not seek power, but to influence the way social or economic issues were thought about. As one 48-year-old finance manager from Liverpool told *The Guardian* during the 2015 leadership contest:

> What is the point of Labour if not to stand up for ordinary working people, whether they are currently in work, sick, disabled or on the scrapheap? There has to be an alternative to pandering to the market. Jeremy offers hope for the future, the promise of a fightback, of resistance to the markets: people and the planet before profit. If it makes Labour less likely to win then so be it. What is the point of winning just to implement Tory-lite policies?                          (Walsh 2015)

Most Corbynite members, however, never quite believed that Labour was inevitably doomed to lose elections under Corbyn. Even in the immediate aftermath of the European Union referendum, when Corbyn's stock among members plummeted owing to what was perceived as his lukewarm campaigning for Remain, a large majority of his supporters within the membership (55 per cent) thought that he would in fact win any subsequent general election. The membership overall did not believe this, by a margin of 50 per cent to 38 per cent, but a slim majority of Corbyn supporters still believed he could take Labour back to power (YouGov 2016b). These members saw Corbyn as principled, honest and courageous, sticking to his beliefs even during an onslaught from his own side. One YouGov survey of the Labour Party selectorate conducted in August 2016 showed that 97 per cent of his supporters thought of him as being "principled", 93 per cent "honest" and 75 per cent "courageous". Even the wider selectorate, including those backing failed leadership contender Owen Smith, for the most part also saw Corbyn in this light: 76, 64 and 48 per cent associated those same words with Labour's leader. The problem remained that Labour voters, and still more the electorate as a whole, did not agree with all this: among Labour voters, only 50, 38 and 21 per cent would use the words "principled", "honest" or "courageous" respectively to describe Corbyn: in terms of the general public, those numbers were only 33, 23 and 13 per cent (YouGov 2016c).

One more key element of these members' electoral worldview was the idea that non-voters might favour a more distinctive, radical offer, and could be drawn back to the polls by the excitement of this new type of politics. As another Corbyn sympathizer told *The Guardian* in 2016: "[Corbyn] can reach out to those who are outside the current voting patterns and disenfranchised" (*The Guardian* 2016). This argument was almost certainly misguided – there is no evidence at all that non-voters think and feel very differently from the rest of the electorate – but it would be churlish not to note that Labour centrists failed to put forward a credible alternative candidate who *would* satisfy most members while attempting to mobilize a new electoral coalition (McDonnell 2016). There was still little sign of any compromise between Labour's warring factions, a new consensus urgently required not so much because of the damage infighting does in public – most of the details never impinge on the public consciousness – but because the party had almost no new ideas or appeal beyond those represented unsuccessfully by Ed Miliband. The party's opinion poll ratings across most of the 2015–17 and 2017–19 parliaments were unprecedently low for a Labour opposition since the Second World War: and with hindsight, Labour's defeat in the February 2017 Copeland by-election was a harbinger of the rout to come (Singh 2017). Recriminations have centred – in some ways rightly – on the leader's underwhelming performance. But unless there is some acceptance that globalized, liberal, "moderate" Labour centrism also seemed unappealing to the working-class voters that Corbyn lost in seats across the North of England and the Midlands, a change of leader alone will do little to revive Labour's fortunes (Bertram 2017; Morris 2017; Chorley 2019; McDonnell & Curtice 2019).

Labour members' views have also evolved over time. They are not set in concrete, and nor should observers either celebrate or despair over some form of hegemonic domination – another of the analytical dangers that arises if one assumes one-dimensional ideological fervour, youthful idealism or activist naivete on the part of "the Corbynites". As Corbyn struggled with crisis after crisis during 2018 and 2019, Labour members' views of his performance, if not his aims, grew less and less approving. Eighty per cent of them thought he was doing "a good job" in March 2018: only 56 per cent of them agreed with the same statement by July 2019. They also placed Sir Keir Starmer, the shadow Brexit secretary, at the top of the list of possible replacements – hardly the view of a membership unwilling to brook any change from the Corbynite line (Smith 2019a). Party members disagreed strongly, for instance, with Corbyn's equivocal stance over Brexit: at the end of 2018, 78 per cent of them told the Party Members Project, funded by the UK's Economic and Social Research Council, that they wanted the party to commit to a second referendum (Walker 2019). Even on the insidious and poisonous issue of antisemitism, there is evidence of at least some change over time in party members' attitudes. Only 10 per cent thought the problem "genuine and serious" in May 2016; that figure had risen to 19 per cent by March 2018. The corresponding number who found the crisis "neither genuine nor serious" dropped from 49 per cent to 30 per cent (Anson 2018). Another survey conducted in the autumn of 2019 showed that the number of members who thought that Labour had a "serious" problem had risen again, to 22 per cent (Welch 2019b). Obviously, given the seriousness of the allegations brought by the Jewish Labour Movement among others, this was a deeply inadequate response (JLM 2019). But the impression given by a small number of tweeters and bloggers who helped to ramp up online hatred against Jews on the left – that most Labour members did not care about the issue at all – seems some way wide of the mark in the aggregate (Community Security Trust 2019: 18–32).

Corbyn's supporters within the Labour Party did not hold monolithic views, and they were not, in the main, far-left entryists or youthful idealists. They were older, more highly educated and more politically experienced than the clichés that abounded in media coverage. Many of their opinions would have seemed mainstream in the Labour Party of the 1980s. In the main, they saw themselves as simply wanting more socialism: public ownership, higher public spending, a more progressive tax system, fewer foreign wars, less scapegoating of migrants, a more integrated NHS. But on touchstone issues – especially in the fields of defence, national security and immigration – and in terms of their overall attitude to government spending and public sector reform, their philosophy and language set them apart from the wider electorate. Their lack of attachment to the party *per se* often issued from at least a recent past outside the Labour Party. Their adherence to a deeply unpopular leader, the cultural gulf of meaning and understanding that has grown between Labour and the voters, and Labour's failure to decide on any clear path forward, mean that this new type of activist will probably need new alliances and coalitions to keep their dreams alive in the years ahead.

# References

Anson, S. 2018. "Labour and the Jews". Medium, 14 April. https://medium.com/@moutajup/labour-and-the-jews-1a6f01138b7e (accessed 18 March 2021).

Bale, T. 2015. *Five Year Mission: The Labour Party under Ed Miliband*. Oxford: Oxford University Press.

Bale, T., P. Webb & M. Polletti 2020. *Footsoldiers: Political Party Membership in the 21st Century*. London: Routledge.

BBC News 2019. "Election 2019: UK results: Conservatives win majority". https://www.bbc.co.uk/news/election/2019/results (accessed 18 March 2021).

Bertram, T. 2017. "The Copeland test: Labour's core bote". Medium, 23 February. https://medium.com/@theobertram/the-copeland-test-labours-core-vote-ddac4fb8ee#.x2tzoynuy (accessed 18 March 2021).

Bolton, M. & F. Pitts 2018. *Corbynism: A Critical Approach*. Bingley: Emerald.

Burton-Cartledge, P. 2017. "What is Corbynism?". Left Futures. https://web.archive.org/web/20190331141600/https://www.leftfutures.org/2017/01/what-is-corbynism/ (accessed 8 April 2021).

Bush, S. 2016. "Corbyn can save Labour from the fate of its European friends". *Financial Times*, 29 August.

Community Security Trust 2019. *Engine of Hate: The Online Networks Behind the Labour Party's Antisemitism Crisis*. London: CST.

Chorley, M. 2019. "General election results: working class switched to Tories". *The Times*, 17 December.

Clarke, C. 2019. *Warring Fictions: Left Populism and its Defining Myths*. London: Policy Exchange.

ComRes 2017. "*Sunday Mirror/Independent* Political Poll, January 2017". http://www.comresglobal.com/polls/sunday-mirror-independent-political-poll-jan-2017/ (accessed 18 March 2021).

Cowley, P. & D. Kavanagh 2018. *The British General Election of 2017*. Basingstoke: Palgrave Macmillan.

Crines, A., D. Jeffery & T. Heppell 2018. "The British Labour Party and leadership election mandate(s) of Jeremy Corbyn: Patterns of opinion and opposition within the parliamentary Labour Party". *Journal of Elections, Public Opinion and Parties* 28(3): 361–79.

Drummond, A. 2015. "Unsurprisingly, Corbyn supporters aren't fans of America". Opinium, 2 November. http://opinium.co.uk/unsurprisingly-corbyn-supporters-arent-fans-of-america/ (accessed 18 March 2021).

Eatwell, R. & M. Goodwin 2018. *National Populism: The Revolt against Liberal Democracy*. London: Pelican.

*The Economist* 2016. "You say you want a revolution". *The Economist*, 1 October.

Gest, J. 2016. *The New Minority: White Working-Class Politics in an Age of Immigration and Inequality*. Oxford: Oxford University Press.

Gray, J. 2016. "The closing of the liberal mind". *New Statesman*, 7 September. https://www. newstatesman.com/politics/uk/2016/11/closing-liberal-mind (accessed 25 March 2021).

*The Guardian* 2016. "Can Labour win an election under Corbyn? Readers debate". *The Guardian*, 3 October.

ICM 2016. "ICM/ *Sun on Sunday* Poll", 21–23 September. https://www.icmunlimited.com/wp-content/uploads/2016/09/2016_sept_sunonsunday_poll.pdf (accessed 18 March 2021).

Ipsos-Mori 2019. "Jeremy Corbyn has lowest leadership satisfaction rating for any opposition leader since 1977". 20 September. https://www.ipsos.com/ipsos-mori/en-uk/jeremy-corbyn-has-lowest-leadership-satisfaction-rating-any-opposition-leader-1977 (accessed 18 March 2021).

JLM 2019. "Redacted JLM closing submission to the EHRC". Jewish Labour Movement. https://www.scribd.com/document/438367082/Redacted-JLM-Closing-Submission-to-the-EHRC (accessed 18 March 2021).

Kellner, P. 2015. "Is rail nationalisation a vote-winner?". https://yougov.co.uk/topics/politics/articles-reports/2015/09/21/is-rail-nationalisation-vote-winner (accessed 18 March 2021).

MacAskill, E. 2016. "Jeremy Corbyn's team targets a Labour membership of one million". *The Guardian*, 27 September.

Mandelson, P. 2015. "Peter Mandelson's memo on how Labour's modernizers lost their way – and where they go next". The Staggers: The New Statesman's Rolling Politics Blog, 25 September. http://www.newstatesman.com/politics/staggers/2015/09/peter-mandelson-s-memo-how-labour-s-modernisers-lost-their-way-and-where (accessed 18 March 2021).

Mason, P. 2015. "That letter: Mark Carney writes to the chancellor". Channel 4 News, 13 January. https://www.channel4.com/news/by/paul-mason/blogs/letter-mark-carney-writes-chancellor (accessed 18 March 2021).

McDonnell, A. 2016. "Could Corbyn win an election by mobilising non-voters? Not if he doesn't win over Conservative supporters too". Democratic Audit, 12 April. http://www.democraticaudit.com/2016/04/12/could-corbyn-win-an-election-by-mobilising-non-voters-not-if-he-doesnt-win-over-conservative-supporters-too/ (accessed 18 March 2021).

McDonnell, A. & C. Curtis 2019. "How Britain voted in the 2019 general election". YouGov, 17 December. https://yougov.co.uk/topics/politics/articles-reports/2019/12/17/how-britain-voted-2019-general-election (accessed 18 March 2021).

Morris, J. 2017. "Working-class desertion of Labour started before Corbyn". *The Guardian*, 25 February.

Murray, L. 2016. "Momentum versus inertia". Medium, 5 December. https://medium.com/@lauracatrionamurray/momentum-vs-inertia-e525c8f9e217#.kr5sp7tji (accessed 18 March 2021).

Nunns, A. 2016. *The Candidate: Jeremy Corbyn's Improbable Path to Power*. London: OR Books.

O'Hara, G. 2015. "Forget the books: Jeremy Corbyn is without historical precedent". The Staggers: The New Statesman's Rolling Politics Blog. http://www.newstatesman.com/politics/staggers/2015/11/forget-books-jeremy-corbyn-without-historical-precedent (accessed 17 March 2021).

Pedley, K. 2017. "Jeremy Corbyn's Donald Trump makeover is risky, but it might just work". *Newsweek*, 9 January.

Poletti, M., T. Bale & P. Webb 2016. "Middle-class university graduates will decide the future of the Labour Party". The Staggers: The New Statesman's Rolling Politics Blog. http://www.newstatesman.com/politics/staggers/2016/07/middle-class-university-graduates-will-decide-future-labour-party (accessed 17 March 2021).

Poletti, M., T. Bale & P. Webb 2016. "Explaining the pro-Corbyn surge in Labour's membership". LSE British Politics and Policy Blog, 16 November. http://blogs.lse.ac.uk/politicsandpolicy/explaining-the-pro-corbyn-surge-in-labours-membership (accessed 18 March 2021).

Poletti, M., T. Bale & P. Webb 2018. *Grassroots: Britain's Party Members: Who They Are, What They Think and What They Do*. London: Queen Mary, University of London, Mile End Institute.

*The Scotsman* 2016. "Poll: support for nationalising Scotland's railway rises". *The Scotsman*, 1 December.

Seyd, P. & P. Whiteley 1992. *Labour's Grass Roots: The Politics of Party Membership*. Oxford: Clarendon Press.

Seyd, P. & P. Whiteley 2002. *New Labour's Grassroots: The Transformation of the Labour Party Membership*. Basingstoke: Palgrave Macmillan.

Singh, M. 2017. "Uncharted territory". Number Cruncher Politics, 24 February. https://www.ncpolitics.uk/2017/02/uncharted-territory.html/ (accessed 18 March 2021).

Smith, M. 2017a. "Maximum earnings limit a 'bad idea', say British public". https://yougov.co.uk/topics/politics/articles-reports/2017/01/11/maximum-earnings-limit-bad-idea-says-british-publi (accessed 18 March 2021).

Smith, M. 2017b. "Voting intention: Conservatives 39%, Labour 28%". https://yougov.co.uk/topics/politics/articles-reports/2017/01/12/voting-intention-conservatives-39-labour-28 (accessed 8 April 2021).

Smith, M. 2019a. "Corbyn's reputation takes a big hit with Labour members, but most still want him to stay". https://yougov.co.uk/topics/politics/articles-reports/2019/07/22/corbyns-reputation-takes-big-hit-labour-members-mo (accessed 18 March 2021).

Smith, M. 2019b. "Labour economic policies are popular, so why aren't Labour?" https://yougov.co.uk/topics/politics/articles-reports/2019/11/12/labour-economic-policies-are-popular-so-why-arent-.(accessed 18 March 2021).

Stewart, H. 2016. "Tom Watson sends Corbyn 'proof' of Trotskyist Labour infiltration". *The Guardian*, 10 August.

Survation 2019. Political Poll for the Daily Mail. https://www.survation.com/wp-content/uploads/2019/10/Daily-Mail-Tables.xlsx (accessed 8 April 2021).

Walker, P. 2019. "Most Labour members believe Corbyn should back second Brexit vote". *The Guardian*, 2 January.

Walsh, J. 2015. "Why Labour voters are turning towards Jeremy Corbyn". *The Guardian*, 24 July.

Welch, B. 2019a. "British public do not believe Jeremy Corbyn will ever end Labour antisemitism". *Jewish Chronicle*, 23 May. https://www.thejc.com/news/uk-news/jc-poll-british-public-do-not-believe-jeremy-corbyn-will-ever-end-labour-antisemitism-1.484592 (accessed 18 March 2021).

Welch, B. 2019b. "YouGov poll: two-thirds of Labour members 'deny party has serious antisemitism problem'". *Jewish Chronicle*, 22 September. https://www.thejc.com/news/uk-news/yougov-poll-labour-members-antisemitism-problem-israel-trade-deal-brexit-survey-1.489039 (accessed 18 March 2021).

Will to Truth 2019. "Reflections on our defeat and the challenges ahead". Will to Truth: Spoken Truths to Powers, 13 December. https://eyalclyne.wordpress.com/2019/12/13/reflections-on-our-defeat-and-the-challenge-ahead/?fbclid=IwAR24nMxm9ARxZe_Ce_PTseI0LxEJOv8DtlL37_dFE7N2EbWPEuXXp0ziofI (accessed 18 March 2021).

Wintour, P. 2015. "The undoing of Ed Miliband – and how Labour lost the election". *The Guardian*, 3 June.

YouGov 2016a. "YouGov/election data survey results". 11–15 February. http://d25d2506sfb94s.cloudfront.net/cumulus_uploads/document/so5om6mzoi/IanWarrenResults_160222_LabourMembersDay1.pdf (accessed 18 March 2021).

YouGov 2016b. "YouGov/*The Times* survey results". 27–30 June. https://d25d2506sfb94s.cloudfront.net/cumulus_uploads/document/eprogs4gmc/TimesResults_160630_LabourMembers.pdf (accessed 18 March 2021).

YouGov 2016c. "YouGov/*The Times* survey results". 25–29 August. https://d25d2506sfb94s.cloudfront.net/cumulus_uploads/document/0cpa7iw5l7/TimesResults_160830_LabourSelectorate.pdf (accessed 18 March 2021).

# 10

# JEREMY CORBYN IN HISTORICAL PERSPECTIVE

*Lise Butler*

In the general election of 1983 the Labour Party, under the leadership of Michael Foot, suffered its worst defeat since 1918.[1] Its manifesto that year – famously dubbed "the longest suicide note in history" by the Labour MP Gerald Kaufman – offered a programme of renationalization, nuclear disarmament and withdrawal from the European Community. In that election three future Labour Party leaders were first elected to parliament: Tony Blair for the Durham constituency of Sedgefield, Gordon Brown for the Scottish constituency of Dunfermline East and Jeremy Corbyn for the London constituency of Islington North. Labour's electoral defeat in 1983, and subsequent defeats in 1987 and 1992, were crucial in driving the party towards the centre in the late 1980s and the 1990s. But the political failures and battles of the early 1980s also shaped the political identity and strategy of the left of the Labour Party and would inform both its successes and its failures under Jeremy Corbyn's leadership between 2015 and 2019.

During and after Corbyn's time as Labour leader, he and his supporters were frequently portrayed as taking Britain "back to the 1970s" for their manifesto promises to renationalize rail and other services, raise taxes on business and higher earners, return more power to trade unions and increase worker control over industry.[2] This account accused the Labour Party under Corbyn's leadership

---

1. I am grateful to Nick Garland for sharing his expertise on this topic and providing valuable advice for researching this chapter, and to Jonathan Leader Maynard, Rick Schwartz and Alison Howson for their very helpful edits.
2. Some easy to find examples include: "Labour leadership: better back to the 1970s with Jeremy Corbyn than 1870s with Tories", *The Observer* (30 August 2015); David Wooding, "Corbyn will take us back to the 70s", *The Sun* (12 September 2015); Joseph Carey, "Jeremy Corbyn stuck in 1970s TIME WARP he should be KILLING Theresa May, blasts Nick Clegg", *The Express* (14 February 2018); Harry Yorke, "Jeremy Corbyn accused of 'turning back clock' to 1970s as he pledges huge power shift towards trade unions", *The Telegraph* (10 September 2019); Frances Elliot and Steven Swinford, "Corbyn bid to launch 1970s-style cash spree", *The Times* (8 November 2019); "Jeremy Corbyn tax plans trigger fears of return to 1970s", *Financial Times* (21 November 2019); Andrew Brown, "Jeremy Corbyn's followers are stuck in the 1970s", *Foreign Policy* (17 December 2019).

of a nostalgic and dysfunctional politics not fit for the modern world, and invoked the industrial strife of the Wilson and Callaghan Labour governments. After the 2019 election another media narrative emerged: that of a Labour Party that had forgotten its working-class roots and "Labour heartlands" in the North of England, and become a party dominated by, as Home Secretary Priti Patel put it at the 2019 Conservative Party conference, a "North London metropolitan elite". Corbynism was portrayed alternately as a movement of an outdated politics of nationalization and labour militancy, and as a movement which appealed primarily to an out of touch urban elite. How, if at all, do we reconcile these visions?

Jeremy Corbyn's life and career have been the subject of numerous accounts – some friendly, and some much less so (some examples include Prince 2016; Perryman 2017; Bower 2018; Nunns 2018). While engaging with various accounts of Corbyn's biography, this chapter does not attempt to provide a detailed reconstruction of the intellectual and political forces that have shaped Jeremy Corbyn, the man. Rather, it seeks to situate Corbyn and Corbynism in terms of recent historical re-understandings and reassessments of left-wing politics and social movements of the 1970s and 1980s, to argue that the politics and political context of the Left in London and other urban centres during that time offer insights for understanding both the successes and failures of Corbynism between 2015 and 2019.

Looking to the 1970s and early 80s *can* help us understand Corbyn and Corbynism. But the vision of a 1970s left wedded to trade union power and tax-and-spend fiscal policies commonly invoked to attack Corbyn and his supporters is inaccurate. The activists and intellectuals of the Labour left in London in the 1970s and early 1980s, the environment in which Jeremy Corbyn's early political career was forged, were in fact motivated by a critique of labourism, or the Labour Party's institutional ties and cultural association with the trade union movement, and sought to develop new networks and political coalitions for a renewed late twentieth-century socialism. For the Labour left of the 1980s, urban centres were spaces where political solidarities could be forged across groups previously overlooked by the PLP, such as immigrant and ethnic minority communities and gay, lesbian and feminist liberation movements. The culturally and socio-economically diverse communities of 1980s London, including Jeremy Corbyn's constituency of Islington North, were central to this vision. Corbyn's early political career, as a councillor in the London borough of Haringey and as MP for Islington North, was shaped by an explicitly modernizing and metropolitan vision of the future of the Left. For Corbyn and other left-wing activists in the 1970s and 1980s, places like North London represented sites of socialist renewal where new political coalitions could be built that reflected the social, economic and demographic transformations of post-industrial Britain.

## Modernization and the Left

In conventional accounts of Labour history, "modernization" has tended to be associated with the reforms of New Labour, often signified by Tony Blair's infamous overturning of Clause IV of the Labour Party constitution, which committed the party to the nationalization of the means of production. Modernization provided a rhetorical strategy for New Labour to position itself against a tradition of state socialism that it portrayed as ill-equipped to tackle the political challenges and demographic realities of the late twentieth century. But the rhetoric of "modernization" conventionally associated with New Labour has much deeper roots within the Labour Party and the British Left – many of which can be located within the left, not the right, of the Labour tradition.[3]

A conventional historical narrative has tended to see the politics of the 1980s as characterized by a right-wing, "neoliberal" rejection of the political norms of the postwar settlement, including a redistributive state, progressive taxation and co-operation between industry and organized labour towards common aims like full employment. But recent scholarship has stressed the continuities between Thatcherism and left social movements, and their common concerns with individual freedom and frustrations with the welfare state (Robinson *et al.* 2017). Important new research has stressed the continuities and interactions between left- and right-wing discourses of "modernization" within Labour circles of the 1980s and 1990s, disrupting narrower accounts of New Labour "modernization" against left-wing resistance (Murphy 2020a). A wealth of recent scholarship on the intellectual Left of the 1980s has also explored the networks associated with the Communist Party of Great Britain journal *Marxism Today*, and the influence of the ideas of continental thinkers such as Antonio Gramsci in providing the ideological apparatus for a left politics that embraced civil society, urban spaces and non-traditional constituencies, including new social movements oriented around racial equality, lesbian and gay rights, and feminism (Shock 2020; Campsie 2017). These accounts have provided a rich portrait of the network of politicians, academics, writers and activists in 1970s and 1980s Britain who "sought to re-think socialism in light of the ideological fragmentation caused by the decline of Marxism as a philosophy of history, the intellectual opportunities opened up by the rise of new social movements, and the strategic possibilities offered by local politics" (Campsie 2017: 181).

The New Left social movements of 1960s Britain were motivated by strong antagonism to both the Wilson government's foreign policy, which attempted to strike a conciliatory tone towards the United States while keeping Britain out of

---

3. For an important recent re-evaluation of discourses of modernization and the British Left see Murphy (2020a).

the war in Vietnam, and the more conservative political culture associated with male-dominated and culturally homogenous trade unions. They also contained an important element of "state critical" thinking, which sought to cultivate spaces of association, co-operation and solidarity in communities, workplaces and other sites of association not formally tied to the state (Ackers & Reid 2016). In the 1960s the Labour left was also influenced by an important critique of parliamentary democracy as a vehicle for socialism. The Labour Representation Committee, which became the Labour Party, was formed in 1900 to represent organized labour in parliament. But in his 1964 *Parliamentary Socialism* the Marxist sociologist Ralph Miliband challenged this premise, arguing that parliamentary politics could only ever support and reinforce rather than challenge capitalism. These various critiques of parliamentary and state socialism contributed to a widespread sense of disillusionment with the Labour Party. As a result of this climate of discontent, many radical socialists turned away from the formal institutional structures of the party in the 1970s to embrace an alternative politics rooted in community activism, local politics and participatory democracy.

A long tradition of political thought on the left has, moreover, emphasized the need for the Labour Party to respond to Britain's changing demographics. In the 1950s and 1960s numerous thinkers on the left pointed out that as the Labour Party's traditional constituency, the industrial working class, acquired higher standards of living, and more and more people moved out of traditional industries and into the public sector or service sector, the party would face declining support.[4] These arguments have tended to be associated with the Labour right and the "revisionist" politics of figures like Anthony Crosland and Roy Jenkins, and are often interpreted as precursors to the Social Democratic Party and New Labour. But the left of the Labour tradition has not been blind to Britain's changing demographics and has certainly not been wedded to a left politics rooted in the representation of the manual working class.

Concerns that a party built on the representation of the manual working class through trade unions was, simply, doomed by demographics re-emerged on the left of the Labour Party in the late 1970s. In his famous 1978 essay, "The forward march of labour halted", Eric Hobsbawm pointed out that trade union membership was stagnating, that the decline of manual occupations and increased standards of living was causing fewer people to identify as working class, and that rising trade union membership in the public sector had resulted in an antagonistic relationship between unions and the public. At the same time, the wider Left was shaped by an important feminist challenge to the Labour Party's

---

4. See Abrams & Rose 1960; Crosland 1956 also famously anticipated a more affluent and materially comfortable society and urged the Labour Party to orient more explicitly toward quality of life, and away from traditional socialist commitments like public ownership.

traditional ties to the manual working class and trade union movement. A key text in envisaging and articulating the need for socialist renewal around democratic, localist and community-oriented organization was a 1978 collection of essays by Sheila Rowbotham, Lynne Segal and Hilary Wainwright entitled *Beyond the Fragments: Feminism and the Making of Socialism.* The essays in *Beyond the Fragments* reflected on the experience of developing a radical feminist politics out of the diverse movements spawned by the New Left, questioned the utility of orienting around "a single democratic centralist party" like the Labour Party and pointed towards more communitarian and localist modes of political engagement (Rowbotham, Segal & Wainwright 1978: 2). At the heart of *Beyond the Fragments'* vision of decentralized socialism was an embrace of local politics. Wainwright described how anti-racist campaigns in Hackney and Islington, organized by the Trotskyist International Socialists, had been central to her political development: community action provided a vital space for developing her politics beyond traditional, worker driven and formal political spaces. Segal's contribution to *Beyond the Fragments*, "A local experience", described her involvement in establishing the Essex Road Women's Centre in 1974 as a space for feminist organizing around principles of autonomy, personal relationships and the rejection of the idea of a revolutionary vanguard of workers.

In 1983, the writer John Gyford described this movement away from the formal institutional structures of the Labour Party, and towards community action and local politics, in an article in the popular social science journal *New Society* entitled "The new urban left: a local road to socialism". Gyford described a new group of local politicians "proclaiming nuclear free zones, discussing Northern Ireland, funding radical community groups, flying red flags, establishing women's committees, appointing political sympathizers to key positions, encouraging workers' cooperatives and municipal enterprise, and questioning the rights and duties of the police and the courts" (Gyford 1983: 91). This group was, in Gyford's words, "the decentralist wing of the extra-parliamentary left". They wrote, he said, in journals like "*Labour Herald*, in *London Labour Briefing* and its provincial counterparts, in *Local Socialism*, in *Marxism Today* and in *Chartist*". In response to "the inadequacy of traditional models of socialist politics" and the political conditions identified by Hobsbawm and others, the "new urban left" sought to replace both revolutionary and parliamentary socialism "with the socialist potential of local government" (*ibid.*: 91–2).

## The GLC and the new urban left

The most famous site of municipal socialism and the "new urban left" in 1980s Britain was the Greater London Council (GLC) (see also Garland, no date).

London had had a long history of left-wing municipal government prior to the GLC (Hatherley 2020). Before the late nineteenth century the capital had been governed by a largely decentralized network of parishes and boroughs, but in 1888 the London Government Act created the London County Council (LCC). The council's seat, County Hall, was opened in 1922 across the river from the Palace of Westminster. While originally Conservative-dominated, the LCC was later controlled by Labour and led by Herbert Morrison in the 1930s, a decade when (like the 1980s) the parliamentary Labour Party was in the political wilderness. Following the London Government Act of 1963, introduced by the Conservative government of Harold Macmillan, the London County Council was replaced by the Greater London Council in 1965. The legislation introducing the GLC expanded the boundaries of London government to include more suburban areas. Although Conservative lawmakers had intended the GLC's expanded constituency to integrate a broader swath of more affluent suburban voters, who tended to vote Conservative, the GLC became a site of ideological and political revival for the Left in the 1970s and 1980s.

In 1981 Ken Livingstone achieved control of the GLC on a left slate. Under Livingstone's leadership the council consciously sought to reach out to the counterculture and liberation movements, to create a political base and build new political solidarities between more traditional Labour activists, community groups, immigrant communities and liberation movements (Kelliher 2014; Robinson 2008: 139–46). Under Livingstone's leadership the GLC pursued a strategy of using rates (or property taxes) paid by wealthier London suburb-dwellers and the City to aggressively fund community organizations, women's centres, immigrant groups and community childcare, and subsidized tube and bus fare through the Fares Fair policy (Wainwright 1987a: 97). It also sought to develop a more open style of administration, seeking to engage members of the public directly in its campaigns and policies: committees such as the Women's Committee, Ethnic Minorities Committee and Planning Committee sought to move beyond both formal representative government, and the formal structures of the Labour Party itself, to engage London residents in an activist-led programme of radical community engagement.

Livingstone presented his political project as an explicit response to changes in British capitalism and London's economy. He saw Thatcher's monetarist policies, and the economic crisis which they had produced, as particularly damaging to London. Unlike the economic crisis of the 1930s, which had hit industrial areas in the North of England, Wales, Scotland and Ireland hardest, London's manufacturing industries suffered severely in the recession of the early 1980s: in 1983 Livingstone noted that while unemployment in the country as a whole had increased by 157 per cent since early 1980, it had risen by nearly 200 per cent in London, because of both the loss of manufacturing jobs and cuts to the public sector (Livingstone 1983: 70–72). The contraction of manufacturing and the changes to London's economy meant that the Labour Party had to organize differently from the way it had done in the past. In a 1984 interview Livingstone reflected that:

> A Labour Party based in the industrial trades unions was credible in the 1940s and 50s, but the contraction of the industrial base means that the Labour Party is going to have to be based on service unions, many of them white collar, which isn't an adequate base on its own.
>
> (Boddy & Fudge 1984: 270)

For Livingstone, the contraction of Britain's industrial base required Labour, both locally and nationally, to rethink its political identity as the parliamentary arm of the trade union movement, and to develop new electoral coalitions. Livingstone argued that the activist networks and ethnic minority organizations that had emerged in urban centres since the 1960s should be formally affiliated to the Labour Party like the trade unions, saying:

> the Labour Party has to change its own structure so that women's organizations, community organizations have a direct input rather than via the trade unions. Black political organizations should be affiliated to the Labour Party, as should various feminist groups. What we should aim for is to build a labour movement that represents not just the trades unions, but also these other sections of society which have been neglected by the labour movement in the past and whose demands have not been articulated.
>
> (Boddy & Fudge 1984: 270)

Livingstone viewed the Labour Party's historic concentration on the "employed male white working class" as its weakness, and called for a politics oriented instead around a coalition of "skilled and unskilled workers, unemployed, women, and black people as well as the sexually oppressed minorities" (Livingstone 1983: 27).

Livingstone's vision of a restructured left coalition oriented around activists and ethnic minority groups rather than trade unions was linked to his anti-imperialist foreign policy commitments. He saw increasing Tory support among the skilled white working class as rooted in "national chauvinism" and deep-rooted imperialist attitudes (Boddy & Fudge 1984: 270–71). In a 1983 interview with Tariq Ali in the *New Left Review*, he noted that during the Falklands War the Labour vote in "more traditional, settled, white working class" areas "collapsed by up to half", but that there had been a swing to Labour in wards with a "substantial Irish, black or unskilled working class community" (Livingstone 1983: 27). As *London Labour Briefing* reported after the GLC elections in 1981, London's

Black and ethnic minority voters had turned out in consistently higher numbers than white voters and produced swings to Labour in Hornsey and Brent South (Amory 1981; Grant 1981).

The GLC took a notoriously antagonistic approach to the Thatcher government: located directly across the Thames from the Palace of Westminster at County Hall, it famously emblazoned London's unemployment figures on its façade in a conspicuous visual protest against the Conservative government across the river. Perhaps unsurprisingly, then, the GLC, and other local authorities across the UK, were key targets for the Thatcher government, which was driven by deep political hostility to the actions of activist councils. As Thatcher put it in 1988:

> we cannot allow anti-enterprise, spendthrift, irrelevant local government to condemn urban areas to deprivation for which the government is then blamed. The attachment of some local authorities to high rates, gay rights, Nicaragua and nuclear free zones does not offer much hope to their residents. (Thatcher 1988)

In the early 1980s the GLC, along with other left-dominated councils across Britain, began to face a sustained media attack and existential threats from the Conservative government in Westminster (Wise 1981). In 1981 Michael Heseltine, the secretary of state for the environment, proposed reforming local government financing to put cash limits on local authority spending, shifting the balance of rate-paying from industrial and commercial sources towards domestic rate-payers, subjecting councils to referenda on taxation that exceeded government limits, and ultimately increasing government oversight over local authority spending (Knight 1981). Between 1979 and 1986 the Thatcher government actually increased spending on the Urban Programme, a programme to help tackle the causes of social deprivation in urban and often immigrant-rich areas set up by the Wilson Labour government in 1968. But it did so while also significantly defunding local authorities: in 1980–81 and 1983–84, cuts to local authority housing schemes amounted to 75 per cent of the government's overall reductions in spending (Murie 1989). And, in an act of political retaliation against the oppositional left politics of municipal governments across the UK, the Conservative government passed the Local Government Act in 1985, which abolished the GLC as well as a number of other municipal councils and privatized County Hall. In 1986 the Thatcher government deregulated the City of London through the "Big Bang", and subsequently introduced an "enterprise zone" with reduced taxes and regulations in the former industrial area of the London docklands. Thatcher's hostility to local councils set the stage for the policy which would lead to her political downfall, the "community charge" or "poll tax" to fund local authority spending. At the heart of the Thatcherite political project was an explicit attack on local authorities (Saumarez Smith 2020). This was also an attack on the municipal socialist movements and left-wing activist coalitions that had embraced local politics, often as an alternative to the parliamentary Labour Party, since the 1970s.

## Jeremy Corbyn and London politics in the 1980s

Jeremy Corbyn's early career as a professional politician was closely intertwined with Livingstone's GLC and the "new urban left" of 1970s and 1980s London. Corbyn had first joined the Labour Party in 1966, optimistic, at the time, about Harold Wilson's leadership, but he soon became disillusioned by the prime minister's accommodationist stance to the United States' war in Vietnam (Wainwright 1987b: 2–3). After a period spent travelling and working in Jamaica and Latin America, he moved to London in 1973 for a course in Trade Union Studies at the Polytechnic of North London, and swiftly joined the Hornsey CLP, becoming chair of its Young Socialists, a key organizer for the local Labour Party and, from 1978, a Haringey councillor. He became a research assistant for the National Union of Tailor and Garment Workers, which represented the tailors in London's East End, then a trade in decline, and in 1975 he became an organizer for the National Union of Public Employees (NUPE), representing the employees of the Inner London Education Authority (Wainwright 1987b: 2).

During his work with NUPE during the "Winter of Discontent" in 1978 and 1979 Corbyn became acquainted with Tony Benn. He supported Benn's campaign for deputy leader of the Labour Party in 1981, although NUPE's votes went to Benn's opponent Denis Healey (Prince 2016). Corbyn became a key ally to Ken Livingstone in his seizure of the GLC leadership in 1981, and a contributor to *London Labour Briefing*, a left-wing newspaper derided by Margaret Thatcher for "encouraging anarchy", which championed Livingstone's GLC, Labour councils and Tony Benn's Alternative Economic Strategy and deputy leadership campaign (Bash 1981).

In 1983 Corbyn was selected as the Labour candidate for Islington North. Corbyn's selection and subsequent election to parliament were the result of a power vacuum created by the defection of several prominent Islington politicians for the Social Democratic Party. The constituency had been represented by the Irish Catholic Labour MP Michael O'Halloran since 1969. O'Halloran, a Catholic and social conservative, spoke infrequently in parliament and was unpopular with local activists. Both O'Halloran and John Grant, the MP for Islington Central, defected to the Social Democratic Party (SDP) before the 1983 election. But when Islington Central was abolished as a result of boundary changes, and Grant was selected as the SDP candidate for Islington North, O'Halloran was forced to run as an independent. In a four-way race against both O'Halloran and Grant, who was supported by the president of the Trades Union Council Frank Chapple, Corbyn, the Labour candidate, won by a majority of 5,607 (Carvel 1983; Prince 2016).

While Islington, today, has become almost a pejorative shorthand for the London metropolitan elite, it was a predominantly working-class and ethnically diverse area in 1983, with only about 20 per cent owner occupation (Carvel 1983: 2). It had also been an important battleground for the municipal left in London. Corbyn's election as MP for Islington North in 1983 followed a gradual increase in strength for the left of the Labour Group in Islington Council. The Islington Council was briefly the only council in Britain controlled by the Social Democratic Party, until SDP candidates were annihilated in the local elections of 1982, and 51 out of 52 seats were won by Labour councillors (*Daily Mail* 1982a). In the early 1980s North Islington Council recruited new members on a platform which included "a radical line on Ireland" and opposition to cuts to council services. The election of Livingstone ally Steve Bundred as GLC councillor for Islington North had caused 16 more establishment Labour candidates to defect to the SDP, and allowed the Labour left to consolidate their position within the local council (Finch 1981; Veness 1981). The council, which was led by Margaret Hodge (who would later become one of Corbyn's fiercest critics over antisemitism), was vilified in the press for flying the Red Flag and the CND's Ban the Bomb flag over Islington Town Hall, establishing a watchdog group to monitor discrimination against gays and lesbians, and telling the mayor of Islington to swap his luxury car for a taxi (*Daily Mail* 1982b–e). Portrayed as the apex of the "loony left", the radicalism of the Islington Council would be a key target in Conservative candidates' attempts to discredit Labour in the 1983 election.

Corbyn's maiden speech to the House of Commons was a strident defence of the local authority in his own constituency against attacks by the media and the government's cuts to local authority spending. "Islington North is only a few miles from the House by tube or bus", Corbyn said, but Westminster seemed "[a] million miles away" from the constituency's "massive unemployment and massive cuts imposed by the Government on the local authorities". He cited a decline in rate support for the borough from £55 to £32 million, high unemployment (he estimated the cumulative unemployment rate between Hackney, Waltham Forest and Enfield to be 20 per cent), and thoughtless urban planning decisions that had resulted in motorway traffic cutting through swathes of the borough en route to the Channel ports that had gradually replaced the London docks since the 1960s. He berated the government for huge cuts to the health service in his constituency, resulting in the closure of multiple hospitals. Corbyn's speech was also, importantly, a defence of the GLC itself, which was already facing threats of abolition from the Thatcher government: "It is clear", Corbyn said, "that the Government are determined to take away all democratic rights of local government in London. They tried to destroy our borough councils. Now they seek to destroy the GLC" (Corbyn 1983).

Corbyn's sense of his purpose as an MP was informed by his political formation in the Haringey CLP and his close links to the GLC. He also shared the same concern about deindustrialization, and the need for the Labour Party to adapt as a political movement in the face of it, that informed Livingstone's political project. In an interview with Hilary Wainwright in 1987 he reflected on the Labour Party's historical role as the political arm of the trade union movement, and the inadequacy of that model for contemporary politics, reflecting that if the party were recreated for the 1980s it would not be "made up of local branches, the Fabian Society, co-ops and the trade unions". Corbyn didn't propose abandoning those institutional pillars of the party: "we'd certainly include those", he said – but he suggested that the party's institutional base should reach "far, far wider", and seek to engage with ethnic minority organizations in particular (Wainwright 1987b: 5). Corbyn also reflected on how the work of being an MP required an awareness of the limitations of what could be achieved either through parliament or through representation in the workplace: he described how as an MP he sought to represent "the issues of the community as a whole", including the unemployed, social security claimants and ethnic minority groups, whose concerns were less directly represented by trade unions (*ibid.*: 4). Corbyn imagined the role of Labour Party MPs and constituency organizers as "activators" rather than "reactors", organizing around the needs of the community rather than acting as "an election machine" (*ibid.*: 5).

For Jeremy Corbyn in 1987, the traditional role of the Labour Party, as the voice of a left-wing coalition of social reformers, socialists and the labour movement in parliament, failed to reflect or represent the rapidly changing demographics of post-industrial Britain. A modernized Labour socialism, he suggested, needed to be based on a more diverse coalition of community groups and social movements, and grounded in local activism. Corbyn's politics have always been highly motivated by his foreign policy commitments, including CND, opposition to apartheid in South Africa, and support for the republican movement in Ireland and liberation movements in South America and Palestine. But the focus of Corbyn's activism during his many years as a backbench MP was on representing, organizing and mobilizing different interest groups in his community and constituency in North London, inspired by and committed to the same vision of urban socialist renewal rooted in a coalition of activists, minority groups and public sector unions that inspired the GLC and the "new urban left" of the 1970s and 1980s.

## Conclusion

Jeremy Corbyn, and the faction of the Labour Party that he has represented in parliament since 1983, should be understood not just as representing the left of the party, but the "urban left". His politics were forged not only in battles between moderates and reformers within the Labour Party, but in reaction to the Thatcher government's hostile attack on left-wing local authorities and the GLC in the early 1980s, and were inspired by a vision of socialist renewal in urban centres.

Livingstone and his allies' idealistic vision of a modern urban socialist coalition rooted in the metropolitan, racially diverse communities of places like London and Sheffield did not prevail. In the late 1980s the Labour Party increasingly turned towards political methodologies based on polling and focus groups, which revealed high rates of distrust for the "loony left" and moved the party towards recapturing "lost skilled working class voters in the South and the Midlands" (Murphy 2020b). And as Gyford acknowledged in 1983, an urban socialist coalition was not an easy recipe for electoral success: when American presidential candidate George McGovern had tried to use the Democratic Party's reformed constitution to build a political coalition of "the young, the black and the poor" in 1972, it had led to "the defection of blue collar and trade union voters, alienated by the style as much as by the substance of the new politics" (Gyford 1983: 92). Indeed, the results of recent UK elections suggest the Labour Party cannot hope to win political power without building a broad coalition across metropolitan and non-metropolitan voters.

However, popular portrayals of Corbynism as a backward-looking political project centred on a 1970s era politics of trade union militancy are inaccurate. The municipal socialism of the 1970s and 1980s represented not a regressive force, but a genuine attempt to build new coalitions, and integrate a broad range of social movements and interest groups into a coherent socialist project. The Left in the 1970s and 1980s held an idealistic vision of cities as a place where new solidarities could be forged which would free the Labour Party, and the Left more generally, from the stultifying domination of trade unions and the limitations of parliamentary democracy. Taking account of the centrality of local politics to the Left of the 1980s supports an important challenge in modern British history to the dominant account of the decade as characterized by a political contest between a Thatcherite embrace of individualism and a Left committed to corporatism, state control and trade union representation. And it shows that the conflicts we continue to see in the Labour Party today – between "Labour heartlands" and "metropolitan elites" – have their origins in competing visions of the future of British socialism in the 1970s and 1980s.

# References

Abrams, M. & R. Rose 1960. *Must Labour Lose?* Harmondsworth: Penguin.

Ackers, P. & A. Reid 2016. *Alternatives to State Socialism in Britain: Other Worlds of Labour in the Twentieth Century*. Basingstoke: Palgrave Macmillan.

Amory, M. 1981. "Black/left alliance strengthened in Brent". *London Labour Briefing* 11: 3.

Bash, G. 1981. "A reply to Thatcher". *London Labour Briefing* 12 (July): 6 .

Boddy, M. & C. Fudge (eds) 1984. *Local Socialism: Labour Councils and New Left Alternatives*. London: Macmillan.

Bower, T. 2018. *Dangerous Hero: Corbyn's Ruthless Plot for Power*. London: Harper Collins.

Campsie, A. 2017. "'Socialism will never be the same again': re-imagining British left-wing ideas for the 'New Times'". *Contemporary British History* 31: 166–88.

Carvel, J. 1983. "Dividing Labour loyalties by five adds up to confusion for voters". *The Guardian*, 1 June.

Corbyn, J. 1983. Maiden speech to House of Commons. 1 July. http://www.ukpol.co.uk/jeremy-corbyn-1983-maiden-speech-in-the-house-of-commons/ (accessed 18 March 2021).

Crosland, A. 1956. *The Future of Socialism*. London: Jonathan Cape.

*Daily Mail* 1982a. "The massacre of Islington". *Daily Mail*, 8 May.

*Daily Mail* 1982b. "SDP fury as Labour starts a 'revolution' under the red flag". *Daily Mail*, 15 May.

*Daily Mail* 1982c. "Left flies more flags". *Daily Mail*, 28 August.

*Daily Mail* 1982d. "Gays get watchdog on the rates". *Daily Mail*, 12 October.

*Daily Mail* 1982e. "Labour mayor is told to cut out the frills". *Daily Mail*, 18 December.

Finch, N. 1981. "The left grows up in Islington". *London Labour Briefing* 13: 3.

Garland, N. "'Socialism is much too important to be left to Labour governments': The Greater London Council, the new urban left and the idea of democracy, 1981–6". Unpublished.

Grant, B. 1981. "Getting the blacks in …". *London Labour Briefing* 12: 18.

Gyford, J. 1983. "The new urban left: a local road to socialism?". *New Society*, 21 April: 91–3.

Hatherley, O. 2020. *Red Metropolis: Socialism and the Government of London*. London: Repeater Books.

Hobsbawm, E. 1978. "The forward march of Labour halted". *Marxism Today* 22(9): 279–86.

Kelliher, D. 2014. "Solidarity and sexuality: lesbians and gays support the miners, 1984–5". *History Workshop Journal* 77(1): 240–62.

Knight, T. 1981. "Our greatest challenge". *London Labour Briefing* 16: 1–2.

Livingstone, K. 1983. "Monetarism in London". *New Left Review* 137(January–February): 68–77.

Livingstone, K. 1983. "Why Labour lost". *New Left Review* 140(July–August): 23–39.

Murie, A. 1989. "Housing and the environment". In D. Kavanagh & A. Seldon (eds), *The Thatcher Effect: A Decade of Change*, 213–25. Oxford: Oxford University Press.

Murphy, C. 2020a. "Futures of socialism: 'modernization' and 'modernity' on the British left, 1973–1997". PhD Thesis, Queen Mary, University of London.

Murphy, C. 2020b. "The rainbow alliance or the focus group: sexuality and race in the Labour Party's electoral strategy, 1985–7". *Twentieth Century British History* 31(3): 291–315.

Nunns, A. 2018. *The Candidate: Jeremy Corbyn's Improbable Path to Power*. London: OR Books.

Perryman, M. (ed.) 2017. *The Corbyn Effect*. London: Lawrence & Wishart.

Prince, R. 2016. *Comrade Corbyn*. London: Biteback.

Robinson, E. *et al.* 2017. "Telling stories about post-war Britain: popular individualism and the 'crisis' of the 1970s". *Twentieth Century British History* 28(2): 268–304.

Robinson, L. 2008. *Gay Men and the Left in Post-War Britain: How the Personal Got Political*. Manchester: Manchester University Press.

Rowbotham, S., L. Segal & H. Wainwright 1978. *Beyond the Fragments: Feminism and the Making of Socialism*. London: Islington Community Press.

Saumarez Smith, O. 2020. "Action for cities: the Thatcher government and inner-city policy". *Urban History* 47(special issue 2): 274–91.

Shock, M. 2020. "'To address ourselves 'violently' towards the present as it is': Stuart Hall, *Marxism Today* and their reception of Antonio Gramsci in the long 1980s". *Contemporary British History* 34(2): 251–72.

Thatcher, M. 1988. "Inner cities launch – presentation". 6 March. The National Archives, Prime Ministerial Private Office files 19/2465.

Veness V. 1981. "SDP score own goal". *London Labour Briefing* 14: 2.

Wainwright, H. 1987a. *Labour: A Tale of Two Parties.* London: Hogarth Press.

Wainwright, H. 1987b. *Labour Party Tapes.* Jeremy Corbyn and Liz Philipson interviewed by Hilary Wainwright. British Library C818/10.

Wise, V. 1981. "As media onslaught mounts: DEFEND THE GLC!" *London Labour Briefing* 14: 1.

11

# LABOUR UNDER CORBYN: ZIGZAGGING TOWARDS BREXIT

*Eunice Goes*

The 2016 referendum on membership of the European Union revealed a Britain fractured along generational, educational, class and regional lines. These cleavages presented substantial electoral problems to the main political parties, but for Labour they also posed an existential challenge.

This chapter explains how the Labour Party led by Jeremy Corbyn responded to these electoral and political challenges and will argue that the party's slow and erratic process of developing a policy that responded to the results of the 2016 referendum and to the tortuous process of withdrawing from the EU contributed to the party's disastrous results at the 2019 general election. In addition, the chapter will argue that the difficult process of agreeing to a "Brexit policy" exposed Labour's divisions and its existential and ideological crisis that had been brewing for the previous two decades.

Three key dilemmas explain Labour's slow, erratic and ultimately unclear response to Britain's decision to leave the EU: (1) the leader's ideological stances and statecraft; (2) electoral considerations; and (3) party cohesion. Seen in this light, Labour's slow response to these dramatic events reflects the challenges faced by power-seeking political parties that need to trade off permanently the not always compatible goals of promoting an ideology, winning elections, maintaining organizational cohesion and ensuring the survival of the party (Panebianco 1988; Harmel & Janda 1994: 248; Berman 2006: 11).

This trilemma was manifested in Labour's response to Brexit. If Corbyn's left-wing Euroscepticism informed most of his slow and indecisive responses to the various challenges the party faced, Brexit also presented Labour with electoral and ideological dilemmas. With an overwhelmingly pro-Remain membership, Labour was becoming a party of the young, educated, urban and cosmopolitan middle classes and was, as a result, more distant from its working-class historical electoral base, which was concerned with immigration and tended to gravitate towards socially conservative values. This diverse but divided electoral base was bluntly expressed in Labour's political geography: 70 per cent of Labour-held seats represented Leave areas (Hanretty 2016). The challenge the party faced was to develop an approach to the Brexit question that could be supported by these two broad sets of voters who held distinctive, if not contradictory, sets of values and priorities.

To show how this trilemma shaped Labour's response to the Brexit question, this chapter will examine the evolution of the party's stance on EU membership from the early days of Corbyn's leadership until the 2019 general election, and it will start by contextualizing Labour's approach to the project of European integration.

## Labour and Europe

For most of Labour's history, the project of European integration did not inspire much Europhilia or interest in the Labour benches and was generally treated as a distraction from the mission of implementing socialism in Britain (Hickson & Miles 2018: 864). In the postwar period Labour politicians tended to view Britain's participation in the European project as, in the memorable words of Hugh Gaitskell, the "end of a thousand years of history" (1962). As Roger Liddle vividly explained, "the roots of Labour's Euroscepticism owe much to two myths: beliefs in both a commitment to a nation state social democracy and in Britain's unique capacity for moral leadership in the world" (2014: 18).

It was only from the 1980s onwards that Labour fully embraced the European project, but even then, its pro-Europeanism was qualified. That is to say, Labour's pro-Europeanism was more about signalling the party's shift to the centre ground of politics than a wholehearted endorsement of the European project (Heffernan 2001: 185). Labour remained, as Richard Heffernan puts it, " 'British' first and 'European' second" (*ibid.*: 188). For Oliver Daddow, the consequence of this stance was that Labour leaders, in particular during the New Labour era, were always more comfortable at "elucidating what they did not stand for on Europe than what they did" (2011: 159). In addition, New Labour leaders also liked to lecture Europe about how they should reform to become more like Britain, and to complain loudly about the EU's shortcomings.

This detached and critical approach to the European project has shaped Labour's policies and attitudes to the EU since the 1990s. For example, in 2008, Prime Minister Gordon Brown was the only EU leader who missed the signing ceremony of the Lisbon Treaty because he did not want to publicize an important moment in the project of European integration. Brown's successor Ed Miliband was less embarrassed about his pro-Europeanism, but reverted to Labour's classic ambivalent approach to the EU when he promised immigration controls in response to voters' concerns about the free movement of EU citizens (Goes 2016: 158).

Labour's embarrassment about Europe was again on display during the 2015 Labour leadership election. In this period, the party changed its stance on the referendum on EU membership, which had been promised by the Conservative government. During Miliband's leadership, Labour had opposed the idea of holding the referendum, but under the temporary stewardship of Harriet Harman the party agreed to support the referendum and the prime minister's negotiating strategy with the EU. This policy change was informed by the party's interpretation of its disastrous electoral results at the 2015 general election. Harman and others felt that Labour's support for the EU had led to electoral losses in seats in the Midlands and Northeast of England, where voters expressed concerns about immigration.

Europe was barely discussed by the different candidates to the leadership in the several hustings organized by the Labour Party; however, Corbyn's stance contrasted with those of his competitors. As David Kogan put it, "Corbyn came from the wing of the left that had always regarded Europe as a capitalist project designed to unify the forces of capital and business in a much larger market" (2019: 269). Reflecting this view, Corbyn voted to leave the then European Communities in the 1975 referendum, and his record as a parliamentarian shows he voted against most European legislation, including the Maastricht and Lisbon Treaties. It is therefore not surprising that he was the only candidate for Labour's leadership who did not rule out voting to leave the EU (Shipman 2017: 73).

Corbyn's unexpected election to the leadership of the Labour Party in September 2015 catapulted him to the centre stage of British politics. Learning the ropes of how to be the leader of the opposition, dealing with a hostile PLP (see Crines, Jeffery & Heppell 2018) and an even more unfriendly media absorbed most of Corbyn's energy in the early months of his leadership (Goes 2018: 61–3). In these challenging circumstances, he had very little time to think about Britain's relationship with the EU, although it is also true that throughout his parliamentary career he had shown little interest in European affairs. In reality, he was encouraged by his team to keep quiet about Europe until Prime Minister David Cameron came back from Brussels with a deal (Shipman 2017: 75). But Corbyn's quiet response to Europe extended beyond this period. For most of the tortuous process of withdrawal from the EU, he was a bystander in the national debate about Britain's most important foreign policy decision of the postwar era; he reacted to events, instead of trying to influence them.

Nonetheless, at his first annual conference as Labour leader Corbyn bowed to the pressure coming from the PLP and trade unions and announced that the party "would stand up for the vision of a social Europe, a Europe of unity and solidarity" (Corbyn 2015). This statement was not the enthusiastic promotion of

EUNICE GOES

the European project that some Labour supporters expected, but at least it was a statement of support for a socialist vision of Europe, which reflected the views of most party members and activists.

## Corbyn and the referendum campaign

While Corbyn's attention was focused on internal Labour politics, the prime minister negotiated new terms of membership with the EU and announced the date of the referendum. When the announcement was made in February 2016, Corbyn contributed little to the debate apart from attacking Cameron's nego-tiating strategy (Corbyn 2016a), and announcing that Labour would be "cam-paigning to keep Britain in Europe in the coming referendum" because "it brings investment, jobs and protection for British workers and consumers" (*ibid.*).

But Corbyn's commitment to Britain's continued membership of the EU was soon questioned. Labour backbenchers and activists as well as Remain campaigners attacked Corbyn's low-key and lukewarm participation in the ref-erendum campaign. To start with, Corbyn and his team refused to plan the referendum campaign until after the local elections of April 2016. When he finally started to campaign, his lack of enthusiasm was notorious. In a much-discussed BBC interview, Corbyn said he was "seven out of ten passionate about the European Union" (Corbyn 2016c). Moreover, it was widely known that his advisers deleted pro-European excerpts from his speeches, and as a result they tended to focus on workers' rights and on the shortcomings of the EU (Corbyn 2016b). More seriously, Corbyn's staff was accused by the chair of the Labour In For Britain campaign, of sabotaging the party's Remain campaign (Wilson 2016).

But if Corbyn's critique of the EU was shared by many other European social democrats, it was not considered to be helpful in the context of a divisive refer-endum, when voters needed to be persuaded of the benefits of EU membership (Shipman 2017: 345). The only European issue that enthused him – freedom of movement – was the most difficult and unpopular one to campaign for on the doorstep. He also refused to appear alongside David Cameron at a Remain campaign event, although he was told that his presence would be an effective tool to persuade Labour voters to vote Remain (Evans & Menon 2017: 66). What informed this decision was the understanding that Labour's involvement in the Better Together campaign in Scotland was the main reason why the party lost most of its Scottish seats at the 2015 general election (Shipman 2017: 74). But Corbyn also refused to appear alongside former Labour leaders, mostly because he did not want to share a platform with the former prime minister, Tony Blair (Evans & Menon 2017: 67). Faced with Corbyn's lacklustre campaign, several past Labour leaders wrote a letter in *The Guardian*, where they asked Labour

166

supporters to vote Remain because "Labour's values are inherent in Europe's virtues" (Kinnock *et al.* 2016).

The critics of Corbyn's campaign strategy not only came from the party's right or centre. Pro-Corbyn activists close to the grassroots movement Momentum felt that Labour needed to develop a different, more positive and dynamic campaign, which would emphasize the benefits of EU membership and of freedom of movement (Kogan 2019: 379). A sign of that discontent was the emergence of the group Another Europe is Possible (AEIP), which was launched by Momentum's treasurer Michael Chessum. In the hope of galvanizing the Labour vote, AEIP organized a very large event – the largest of the Remain campaign – that included the participation of John McDonnell, Clive Lewis and other left-wing politicians like the Green MP Caroline Lucas and the commentator and activist Owen Jones. The event was well attended but Corbyn's absence was duly noted.

However, Corbyn's ambivalence about the EU was not the only problem. The PLP was also divided over Brexit. There were frontbenchers and backbenchers who had reservations about the EU and in particular about the principle of freedom of movement for EU citizens. During Miliband's leadership, frontbenchers like Yvette Cooper and Rachel Reeves, and other backbenchers and activists associated with the group Blue Labour, defended restrictions to the EU's freedom of movement as well as new immigration controls. These issues continued to divide the party, the PLP and the shadow cabinet during and after the 2016 referendum.

The combination of Corbyn's ambivalence and Labour's divisions affected the referendum's result. Corbyn's lack of enthusiasm and visibility in the campaign meant that many voters were unsure about Labour's position on the referendum (Cowley & Kavanagh 2018: 83). This being said, two-thirds of Labour voters voted Remain, including in areas that voted overwhelmingly to leave the EU (Fieldhouse 2019).

## Post-referendum blues

Labour Remainers were quick to blame Jeremy Corbyn for the result of the referendum. At the Pride march in London, an activist confronted Corbyn and blamed him for the result. His response of "I did all I could" was unconvincing (Stewart 2016). It did not help that on the day after the referendum he called for the immediate triggering of Article 50 (Pine 2016). The perception that Corbyn was responsible for the result of the referendum "set in train multiple attempts to unseat" the Labour leader (Cowley & Kavanagh 2018: 45). In a matter of days, 20 members of the shadow cabinet resigned while the PLP launched a motion of no confidence against the leader. Despite losing that motion of no confidence by 172 to 40, Corbyn refused to budge.

The PLP realized then that the only way to unseat Corbyn was through a leadership challenge. With that goal in mind, Angela Eagle announced in early July that she was standing against Corbyn in a formal leadership contest. She eventually pulled out of the race when the MP for Pontypridd, Owen Smith announced he was a candidate for the leadership of the party. Roughly two months later, Corbyn emerged as the winner of that contest with a bigger majority than in 2015.

These internal party manoeuvres meant that Labour did not have time to develop a Brexit policy, beyond its commitment to respect the referendum's results. In his speech to the party conference in Liverpool, Corbyn advised party members to refrain from "patronising and lecturing those in our communities who voted leave" and to accept "the decision of the British people". He then pivoted to announce that Labour could negotiate a "better Britain out of Brexit" (Corbyn 2016d).

To the dismay of Labour Remainers and to the delight of pro-Leave MPs, he also said that Labour was "not wedded to freedom of movement for EU citizens as a point of principle" and that voters' concerns with immigration "should be addressed" (Corbyn 2017a). Interestingly Corbyn's position was shared by all the shadow cabinet and by a majority of Labour MPs. Even the shadow Brexit secretary Keir Starmer, who later became associated with the Remain cause, argued that Labour had to accept Brexit (Pogrund & Maguire 2020: 128).

Corbyn's positioning was informed by polling analysis, which showed that Brexit was shaping voting behaviour across the country, and crucially in the many marginal seats in the Midlands and in the Northeast of England that the party needed to retain. The leader's office was particularly concerned with the possibility of losing the seats of Copeland and Stoke-on-Trent in forthcoming by-elections (Bush 2017). His team was also acutely aware that most Labour seats were located in Leave areas, although only ten of them were represented by pro-Leave MPs (Evans & Menon 2017: 104).

In the meantime, Prime Minister Theresa May had already ruled out membership of the Single Market and was preparing to trigger Article 50, a move that would officially start the process of Britain's withdrawal from the EU. This created problems for Labour, as the option of a soft Brexit, which implied membership of the Single Market, was no longer on the table. Unable to shape the terms of Britain's future relationship with the EU and aware of immediate electoral challenges, Corbyn was more sensitive to the pressure coming from backbenchers who represented Leave constituencies, and he therefore imposed a three-line whip on the PLP to vote in favour of triggering Article 50 (Stewart & Mason 2017).

In an attempt to convince Labour Remainers to accept the argument that supporting the triggering of Article 50 did not amount to endorsing May's deal with the EU, he guaranteed that the party would "use every means at our disposal to make sure jobs, living standards, workers' rights and environmental protections are protected in the negotiations that follow" (Corbyn quoted by Brinded 2017; see also Corbyn 2017b). To help distinguish Labour's stance from the one defended by the government, the shadow Brexit secretary Keir Starmer announced six tests for Labour to support any Brexit deal (Starmer 2017a).[1]

Although not all members of the shadow cabinet supported Starmer's "six tests" (Pogrund & Maguire 2020: 69), they allowed Labour to present what it defined as "constructive ambiguity" about Brexit at the 2017 general election. The party's manifesto *For the Many Not the Few* specified that Labour accepted the referendum result and promised that a Labour government "would build a close relationship with the EU, protect workers' rights and environmental standards" (Labour Party 2017: 24).

The manifesto also committed the party to negotiating a new trade deal with the EU "that puts jobs and the economy first" (*ibid.*: 14), which implied access to the Single Market. However, the manifesto also stated that "freedom of movement will end when we leave the EU". In its place, Labour proposed a "reasonable management of migration" (*ibid.*: 28). To some extent, Labour's manifesto declared the desire to have an "à la carte" relationship with the EU, although it was unlikely that Britain's European partners would ever agree to it.

But if Labour's approach raised important questions about its feasibility, in electoral terms the party's "constructive ambiguity" on Brexit proved to be astute. At this election, Labour obtained a 40 per cent share of the vote and elected 262 MPs, the party's best result since 2001. As Mellon *et al.* showed, "Labour managed to claim voters from both the Leave and Remain side in substantial numbers, but particularly among respondents who had said 'don't know' prior to the general election campaign" (2018: 735). In particular, Labour benefitted from a swing across Remain areas, which proved to be sufficient to overturn huge Conservative majorities in Battersea, Kensington, Canterbury and Enfield Southgate and which was also able to retain seats in Leave areas

---

1. Those tests were: (1) Does it ensure a strong and collaborative future relationship with the EU?; (2) Does it deliver the "exact same benefits" as we currently have as members of the Single Market and Customs Union?; (3) Does it ensure the fair management of migration in the interests of the economy and communities?; (4) Does it defend rights and protections and prevent a race to the bottom?; (5) Does it protect national security and our capacity to tackle cross-border crime?; (6) Does it deliver for all regions and nations of the UK? Keir Starmer, "What next for Britain?", Chatham House, 27 March 2017. https://www.chathamhouse.org/sites/default/files/events/2017-03-27-StarmerPREP.pdf (accessed 19 March 2021).

(Evans & Menon 2017: 102–3), perhaps because the party promised to respect the results of the referendum.

## The slow march of Labour Remainers

The results of the 2017 general election led to a slow evolution in Labour's Brexit position. The party's leadership knew that most of the electoral advances had been led by the rise of the youth vote in Remain constituencies, but Corbyn and his team were still committed to respecting the results of the 2016 referendum. This stance would imply that the party would abstain on votes calling for Britain to remain within the Customs Union and the Single Market.[2]

But for pro-Remain groups like Another Europe is Possible, Open Britain and Best for Britain, the electoral results showed that Labour had to change policy. For instance, Michael Chessum from AEIP explained that the Labour's 2017 results "opened a window of opportunity" to force Labour to support a second referendum on EU membership.[3] At this time, it was clear that most Labour members and voters supported proposals to hold a second referendum on EU membership. Research conducted by Bale, Webb and Poletti showed that 86.3 per cent of Labour Party members were in favour of a second referendum on a final deal, and 92 per cent defended Britain's membership of the Single Market (2020: 66).

There was also movement within the shadow cabinet. By the end of August 2017, Keir Starmer started to push for a time-limited transitional period following Britain's withdrawal from the EU. In an article published in *The Observer*, he revealed that Labour would support membership of the Single Market and Customs Union in a transitional period after March 2019, the date when Britain was expected to leave the EU (Starmer 2017b). Crucially, he hinted that the party might support membership of the two on a permanent basis. "Remaining in a form of customs union with the EU is a possible end destination for Labour", he wrote.

However, Starmer's efforts to move the party into a more pro-European direction were blocked by Corbyn's office and by the leadership of Momentum, who did not allow Brexit to be discussed at the 2017 annual party conference. This decision reflected the pressure raised by MPs who represented Leave constituencies and Corbyn's office's scepticism towards the project of European integration. According to the testimony of a senior Labour figure who attended shadow

---

2. In June, 49 Labour MPs defied the whip and voted for the amendment calling for Britain to remain in the Customs Union and Single Market.
3. Michael Chessum, Director of Another Europe is Possible, private interview, 17 September 2019.

cabinet meetings, figures like Seumas Milne wanted to keep a balance on Brexit between Leave and Remain supporters.[4] Despite this, Starmer made a speech in which he advocated for a withdrawal deal with the EU that retained the benefits of a customs union (2017c).

As a no-deal Brexit was being discussed as a viable and desirable option in Conservative circles, Labour started to change its stance. McDonnell started to voice his concerns about the economic consequences of Brexit and by December 2017 Corbyn had agreed that Britain should remain in the Customs Union indefinitely.[5] However, despite this open change of mind, Corbyn let his office draft Brexit policy that ignored the input of the shadow Brexit secretary (Pogrund & Maguire 2020: 71–2). Following some angry exchanges at shadow cabinet meetings, by February 2018 Labour's leadership was openly committed to the direction suggested by Keir Starmer the previous summer.

The party's new position aimed to prepare the ground to defeat in parliament the withdrawal agreement negotiated by May. In a speech delivered in Coventry, Corbyn said that Labour would seek a "bespoke agreement" that would retain most of the advantages of EU membership and would defend membership of the Customs Union and Single Market during the transition period. He also announced that freedom of movement would end with Britain's withdrawal from the EU, but in rather nebulous terms he claimed that "Labour would negotiate a new and strong relationship with the Single Market that included full tariff-free access and a floor under existing rights, standards and protections" (Corbyn 2018a).[6]

Labour's new position represented a significant shift. However, the fact that the "new and strong relationship" with the EU fell short of membership of the Single Market suggested that Corbyn was trying to find a compromise for Labour's internal divisions, in particular regarding immigration policy and freedom of movement. Although the Labour leader was a staunch supporter of immigration, many MPs representing Leave constituencies and several powerful trade unions (notably Unite and the GMB) opposed the principle of freedom of movement for EU citizens.

The speech also contained some interesting Eurosceptic lines, which showed that concerns with party unity and electoral prospects were not the only factors influencing his approach to Brexit. Corbyn was explicit about the areas where he

---

4. Written testimony of senior Labour figure.
5. Written testimony of senior Labour figure.
6. Starmer wanted to avoid a "Norway deal", which involved membership of the Customs Union and Single Market. He considered such a deal disadvantageous because Britain would become a "rule-taker" instead of a "rule-maker". He had specific concerns about the impact of a Norway-style deal on Britain's agricultural sector, immigration policy and Northern Ireland.

would like Britain to diverge from the EU. The main target of his attack was the European Court of Justice, whose authority over competition law and state aid rules was seen by Corbyn's advisers as a threat to Labour's plans to nationalize utilities and invest in the economy (Kogan 2019: 387). This reasoning informed the May 2018 decision to ask Labour peers to abstain on the votes associated with the EU Withdrawal Agreement bill, namely on the vote to keep Britain in the European Economic Area.[7]

While Corbyn's allies were concentrating on finessing Labour's position on Brexit, pro-Remain advocates manoeuvred to use the collapse of the prime minister's Chequers Plan (at the summit in Salzburg in the summer of 2018) to force Labour to endorse the campaign for a second referendum on EU membership. Groups like AEIP, For Future's Sake, Our Future Our Choice, Labour for a People's Vote and several trade unions sensed that public opinion was softening around Brexit. A survey conducted by NatCen revealed that 60 per cent of voters believed that Britain should allow freedom of movement from the EU (Curtice 2018). Signs of that growing impatience were the 151 motions (out of 272) submitted by the constituency parties to Labour's annual conference asking for a second referendum on Britain's future relationship with the EU.

Corbyn resisted the pressure coming from the grassroots of the labour movement, and in his speech McDonnell insisted that a new referendum would not offer an option to vote Remain, but in an unscripted moment Starmer told delegates that "no one is ruling out Remain as an option". This spontaneous ad-libbing,[8] which was greeted by massive applause by the delegates, was immediately attacked and dismissed by Unite's leader Len McCluskey and by Corbyn's office.

In November, several polls showed that there was growing popular support for a second referendum. Moreover, Momentum members were supportive of a second referendum and 92 per cent wanted all Labour MPs to vote against May's Brexit deal if it did not meet Labour's six tests (Schofield 2018). By late November, Labour seemed to be succumbing to this pressure. McDonnell said that if Labour failed to force a general election, the party would "inevitably" support a second referendum (Elgot & Stewart 2018). Interestingly, Corbyn did not second McDonnell's comments and in an interview with a German magazine he said that "we can't stop Brexit" (Schindler 2018).

---

7. Despite Corbyn's request, 83 peers voted for the amendment. When the bill came back to the House of Commons, the Labour line was to abstain, but 74 backbenchers challenged the whip.
8. Starmer was not a natural Remainer. He had accepted the referendum results and was committed to negotiating a Brexit deal, but with time he changed his mind and started to gradually convince Corbyn of the need to accept a second referendum on EU membership (Pogrund & Maguire 2020: 136–8).

The tension between Corbyn and McDonnell was personal and reflected different approaches to Labour's electoral strategy, but they also suggested divisions in the shadow cabinet and in the PLP about Brexit. In the shadow cabinet, figures like Starmer, Emily Thornberry and Tom Watson argued for a second referendum, whereas frontbenchers like Angela Rayner, Ian Lavery and Richard Burgon resisted such proposals and insisted that Labour had to respect the results of the 2016 referendum. Similarly, Nia Griffiths reminded the party that most of the marginal seats Labour needed to win had voted Leave.

Corbyn tried to mediate and develop a compromise position that considered the different strands of opinion in the party, but his own opinion about the EU started to change too. By 2018, he was acutely aware of the economic impact of Brexit and he started to understand that membership of the EU was not necessarily a neoliberal straitjacket. By January of 2019, Corbyn realized that it was possible to launch a programme of public investment under the EU's state aid rules.[9]

In the PLP disagreements were tetchier. In a major blow to Corbyn's leadership, seven Labour MPs, including Chuka Umunna, Luciana Berger, Chris Leslie and Angela Smith, defected from Labour and joined The Independent Group in February 2019. The reasons for the defections were Corbyn's slow and inadequate response to the charges of antisemitic behaviour by party members and officials (see Heppell 2021a) and his refusal to support a second referendum on EU membership.

In the meantime, Theresa May submitted her withdrawal agreement to a vote in the House of Commons. At this stage, the Labour leader tried belatedly to claim that there were alternatives to May's plans (Corbyn 2018b) and whipped the party to vote against May's deal. In the three times May's withdrawal agreement was subject to a vote, Labour voted overwhelmingly against it, but there was dissent in the PLP. In the first vote, 19 Labour MPs voted for May's deal, and in the second vote, three Labour backbenchers supported the prime minister.

But the defeat of May's withdrawal agreement meant that the prime minister was forced to ask the EU for a six-month extension. The extension meant that Britain had to participate in the European Parliament (EP) elections that had been scheduled for 23 May. Labour found itself again at the mercy of events, having now to quickly select candidates and draft a manifesto for an election it had neither foreseen nor wanted.

Electoral considerations and pressure from MPs representing Leave constituencies and from Unite shaped Labour's unclear position on Brexit during the campaign for the EP elections. In its EP manifesto, Labour promised to deliver a "comprehensive customs union with the EU with a UK say, close Single

---

9. Written testimony of senior Labour figure.

Market alignment, guaranteed rights and standards and the protection of the Good Friday Agreement in Northern Ireland" (Labour Party 2019a). The party only backed the proposal for a second referendum if the options of an alternative negotiation with the EU or a general election were rejected (*ibid.*).

Perhaps as a result of that ambiguous position, Labour obtained disappointing results in the EP elections, attracting only 14.1 per cent of the vote with only ten MEPs being elected (and losing ten others). Crucially, the party lagged behind the Brexit Party and the Liberal Democrats, was annihilated in Scotland and experienced considerable decline in support in the Northeast of England and the Midlands. Activists who campaigned during the European elections claimed that the party's ambiguous position on Brexit was the main reason why Labour obtained such dismal results. This conclusion was supported by the fact that 57 per cent of Labour voters in Leave constituencies voted for Remain in the 2016 referendum (Fieldhouse 2019).

Similar conclusions were reached by several frontbenchers. The then deputy leader Tom Watson and the shadow foreign secretary, Emily Thornberry, blamed Labour's equivocations about a second referendum on EU membership for the party's dismal results (Schofield 2019). Similarly, John McDonnell accepted that the only way to break the deadlock on Brexit and prevent a no-deal Brexit was "to go back to the people" (McDonnell quoted in BBC News 2019).

However, members of the shadow cabinet like Richard Burgon, Ian Lavery, Rebecca Long-Bailey and Angela Rayner were against the idea of a People's Vote (as the campaign for a second referendum became known) on the grounds that Labour's ambiguous position was an asset to the party. Equally, Corbyn's advisers Seumas Milne, Karie Murphy and the Unite leader Len McCluskey opposed the idea of another referendum on EU membership. Corbyn listened to arguments on both sides of the debate, and he hesitated, even though he was leaning in favour of supporting a second referendum. In private, Corbyn suggested that he was ready to support a new public vote on Brexit.

## Change again

Despite the internal divisions, the electoral results of the European elections marked a turning point in Labour's Brexit approach.[10] If the results were to be replicated at a general election, Labour was in danger of losing many seats in London and other urban centres. Taking advantage of the new mood in the party, groups like AEIP, the People's Vote and the left-wing commentators Paul

10. Luke Cooper, Convener of Another Europe is Possible and Labour Party activist, private interview, 27 November 2019.

Mason and Owen Jones intensified their efforts in trying to convince Labour to become a Remain party.

Most trade union leaders also agreed that Labour should demand a second referendum and campaign to remain in the EU. The efforts of the pro-Remain activists, and in particular of the People's Vote campaign, had the effect of, to use the words of a Labour backbencher, "putting Corbyn in a corner".[11] From then on, the leadership of the party started a slow shift towards a position that supported a second referendum.

The wider context of British politics also played a role in Labour's shifting position. Theresa May's resignation, and the appointment in July of Boris Johnson as prime minister opened again the possibility of a no-deal Brexit (especially as the six-month extension of Article 50 was nearing its end) (for a discussion on May's vulnerability as Conservative Party leader, see Roe-Crines, Heppell & Jeffery 2021, and on the selection of Johnson as her replacement, see Jeffery, Heppell & Roe-Crines 2021). This was an outcome that Labour and most trade unions vehemently opposed. In response to this pressure, Corbyn said that he was "listening very carefully" to both sides of the debate and accepted that, if a general election was not possible, a new deal had to be approved by the people in a referendum (Mason & Elgot 2019).

In July, Corbyn announced that he would support a referendum and that Labour MPs would be free to campaign for either side. According to revelations made by Channel 4's *Dispatches* programme, but which have been denied by the Labour Party, Jeremy Corbyn, Diane Abbott and John McDonnell met secretly at the leader's allotment in East Finchley and agreed to turn Labour into a Remain party. They also agreed that Corbyn would write an article to announce the new position. The article was written, but his adviser Seumas Milne convinced Corbyn not to publish it (Channel 4 2019).

At the grassroots level, the People's Vote campaign, together with AEIP and Momentum (in particular the wing closer to Laura Parker), intensified their efforts to convince the Labour leader to adopt a new position at the annual conference that supported a second referendum on EU membership. They coordinated efforts with constituency parties to submit a record number of motions proposing to turn Labour into a Remain party.

However, many activists were concerned about backroom manoeuvring, especially by Corbyn's team and by some of the big trade unions. For example, Michael Chessum from AEIP criticized the undemocratic decision-making structures of the Labour Party, in particular the block vote of the trade unions. As he put it, "literally four men wearing suits can decide Labour's position on Brexit".[12]

---

11. Jon Cruddas, Labour MP for Dagenham and Rainham, private interview, 8 October 2019.
12. Chessum, private interview.

After much manoeuvring behind the scenes, at Labour's annual party conference in September Jeremy Corbyn announced the party's new position on Brexit, which no longer insisted on the condition of holding a new general election. Labour now proposed renegotiating a new withdrawal agreement with the EU and then subjecting that deal to a referendum in which voters would be given the option of voting for Labour's negotiated withdrawal agreement or to remain in the EU. Crucially, Corbyn did not reveal on which side of the referendum he would campaign. He simply said that he would be neutral and would "carry out whatever the people decide" (Corbyn 2019a). But there was another fatal flaw in Corbyn's plan. He never tried to explain why a second referendum was required. To claim, as he did, that the government's Brexit deal would harm Britain's economy and jobs was not (as the results of the 2019 general election showed) a sufficiently strong argument to convince Leave supporters in the party's heartlands to support Labour's strategy.

Corbyn's new position was welcomed by most trade unions and pro-European activists. It helped that key figures in the shadow cabinet, like Starmer, Abbott, and crucially McDonnell and Long-Bailey, announced they would campaign to remain in the EU. But there was some palpable disappointment in the Remain wing of the party. Michael Chessum told *The Guardian* that it was "utterly absurd for Labour in those circumstances, for Labour not to campaign for remain when 90% of its members want to stay in the EU" (Mason 2019).

More seriously, Labour's new position was not welcomed by MPs who represented Leave constituencies, like Cruddas, for whom the new position was "unsustainable" and "risky". As he put it, "Labour risks losing the support of working-class voters".[13] Cruddas' view was echoed by other backbenchers who represented Leave constituencies and who believed that Labour needed to respect the result of the 2016 referendum.

Those reservations led backbenchers like Stephen Kinnock and Caroline Flint to launch a campaign in favour of a compromise Brexit deal. However, when Boris Johnson finally presented his deal in parliament in October, many of those Labour backbenchers refused to support it on the grounds that it did not protect labour rights and environmental standards. Failing to get his deal approved, the prime minister was forced to asked for a third extension to Article 50, but he also triggered his nuclear option and called an early election to be held on 12 December.

The announcement of an early election with the explicit goal of "getting Brexit done" put Labour in a very difficult position. As Angela Rayner warned the shadow cabinet, the Conservatives would frame the election as a "people versus parliament" contest. Such framing would add to Labour's electoral challenges.

---

13. Cruddas, private interview.

Opinion polls showed that the party was trailing behind the Conservatives, Corbyn was a very unpopular leader of the opposition and the party had had very little time to explain to its traditional voters the recently approved Brexit policy. In these circumstances, it did not help the party's chances that neither Corbyn nor any of other frontbencher tried to explain to voters why a new referendum on EU membership was necessary.

However, at this stage Labour had little choice but to include the party's new policy on Brexit in the 2019 manifesto, which specified that Labour would negotiate a new deal with the EU that would protect "jobs, rights and the environment", protect peace in Northern Ireland and avoid "a hard border in Northern Ireland". Labour's negotiated new deal would include a "permanent and comprehensive UK-wide customs union and close alignment with the single market" (Labour Party 2019b). Crucially, Labour promised a legally binding "final say on Brexit" in the shape of a referendum on Labour's negotiated deal and which would include the option of voting for Remain (*ibid.*). Unlike Labour's 2017 manifesto that accepted that Brexit meant the end of free movement, the 2019 manifesto did not make such a stark statement and instead asserted that Labour recognized "the huge benefits of immigration to our country", and that "many British citizens have benefitted from freedom of movement"(*ibid.*: 91).

Labour strategists were aware that the party's stance on Brexit would be hard to sell on the campaign trail. The long and convoluted policy contrasted with the Conservatives' short, clear and powerful "Get Brexit Done" slogan. To make matters worse, Corbyn's neutral stance on the referendum looked weak and opportunistic. To address the shortcomings of Labour's Brexit policy, Momentum launched a short video in which the party's Brexit stance was explained in less than 30 seconds by a young Labour supporter. Moreover, Jeremy Corbyn devoted the second speech of the campaign to claiming that Labour's position was not "really complicated", but failed to explain why a new withdrawal agreement and new referendum were necessary (Corbyn 2019b). Corbyn was also trying to deflect attention from Brexit by focusing on the radical manifesto and by associating the Conservatives' Brexit deal with a free-trade deal with the US that would result in the privatization of the NHS.

The results of the 2019 general election show that this strategy was disastrous. As a Labour backbencher put it, the party "failed to put a compelling narrative".[14] Labour not only obtained its worst result since 1935 (in terms of seats), winning only 202 seats on a 32.1 per cent share of the vote, but it lost many seats in the party's historic strongholds like Bishop Auckland, Workington, Ashfield and Blyth Valley, that is, areas that had voted to leave the EU in 2016. Interestingly,

---

14. Bridget Phillipson, Labour MP for Houghton and Sunderland South, private interview, 10 March 2020.

however, Labour's share of the vote also declined in many Remain areas, and in Scotland, Wales and the Southeast of England. In reality, according to research conducted by Luke Cooper and Christabel Cooper, Labour lost votes in all parts of Britain and "across every social class and nearly every age group" (2020).

Polling data suggests that the party's position on Brexit was not the main reason why so many voters deserted Labour, although it played an important role. Polling analysis from YouGov shows that Corbyn's credibility was the main reason why so many Labour voters deserted the party: 35 per cent of former Labour voters invoked Corbyn as the reason why they did not vote Labour at the election, 19 per cent claimed that Brexit was the reason and 16 per cent claimed that the party's reputation for competence was the reason they stopped voting for Labour (Curtis 2019). Similarly, Lord Ashcroft's analysis of Labour's defeat showed that "two thirds of Labour Party members – including three quarters of Corbyn leadership voters – said that Brexit dominated the election and had a bigger effect on the result than on how people felt about the parties, leaders, and other policies" (Ashcroft 2020). It is important to stress that Labour losses in the so-called "Red Wall" did not start in 2019. Labour's support in those areas had been in decline since 2005 (Goes 2020). These losses are related to the effects of deindustrialization and the concomitant withdrawal of the trade unions from the region, as well as to Labour's complacent response to its decline in those areas.

If it is clear that Brexit played a role in Labour's catastrophic electoral results, it will take time to ascertain exactly how it affected the party's electoral fortunes. Labour MPs representing Leave constituencies blamed the commitment to hold a second referendum for the loss of many seats in the Northeast of England and in the Midlands. Some Corbynites blamed Starmer for forcing the party to abandon Labour's policy to accept the results of the 2016 referendum. Pro-Remainers on the other hand blamed the leadership of the party for taking so long to adopt a position which in the end remained unclear to many voters. For others, the party's position on Brexit and Corbyn's unpopularity cannot be disentangled from each other.[15] In addition, Corbyn's unwillingness to choose a side in the referendum was problematic because it was perceived by voters as expedient and opportunistic. Regardless of who is right in this debate, the fact remains that Labour's catastrophic defeat meant that the United Kingdom officially left the EU on 31 January 2021. Moreover, as an opposition party, Labour had no influence in shaping Britain's future relationship with the EU.

---

15. Phillipson, private interview.

## Explaining Labour's evolving Brexit approach

Labour's zigzag approach to Brexit since 2015 can be explained by three key factors. First, Corbyn's lack of interest in Europe and his long-standing left-wing Euroscepticism (as well as the influence of his Eurosceptic advisers) led to an unenthusiastic referendum campaign and also to a very slow and inconsistent response to the changing circumstances. Put simply, Corbyn was not interested in European affairs and took time to understand the significance of Brexit. On the other hand, Corbyn's inability to lead the party on this crucial issue and his unwillingness to explain the merits of Labour's pro-EU policy led to an erratically evolving stance that culminated in the adoption of a confused and ambivalent Brexit policy just a few weeks before the 2019 general election, which left voters confused and unimpressed.

But Labour's lack of clarity over Brexit cannot be explained exclusively by Corbyn's own Eurosceptic views or indecisive and ineffective statecraft. Labour's complex internal divisions over Brexit, and in particular over immigration, were a second factor contributing to the party's ambivalence. Following the 2016 referendum on EU membership, the party was divided over how to react to the result. Corbyn tried to bridge these differences, but his compromise positions left all sides frustrated and resulted in policies that seemed opportunistic.

Backbenchers who represented Remain areas wanted Labour to either support a second referendum on EU membership or to support a soft Brexit, which implied membership of the Single Market and the acceptance of EU citizens' freedom of movement. By contrast, MPs who represented Leave areas (the equivalent of 61 per cent of Labour seats), such as Lisa Nandy and Caroline Flint, claimed that Labour had to accept the results of the referendum and campaign for the least damaging Brexit. Among this group there were MPs who were more concerned with immigration and who objected to a Labour Brexit deal that supported freedom of movement, while others, like Stephen Kinnock and Lucy Powell, were supportive of a deal with the EU that encompassed membership of the Single Market. For others, like Cruddas, the problem was more existential. Turning Labour into a Remain party risked losing not only working-class voters but also its historic working-class identity.

The third factor follows directly from the second. Labour's internal divisions reflected above all (but not only) concerns with Labour's electability. Indeed, discussions in the shadow cabinet about Brexit were heavily influenced by electoral considerations. The adoption of a clear Brexit stance, either in favour of remaining or of leaving the EU would have led to electoral losses that would have undermined Labour's chances of forming a government. If Labour had adopted a clear Leave position it would have lost many seats in London and other urban areas to the Liberal Democrats and Greens in the 2017 and 2019 general elections. But a clear Remain position, on the other hand, would have led to dozens of losses in both elections in Labour's historic strongholds.

At the 2017 general election Labour's "constructive ambiguity" on Brexit proved to be effective. Labour registered many gains in London, university towns and in constituencies like Canterbury and Kensington that had never elected a Labour MP. Conversely, Labour retained many seats in Leave areas, albeit with shrinking majorities. At the time, it was clear that Corbyn sought to accommodate Labour's opposing tribes on Brexit by adopting an ambiguous position. For instance, Jon Cruddas argued that Corbyn "tried to square the circle; he tried to forge a position that considers the different currents of opinion in the party".[16]

But following three years of parliamentary deadlock over Brexit and voters' fatigue over the issue, Labour's ambiguous position became a liability in 2019. The party lost 47 seats in England including in its industrial heartlands, namely in places like Sedgefield, Bishop Auckland, Darlington, Redcar, Stockton South and Blyth Valley, although it also lost votes in all areas of the country, including in Corbyn's own constituency of Islington North.

What is clear is that Brexit exposed Labour's structural problems and forced the party to confront the identity crisis that had been affecting its electoral fortunes for some time and that turned into an existential crisis after the 2015 general election. In 2005 Labour started to lose the support of working-class voters in its heartlands in the Northeast of England and Midlands, but the trend intensified after the 2016 referendum. As Mellon *et al.* noted, following the referendum the Brexit cleavage created a new polarization among the British electorate, "with the Conservatives disproportionately attracting Leave voters and Labour disproportionately losing Leavers" (2018: 720). Labour's story of electoral decline in its working-class heartlands happened in parallel with the party's growing popularity in urban centres, in particular in university towns, populated by young university graduates (Sobolewska & Ford 2020: 212–14).

The transformation of Labour's electoral map raises important questions about the party's future direction. As the pro-European peer Roger Liddle argued in an article, Labour's dilemmas with Brexit are at "root ideological" as they "raise existential questions about the party's identity and mission" (2018). Cruddas reached a similar conclusion, although he added that by transforming Labour into the party of young, urban, middle-class cosmopolitans Corbyn had paradoxically managed the feat of completing New Labour's project.[17] What is clear is that in the years to come Labour will struggle to develop a programme that will be supported by voters on both sides of the Brexit divide.

---

16. Cruddas, private interview.
17. Cruddas, private interview.

The phenomenon that Liddle and Cruddas allude to is not unique to Britain. Brexit is merely the manifestation of the impact of the globalization cleavage in European party systems. As Kriesi *et al.* explained, globalization has created winners and losers in politics who have very distinct values and priorities (2006: 1260). The "winners" of globalization tend to cherish liberal and cosmopolitan values and embrace immigration, whereas the "losers" of globalization typically tend to defend socially conservative values. Unless political parties are able to identify a cause that will unite these two sets of voters, it will be very difficult for parties like Labour to win a majority at a general election.

Labour faced difficult dilemmas throughout the Brexit saga. The task of choosing a side in the Brexit debate amounted to choosing a worldview that would inevitably result in electoral losses. But in the meantime, the party found that sitting on the fence also resulted in electoral losses and crucially, it contributed to Brexit.

As Britain ventures into the world outside the EU, Keir Starmer, who replaced Corbyn as Labour leader (see Heppell 2021b), no longer has to develop strategies to prevent or mitigate the implementation of Brexit, but it would be a serious mistake to think that this issue no longer matters for British politics. The globalization cleavage, vividly exposed by the 2016 referendum, will continue to pose considerable electoral, ideological and existential challenges to the Labour Party.[18]

## References

Ashcroft, M. 2020. "Diagnosis of defeat: Labour's turn to the smell the coffee". Lord Ashcroft Polls, February. https://lordashcroftpolls.com/wp-content/uploads/2020/02/DIAGNOSIS-OF-DEFEAT-LORD-ASHCROFT-POLLS-1.pdf (accessed 19 March 2021).

Bale, T., P. Webb & M. Poletti 2020. *Footsoldiers: Political Party Membership in the 21st Century.* Abingdon: Routledge.

BBC News 2019. "John McDonnell: Brexit 'needs to get back to the people'". 27 May. https://www.bbc.co.uk/news/av/uk-politics-48424278/john-mcdonnell-brexit-needs-to-go-back-to-the-people (accessed 19 March 2021).

Berman, S. 2006. *The Primacy of Politics: Social Democracy and the Making of Europe's Twentieth Century.* Cambridge: Cambridge University Press.

---

18. I am very grateful for the time and insights from Jon Cruddas, Bridget Phillipson, Sienna Rogers, Richard Corbett, Lord Liddle, Michael Chessum, Luke Cooper, Natalie Sedacca and many other Labour activists, party workers and councillors who spoke to me but who asked to remain anonymous. I am particularly grateful to the senior Labour politician who shared with me extensive notes of many shadow cabinet, NEC and PLP meetings and other Labour Party events. These notes confirmed facts, events and interpretations that had been voiced by other Labour activists I spoke to while researching this chapter. The mistakes in the narrative are of course my own.

Brinded, L. 2017. "Jeremy Corbyn emailed all Labour members telling them why the party is voting to start the Brexit process". *Business Insider*, 28 January. https://www.businessinsider.com/jeremy-corbyn-letter-to-labour-members-on-article-50-brexit-vote-2017-1?r=US&IR=T (accessed 19 March 2021).

Bush, S. 2017. "Why has Jeremy Corbyn committed Labour to voting for Article 50?" *New Statesman*, 26 January. https://www.newstatesman.com/politics/staggers/2017/01/why-has-jeremy-corbyn-committed-labour-voting-article-50 (accessed 17 March 2021).

Channel 4 2019. "Puppet Masters: The Men Who Really Run Britain". *Dispatches*, 4 November.

Cooper, L. & C. Cooper 2020. "The devastating defeat: why Labour lost and how it can win again". Europe for the Many, January 2020. https://www.europeforthemany.com/tdd-web.pdf (accessed 19 March 2021).

Corbyn, J. 2015. "Speech to the Labour Party Annual Conference, 29 September". https://www.policyforum.labour.org.uk/news/speech-by-jeremy-corbyn-to-labour-party-annual-conference-2015 (accessed 19 March 2021).

Corbyn, J. 2016a. "Jeremy Corbyn's statement on David Cameron's statement on the EU deal". 18 February. https://jeremycorbyn.org.uk/response-to-camerons-statement-about-his-eu-renegotiations (accessed 26 March 2021).

Corbyn, J. 2016b. "Leaving the EU would lead to bonfire of rights". *The Guardian*, 14 April. https://www.theguardian.com/politics/2016/apr/14/jeremy-corbyn-leaving-eu-would-lead-to-bonfire-of-rights (accessed 19 March 2021).

Corbyn, J. 2016c. "Corbyn: I'm seven out of 10 on the EU". BBC News, 11 June. https://www.bbc.co.uk/news/av/uk-politics-eu-referendum-36506163/corbyn-i-m-seven-out-of-10-on-eu (accessed 19 March 2021).

Corbyn, J. 2016d. "Speech to the Labour Party Conference". 28 September. https://www.policyforum.labour.org.uk/news/jeremy-corbyn-s-speech-to-annual-conference-2016 (accessed 19 March 2021).

Corbyn, J. 2017a. "Speech in Peterborough". 10 January. https://labour.org.uk/press/jeremy-corbyns-speech-in-peterborough/ (accessed 19 March 2021).

Corbyn, J. 2017b. "Labour will challenge the government's plan for a bargain basement Brexit". 14 March. https://labour.org.uk/press/labour-will-challenge-the-governments-plans-for-a/ (accessed 19 March 2021).

Corbyn, J. 2018a. "Speech on Britain after Brexit". Coventry, 26 February. https://labour.org.uk/press/jeremy-corbyn-full-speech-britain-brexit/ (accessed 19 March 2021).

Corbyn, J. 2018b. "Labour could do a better Brexit deal: give us the chance". *The Guardian*, 6 December. https://www.theguardian.com/commentisfree/2018/dec/06/jeremy-corbyn-general-election-brexit-labour-theresa-may (accessed 19 March 2021).

Corbyn, J. 2019a. "Speech to the Labour Party Annual Conference". 24 September. https://labour.org.uk/press/jeremy-corbyns-labour-party-conference-leaders-address/ (accessed 19 March 2021).

Corbyn, J. 2019b "Brexit Speech". Harlow, 05 November. https://labour.org.uk/press/jeremy-corbyns-brexit-speech-in-harlow/ (accessed 19 March 2021).

Cowley, P. & D. Kavanagh 2018. *The British General Election of 2017*. Basingstoke: Palgrave Macmillan.

Crines, A., D. Jeffery & T. Heppell 2018. "The British Labour Party and leadership election mandate(s) of Jeremy Corbyn: patterns of opinion and opposition within the parliamentary Labour Party". *Journal of Elections, Public Opinion and Parties* 28 (3): 361–79.

Curtice, J. 2018. "Do voters still want to leave the EU? How they view the Brexit process two years on". Natcen/UK in a Changing Europe. https://ukandeu.ac.uk/wp-content/uploads/2018/09/Do-Voters-Still-Want-to-Leave-the-EU.pdf (accessed 19 March 2021).

Curtis, C. 2019. "In their own words: why voters abandoned Labour". YouGov, 23 December. https://yougov.co.uk/topics/politics/articles-reports/2019/12/23/their-own-words-why-voters-abandoned-labour (accessed 19 March 2021).

Daddow, O. 2011. *New Labour and the European Union: Blair and Brown's Logic of History*. Manchester: Manchester University Press.

Elgot, J. & H. Stewart 2018. "Labour will inevitably back second Brexit referendum, says McDonnell". *The Guardian*, 28 November. https://www.theguardian.com/politics/2018/nov/28/labour-seize-second-brexit-vote-option-john-mcdonnell (accessed 19 March 2021).

Evans, G. & A. Menon 2017. *Brexit and British Politics*. Cambridge: Polity.

Fieldhouse, E. 2019. "Labour's electoral dilemma". British Election Study, 17 October. https://www.britishelectionstudy.com/bes-findings/labours-electoral-dilemma/#.XeqGkJP7Ts0 (accessed 19 March 2021).

Gaitskell, H. 1962. "Speech to the Labour Party Annual Conference". 3 October. https://www.cvce.eu/content/publication/1999/1/1/05f2996b-000b-4576-8b42-8069033a16f9/publishable_en.pdf (accessed 19 March 2021).

Goes, E. 2016. *The Labour Party under Ed Miliband: Trying but Failing to Renew Social Democracy*. Manchester: Manchester University Press.

Goes, E. 2018. "'Jez, we can!' Labour's campaign: defeat with a taste of victory". In J. Tonge, C. Leston-Bandeira & S. Wilks-Heeg (eds), *Britain Votes 2017*, 59–71. Oxford: Oxford University Press.

Goes, E. 2020. "Labour's 2019 campaign: a defeat of epic proportions". In J. Tonge, S. Wilks-Heeg & L. Thompson (eds), *Britain Votes: The 2019 General Election*, 84–102. Oxford: Oxford University Press.

Hanretty, C. 2016. "Revised estimates of Vote Leave in Westminster constituencies". Medium, 16 August. https://medium.com/@chrishanretty/revised-estimates-of-leave-vote-share-in-westminster-constituencies-c4612f06319d (accessed 20 January 2020).

Harmel, R. & K. Janda 1994. "An integrated theory of party goals and party change". *Journal of Theoretical Politics* 6(3): 259–87.

Heffernan, R. 2001. "Beyond Euroscepticism: exploring the Europeanisation of the Labour Party since 1983". *Political Quarterly* 72(2): 180–89.

Heppell, T. 2021a. "The British Labour Party and the Antisemitism Crisis: Jeremy Corbyn and Image Repair Theory". *British Journal of Politics and International Relations*.

Heppell, T. 2021b. "The Labour Party Leadership Election: The Stark Model and the Selection of Keir Starmer". *British Politics*.

Hickson, K. & J. Miles 2018. "Social Democratic Euroscepticism: Labour's neglected tradition". *British Journal of Politics and International Relations* 20(4): 864–79.

Jeffery, D., T. Heppell, and A. Roe-Crines 2020. "The Conservative Party leadership election of 2019: An analysis of the voting motivations of Conservative parliamentarians". *Parliamentary Affairs*.

Kogan, D. 2019. *Protest and Power: The Battle for the Labour Party*. London: Bloomsbury.

Kinnock, N. *et al.* 2016. "Labour Party's purpose is aligned with Europe". *The Guardian*, 3 June. https://www.theguardian.com/politics/2016/jun/03/kinnock-beckett-blair-brown-harman-and-miliband-labour-partys-purpose-is-aligned-with-europe (accessed 19 March 2021).

Kriesi, H. *et al.* 2006. "Globalisation and the transformation of the national political space: six European countries compared". *European Journal of Political Research* 45(6): 921–56.

Labour Party 2017. *For the Many Not the Few: The Labour Party Manifesto 2017*. London: Labour Party.

Labour Party 2019a. *Transforming Britain and Europe: For the Many and not the Few*. London: Labour Party. https://labour.org.uk/wp-content/uploads/2019/05/Transforming-Britain-and-Europe-for-the-many-not-the-few.pdf (accessed 19 March 2021).

Labour Party 2019b. *It's Time for Real Change: The Labour Party Manifesto 2019*. London: Labour Party. https://labour.org.uk/wp-content/uploads/2019/11/Real-Change-Labour-Manifesto-2019.pdf (accessed 19 March 2021).

Liddle, R. 2018. "Brexit: what should Labour commit to?". UK in a Changing Europe, 26 February. https://ukandeu.ac.uk/brexit-what-should-labour-commit-to/ (accessed 19 March 2021).

Liddle, R. 2014. *The Europe Dilemma: Britain and the Drama of EU Integration*. London: I. B. Tauris.

Mason, R. 2019. "Jeremy Corbyn: I'll stay neutral and let the people decide on Brexit". *The Guardian*, 17 September. https://www.theguardian.com/politics/2019/sep/17/corbyn-vows-to-put-sensible-brexit-deal-to-voters-in-referendum (accessed 19 March 2021).

Mason, R. & J. Elgot 2019. "Corbyn 'listening very carefully' to Labour calls for second referendum". The Guardian, 27 May. https://www.theguardian.com/politics/2019/may/27/corbyn-pressed-by-senior-labour-mps-to-back-a-second-referendum (accessed 8 April 2021).

Mellon, J. *et al.* 2018. "Brexit or Corbyn? Campaign and inter-election vote switching in the 2017 UK general election". *Parliamentary Affairs* 71(4): 719–37.

Panebianco, A. 1988. *Political Parties: Organization and Power*. Cambridge: Cambridge University Press.

Pine, S. 2016. "Corbyn: Article 50 has to be invoked now". LabourList, 24 June. https://labourlist.org/2016/06/corbyn-article-50-has-to-be-invoked-now/ (accessed 19 March 2021).

Pogrund, G. & P. Maguire 2020. *Left Out: The Inside Story of Labour Under Corbyn*. London: Bodley Head.

Roe-Crines, A., T. Heppell, and D. Jeffery 2021. "Theresa May and the Conservative Party Leadership confidence motion of 2018: analysing the voting behaviour of Conservative parliamentarians". *British Politics*.

Schindler, J. 2018. "Interview with Labour leader Jeremy Corbyn: 'we can't stop Brexit'". *Der Spiegel*, 9 November. https://www.spiegel.de/international/europe/interview-with-labour-leader-corbyn-we-can-t-stop-brexit-a-1237594.html (accessed 19 March 2021).

Schofield, K. 2018. "Labour MPs warned as 92% of Momentum members call on them to vote down Brexit deal". PoliticsHome, 6 November. https://www.politicshome.com/news/uk/political-parties/labour-party/news/99659/labour-mps-warned-92-momentum-members-call-them (accessed 19 March 2021).

Schofield, K. 2019. "Emily Thornberry launches furious attack on Labour's Brexit policy after election losses". PoliticsHome, 26 May. https://www.politicshome.com/news/uk/foreign-affairs/brexit/news/104161/emily-thornberry-launches-furious-attack-labours-brexit (accessed 19 March 2021).

Shipman, T. 2017. *All Out War: The Full Story of Brexit*. London: William Collins.

Sobolewska, M. & R. Ford 2020. *Brexitland*. Cambridge: Cambridge University Press.

Starmer, K. 2017a. "What next for Britain?" Chatham House, 27 March. https://www.chathamhouse.org/sites/default/files/events/2017-03-27-StarmerPREP.pdf (accessed 19 March 2021).

Starmer, K. 2017b. "'No constructive ambiguity': Labour will avoid Brexit cliff edge for UK economy". *The Observer*, 26 August. https://www.theguardian.com/commentisfree/2017/aug/26/keir-starmer-no-constructive-ambiguity-brexit-cliff-edge-labour-will-avoid-transitional-deal (accessed 19 March 2021).

Starmer, K. 2017c. "Speech to the 2017 Labour Party Annual Conference". Brighton, 25 September. https://labour.org.uk/press/keir-starmer-speech-to-labour-party-conference/ (accessed 19 March 2021).

Stewart, H. 2016. "Jeremy Corbyn tells Pride heckler 'I did all I could' against Brexit". *The Guardian*, 25 June. https://www.theguardian.com/politics/2016/jun/25/jeremy-corbyn-vows-to-face-down-any-leadership-challenge-brexit (accessed 19 March 2021).

Stewart, H. & R. Mason 2017. "Corbyn to order Labour MPs to vote for Article 50 trigger". *The Guardian*, 19 January. https://www.theguardian.com/politics/2017/jan/19/corbyn-to-impose-three-line-whip-on-labour-mps-to-trigger-article-50 (accessed 19 March 2021).

Wilson, P. 2016. "Corbyn sabotaged Labour's Remain campaign. He must resign". *The Guardian*, 26 June. https://amp.theguardian.com/commentisfree/2016/jun/26/corbyn-must-resign-inadequate-leader-betrayal (accessed 19 March 2021).

## 12

## CORBYN, THE CONSTITUTION AND CONSTITUTIONAL PREMIERSHIP: BREAKING BENNISM?

*Steven Daniels*

Given Corbyn's politics, firmly on the left of the wider Labour Party, it could reasonably have been assumed initially that any proposals that he might have put forward for constitutional reforms would have been quite radical in nature. Indeed, his close personal and political relationships with other party grandees, such as Tony Benn, offer a political window on what Corbyn's thinking on constitutional reform would have been had he been elected. However, a prime minister as far to the left as Corbyn remains untested in British political history, and any such reforms would also have to be measured against the successes and failures of previous Labour governments. What would a Corbyn government have meant for the British constitution?

To explore this, given the political similarities between Corbynism and Bennism (Bolton & Pitts 2018), this chapter explores Benn's framework for the establishment of a constitutional premiership, intended to strengthen the role of the legislative branch of the British constitution at the expense of the executive. Benn's constitutional premiership is rooted in the socialist principles that guide the Labour Party, advocating for a greater role for the party and its affiliates. Previous Labour governments have made some progress (or regression) in advancing constitutional premiership, although some actively resisted some elements of it. As such, this chapter determines if a Corbyn government would have represented an adherence to constitutional premiership, or continuity with the efforts of previous prime ministers to resist it.

The constitution has long been viewed as a tool through which to advance socialism. At the beginning of the twentieth century, the Labour Party emerged as a political force with a dual mandate: the socialist organizations that co-founded it sought greater common ownership of the means of production, and the trade union groups sought representation for their members within the institutions of state so that their lot might be improved (Harvey & Bather 1963: 92). This correlates with the wider aims of Bennism to promote greater political participation to advance socialism. The aims of the party were clear: to "promote socialism (whatever that may mean) by democratic means [...] within the constraints of the present framework of parliamentary democracy". If these aims were to be achieved in earnest, then it would undoubtedly raise constitutional questions, and a "paradoxical enthusiasm" to answer these questions with reform: "paradoxical because democratic socialism in government needs to harness rather than clamp the power of the State as an engine of social reform" (Ewing 1995: 103–4).

Given the socialist underpinnings and origins of the Labour Party, such paradoxes are to be expected, given the conservative and entrenched nature of the constitution. One of the groups that contributed towards the foundation of the party, the Fabians, expressed satisfaction with the constitution (save for the House of Lords), as it allowed for "not obstacle but opportunity" in advancing political democracy into a wider social and economic democracy (Wright 1990: 324). Given such paradoxical influences on the party's constitutional position, Ewing distilled the party's aims in constitutional reform into three distinct goals:

[1] the sovereignty of the people exercised through elected representatives is the primary sources of constitutional authority;

[2] the authority of the State so derived shall be engaged for the principal purpose of promoting the social, economic and cultural welfare of the citizens;

[3] the socio-economic objectives of the State shall be promoted in a manner which respects the civil liberties and political freedom of individuals.

(Ewing 1995: 105)

Constitutional premiership undoubtedly provided opportunities to advance these aims.

Unlike Benn, before becoming leader in 2015, Corbyn had never held a single role, post or position in or out of government. The eternal backbencher, in 1996 Corbyn was even threatened with losing the party whip by Blair. Benn defended Corbyn (Benn 2002: 383–4). Benn and Corbyn remained close, both politically and personally. Their shared political stance and interests made Corbyn a regular fixture in his published diaries, with Benn mentioning Corbyn on at least 49 pages, attending and supporting events together as varied as visits to local hospitals, meeting with the Quaker Peace Centre, walking around a nature reserve in Stansgate and having lunch with their families (Benn 1994, 2002).

Given Corbyn's status as the protégé of Benn (Stafford 2016: 74), their near-identical position on the political spectrum and their long history of sharing policy platforms, it is reasonable to assume that they would have had similar aims in constitutional reform. In terms of theoretical framework, this chapter therefore adopts and advances Benn's proposals for constitutional reform, as detailed in *Arguments for Socialism* (1979) and *Arguments for Democracy* (1981), and extrapolates their similarities to the aims and proposals of a Corbyn government. This chapter also explores how previous Labour governments have fared with constitutional premiership, given the party's wider aims of advancing socialism. However, this chapter ultimately reveals that Corbyn's advancement of constitutional premiership would have been mixed at best. Indeed, when removing the questionable elements of Corbynite proposals, a Corbyn government would have represented greater continuity with previous Labour prime ministers in maintaining the authority of the executive, rather than a break with the past and a new political journey of left-wing constitutional reform along Bennite lines. This continuity is notable, given Corbyn's reputation for tackling elite and entrenched interests, including those within Labour; Bolton and Pitts go so far to describe the success of the Corbyn leadership as relying on representing "a clean break with everything that has come before in Labour history" (2018: 42–3). Such a continuity with the historical Labour Party leadership provides an interesting counterpoint to the party populism from which Corbyn is said to have drawn "strength, utility and coherence" (Watts & Bale 2018: 100–1). This is paradoxical: such an adherence to his predecessors, and *not* to the Bennism that informed his own politics, is clearly at odds with what the wider membership expected of him and how he would have governed.

**The framework: advancing Bennism?**

Tony Benn's relationship with the constitution is a complex one and, despite never having become prime minister, his experiences qualify him to comment on its functions and offer his suggestions for amendments, so that the socialist aims underpinning the Labour Party might be advanced. As a politician, Benn did achieve high office. In the Wilson and Callaghan governments, Benn served in various posts, including cabinet positions: postmaster general in 1964, minister of technology in 1966, minister of power in 1969, secretary of state for industry in 1974 and energy secretary in 1975. Benn even stood, unsuccessfully, for leadership positions within the party, failing to become deputy leader in 1971 and 1981, and leader in 1976 and 1988 (Benn 1981: i; Gibson & Assinder 1988: 1–2).

Benn's most significant contribution to constitutional reform in pursuit of socialist aims came not from government, but from the backbenches. In 1941, Benn's father, William Wedgwood Benn, was created Viscount Stansgate by Churchill's wartime government, a hereditary title that passed to Benn on his father's death in 1960. Benn, an elected MP at the time, described the struggle to shed the peerage as the event that "taught me more about the British establishment and how it really works, and how to defeat it, than any other episode in my life". It had given Benn a "taste of what happens when authority decides to crush dissent", particularly when he was promptly expelled from the Commons (Benn 1979: 15–16). Benn's struggles took on both a legal and political dimension. Legally, Benn asserted his right to renounce his peerage and lost, with the courts citing a 1626 statement that a peerage was an "incorporeal hereditament affixed in the blood and annexed to the posterity". Benn was unable to return to the Commons until 1963, when the Macmillan government introduced legislation allowing peers to renounce their titles, which Benn did within five minutes of it passing (Benn 1979: 15–16; Freeman 1982: 22). He had taken on the constitution and, eventually, won. Benn noted that the incident had far-reaching consequences for the British constitution as a whole, and was undoubtedly a major factor in developing his ideas for socialist reform of the constitution:

> it tested the House of Commons and its Committees, the House of Lords and its Committees, the Crown insofar as it was involved, the press, local government, the Labour Party, the Conference, the Constituency [...] it was the most extraordinary way of learning how the British constitution worked and where power resided, and I learned a lot of things that shocked me very much, particularly the ideas of those who ran the parliamentary government – I learned that they were not particularly democratic at all. (cited in Freeman 1982: 22)

Like other actors and groups mentioned in this chapter, Benn sought to promote his own vision of democratic socialism within the party, in order to advance wider socialist goals. Benn's version of socialism was to be open, libertarian, pluralistic, humane and democratic. He believed that only democratic socialism could combine public investment in industry, expanded public expenditure and the protection of personal freedoms (Benn 1979: 17, 140).

It is in these experiences and beliefs that Benn developed his own framework for constitutional change, to ensure that such tenets of democratic socialism could safely be advanced, executed and implemented. At its core, Benn sought to develop a "constitutional premiership", to replace an "absolute premiership" that had, in his view, amassed far too much power of patronage. He believed such a transition would happen no more naturally than other major developments in British constitutional history. Benn noted how an absolute monarch had ceded power to the House of Lords, who in turn had recognized the power of the House of Commons after 1688, eventually reaching the current constitutional arrangement (Benn 1980: 7–8, 11–14).

Benn's constitutional premiership was designed to ensure that groups and supporters of socialism would have the ability to influence the decision-making process of the Labour Party and Labour governments, thus creating a far more participatory and democratic constitution. Benn feared that if pent-up demands for economic, industrial and social change were not able to be expressed through a Labour Party and/or government, then they would be expressed through other channels, damaging the role of Labour as the democratic voice of working people and their families (Benn 1981: 38). He believed that seven key changes could ensure the emergence of a constitutional premiership, and it is from this that a working framework can be constructed against which to test Corbynite proposals.

The first constitutional change designed to prevent "the immense concentration of power in the hands of the prime minister" is by far the simplest, namely the total abolition of the House of Lords, which Benn described as an obsolete and unnecessary part of the constitution. Furthermore, it was not to be replaced with a new second chamber ("The Labour Party does not support the idea [...] Nor do I"; Benn 1979: 172). Removing the opportunity for a prime minister to nominate peerages would dent his powers of patronage (Benn 1981: 38–9). Given Benn's own experience with the Lords, this change is perhaps the least surprising of all.

The second constitutional change calls for the confirmation of portfolio allocations by Labour MPs. By requiring ministers to be confirmed in post by parliamentarians before the Crown, "there would be a real sharing of power that would greatly strengthen the role of the government's supporters". Such changes to the cabinet system would enhance their accountability as ministers and weaken prime ministers' power of patronage and "personal preference". Benn also envisaged greater transparency of these briefs, as the cabinet as a whole would have access to information that would allow them to make an informed decision. Conscious of shifting the balance of power away from the House of Commons as a whole, Benn stressed that the House should not lose its power to overthrow a government, "if they wish". Such reforms were to be mirrored internally within the Labour Party to advance socialist voices (Benn 1979: 173–4; 1981: 39–40).

The third constitutional change was to develop further the Commons select committee system, granting it the right to summon ministers, access their documents and further enhance transparency in the workings of government. Benn even believed that such committees should be given sufficient powers as to act as a counterbalance to the power of the executive, and that there should be a minimum of six committees, covering economic, industrial and defence policies, foreign affairs, agriculture and the machinery of government. For socialism to be advanced, they would form part of wider open government, with the power to hold hearings in public and with the press present (Benn 1979: 129–30; 1981: 40).

The fourth constitutional change related to major public appointments. Benn advocated a greater role for the enhanced committee system and the House to comment on appointments, with the Commons having the final say. For example, Benn notes the Wilson governments appointed 24 chairmen of nationalized industries collectively worth 20 per cent of GDP, and 16 chairmen of Royal Commissions with significant influence over future policy: "For not one of these appointments [... was Wilson] constitutionally required to consult Cabinet, Parliament, public or party" (Benn 1979: 126; see also Benn 1981: 40). Such a system would be particularly prudent in the case of (heavily unionized) nationalized industries. A greater involvement in the management of their industry would undoubtedly represent an opportunity to advance socialism. Given the extensive privatization programmes enacted by the Thatcher and Major governments between 1979 and 1997 (Parker 2012), this has provided significantly fewer opportunities for comment on public appointments.

The fifth constitutional change was the creation of a Freedom of Information Act, in order to reduce the power of the prime minister to the advantage of the public. Benn's advocating for freedom of information is a key tenet in the creation of an open democracy, with free access to information, including sensitive information (with military security or personal information the only exceptions), a crucial step in freeing democracy from its current mechanisms of control, such as the media. This was to be part of open government, and the growth of accountability of the prime minister to the House of Commons (Benn 1979: 171–2; 1981: 40).

The sixth constitutional change was the return of law-making powers from the EU to parliament. Benn was hypercritical of the supranational organizations comprising what was then the EEC, believing that law-making powers had been siphoned from the House of Commons to the Council of Ministers, who met privately. Such meetings also enhanced the royal prerogative invested in the prime minister, at the expense of the Commons. Benn feared that, as the EEC developed common goals in areas such as foreign policy, nationality, elected assemblies and monetary policies, this would mark "the end of Britain as a completely self-governing nation and of our democratically elected parliament as the supreme law-making body" (Benn 1979: 95; see also Benn 1981: 40) With EEC laws taking precedence over British ones, even in a circumscribed capacity, Benn believed it limited opportunities for the advancement of socialism.

The seventh and final constitutional change was the strengthening of the PLP at the expense of the party leader. Benn believed that the PLP should represent the primary forum of debate for the various factions within the party, and that MPs should advance policies agreed through channels such as the annual conference. The PLP should engage regularly with the NEC (who would have final say on the Labour manifesto) to ensure that all voices and issues were heard. Party leadership would still play a prominent role, however. Benn believed it vital for the leadership to protect dissenting voices, and to ensure that no "witch-hunts" occurred, even from domestic agencies such as MI5 or Special Branch. Benn summarized the new leadership structure thus:

> This is not a charter for anarchism, nor a dream of creating a wholly self-regulating economic and political system. Leadership there must be, but not all from the top. Leadership is inseparable from responsibility and responsibility is inseparable from power, and if power is not being disseminated more widely, leadership will have to be more widely shared too.                    (Benn 1979: 178–9; see also Benn 1981: 41)

Benn was not naive enough to suggest that his plans for a constitutional premiership are a silver bullet. He stressed that all systems of government require goodwill, common sense and trust by both the governing and the governed. "But our history has taught us that even good kings were not good enough to make an absolute monarchy acceptable" (Benn 1981: 39). Nonetheless, a clear Bennite framework on which to build constitutional change has now been established, one that allows for the advancement of socialist aims using the Labour Party as a democratic vehicle, with such progress coming at the expense of the powers and scope of the executive.

## Previous Labour governments and the constitution: resisting Bennism?

Before exploring how successful Corbynism was in advocating Benn's constitutional premiership, it is first prudent to understand the wider constitutional and political context at the time when Corbyn took office. British political history has so far produced six Labour prime ministers, all of whom have wrestled with the constitution in some fashion. Given the wider aims of the Labour Party, all six have a mixed record regarding constitutional reform: some met with success, others failure. The most common theme among them in meeting the challenges of the constitutional premiership is their refusal to surrender the powers of the executive. This section is not intended to be comprehensive, but rather to provide a flavour of the natural progress of Benn's constitutional premiership, and the various challenges Labour governments have faced in implementing constitutional reform.

It is clear that Benn's constitutional premiership is firmly situated within the establishing principles of the Labour Party as a whole. The first two Labour governments (1924, 1929–31), both minority administrations under Ramsey MacDonald, trod carefully in such matters. Wright notes that prior to taking office, MacDonald advocated for a gentler approach towards the use of the state and the constitution for advancing social democracy. Even to fellow socialists, MacDonald encouraged "an affirmation of a constitutional collectivism which reflected an economic collectivism" (Wright 1990: 324–5).

On achieving office as the first Labour prime minister, MacDonald focused on pragmatic achievements instead of the wholesale advancement of socialism. He sought to convince the electorate, and indeed the labour movement itself, that it could be trusted to govern in good faith. In the second Labour government, minor constitutional reform was a political possibility. However, in 1930, MacDonald found his Representation of the People Bill frustrated by the Lords, who introduced a "wrecking amendment" designed to protect smaller towns and rural districts, "clearly intended to benefit the Conservative Party" (Dorey 2008: 18, 20–21). Even from its very first governments, the Labour Party and the House of Lords had a difficult relationship. Given their minority status and short duration, the MacDonald governments, although well intended, failed to achieve any significant constitutional reform, falling at the first hurdle of Benn's constitutional premiership.

Clement Attlee's government, the first to achieve a parliamentary majority (1945–51), was far more successful in achieving constitutional reform, particularly concerning the Lords. Loewenberg noted that, not unlike MacDonald, Attlee faced several internal pressures from extra-parliamentary bodies questioning his constitutional authority as prime minister. Yet, the constitutional powers afforded to the Attlee government by virtue of its majority soon quelled any competing source of power, allowing the PLP to lead the labour movement in achieving its socialist aims (Loewenberg 1958: 771, 790). The largest contribution of the Attlee government towards constitutional premiership was in reforming the House of Lords. Dorey notes that the promise of such reform was quite strongly worded in the 1945 Labour Manifesto, potentially as a warning: "we give clear notice that we will not tolerate obstruction of the people's will by the House of Lords". It seemed to have the intended effect, as Attlee received little in the way of opposition between 1945–7. However, this was to change on the expansion of nationalization programmes (Dorey 2008: 104–5).

Desires to reduce the power of the Lords sparked a wider debate within the party, particularly over the power, functions, rationale and overall composition of the Lords (*ibid.*: 106). Debates centred around ensuring that the Lords did not represent a permanent majority for one party, that heredity by itself should not qualify for admission and the creation of life peers be based upon public service or personal distinction: all reforms designed to allow for a greater representation of social and economic changes nationwide within parliament, somewhat befitting the spirit of constitutional premiership. The Attlee government passed the 1949 Parliament Act, reducing the delaying power of the House of Lords, thus further promoting the Commons (Harvey & Bather 1963: 35–6, 46–7). More significant reform of the Lords would have to wait. For now, the government had secured an advancement of legislative power without any significant loss of executive power.

The Wilson governments (1964–70, 1974–76), in which Benn served, took steps towards the creation of open government as a precursor to the Freedom of Information Act. There were two key reforms: a reduction in the waiting time for government records to be made public from 50 to 30 years and the greater use of consultative publications (Dorey 2008: 185–6). Efforts at expanding open government through enhanced select committees met with resistance from ministers, including James Callaghan, who reportedly viewed them as a threat to strong and effective government, not least because avoiding their questioning was more difficult than in Prime Minister's Questions (Dorey 2008: 75). Such difficulties continued into Callaghan's own government (1976–79), which, conscious of the parliamentary arithmetic, acceded in 1978 to backbencher demands for a debate on the strengthening of select committees. The belief was that a more coherent system of committees would allow for a "new balance" in the House, enabling it to "exercise effective control and stewardship over Ministers" (Dorey 2008: 76).

Further to the satisfaction of the constitutional premiership during this time period was the proposed expansion of Labour's own machinery, to allow for "investigative" and "legislative" committees to be granted powers to interview witnesses and material regarding new proposals, and, crucially, to do so before the government introduced such material to the House. Although these proposals were "not universally or unanimously supported" by Labour MPs, their introduction would have resulted in a significant extension of the powers of the wider party and NEC to influence the executive (Dorey 2008: 76–7). Despite their best efforts, the third and seventh reforms required for constitutional premiership had failed to take hold, and the executive remained in control.

The reforms of the Blair government (1997–2007) are described by Dorey as radical, "in so far as they went much further than any [previous Labour] constitutional reforms", with "serious implications for both the British system of governance and Britain's unitary state tradition" (2008: 1). Indeed, given the length and large majorities of the Blair government, it is unsurprising that reform was so far-reaching, into many areas of interest to constitutional premiership.

Various reforms took place that would have interested and affected the development of constitutional premiership. In terms of select committees, the Blair years were something of a disappointment. It remained non-committal to their strengthening, something about which Labour MPs expressed their displeasure, despite requests in March 2000 for greater resources and independence from party whips. The government refused to even provide parliamentary time to vote on the matter (Dorey 2008: 89). The transfer of powers to European supranational institutions continued apace, and with a greater significance. For example, the

European Convention on Human Rights became part of domestic British law, further entrenching the supremacy of European courts and their ability to over-rule. The Freedom of Information Act was introduced in full, seemingly confirming open government. However, Bevir notes the Act had its critics, with the Department of Constitutional Affairs acting as a "clearing-house for requests of information", refusing access to sensitive documents (2007: 5–6).

Blair's largest contribution to constitutional reform and the development of constitutional premiership was House of Lords reform. Cockerell notes that Blair originally sought its outright abolition (2001: 119). Blair himself noted his concerns with having an appointed upper chamber, fearing it could encourage cronyism, although he did accept the benefits of being able to appoint those with different backgrounds, undoubtedly encouraging a more diverse chamber as a whole (2010: 649). Ultimately, the House of Lords Act 1999 removed all but 92 hereditary peers and was designed to be the first step towards the eventual full replacement of the Lords with an elected upper chamber (Flinders 2005: 79). It was undoubtedly the furthest any Labour government had gone in seriously denting the Lords as a major constitutional player. As in the case with Attlee, it further enhanced the power of the legislature while retaining the powers of the executive.

The most recent Labour government, Brown's (2007–10), came into conflict in the advancement of the constitutional premiership in relation to further European integration, particularly the Lisbon Treaty. Cowley and Stuart note that the passage of the Bill to ratify the treaty took a considerable amount of time in the House, rather than in committee, reducing time and opportunities for scrutiny. As a result, Brown suffered some 32 separate rebellions over the bill, the most the government suffered over a single bill (Cowley & Stuart 2014: 7–8). It was clear that the wider Labour Party did not cherish being excluded, and that the Brown executive, much like its predecessors, valued a lack of scrutiny.

It is therefore clear that significant progress was made by previous Labour governments in advancing constitutional premiership, although their progress as a whole was contingent on the executive retaining its power and influence. There were successes. For example, a Freedom of Information Act had been introduced, and the scope and powers of the Lords significantly reduced. However, efforts to expand the role and powers of select committees or to integrate the Labour Party further into the democratic processes of the House met with failure, often because of the eagerness of the executive to limit such challenges to its power. Integration into European supranational institutions continued, with a further transfer of law-making powers to the EU. In the case of most Labour governments, the executive repeatedly sought to maintain control, largely to the exclusion of others, including the Labour Party. It is clear that a Corbyn government would have faced significant challenges in introducing constitutional premiership wholesale. It is prudent to determine if a Corbyn Labour government would have had more in common with its predecessors.

## The Corbynite constitution: breaking Bennism?

At the beginning of the Corbyn years, it is clear that some progress had been made in the advancement of Benn's constitutional premiership, although progress was mixed depending on the area of focus. Of Benn's seven proposed reforms, only two had seen any significant progress by 2015: House of Lords reform (crippled but not abolished) and the establishment of a Freedom of Information Act (although with strings attached). This section, although seeking to avoid indulging in counterfactual history, explores Corbyn's attitudes to, actions towards and proposals for constitutional reform, to determine how they advocated Benn's framework and how they correlated with the efforts of previous Labour prime ministers. It determines if, when it comes to constitutional matters, Corbynism represented continuity with previous Labour governments in valuing the power of the executive, or if it represented Bennism and the establishment of constitutional premiership, largely at the expense of the power of the executive.

The two manifestos under which Corbyn ran as prospective prime minister list indications of constitutional reforms that could be expected. They provide the most concrete evidence of what a Corbyn government would have implemented, had he succeeded in either 2017 or 2019. For example, the 2019 manifesto promised an end to the Fixed-term Parliaments Act 2011 (which would have been to the benefit of the executive). In 2017 Labour offered greater opportunities for socialist advancements. For example, the manifesto promised to audit all policy and legislation for its impact on women or provide opportunities for greater legislative involvement (Labour Party 2017: 109; 2019: 82). These manifestos themselves were divisive in signalling the direction of Corbyn and Corbynism, with Manwaring and Smith noting that the 2017 manifesto was simultaneously described as a "dangerous throwback" to the politics of the 1970s, and yet also as representing "fairly conventional" social democratic politics (2020: 26): this is ironic, given Corbyn's struggle with constitutional premiership. Such a link between the 1970s and 2010s is clearly of interest in determining Corbyn's direction of travel, and Byrne is clearest in noting the firm connection between Bennism and Corbynism in the manifesto, with Corbyn pledging to broaden democratic participation and engagement, particularly to the benefit of those "politically blooded in the Labour left of the late 1970s and early 1980s" (Byrne 2019: 261–2). It is appropriate to explore each of Benn's criteria in turn, to determine how committed a Corbyn government would have been to Benn, Bennism and constitutional premiership and whether Corbynism's approach to each criterion represented an advancement or was instead closer to the governance style of previous Labour governments.

In terms of the first criterion, the abolition of the House of Lords, Corbyn's record is mixed. The 2017 manifesto promised to further restrict the powers of the House of Lords, by completely ending the hereditary principle and reducing the overall membership of the upper chamber (Labour Party 2017: 102). The 2019 manifesto went further, proposing to abolish the Lords entirely, and instead replace it with an elected Senate of the Nations and Regions (2019: 81). Corbyn's relationship with the House of Lords during his leadership was difficult, least of all because of his wider issues with party management, in which, according to Shaw, Corbyn had been reliant both on traditional pluralism and (at times empty) threats, critically noting that leadership "requires some agglomeration of power at the centre – which Corbyn notably lacks" (Shaw 2016). Ewing goes so far as to suggest that having a directly elected Lords would have produced further electoral headaches for a Labour government, as either the necessary legislation would consume too much time and capital, or a new upper chamber might create "obstacles" to the implementation of a progressive manifesto (2017: 351). Indeed, Watts (2018) notes it is no coincidence that Corbyn only finally committed the 2019 manifesto to abolishing the Lords after Labour peers rebelled and voted with the May government over her EU Withdrawal Bill. It is clear that Corbyn's support for the abolition of the Lords was driven by, or concerned with, a desire to remove roadblocks on the power of the executive. For the most part, this indicates a total commitment to the first step in establishing Benn's constitutional democracy, although it does demonstrate some divergence. Benn did not believe the second chamber should be replaced, something which, by 2019, Corbyn was prepared to support, perhaps for wider party coherence. In terms of the wider Labour canon, Corbyn's proposals were not that radical. They represented, at best, a gradual continuation of the policies and reforms enacted by the Blair government. In terms of adherence to Bennite proposals, Corbynism came close, but could not be considered a total adoption. It did, however, represent a total continuity with previous Labour governments: Corbyn undoubtedly sought a weakening of the Lords to the benefit of, ultimately, the executive.

The second criterion called for ministers to be confirmed in post by Labour MPs. Neither manifesto makes any commitments in this regard, save for promising to "overhaul the system of ministerial appointments to public office" in 2019 (Labour Party 2019: 82). Yet allowing a greater role for Labour MPs was clearly something that Corbyn was not too prepared to engage with, if his record as leader of the opposition is any indication. For example, his October 2016 shadow cabinet reshuffle was perceived as weakening the number of Labour moderates in order to boost his own support, with some Labour MPs requesting a return of elections to the shadow cabinet (Stone 2016) to ensure wider representation of various factions and voices. Clearly, Corbyn was not as interested or committed to the broad-church approach as Benn had been. Corbyn later (in November 2016) refused to reintroduce shadow cabinet elections (Merrick 2016). Given the perceived "civil war" between the Corbynite and Blairite wings of the party (Rawnsley 2015), it is reasonable to assume that a Corbyn premiership would not have consulted with Labour MPs over the allocation of portfolios, lest it further expand the rift in the party, or provide an opportunity for Blairite and other "moderate" MPs to regain lost ground. Indeed, keeping the PLP at arm's length and reducing their potential impact may have benefitted his fractious leadership, especially in the early days. Richards notes that Corbyn and his MPs felt simultaneously trapped by and at odds with each other, with the friction causing Corbyn to struggle with his convictions in order to maintain a semblance of party unity, suggesting Trident as one example. Richards suggests further that it is in the membership that Corbyn felt "liberated" and able to act (2016: 12). It is clear that, had this stand-off continued, which it most certainly would have done had a Corbyn government materialized, the smaller the role for the wider PLP, the better. Allowing the executive to continue dominating the party represents a clear break with Benn's constitutional premiership, and yet further continuity with previous Labour governments.

Benn's third criterion for advancing constitutional premiership saw a greater role and powers for committees, with enhanced ability to scrutinize the executive. This criterion is the easiest to determine, and the 2019 manifesto is crystal clear in this regard, as it suggests that a Corbyn government would have taken a significant step towards constitutional premiership. It promised to empower the Committee on Climate Change to assess and recommend policies to tackle the UK's carbon footprint, as well as creating a Climate Change Sustainability Committee. It would have strengthened the powers of the Joint Intelligence and Security Committee, while simultaneously restricting the prime minister's power to suppress the publication of committee reports. A new Business Commission was to be created to streamline regulation and be answerable to select committees. The Advisory Committee on Business Appointments was to be replaced, with the new body "sufficiently resourced and empowered", and governed by a "diverse and representative board" established in law (Labour Party 2019: 16, 44, 64, 82, 102). By clearly committing to and allowing a greater role for such bodies at the nominal expense of the executive, this represents the strongest example yet of Corbyn's commitment to constitutional premiership, and Corbynism's continuation of Bennism. It is also the first major break with previous Labour prime ministers and the fear of a weakening of the executive, as the experiences of Wilson and Callaghan demonstrated.

Adoption of the fourth criterion, regarding major public appointments, particularly in (formerly) nationalized industries, is difficult to determine because of wholesale privatization in the 1980s and 1990s. However, it is likely that a Corbyn government would have ultimately been in a position make such decisions, had the 2019 proposals to renationalize rail, mail, water and energy been implemented (Labour Party 2019: 7). It is also curious to note that the nationalization programme itself might have met with further challenges, with polling data suggesting the wider public remained concerned with how it would have been funded (Manwaring & Beech 2018: 32). Paul Mason (2018) suggested that the Corbynite approach to the nationalization of industries would not see a wholesale replacement of neoliberalism with Keynesianism, but rather a mixture of the two that would, for example, replace asset-driven growth with productivity-driven growth, and that such an approach "shouldn't flinch" from having to increase investment or expand the workforce to achieve that. Clearly, those receiving major public appointments would have to demonstrate a commitment to the Corbynite way of thinking, and indeed to the implementation of ultimately socialist policies, as would those heading up the proposed new National Investment Fund tasked with investing £250 billion into declining regions (Byrne 2019: 260). Given Corbyn's actions in line with second criterion, it is reasonable to assume such appointments would have been made without further input, particularly given the resistance this policy faced from other sources, not least those within the wider Labour Party, such as those on the Blairite wing. This would represent a further break with constitutional premiership, and again a greater commitment to the power of the executive and continuity with previous Labour governments.

As noted, the fifth criterion, the Freedom of Information Act, had already been introduced in full by the Blair government. However, Corbyn's government would have expanded the Act's powers as part of a wider commitment to open government, to the larger satisfaction of Bennism. Both manifestos proposed an extension of the powers and scope of the Act. The 2017 manifesto proposed extending the Act to include private companies running public services. This proposal was retained in 2019 and also sought to set "new standards of consistent disclosure practice", such as by ending the information commissioner's six-month limit on the deliberate destruction of public records (Labour Party 2017: 102; 2019: 83). Such proposals would undoubtedly have contributed towards the Bennite constitutional premiership aim of open government, as would Corbyn's proposals to introduce a constitutional convention on extending democracy nationally, regionally and locally. Such plans would have seen the introduction of a policy forum enhancing democratic ownership and accountability (Martell 2018: 6). As noted by Martell, a Corbyn government would have required far greater transparency, given the proposed involvement of the public in local budget decisions, as part of a wider drive for "bottom-up democracy" (*ibid.*). Furthermore, such drives would have fitted within the wider progress made by previous Labour governments. It is the first criterion that Corbynism would have satisfied on both accounts: a Corbyn government would have both advocated and advanced constitutional premiership, and also fitted in with the actions of its predecessors.

Labour's approach to the sixth criterion, namely the repatriation of powers from EU institutions, is complicated, not least by conflict within the Labour Party over a Brexit approach (Blitz 2017), requiring Corbyn to maintain an ambivalent position (Room 2019). Indeed, both he and Benn had defied the Labour whip to vote against the Maastricht Treaty in 1992 (Cawthorne 2015: 65), suggesting a shared Eurosceptic position. However, the 2019 manifesto promised a "final say on Brexit", promising to hold a second referendum including an option to Remain. The 2017 manifesto also promised not only to protect the 1998 Human Rights Act, but to extend it, by making the Human Rights Commission "truly independent", further entrenching the European Convention on Human Rights deeper into British law (Labour Party 2017: 108; 2019: 89). Ewing (2017: 358–9) notes, ironically, that EU law had actually further entrenched the powers of trade unions and their influence (such as collective bargaining) as wholly legitimate, and that they deeply penetrated into existing political and legal structures, an avenue a Corbyn government could have explored to further support and legitimize extra-party actors. On the surface, this greater commitment to supranational instruments demonstrates a break with Bennism and constitutional premiership, and at least maintaining the position of previous Labour governments, if not making a small advancement. It also offers some further evidence of the greater role of parliamentary committees in being able to challenge the executive, as per the third criterion.

In the seventh and final criterion, namely a greater role for the wider Labour Party itself in government, Corbyn's aims in this regard are evidenced as far back as his initial candidacy for leader. He promised to answer the "overwhelming" call of party members eager to see a "broader range of candidates and thorough debate about the future of the Party". His position was clear: "I am standing to give Labour Party members a voice in this debate" (Cawthorne 2015: 111). Despite this, in November 2016, Corbyn refused to advance proposals for party members to participate in policy-making through "digital consultations" (Merrick 2016). Indeed, efforts were even made to directly remove critics of his leadership from within the party itself, for example with the proposals to abolish the deputy leadership in September 2019, the negative response to which forced Corbyn to downgrade to a "review" (Mohdin 2019). Bassett (2020) is more critical of the Corbyn leadership. He notes that a promising start was made, but that even by 2018 any serious efforts to expand party influence via rule changes had amounted to "little more than tinkering", such as the widening of the party's franchise to give greater power to trade unions. Bassett does offer some praise for the slow move away from the executive-centred bureaucratic approach of the New Labour years. However, ultimately, Bassett suggests that despite extensively promoting his desire to improve the role and status of party membership, constitutionally Corbyn "will leave the Labour Party in a similar state to how he found it". These incidents suggest further correlation with Corbyn's preference for executive dominance, with any efforts to expand the influence of the party being token at best.

Outside of the Labour Party itself, manifestos hint at, but are non-specific and non-committal towards, a greater role for party institutions and allies through non-governmental bodies through which to influence the wider parliamentary party. The 2017 manifesto proposed to create an industrial strategy council, specifically modelled on the "highly successful" Automotive Council. It promised the establishment of a constitutional convention designed to advise on reforming how "Britain works at a fundamental level" and, in 2019, this was specified to be led by a citizen's assembly. A network of smaller, community-led regional development banks was to complement cooperatives (themselves set to double in size) and small businesses. In 2019, a direct link between such groups was to be established in cabinet, with the creation of a ministry for employment rights. A national Women's Commission was to act as an independent advisory body, "to contribute to a Labour government" (Labour Party 2017: 14, 16, 19, 102; 2019: 60, 65, 81). Furthermore, the role of extra-party actors such as Momentum cannot be ignored in offering an avenue of influence over the Labour Party, and its founders were very clear in this regard: they believed that Momentum was founded to "radically reshape" the political terrain around the Labour Party to transform government as a whole, citing the 1945 Attlee government (or indeed, the 1979 Thatcher government) as examples. In particular, they envisaged a broad coalition with Corbyn at its head, in which extra-party actors were to be as important as the traditional arms of Labour, such as trade unions. Crucially, Corbyn's executive leadership was vital in driving the campaign (Klug *et al.* 2016: 36–7).

Given that a Corbyn government would have resulted in a greater number and range of powers for select committees and extra-parliamentary bodies, and indeed a greater voice and role for such bodies, it is clear that on the seventh criterion, Corbynism represents a break with established Labour governments, who would not have tolerated such a burden on their executive power. It instead correlates more closely – although not fully – with Benn's constitutional premiership, by creating new avenues for party members to engage with a Corbyn government.

## Conclusion

In conclusion, had a Corbyn government taken power, the Corbynite approach towards constitutional reform would have demonstrated near-balance in terms of ideological commitments towards Bennism and the strengthening of the legislature, while also representing continuity with the actions and reforms of previous Labour governments in protecting the power of the executive. As was the case with Corbyn's actions as leader, his proposals for government found themselves trapped between the old and the new world. Unable to commit fully to one or the other, Corbynite constitutional proposals struggled to establish themselves as firmly as his supporters would have liked, while simultaneously being far more radical than his critics would have tolerated.

Benn's constitutional premiership framework was established to allow for a greater influx and influence of socialism within the British constitution, and to allow the constitution to contribute towards wider socialist aims. Of Benn's seven key changes, Corbyn's proposed reforms would have advanced four. Based on his actions and proposals, a Corbyn government would have overseen the abolition of the House of Lords; greatly enhanced, empowered and extended select committees; retained and extended the powers and scope of the Freedom of Information Act; and would have provided extra-parliamentary opportunities for party members and affiliate institutions to influence the party and the executive. Corbyn broke with Benn's constitutional premiership in three areas: his management of the shadow cabinet suggests he would not have allowed Labour MPs a say on ministerial appointments; his executive would probably have retained patronage and influence over senior appointments in the newly (re-) nationalized industries; and his troubled Euroscepticism was not fully realized, with the full and total repatriation of law-making powers to parliament unlikely to occur, because of a greater commitment to existing supranational instruments. Viewed in this way, a Corbyn government would have advocated a (bare) majority of Benn's reforms towards constitutional premiership.

However, countering the Bennite position on constitutional reform is the orthodox position of previous Labour governments, with its greater commitment to executive power and a subservient party machine behind it. A Corbyn government would probably have demonstrated a continuity with previous Labour prime ministers. Like MacDonald, Attlee and Blair, he sought to further weaken the Lords to strengthen the Commons, but without weakening the power of the executive. Like Attlee, Wilson and Callaghan, he resisted and minimized attempts to influence his appointments, securing his power of patronage. Like Attlee, Wilson and Callaghan, he would have acted alone in appointing chairmen to (re-)nationalized industries, further entrenching patronage. Like Blair, he supported a push for open government via the Freedom of Information

Act. Finally, like Blair and Brown, he envisaged a role for supranational European legislation with supremacy over British law, particularly the Human Rights Act. Despite introducing large swathes of constitutional premiership, the governing style of a Corbyn government undoubtedly would have followed, firmly and neatly, in the footsteps of its predecessors, and not forged a (wholly) new path as his supporters would have hoped. This would undoubtedly have been of great disappointment to them, and perhaps even to Benn himself.

## References

Bassett, L. 2020. "Constitutionally, Corbyn will leave the Labour Party in a similar state to how he found it". LSE Blog, 20 February. https://blogs.lse.ac.uk/politicsandpolicy/corbyn-reforms/ (accessed 19 March 2021).

Benn, T. 1979. *Arguments for Socialism*. London: Penguin.

Benn, T. 1980. "The case for a constitutional premiership". *Parliamentary Affairs* 33(1): 7–22.

Benn, T. 1981. *Arguments for Democracy*. London: Penguin.

Benn, T. 1994. *Tony Benn Diaries 1980–90*. London: Hutchinson.

Benn, T. 2002. *Tony Benn Diaries 1991–2001*. London: Hutchinson.

Bevir, M. 2007. "Socialism and democracy: New Labour and the constitution". *Observatoire de la société britannique* 3: 1–19.

Blair, T. 2010. *A Journey*. London: Hutchinson.

Blitz, J. 2017. "Jeremy Corbyn is a Brexit bystander". *Financial Times*, 29 June.

Bolton, M. & F. Pitts 2018. *Corbynism: A Critical Approach*. Bingley: Emerald.

Byrne, L. 2019. "How Jeremy Corbyn brought labour back to the future: visions of the future and concrete utopia in labour's 2017 electoral campaign". *British Politics* 14(3): 250–68.

Cawthorne, N. 2015. *Jeremy Corbyn: Leading from the Left*. London: Endeavour Press.

Cockerell, M. 2001. "The politics of second chamber reform: a case study of the House of Lords and the passage of the House of Lords Act 1999". *Journal of Legislative Studies* 7(1): 119–34.

Cowley, P. & M. Stuart 2014. "In the brown stuff: Labour backbench dissent under Gordon Brown, 2007–10". *Contemporary British History* 28(1): 1–23.

Dorey, P. 2008. *The Labour Party and Constitutional Reform*. Basingstoke: Palgrave Macmillan.

Ewing, K. 1995. "Democratic socialism and labour law". *Industrial Law Journal* 24(2): 103–32.

Ewing, K. 2017. "Jeremy Corbyn and the law of democracy". *King's Law Journal* 28(2): 343–62.

Flinders, M. 2005. "Majoritarian democracy in Britain: New Labour and the constitution". *West European Politics* 28(1): 61–93.

Freeman, A. 1982. *The Benn Heresy*. London: Pluto.

Gibson, R. & N. Assinder 1988. "Kinnochio!". *Daily Express*, 3 October.

Harvey, J. & L. Bather 1963. *The British Constitution*. London: Macmillan.

Klug, A. *et al.* 2016. "Momentum: a new kind of politics". *Renewal* 24(2): 36–44.

Labour Party 2017. *For the Many, Not the Few: The Labour Party Manifesto 2017*. https://labour.org.uk/wp-content/uploads/2017/10/labour-manifesto-2017.pdf (accessed 19 March 2021).

Labour Party 2019. *It's Time for Real Change: The Labour Party Manifesto 2019*. https://labour.org.uk/wp-content/uploads/2019/11/Real-Change-Labour-Manifesto-2019.pdf (accessed 19 March 2021).

Loewenberg, G. 1958. "The British Constitution and the structure of the Labour Party". *American Political Science Review* 52(3): 771–90.

Manwaring, R. & M. Beech 2018. "The case of the British Labour Party: back to the wilderness". In R. Manwaring & P. Kennedy (eds). *Why the Left Loses* 25–38. Bristol: Policy Press.

Manwaring, R. & E. Smith 2020. "Corbyn, British labour and policy change". *British Politics* 15(1): 25–47.

Martell, L. 2018. "Corbyn, populism and power". *Hard Times* (January): 1–11.

Mason, P. 2018. "Neoliberalism has destroyed social mobility. Together we must rebuild it". Open Democracy, 2 February. https://neweconomics.opendemocracy.net/neoliberalism-destroyed-social-mobility-together-must-rebuild/ (accessed 19 March 2021).

Merrick, R. 2016. "Jeremy Corbyn drops plans for shadow cabinet elections and for Labour members to help decide policy". *The Independent*, 22 November. https://www.independent.co.uk/news/uk/politics/jeremy-corbyn-drops-plans-for-shadow-cabinet-elections-and-for-party-members-to-help-decide-policy-a7432756.html (accessed 19 March 2021).

Mohdin, A. 2019. "Explained: the attempt to remove Tom Watson as deputy Labour leader". *The Guardian*, 21 September. https://www.theguardian.com/politics/2019/sep/21/explained-attempt-to-remove-tom-watson-deputy-labour-leader (accessed 19 March 2021).

Parker, D. 2012. *The Official History of Privatisation, Volume II: Popular Capitalism, 1987–1997*. Abingdon: Routledge.

Rawnsley, A. 2015. "Labour is really two parties. And they simply can't stand each other". *The Guardian*, 2 August. https://www.theguardian.com/commentisfree/2015/aug/02/labour-split-corbyn-blairites (accessed 19 March 2021).

Richards, S. 2016. "Leadership, loyalty and the rise of Jeremy Corbyn". *Political Quarterly* 87(1): 12–17.

Room, G. 2019. "Why has Corbyn remained so ambivalent about Brexit?" LSE Blogs, 11 February. https://blogs.lse.ac.uk/brexit/2019/02/11/why-has-corbyn-remained-so-ambivalent-about-brexit/ (accessed 19 March 2021).

Shaw, E. 2016. "Fractured and unmanageable? Labour Party management under Blair and under Corbyn". LSE Blogs, 7 June. https://blogs.lse.ac.uk/politicsandpolicy/labour-party-management-under-blair/ (accessed 19 March 2021).

Stafford, J. 2016. "The Corbyn experiment". *Dissent* 63(1): 69–76.

Stone, J. 2016. "Jeremy Corbyn completes shadow cabinet reshuffle and wrests control of NEC". *The Independent*, 7 October. https://www.independent.co.uk/news/uk/politics/jeremy-corbyn-labour-shadow-cabinet-reshuffle-nec-a7351241.html (accessed 19 March 2021).

Watts, J. 2018. "Jeremy Corbyn commits to abolishing House of Lords". *The Independent*, 23 May. https://www.independent.co.uk/news/uk/politics/jeremy-corbyn-house-lords-abolish-labour-leader-a8365401.html (accessed 19 March 2021).

Watts, J. & T. Bale 2018. "Populism as an intra-party phenomenon: the British Labour Party under Jeremy Corbyn". *British Journal of Politics and International Relations* 21(1): 99–115.

Wright, A. 1990. "British socialists and the British Constitution". *Parliamentary Affairs* 43(3): 322–40.

# 13

# JEREMY CORBYN'S FOREIGN POLICY

*Mark Garnett and Richard Johnson*

No account of Jeremy Corbyn's political career could be complete without an assessment of his approach to foreign policy. His professed mission to create a fairer and more equal Britain has been matched by a desire to transform the country's international relations. Prior to becoming Labour's leader, Corbyn's public profile chiefly arose from his stance on a foreign policy issue: his opposition to the Iraq War. Indeed, according to one well-placed source, he would have preferred to serve as foreign secretary rather than as prime minister (Bush 2018). The Orwell Prize-winning journalist Steven Bloomfield summarized, "Foreign policy is Corbyn's passion. While the ins and outs of NHS reform don't tend to interest him, a conversation about healthcare in Latin America can last for hours" (Bloomfield 2018).

While foreign policy brought Corbyn to public notice, his views on controversial international issues provided considerable ammunition for critics at home and abroad. To his opponents, his "terrorist" groups, such as the IRA and Hamas, made him an enemy to his country, and a security risk even as leader of the opposition. Our present purpose is to offer a more general overview and evaluation of Corbyn's foreign policy, in the light of the most cogent criticisms of his detractors. In recent years, a failed leader of the opposition (William Hague) has ended up serving as foreign secretary. It is unlikely (not least on grounds of age) that Jeremy Corbyn's career will follow the same course. But it is permissible to pose the hypothetical question of whether or not Corbyn was really equipped to realize his ambition of serving in this senior ministerial role, not least because in his relatively brief spell as a major political player he had the chance to inspire others who might seek to shape British foreign policy along "Corbynista" lines.

## The case against Corbyn

In September 2019, the Washington-based think tank the Hudson Institute published *The Prospective Foreign Policy of a Corbyn Government and its US National Security Implications*. Since the Institute has strong "conservative" affiliations it was most unlikely to commission a sympathetic study of Corbyn's views. However, the author of *The Prospective Foreign Policy of a Corbyn Government*, Azeem Ibrahim, is a reputable scholar with excellent knowledge of the political context on both sides of the Atlantic. His critique of Corbyn is therefore much better suited to the present purpose than the productions of journalists working for more blatantly partisan British newspapers. Indeed, the most polemical passages in the pamphlet were contributed by the author of the foreword, the former British foreign secretary Malcolm Rifkind, who congratulates Ibrahim for having shown that "Corbyn's worldview is warped and lacks any ethical foundation", so that "Corbyn, if he were to obtain power, would do grave damage not only to the United Kingdom and the West but to the cause of democracy and liberal values throughout the world" (Ibrahim 2019a: 6).

In reality, Ibrahim presents Corbyn's worldview as distorted rather than "warped"; it is "binary [...] with imperialism and capitalism on one side and opposition to them on the other". From this basic position, Ibrahim alleges, Corbyn automatically sides with states "such as Russia, Venezuela, Syria, Iran, and, sometimes, China", as a reward for their apparent resistance to "Western imperialism". As a corollary, Corbyn is selective in his identification of human rights abuses, stigmatizing those committed by Western and pro-Western regimes while minimizing or overlooking similar actions when perpetrated by his favoured regimes. He regards protests against these regimes as illegitimate. There is, Ibrahim claims, "never any nuance in his positions, so the messy, brutal civil war in Syria is reduced to an anti-imperialist Assad government struggling against jihadi and Western-sponsored opposition groups" (*ibid.*: 9–10).

On the basis of this analysis, Ibrahim offers some predictions about the likely nature of a Corbyn-led government's foreign policy. In terms of attitudes towards specific states and regions, Britain would switch its support in the Middle East from Israel and Saudi Arabia to Iran and would show "a greater tolerance for the Putin regime's actions and worldview". Rather than embracing "globalization" and transnational institutions, Corbyn would try to impose "a degree of autarky", ensure that Britain leaves the EU, and would be at best a disruptive influence within NATO, the United Nations (UN), the International Monetary Fund and the World Bank (*ibid.*: 10).

Ibrahim attributes Corbyn's approach to his exposure to arguments from various "leftist" elements in the 1970s, including the Communist Party of Great Britain and the intellectual "New Left", as well as elements within the Labour

Party at that time (*ibid.*: 15–16). He accepts that in some instances Corbyn is right to criticize Britain's existing foreign policy stances, particularly its tendency to refrain from criticizing "friendly" regimes with questionable records on human rights. However, although Ibrahim concedes that a rebalancing of Britain's alliances might be appropriate in these instances, in his view a Corbyn-led government would merely create a different kind of imbalance, turning well-known adversaries of the West into allies. Accordingly, Ibrahim's critique was cited as an authoritative account by the authors of serious pieces in periodicals such as *The Atlantic*, and Ibrahim himself wrote several follow-up articles for journals like *The Spectator* (Ibrahim 2019b).

In the remainder of this chapter, we build our own analysis of Corbyn's approach on a sample of key speeches and statements throughout his career, before comparing our findings to Ibrahim's conclusions. At the outset, however, it is worth noting that Ibrahim's criticism of Corbyn's "binary worldview" can be applied with at least equal justice to most US presidents since 1945, with their Cold War mentality and their "Axis of Evil". Thus, the predicted transformation of Britain's alliances would have resulted from a style of thinking characteristic of the US itself; the world, for Corbyn, merely spins in a different direction on its "axis". In this respect his worldview actually has more in common with that of US governments since 1945 than with the traditional approach of British foreign policy-makers, who have *always* included a degree of "nuance in [their] positions" unless over-ridden by hyperactive prime ministers (like Eden in relation to Suez, and Blair in relation to almost every foreign policy question).

Finally, unlike Ibrahim we have little interest in guessing what a Corbyn-led government would have done, for the obvious reason that this supposed "threat to Western security" was lifted forever by the 2019 general election. Our discussion focuses chiefly on evidence for Corbyn's position *before* he became Labour leader in 2015. However, it is also relevant to consider any signs of modification in his stated positions after his transition from backbench dissident to potential prime minister. Thus, our discussion also includes an evaluation of a key speech Corbyn delivered as opposition leader before the 2017 general election, and policy positions in Labour's manifestos of 2017 and 2019.

## Case studies of Corbyn's foreign policy approach

When appraising the foreign policy positions of senior political figures, one usually needs to take account of an evolution in their views over time, in response to changes in the international and domestic context as well as personal experience. In this respect, as in so many others, Corbyn is different. Almost the only point of agreement between his admirers and his detractors is the consistency of his outlook. For example, the former Labour MP Mike Gapes observed that, "Most of Corbyn's foreign-policy positions are identical today to what he always had: a pro-Castro, pro-Chávez, anti-imperialist view of the world" (Serhan 2019). If we accept these remarks at face value, we can place equal emphasis in our discussion on speeches and statements taken at various times in Corbyn's political career, starting soon after his election to parliament in 1983. Corbyn's more than three decades as a backbench Labour MP (1983–2015) provide a rich, unvarnished collection of evidence that can be used to understand his foreign policy approach.

## Grenada

Although Corbyn devoted his maiden speech to domestic issues, it was not long before an occasion arose for him to exercise his eloquence on international developments. On 26 October 1983, he spoke in a debate on the US invasion of Grenada, a Commonwealth territory in the West Indies (*Hansard* 1983). Corbyn denounced the invasion but was no less critical of the "scandalous role of British foreign policy in the region", which had been to follow the American lead without question, at least until the Grenada invasion. This had presented the government with an acute dilemma, not only because the invasion was viewed by many to be illegal, but also because the UK had been given very belated notice of an ally's action against a sovereign Commonwealth state. Corbyn drew the attention of the House to the avowedly-Marxist "New Jewel" movement, initially led by Maurice Bishop, which since a bloodless coup in 1979 had been responsible for significant social reforms.

As a set-piece attack on US policy towards Grenada, Corbyn's speech was powerful. The country, he argued, "has demonstrated that it believes that the Caribbean is its own basin". He remarked upon US attempts to destabilize neighbouring regimes, particularly that of Nicaragua, purportedly because it feared the growing influence of Cuba and the Soviet Union, but in reality because it felt threatened by the "ideas and inspiration" of radical movements like New Jewel and Nicaragua's Sandinistas. However, his case against his own government was far less clear. He claimed that its "Uriah Heap diplomacy" towards the US had made the UK look "incredibly stupid and shortsighted". As well as condemning the Americans, the House should censure the British government "for standing by and allowing a foreign power to invade Grenada". The government should be forced to condemn the US action at the UN Security Council and to demand the immediate withdrawal of its forces.

There was, naturally, no possibility that the Commons would follow Corbyn's advice and, judging from subsequent contributions to the debate, his speech was regarded as an irrelevance. Most probably, the effect of his critique of the US action was dissipated by his impractical recommendations. In truth, the British government was embarrassed by the Grenada invasion – coming as it did so soon after the brief national intoxication provoked by the Falklands conflict – because it brought into sharp juxtaposition two legacies of Britain's postwar attempt to sustain some kind of global role. On the one hand, it exposed Commonwealth responsibilities that the country could no longer sustain; on the other, it exposed a degree of subservience towards the US, which had not been anticipated by those (notably Churchill) who promoted the idea of a "special relationship" between the countries, and which was particularly unwelcome to a government that had agreed to the siting of US cruise missiles on British soil. In effect, by accusing the British of pursuing a policy that was both weak and ill-intentioned, Corbyn was criticizing ministers for failing to prevent an action of which they approved: an example of having one's critical cake and eating it.

The impression that Corbyn had prepared a speech in order to testify to his opinions rather than trying to influence (let alone persuade) his parliamentary colleagues is enhanced by the fact that he spoke immediately after contributions from two veteran right-wing MPs: Enoch Powell (now an Ulster Unionist) and Julian Amery. Both of these speeches were worthy of comment, but Corbyn ignored them. Powell had exhibited his idiosyncratic brand of anti-Americanism, arguing that over Grenada the US had treated Britain as it usually did, that is, ignoring its views when it was intent on pursuing what it regarded as its national interests.

If Corbyn had been an experienced parliamentarian like his fellow Labour MP Tony Benn, he would have taken note of these speeches, which implied that Britain should react in very different ways to an assumed reduction of its role in the world. Instead, he ploughed on as if no one else had spoken. In addition, while his praise of Maurice Bishop's regime was largely justified, under his rule Grenada's observation of human rights had not been impeccable; and the pretext for the US invasion had been the toppling (and subsequent assassination) of Bishop at the hands of a former ally whose actions had undoubtedly injected a new element of instability into a region that was considered crucial to US interests. Corbyn made no reference to Bishop's displacement, although this sequence of events was alarming to genuine well-wishers of the New Jewel movement.

## Rwanda and Sierra Leone

On 6 April 1994, the presidents of Rwanda and Burundi were killed when their plane was blown up by a surface-to-air missile as it approached Kigali Airport.

Fourteen hours later, Rwanda's Prime Minister Agathe Uwilingiyimana was killed as she emerged from her home. In the power vacuum that followed, extreme Hutu elements moved quickly to begin exterminating the ethnic minority Tutsis and sympathetic Hutus. Between 7 April and 15 July, over 800,000 people, in a country with a population of 8 million, were slaughtered.

The situation in Rwanda before the presidents' deaths was already delicate. The country had been embroiled in a civil war since 1990. A UN peacekeeping force, known as the United Nations Assistance Mission for Rwanda (UNAMIR), had been sent to the country in October 1993 to enforce peace accords and were still present in the country at the time when the slaughter began. Ten members of this force were killed when they tried to protect Prime Minister Uwilingiyimana. In response, the UNAMIR was reduced from 2,500 to 270 troops as alarmed countries, still chastened by the "Black Hawk Down" affair in Somalia, withdrew their support from the mission. Western governments refused to act; the US and UK governments were focused on the situation unfolding in Bosnia. The very same month, NATO forces had begun conducting airstrikes, for the first time in its history, on Serbian forces (discussed below).

A UN resolution was passed in May 1994 to bolster the number of troops in the UNAMIR to 5,500. However, as the weeks dragged on, troops had not arrived (Dallaire 2004). The United Kingdom refused to acknowledge urgent requests from the Secretariat for troops and logistical support. A report from the special rapporteur on 28 June 1994 described the situation as a genocide, but as late as July 1994, Foreign Secretary Douglas Hurd was still "thumping the table" and insisting, "We will not call this a genocide" (Cameron 2012: 79).

On 7 July, John Major was rebuked by the Christian socialist Labour MP Norman Godman, who called the UN Security Council "disgracefully inept and irresponsible" and urged for increased support for the operation in Rwanda. Major reported that he did "share the horror and revulsion felt by many people, including the honourable Gentleman, about the terrible suffering in Rwanda". Yet he went on to say that the Security Council "simply does not have the resources in terms of cash or money" to provide for troops in Rwanda. Major concluded that, "It simply is not practicable for it to become the policeman of every part of the world" (*Hansard* 1994a).

Ordinarily, one might expect Jeremy Corbyn to express some sympathy with Major's non-interventionist position. Corbyn's foreign policy pronouncements have typically been highly critical when UK governments act as "the policemen of the world", launching military interventions in countries and telling them how to run their own affairs. Yet the Rwanda conflict facially implies some nuance to Corbyn's non-interventionism. On 27 April 1994, Jeremy Corbyn had signed a cross-party Early Day Motion, expressing deep concern about the slaughter in Rwanda, which by this time had claimed at least 100,000 victims. The motion condemned the reduction in the peacekeeping mission and demanded "that the Security Council should urgently increase UNAMIR's strength and mandate allowing it to protect civilians" (UK Parliament 1994). The motion was signed by 105 MPs, representing a wide section of the Labour Party from Audrey Wise to Peter Shore to Mike Gapes, as well as a handful of MPs from other parties, including Liberal Democrats, Scottish and Welsh nationalists and Conservatives.

In Rwanda, Corbyn apparently saw a role for the UN to use force to stop the unfolding genocide. Admittedly, Corbyn's public interventions about Rwanda in 1994 are scarce, but it is clear that he did not support the government's inaction. He asked Hurd in July 1994 to account for how much foreign aid the British government had spent in Rwanda and its neighbours since the conflict began, possibly a riposte to Hurd and Major's assertions that the UK lacked the funds to support the UN peacekeeping mission (*Hansard* 1994b). In the years to follow, Corbyn asked questions relating to the Great Lakes refugee crisis and offered criticism about the British government's failure to help enforce a UN arms embargo.

Corbyn was clearly moved by the plight of the Tutsis. In a debate on the twentieth anniversary of the genocide, Corbyn spoke about visiting memorials to the victims on trips to Kigali. He told the House, "Talking to schoolchildren in Rwanda about what they have been through, one realises that horror, [one] wonders what more could have been done to prevent it and can still be done to defend and protect human rights and democracy" (*Hansard* 2014). Given the murderous climate in Rwanda in 1994, the prospects of effectual intervention that stopped short of military action were vanishingly slight.

For many Western leaders, the tragedy in Rwanda showed the terrible costs of international inaction. In his memoirs, President Bill Clinton reflected, "neither I nor anyone on my foreign policy team adequately focused on sending troops to stop the slaughter". He admitted, "The failure to try to stop Rwanda's tragedies became one of the greatest regrets of my presidency" (Clinton 2004: 593). The Rwanda tragedy became justification for subsequent Western "liberal" interventions.

These lessons appeared to have been learned during the civil war in Sierra Leone, by which time Major had been replaced as British prime minister by Labour's Tony Blair. In October 1999, the UN Security Council created the United Nations Mission in Sierra Leone (UNAMSIL), which was designed to enforce a fragile peace agreement signed between the warring parties earlier that summer. About 6,000 UN troops were sent to the west African nation. However, this force could not prevent the advance of the rebel army (the Revolutionary United Front) as they advanced on the capital Freetown in May 2000. This time, the British government sent a significant military contingent to bolster the UNAMSIL and within a matter of months the RUF were forced to disarm.

Once more, Jeremy Corbyn delivered barbed comments about the actions of the British government; but this time he was irate that the government had been *too* proactive. He asked Defence Secretary Geoff Hoon, on 15 May 2000, "Why cannot British troops be placed under UN command, so that it is clear that they are part of the UN?". Hoon replied that British troops "have a particular and limited objective, which is precisely why they will not come under the control or command of the United Nations". Corbyn disagreed: "Although British troops went in with a clear mission to extract Commonwealth and European nationals, their objective seems now to have changed to that of a support mechanism for the United Nations". Corbyn worried that British troops would become a long-term presence in the country, perhaps even supporting the new regime. Corbyn warned, "they may be asked by President Kabbah's Government to undertake economic objectives, such as securing the diamond-producing areas for his Government. We need serious clarity on what the British troops are there for in the longer term" (*Hansard* 2000a). Reverting to his usual form, Corbyn's greatest concern seemed to be the size of the Western footprint in a former British colony.

## Bosnia and Kosovo

At the same time that genocide was taking place in Rwanda, ethnic warfare was raging in the former Yugoslavia. The once delicately balanced federation was collapsing, as constituent units declared independence and ethnic Serbs were determined to re-assert their dominance. Yet another poorly resourced UN peacekeeping mission failed to protect thousands of Muslim Bosnians from mass slaughter and displacement.

The Major government was once more sedentary. Indeed, Foreign Secretary Douglas Hurd was "a stumbling block" to Western action (Turner 2013: 477). Hurd insisted in his memoirs that inaction was the correct course because "Britain had no substantial commercial or strategic stake" in the region (Hurd 2003: 444). British political reaction to the bloodshed in Bosnia did not follow obvious partisan or ideological lines. Hurd's former boss, Margaret Thatcher, said that the killings "in the heart of Europe [...] should be in Europe's sphere of conscience" and that by being inactive, the British "were like an accomplice to massacre" (Thatcher 1993). Malcom Rifkind, the contributor to the aforementioned Hudson Institute critique of Jeremy Corbyn's foreign policy, dismissed Mrs Thatcher's comments as "emotional nonsense" (Norman 2013).

Discerning Jeremy Corbyn's view on this foreign policy crisis is not easy. He made no interventions on the matter in parliament at the time, although he did comment on it later. In a foreign policy debate in November 1995, when

"Bosnia" was mentioned 40 times and "Serbs" were raised 25 times, Corbyn managed to give a ten-minute speech without mentioning either. The Socialist Campaign Group, to which Corbyn belonged, was "split down the middle" (Mullin 2011: 105). Figures on the Labour Party's right were harshly critical of the Major government. The Blairite MP Calum MacDonald compared Serbian leader Slobodan Milošević to Hitler and compared non-intervention to appeasement. Peter Mandelson accused John Major of "dithering incompetence" and blamed him for "Bosnian Muslims seeing their houses burned and their women raped" (quoted in Turner 2013: 477). Some on the Labour left took a similar view. Chris Mullin likened the situation to the Spanish Civil War. He wrote passionately in his diary, "ethnic cleansers are on the brink of triumph in Europe and no one wants to lift a finger. My view is the same as it has always been: overwhelming force" (Mullin 2011: 103). Fellow left-wingers Lynne Jones and Bernie Grant were strongly in favour of arming the Bosnians and bombing the Serbs (Benn 2002: 228). On the other side, Tony Benn argued "you shouldn't bomb or arm". Left-wingers Alice Mahon and Diane Abbott founded a "Committee for Peace in the Balkans", which issued a statement calling the subsequent NATO bombing of the Serbs "one sided" and denounced it as an "atrocity" (Unkovski-Korica 2019).[1] Yet, for all of Jeremy Corbyn's professed passion about foreign policy, he did not seem to have made up his mind about the matter. At a February 1994 meeting of the Socialist Campaign Group, Benn puzzled, "We had an interesting meeting of the Campaign Group on Bosnia [...] The debate went backwards and forwards [...] Jeremy Corbyn's position I didn't quite gather" (Benn 2002: 228).

On becoming Labour leader, Corbyn became much more forthright on the matter. In 2017, he travelled to Sarajevo to attend a commemoration of the massacre of 8,000 Bosnian Muslims in Srebrenica in July 1995. In 2018, Corbyn wrote in a letter to the London Muslim Centre: "As anyone who remembers or has learned about the events at Srebrenica, I was horrified by the inhuman brutality of the massacre and determined to do what I could to help future generations remember and learn from what took place" (East London Mosque 2018). In July 2020, now returned to the backbenches, Corbyn tweeted, "Today is #Srebrenica Memorial Day. We remember the thousands killed. Together, we must learn the lessons of history and ensure that such horrific acts never happen again" (Corbyn 2020). Corbyn's moral clarity was perceptible, but only in hindsight.

When it came to intervention in Kosovo four years later, Corbyn had sharpened his opinion somewhat. In May 1999 he spoke in a debate on the ongoing NATO intervention (*Hansard* 1999b). The context for this speech was in marked contrast to the Grenada debate. On this occasion, the British government was

---

1. See https://greatersurbiton.files.wordpress.com/2020/06/corbynsrebrenica.jpeg?w=574&h=579 (accessed 22 March 2021).

a leading advocate for action, rather than being embarrassed and impotent. Furthermore, the governing party was Labour, led by Tony Blair, rather than the Conservatives.

True to his reputation, there is no sign that these factors made any difference to Corbyn's analysis. The West, he claimed, was responsible for the problems of the former Yugoslavia. After the Cold War: the fragmented country was "allowed to get into enormous debt and to develop huge economic problems, on the back of which petty nationalists such as [Croatia's president] Tudjman and [his Serbian counterpart] Milošević rose to power". Having sown the original seeds of conflict, the West's response, through its NATO military arm, was making matters far worse; in particular Serbia, which had looked set to rid itself of Milošević through peaceful protests just two years previously, was now united behind its president. The proper solution, as promoted at a recent conference at the Hague which Corbyn himself had attended, was a peaceful negotiated settlement.

This was a particularly informative speech, foreshadowing Corbyn's stance during the Iraq War. On the face of it, the criticism of Milošević refutes Ibrahim's inclusion of Serbia among the states that Corbyn actively supported. However, Corbyn was careful not to single out Serbia when referring to the most notorious crimes (e.g. "ghastly ethnic cleaning") committed during the conflict; by implication, since "our actions have resulted in a brutalisation of the people of Yugoslavia", the identity of the worst offenders was less important than cutting off the process of "brutalisation" at its source.

Corbyn's speech is also noteworthy in respect of another of Ibrahim's claims – that if he had become prime minister Britain's membership of NATO would have come into question. On the basis of this speech there would have been no doubt on the matter. In his view, at the end of the Cold War NATO should have followed its rival, the Warsaw Pact, into oblivion. Instead, "under the cloak of the 50th anniversary of the establishment of the North Atlantic Treaty Organization, there has been a vast expansion of [its] work". Whether or not it had been justified back in 1949 as a framework for mutual defence, NATO's survival and growth after the disappearance of its initial rationale suggested a more aggressive purpose. In addition, "NATO knows no democratic control whatever; at any one time, 90 per cent of British troops are under the control of NATO generals, answerable only to the President of the United States"; the more inter-governmental Organization for European Security and Co-operation would be far preferable as a forum for conflict resolution. NATO had become – indeed, on Corbyn's logic, always had been – a threat to Britain's traditional understanding of itself as an independent state with parliament as its sovereign decision-making body. The pro-American Blair government was playing its own part in undermining Britain's democracy and autonomy, by preventing a meaningful parliamentary debate on the Kosovan intervention for almost two months (*Hansard* 1999a).

Apart from its other thought-provoking features, Corbyn's speech on Kosovo seemed rather odd for a supposed champion of parliamentary democracy, since it contained no reference to earlier contributions to the debate on that day. As with his speech on Grenada, Corbyn's effort on this occasion was not cited by subsequent speakers. Once again, it was as if he had testified to his views because he could not remain silent, rather than hoping to persuade anyone in his immediate audience. By sharp contrast, in the previous month his party leader and prime minister, Blair, had delivered a speech to the Chicago Economic Club – a body with global reach – that set out his conditions for "liberal intervention" in the affairs of delinquent sovereign states. From Corbyn's perspective, the "Chicago speech" merely confirmed what he had always believed: the forces which had never relented in their attempts to "unmake" the world during the Cold War were showing their true colours, seizing the opportunity to reshape it in their own interests while resistance was weak. By delivering defiant speeches in parliament – even if no one was giving him a respectful hearing – Corbyn was proving that the sins of the West were not being committed in his name.

When he became Labour's leader, Corbyn's earlier orations were on the record to show his supporters that even if no one had heeded him at the time he had always been on the right side of history. However, in the case of Kosovo, at least, the final verdict is less certain. If NATO had not convinced Milošević that it was in deadly earnest, it is very debatable that the various parties to the conflict in former Yugoslavia would have desisted in their "ghastly" ethnic cleansing. Certainly in the absence of an armed infringement of "national sovereignty" it seems unlikely that fanatical Serbian militants, whose hatred of other nationalities within the former Yugoslavia went far enough to motivate cold-blooded murder of non-combatants, would have changed their attitude towards a practice that an objective observer would have described as "genocide". The fact that the targets of genocidal mania in Kosovo tended to be of the Muslim faith makes it particularly poignant that Corbyn should choose to speak out against NATO intervention at this particular moment.

## Sri Lanka

In the following year Corbyn delivered a speech on Sri Lanka in Westminster Hall. In these different surroundings – away from the partisan rancour of the Commons – Corbyn was far more sensitive to his fellow debaters, apologizing to the Liberal Democrat MP Simon Hughes, who had organized the occasion, for having missed part of his speech. This was not the only contrast between this speech and Corbyn's previous efforts on Grenada and Kosovo. Although Corbyn did draw attention to the colonial roots of the civil strife in Sri Lanka, he did not dwell on the details and refused the obvious opportunity to stigmatize the UK's (very prominent) role in creating the ethnic tensions that spilled over after Ceylon's independence (*Hansard* 2000b).

Corbyn began by noting his long-standing interest in the Sri Lankan conflict and his contacts with representatives of the Liberation Tigers of Tamil Eelam (LTTE). Those who expected Corbyn, the alleged "friend of terrorists", to embrace the cause of the "Tigers" would have been astonished by his stated position:

> In a sense, one can understand the strong feelings that both sides express. The national pride that is exemplified in many of the statements made by the Sri Lankan government is understandable. They do not want foreign interference or outside influences. They say that they will sort the issue out. Also involved is the integrity of Sri Lanka.
>
> (*Hansard* 2000b)

"In a sense" was a very strange prelude to this passage. The evasive phraseology makes more sense in view of his later comments. "Pride" is not a word Corbyn would have used in connection with similarly repressive governments, like those of Israel or South Africa. It is clear that, whatever his personal sympathies, his over-riding concern in relation to Sri Lanka was to avoid giving succour to any foreign power (such as India as well as the usual Western/imperialist suspects) that might wish to impose a "solution" on the island. In his desperation to avoid giving anything like a green light to the advocates of military intervention to impose a settlement, he accepted at face value the Sri Lankan government's assertion "that they will sort the issue out" (which in 2009 they ultimately did by massacring the LTTE, after years of officially sponsored terror against the Tamil population). His reference to the "integrity of Sri Lanka" was particularly telling, since the government's most fanatical Buddhist supporters believed that the island could not be divided for religious reasons while the LTTE's case was that partition was the only just outcome for the struggle.

Corbyn's preferred solution of a negotiated peace (preferably brokered by Norway) leading to meaningful devolution rather than partition was, perhaps, a plausible "middle way" that might have prevented some of the bloodshed. However, given the clamour among Singhalese extremists for a campaign of extermination against the LTTE, the only way in which a compromise could be reached would be by the means of external intervention; not from Norway, despite its honourable part in the process, but from some combination of the "great powers". In this context Corbyn warned against US economic (let alone military) interest in the region, but seemed oblivious to the possibility of an impending Chinese initiative to make Sri Lanka into an economic colony.

## Afghanistan and Iraq

Corbyn found his foreign policy stride – and notoriety – in his staunch and consistent opposition to British intervention in Afghanistan and Iraq in the 2000s. We argue that Corbyn's rebellions against the Labour government were instrumental in laying the ground for his leadership victory in 2015.

In the wake of the horrific killings of 2,000 civilians in the United States on 11 September 2001, a broad group of countries agreed to join forces with the US to invade Afghanistan and overthrow the Taliban government, which had sheltered the responsible al-Qaeda terrorist network of Saudi national Osama bin Laden. On 7 October 2001, British and American forces began their attack from the air. British ground troops were deployed the following month, and on 13 November the capital city of Kabul fell to anti-Taliban forces. The UK parliament was not invited to vote on the invasion of Afghanistan, a point which incensed the member for Islington North. Three days before the airstrikes began, Corbyn told his fellow members of parliament, "we should be slightly careful about parading British democracy all around the world, when this parliament is almost unique in having no right to vote on the deployment of British forces anywhere in the world" (*Hansard* 2001). Corbyn went on to point out that the Taliban's predecessors, the *mujahideen*, had been funded by the US government in the 1980s, as they resisted the Soviet invasion of Afghanistan. Corbyn then raised the matter of the "CIA's funding of the bin Laden organisation. Bin Laden used that money to build bunkers throughout Afghanistan". Corbyn then added, somewhat insensitively given the events of only two weeks earlier, "What goes around comes around" (*ibid.*).

Consequently, Corbyn argued that a US-led invasion was illegitimate, even under the auspices of NATO, and rejected George W. Bush's contention that he would bring the perpetrators of 9/11 to justice: "I do not believe that the Pentagon or NATO can administer world justice. The United Nations provides the basis and principle that are needed". Instead, Corbyn argued that the United Kingdom should pressure the United States to resist the temptation to invade Afghanistan. Efforts should be made to arrest Osama bin Laden and bring him before the International Criminal Court, of which, Corbyn noted, the United States was not a member. Corbyn saw this as the best way to avoid bloodshed: "in the interests of justice and of causing no more needless deaths, we must have an international rule of law and a proper international court at which criminals can be brought to justice" (*ibid.*).

Jeremy Corbyn's opposition to the war in Afghanistan was a minority position, to say the least. The leaders of all major parties backed the invasion, as did the major newspapers. Douglas Kriner and Graham Wilson identified that the "British political elite united behind the Afghan War early and that this elite consensus remained unshaken" (Kriner & Wilson 2016: 565). Across 16 polls in 2001, British public support for military action in Afghanistan averaged at two-thirds (*ibid.*: 568).

Corbyn made nine interventions on Afghanistan in the final three months of 2001, criticizing the invasion and its conduct, as well as raising the alarm about the treatment of Muslims and terrorist suspects in the United Kingdom. At the same time, he began working with fellow activists on the left – including figures from the Socialist Workers Party, the Alliance for Workers' Liberty, the Communist Party of Great Britain as well as the Labour Party – who opposed the war effort. Together, they formed the Stop the War Coalition. Corbyn would remain at the centre of this organization, becoming its chairperson in 2011, until his election as Labour leader in 2015.

The following year, the British and American governments turned their attention to Saddam Hussein's Iraq. In stark contrast to Afghanistan, elite attitudes on Iraq were divided from the start (Clarke, Saunders & Stewart 2009). Stop the War's early formation made it well suited to becoming a leading organization in the efforts to oppose the Iraq invasion. Stop the War in Afghanistan simply repurposed itself to become Stop the War in Iraq. In the summer of 2002, Stop the War helped to organize a protest of 400,000 people. *The Mirror*, heretofore loyal to Tony Blair, came out against the prospect of war. By February 2003, as the parliamentary vote on the invasion was taken, about 1 million demonstrators gathered in London to show their opposition to the war and Corbyn was invited to speak to the assembled throng.

The fact that Corbyn was "right" about Iraq has been hugely important for his political career and for his foreign policy approach. It gave him a moral vindication for his foreign policy outlook, which his muddled reaction to Sierra Leone, Kosovo and Sri Lanka simply had not. Stop the War became a major vehicle for Corbyn to build a national profile as a backbencher. He travelled around the country speaking to large audiences, especially as disaffection with the war grew, condemning Western intervention. Tony Benn oozed in his diaries after one such event in February 2004, "Jeremy Corbyn made a brilliant speech. I must say, Jeremy is so thoughtful and experienced and clear" (Benn 2007: 171).

More importantly, Iraq became a powerful symbol for Corbyn's relationship with the Labour Party membership. He was on "their" side, from the start. In spite of an unprecedented rebellion, most Labour MPs supported the war, which appalled the majority of party members. Only one in three Labour supporters in March 2003 supported the invasion without UN backing (Ipsos-Mori 2003).

Iraq symbolized an enormous chasm between the PLP and ordinary Labour members that had been growing since the establishment of New Labour in 1994. One long-standing Labour Party activist reflected that among the membership there was "much latent hostility to Blair, which had been there since 1994, and what New Labour stood for […] The range of issues associated with Blair came home to roost with the Iraq War" (Johnson & Walsh 2012: 230). One Labour Party councillor recalled, "Blair was just walking on water and you could see that he was just dismissive of [the anti-war] position […] I blame the Parliamentary Labour Party. What a bunch of cretins to not make a judgement. [Blair's] judgement was appalling, and so was theirs" (*ibid.*: 228).

In the 2015 Labour leadership contest, Jeremy Corbyn was the sole candidate who had opposed the Iraq War; Andy Burnham and Yvette Cooper had both voted for the invasion, while the other candidate Liz Kendall, not yet an MP in 2003, hailed from the party's Blairite right. Although the invasion had occurred 12 years earlier, the war itself lasted into the 2010s and the issue remained salient in the leadership contest. In one interview while running for leader, Corbyn called for Tony Blair to be tried for war crimes and denounced Iraq as "an illegal war" (Smith 2015). Corbyn's commanding 60 per cent support among first-preference votes was partly, if not chiefly, attributable to his stance on this key foreign policy question.

Syria

Between Corbyn's speech on Sri Lanka and his contribution to a Commons' debate on Syria in May 2013 the world had experienced 9/11, the "War on Terror" and the Arab Spring. But in key respects Corbyn's approach was just the same. Western intervention in the Syrian civil war was being mooted, in the form of arms supplies to the Syrian National Coalition, which had been identified as the chief opposition grouping to President Assad's regime. Early in the debate Corbyn made a very effective intervention during the speech of the Foreign Office minister Alistair Burt, suggesting that if the government supplied arms to one opposition group rather than others it risked "fuelling a civil war within a civil war" (*Hansard* 2013a).

In his own speech, Corbyn argued that the National Coalition consisted of "people we do not know". Those who sought regime change in Damascus and identified the Coalition as the most appropriate vehicle, without conducting due diligence, had "a very selective memory", since not long ago the West had been very happy to co-operate with Assad. In addition, Britain was proposing to add to the machinery of death in an area that was already over-stocked. The conflict in Syria was "a proxy war for all kinds of interests":

The Gulf Co-operation Council countries, particularly Saudi Arabia and Qatar, are supplying vast amounts of money and arms to the area. Iran feels under threat and thinks that it is next on the western countries' hit list, so it is presumably helping the Assad regime in some form.

(*Hansard* 2013b)

This is a characteristic Corbyn statement on the endemic conflict in the Middle East. Russia's support for Assad is noted as a matter of fact, free from any moral judgement from Corbyn. Saudi Arabia and Qatar are undoubtedly fuelling the conflict, but their motives are unexplored in the speech. Iran's involvement, by contrast, is presented as unproven; but if that state had indeed decided to intervene in the affairs of another country it would be doing so for what Corbyn considers to be a respectable reason: it "thinks it is next on the western countries' hit list". For a person like Corbyn, who purportedly rejects the idea of lethal interference across state boundaries, this is pretty lame; indeed, the implicit logic of his argument could be used to justify the position of US "hawks" who regarded Iranian involvement in the conflict as a pretext to attack the real Middle Eastern organ grinder rather than the Syrian monkey.

When discussing the murderous Singhalese regime in Sri Lanka, Corbyn had accepted that the government was anxious to resolve the conflict on its own but that the peaceful Norwegian initiative could help. As in the Sri Lankan case, by May 2013 it was clear to objective observers that the Syrian government was trying to sponsor a "solution" which involved the violent elimination of any potential sources of opposition. However, while conceding that the Assad regime had "committed enormous human rights abuses", Corbyn still tacitly considered that it would be a suitable partner for a negotiated settlement.

In August 2013, the House of Commons voted against a motion designed to pave the way for direct British intervention against the Assad regime. Corbyn did not speak in this debate, but when the vote was taken it seemed that his propensity to choose "the right side of history" had been demonstrated more rapidly than usual. The prime minister, David Cameron, regarded the vote as a definitive veto on his plan to join the US in action against Assad. The cause of non-intervention had been vindicated without the alternative being attempted and resulting in a catastrophic failure.

## Ukraine

Corbyn's speech on Syria followed closely after a statement he had released in his capacity of national chair of the Stop the War Coalition, regarding another of the world's trouble-spots – this time Russia's annexation of the Crimean region of

Ukraine. His main purpose was to present the argument against armed Western intervention to stall and/or reverse Russia's aggression. As usual, Corbyn found reasons to blame the West for the outbreak of hostilities: NATO and the EU had sought to interfere in Ukrainian politics, triggering an understandable reaction from Russia, which felt threatened.

Corbyn's statement rehearsed a series of recent events, including elections which had reflected the complex ethnic origins of the Ukrainian population. However, although he admitted that Russia had "gone way beyond its legal powers" in its response to the crisis in Ukraine, he took pains to set out the ethnic balance, giving the impression that interventions by a foreign power (Russia) might after all be justified, on grounds that bore an unsettling resemblance to those used by Neville Chamberlain to salve his conscience after selling out the Sudetenland (Corbyn 2014).

*Inter alia*, in this statement Corbyn reaffirmed his preference for the Organization for Security and Co-operation in Europe as a conflict-resolving forum in questions relating to Europe and its near-neighbours. However, this element of consistency in his approach to international crises was overshadowed by his response to demonstrations in the Ukraine against its narrowly elected pro-Russian president, Viktor Yanukovych. Presumably for the first time in his life, this indefatigable protester against Western actions across far-flung continents introduced a qualifying clause to his consistent principles: "We must defend the right of people to demonstrate against their governments, but ...". The qualification turned out to be a telling non-sequitur:

> ... but it was remarkable that the EU leadership in the person of Baroness Catherine Ashton and the US political establishment in the guise of Senator John McCain both chose to give very strong support to demonstrations in Kiev which were far from representing all Ukrainians. Neither did they make any comments about far-right and racist involvement in the uprising.                (Corbyn 2014)

Ironically, Corbyn followed this passage, which implied that the non-negotiable right to protest was in fact limited in cases where it was supported by Western governments, by noting that "Double standards come to the fore in times of crisis and none could be more obvious than those of the Western media over the past week".

## Corbyn as leader

Although Corbyn's foreign policy stances – particularly his association with the Stop the War Coalition – were crucial to his credentials as the candidate of radical change in the contest to replace Ed Miliband as Labour leader, his political opponents expected to exploit this subject to their advantage in the 2017 general election. Indeed, Conservative strategists could be forgiven for thinking that his views offered them an embarrassment of point-scoring riches.

Labour strategists decided that the best way to counter Conservative charges was to find an opportunity for Corbyn to speak for himself. On 12 May 2017, almost a month after Theresa May had called a "snap" election, the opposition leader delivered a speech at London's Royal Institute of International Affairs ("Chatham House"). The choice of venue was highly significant; Ed Miliband had also appreciated the value of association with this highly respected think tank, and had spoken there before the 2015 election.

Corbyn's speech attracted far more attention than Miliband's effort. He duly raised the nuclear weapons issue, mentioning that he was often asked if, as prime minister, he would ever order their use. His response was not really an answer to that question: he argued instead that if Britain ever found itself in a situation where the use of such weapons became an option, "it would represent complete and cataclysmic failure. It would mean world leaders had already triggered a spiral of catastrophe for humankind" (Corbyn 2017). Before his audience could consider whether or not this implied a negative response to the purported question, Corbyn insisted that he was not a pacifist; there were circumstances in which violence might be necessary as a last resort. Although these circumstances were left unspecified, he reassured voters that, "If elected prime minister I will do everything necessary to protect the safety and security of our people and our country". Characteristically, he insisted that, "The best defence for Britain is a government actively engaged in seeking political solutions to the world's problems".

For Corbyn this section of the speech was an unpleasant necessity arising from his new status; by "fudging" the nuclear issue (and neither confirming nor denying that a Labour government would renew the Trident "deterrent") he was putting at risk his reputation for fearless radicalism as well as his image as a refreshing, plain-speaking contrast to Britain's colourless "career politicians". However, the central theme of the speech gave him the opportunity to speak from the heart. His message was that, far from achieving its stated objectives, the "war on terror" had made Britain, and the world in general, far less secure. Apart from the new threats it had created and the chaos it had spawned in countries like Afghanistan, Iraq and Libya, it deflected attention from the real issues confronting humanity: "ethnic conflicts, food insecurity, water scarcity and the fast-emerging effects of climate change". Underlying these critical sources of concern was grotesque and ever-increasing economic inequality at home and abroad.

To no one's surprise, Corbyn's analysis suggested a radical reappraisal of Britain's recent foreign policy decisions. "The 'bomb first, talk later' approach to security has failed", he announced. But what would this entail for the country's existing alliances? Corbyn pledged that "A Labour government will want a strong and friendly relationship with the United States. But we will not be afraid to speak our mind". Since "the security threats and challenges we face are not bound by geographic borders, it is vital that as Britain leaves the EU, we maintain a close relationship with our European partners alongside our commitment to NATO and spending at least 2 per cent [of GDP] on defence".

Compared to Corbyn's pre-leadership utterances this agenda was breathtakingly modest. The new accord with the US would be almost identical to the one foreshadowed by the 2010 Conservative Party manifesto, which studiously avoided the notorious phrase "special relationship" while accepting the US-inspired target of spending at least 2 per cent of GDP on defence (Garnett, Mabon & Smith 2017: 303). Whatever they had done in practice, no major British political party had ever fought an election on a promise to adopt a posture of unquestioning obedience to the US; Corbyn was thus following a trend rather than blazing a new trail. More serious, perhaps, was the fleeting allusion to NATO. While this was followed by discussion of the situation in relation to Russia, and the need to establish a much less confrontational attitude, there was no suggestion of what a Corbyn-led government might do to secure this change in NATO policy. The implications for national sovereignty of continuing membership of NATO were not addressed, despite Corbyn's objections to the organization's undemocratic decision-making structures. The same was true of his comments concerning future defence (and, by implication, foreign policy) cooperation with the EU.

In his peroration, Corbyn promised that a Labour government would "advance a security and foreign policy with integrity and human rights at its core". Once Britain was set on its new course, "We can walk the hard yards to a better way to live together on this planet". Corbyn's closing remarks suggested undiminished idealism, which he attributed to the example of his parents, who had met while campaigning in support of the democratic government of Spain during the civil war. While this – rather than the milieu of 1970s leftist agit-prop cited by Ibrahim (2019a) – provided an accurate provenance for Corbyn's worldview, the remainder of the text could not escape criticism. For example, John Bew (writing for the Conservative-linked think tank Policy Exchange) attacked Corbyn for departing from Labour's internationalist tradition. According to Bew, the Labour leadership (including the shadow chancellor John McDonnell and Corbyn's special adviser Seumas Milne) had presented a foreign policy agenda that was not only "incoherent", but "disingenuous because they are failing to tell the public what they really think", particularly about NATO (Bew 2017).

Bew argued that Corbyn would pay a heavy electoral price for his views on international politics and their implications closer to home: "it is on national security that the distance in public trust between Corbyn and Theresa May is most pronounced. His speech at Chatham House will have done very little to close the gap". Bew was writing on 15 May 2017. Less than a week later, a suicide bomber attacked concert-goers at the Manchester Arena, killing 22 and injuring many more, mainly young people. Understandably, the incident increased the salience of terrorism as an electoral issue; on polling day (8 June) it was named by voters as the second most important consideration, behind the ubiquitous Brexit (Fieldhouse & Prosser 2017). However, contrary to Bew's expectation, the Conservatives were not the beneficiaries, partly owing to Corbyn's skilful response, which contextualized the foreign policy implications and blamed Theresa May for damaging cuts to police and security services.

The accusation that Corbyn and his closest colleagues had been "disingenuous" seems unfair. Indeed, Bew's Policy Exchange piece suggested as much, since he highlighted that Labour's divisions on foreign policy excluded the possibility that Corbyn could say what he really meant; a position which, presumably, the leader would have been forced to live with even if his party had secured a parliamentary majority at an ensuing election. The section on foreign policy and security in the 2019 Labour manifesto was entitled "A New Internationalism", as if taking direct aim at Bew's criticisms. The manifesto's headline pledges were the introduction of a US-style war powers act to curb the executive's prerogative powers; an unflinching audit of Britain's colonial crimes; and more resources for the diplomatic service (another policy that the Tories had promised in their 2010 manifesto). Arms sales to Saudi Arabia, Yemen and Israel would be ended. However, the manifesto pledged:

> We will maintain our commitment to NATO and our close relationship with our European partners [...] Labour supports the renewal of the Trident nuclear deterrent [...] Labour's commitment to spend at least 2% of GDP on defence will guarantee that our armed forces are versatile and capable of fulfilling the full range of roles and obligations.
>
> (Labour Party 2019).

Having won the Labour leadership at least in part because of his reputation as a person of principle in matters of foreign policy – and despite the apparent strengthening of his position within the party after overcoming a vote of no confidence from his parliamentary colleagues provoked by his unconvincing contribution to the Remain campaign in the 2016 referendum – Corbyn had found that the price of his sensational elevation from the backbenches was at least a partial compromise of those principles.

## Summarizing Corbyn's foreign policy

We would argue that there are four common themes that characterize Jeremy Corbyn's foreign policy: (1) anti-"Western imperialism", (2) pacifism, (3) anti-capitalism, and (4) the tradition of dissent.

### Anti-"Western imperialism"

The first theme is the "anti-imperialism" identified by critic Mike Gapes, or more specifically anti-*Western imperialism*. This appears to be at the core of Jeremy Corbyn's self-conception of his foreign policy outlook. Corbyn believes that Western governments – especially the United States, the European Union and those countries that fall within their orbits – have conducted their international relations irresponsibly and immorally. Too often, these states have plundered resources from indigenous peoples for material gain and waged wars for territorial self-aggrandizement and enrichment. It is worth noting that Jeremy Corbyn came of age when many on the left regarded the United States as the biggest threat to world peace. His first marches were against the Vietnam War and for CND in the 1960s.

In 2011, Corbyn wrote a foreword to a new edition of J. A. Hobson's *Imperialism: A Study*, a 1902 text that argued that the expansion of British, American, French and German rule to Latin America, Africa and Asia was driven by elite financial interests. Hobson insisted that imperialism did not even serve the interests of the common people in the imperial nations, who were encouraged to overlook their own oppression by the intoxication of national aggrandizement. While Hobson could have made his point without resorting to antisemitic tropes, he could not restrain himself from criticizing Jews. Hobson wrote that these elite financiers were "men of a single and peculiar race, who have behind them many centuries of financial experience". Hobson pondered, "Does anyone seriously suppose that a great war could be undertaken by any European state, or a great State loan subscribed, if the house of Rothschild and its connections sets their face against it?" (Hobson 1902: 57). Admittedly, Hobson did not mention Judaism explicitly, nor did he dwell on this point in the book (Donald Sassoon has written that Hobson's anti-Jewish bigotry was "completely marginal" to his argument), but Corbyn's description of Hobson's work as "correct and prescient" in his 2011 foreword did him no favours (Sassoon 2019).

Corbyn's anti-Western imperialism is not quite the same as always rooting for the "underdog" or the "oppressed", as his supporters might contend. The Serbs were not the underdogs in the Balkans, nor was Assad the underdog in Syria.

The Russians were decidedly the "overdogs" in the Crimea. Yet, in all of these instances, Corbyn either sided with or (uncharacteristically) failed to condemn outright the aggression of these actors. The explanation is that for Corbyn, the underdog is not the group that has the least power within a given theatre of conflict. It is the group that is opposed to the United States, which Corbyn believes has an almost unlimited reservoir of international power.

Pacifism

The second theme is pacifism. Jeremy Corbyn's friend and former colleague George Galloway described him as "a pacifist who'll speak to anyone" (Quoted in Whittell 2019). As we have seen, before becoming Labour leader, Jeremy Corbyn was one of the leading lights of the anti-war left, especially in his role as chair of the Stop the War Coalition. Corbyn only resigned from Stop the War after he became Labour leader. In his resignation speech, Corbyn explained, "I hardly need to say, in stepping down as chair, I want to make absolutely clear my continuing solidarity with the Coalition and its work against wars of intervention" (Corbyn 2015). Around this time, Corbyn created the first-ever shadow ministership for peace and disarmament, held by Leeds MP Fabian Hamilton.

During his long career as a backbench Labour MP, Corbyn voted against every proposed military action put before parliament. While in itself not evidence of pacifism, Corbyn's consistent anti-war position suggested a kind of pacifist position. During his leadership campaign, Corbyn was more ambiguous than his subsequent Chatham House speech suggested. In an interview with a Christian magazine in July 2015, he was asked about the circumstances in which he would support war. Mulling over action in the Second World War, Corbyn replied, "I do have respect for those people that were conscientious objectors in the war. Does that make me a pacifist? I can't really answer that. I'm not sure" (Spanner n.d.). One wonders if Corbyn knows how he would have voted in the May 1940 special Labour conference in Bournemouth, which agreed that the party could join a wartime coalition led by Winston Churchill. The dissenting delegates were described by Hugh Dalton as "freaks talking pathetic rubbish" (quoted in Pugh 2010: 259). As a backbencher, Corbyn lavished praise on the "heroic" E. D. Morel, a pacifist Labour MP who was imprisoned for breaching the Defence of the Realm Act during the First World War. For someone who should have known his Labour Party history – at least in so far as it celebrated radical figures – Corbyn made a surprising factual slip when he told the House of Commons in 2014 that, "I think [Morel] was the first Labour Foreign Minister, in the 1920s" (*Hansard* 2014). Morel was indeed considered for the position, but it was taken by a pacific-minded politician whom Corbyn presumably regarded as less "heroic" – the prime minister, Ramsay MacDonald.

Of all of Labour's leaders, the one to whom Jeremy Corbyn is most often compared is George Lansbury (Seymour 2016: 2). Lansbury was an ascetic, dissenting vegetarian who had forged his career as a principled local politician and activist in London. Lansbury was also a staunch pacifist, which was borne out of his Christian faith. As party leader, Lansbury wrote to the electors in Fulham East in 1933, "I would close every recruiting station, disband the Army, and disarm the Air Force. I would abolish the whole dreadful equipment of war, and say to the world, 'Do your worst!'" (quoted in Benn 2009).

But Lansbury found himself in a similar predicament to Corbyn as leader, after taking the position almost by accident. He had been excluded from the 1924 Labour government in part because of concerns about Bolshevik sympathies, outlined in his book *What I Saw in Russia* (1920). In the 1929 government he was given the relatively modest position of first commissioner of works, in which he spent most of his time tending to the royal parks. He ascended to the party leadership in 1932 when virtually every other Labour MP of significance had either lost their seat in the 1931 election rout or joined the Conservative-backed national government.

Lansbury had a strong sense of his own conscience, but that conscience did not always align with the opinions of other Labour MPs or leaders of the wider movement. His dithering over rearmament led a furious trade union leader (and, later, foreign secretary) Ernest Bevin to accuse Lansbury at the 1935 Labour conference of "hawking your conscience around from body to body asking to be told what to do with it" (quoted in Pugh 2010: 240). Similarly, Corbyn's personal pacifist convictions ran contrary to the exigencies faced by a major party leader and a potential prime minister. However, Lansbury resigned a few weeks before the 1935 general election, while Corbyn did not follow suit until he had led his party to two general election defeats.

As Corbyn suggested at Chatham House, his pacifism was not the kind of absolute principle that it was for Lansbury. As a backbencher, Corbyn supported some UN peacekeeping missions. He supported the UN-backed intervention in East Timor in 1999, where he had come under fire while working as an election observer during the referendum on independence from Indonesia. In 1994, as we have seen, he signed the Early Day Motion calling for a more robust UN military presence in Rwanda to end the ethnic violence. In Sierra Leone, he opposed British troops operating under the British flag, but a question he posed in the Commons to Defence Secretary Geoff Hoon suggests that he would have been comfortable if they had formed part of a UN force.

## Anti-capitalism

Perhaps unsurprisingly for a man of the Left, Jeremy Corbyn has typically aligned himself with countries led by left-wing leaders. This is true of many Labour leaders, but Corbyn has aligned himself with a slightly different cadre than his predecessors. In the 1990s, many Labour Party MPs looked enviously to the electoral success of Bill Clinton's Democratic Party in the United States. After the financial crisis, Labour elites' love affair with Democrats' liberal centrism fizzled out. The post-New Labour leadership of Ed Miliband drew inspiration from European social democratic leaders (BBC 2013). Munching Danish pastries in Copenhagen with Prime Minister Helle Thorning-Schmidt, who happened to be the daughter-in-law of former Labour leader Neil Kinnock, Miliband declared, "I will be talking to allies across Europe – in Denmark, Sweden and Holland – about how we change it to make the EU work for working people and help us all begin building for the future" (Ross 2013).

Jeremy Corbyn did not find inspiration from socialist leaders in the United States or in Western Europe. Instead, he spoke with much greater enthusiasm about the populist left-wing leaders of Latin America. His critic Mike Gapes conceded, "I've known him since the seventies and I think his instinctive world view is that of anybody who has supported Chavez, Maduro and Castro as he has. It's the romantic view of revolutionary third world liberation movements" (Whittell 2019).

Corbyn first visited Latin America in the late 1960s, visiting Brazil, Argentina, Paraguay, Chile and Bolivia. He kept, as yet unpublished, diaries during this trip. By the time he became leader, Corbyn had visited nearly every Latin American country. Undoubtedly impactful was his exposure to life in Allende's Chile, before hopes for a more just society in that country were extinguished by General Pinochet with Western backing. The journalist Matt Kennard described Corbyn as "the first leading British politician since Judith Hart in the 1970s to have detailed knowledge of the region and sympathy for its struggles" (Kennard 2018). Hart, like Corbyn until he became party leader, was a leading member of the Labour Party's inter-nationalist Eurosceptics, who argued that the party's sympathies should be placed with the post-colonial governments of Latin America, Africa and Asia rather than the privileged governments and peoples of Europe. Corbyn similarly promoted a kind of socialist internationalism, arguing that Britain should link arms with anti-capitalist governments in the developing world. Corbyn explained, "I'm very clear that we have to build an international movement, which deals with economic injustice and inequality, and challenges the neoliberal agenda" (*ibid.*).

Over the years, Corbyn led campaigns in solidarity with socialists in a variety of Latin American countries, including Cuba, Venezuela, Chile and Bolivia. In Bolivia, he led a parliamentary delegation: "We were looking there at the control of water, and mining industries", he explained (LAB 2018). Corbyn has personal ties to the region, as well. He speaks fluent Spanish. His second wife – and mother of his children – is from Chile. His third wife Laura Alvarez is Mexican. Corbyn displayed a little Mexican flag on his desk when he was Labour leader (he did not fly a British one). Corbyn travelled to Mexico in December 2018 to attend the inauguration of Mexico's left-wing president Andrés Miguel López Obrador, with whom he developed a friendship (*The Economist* 2019). Corbyn explained that his travels in Latin America demonstrated to him a range of alternative political possibilities. "Look at popular movements in Latin America. Look at that form of democracy. Policy-making in Britain is too narrow, too elitist" (TeleSur 2017).

## The tradition of dissent

For most of his career, Corbyn understood his role as someone who should speak truth to power. Bob Clay, a left-wing Labour MP from 1983 to 1992 who shared a parliamentary office with Corbyn and sat with him through hundreds of meetings, characterized him as "something of a gadfly" (Knight 2016). In this respect, Corbyn can be said to fit in a long tradition of dissent in British foreign policy, detailed memorably by A. J. P. Taylor in his book *The Trouble Makers*. The aforementioned 1920s Labour politician E. D. Morel, whom Corbyn described as "heroic", is one of the Dissenters profiled in Taylor's book.

According to Taylor, a "Dissenter" is not just someone who disagrees with a particular foreign policy position. Taylor acknowledges that many individuals will oppose one policy over another "while still accepting its general assumptions". A Dissenter, in contrast, "repudiates its aims, its methods, its principles". Taylor writes that a foreign policy Dissenter "claims to know better and to promote higher causes; he asserts a superiority, moral or intellectual" (Taylor 1957: 13). Taylor did not mean that Dissenters were hypocrites. He admired this dogged-ness, writing that they are were among "the Englishmen I most revere" (*ibid.*: 9).

Corbyn's approach to foreign policy can be located in this tradition. Corbyn does not question whether a particular intervention is right or wrong on its own merits alone. Instead, he questions the entire premise of British interven-tion in international affairs and offers a fundamental challenge to the type of order Britain should see itself championing. Looking over two centuries of for-eign policy dissent, Taylor argues, "they have all been contemptuous of those in authority" (*ibid.*: 13), much as Corbyn's many parliamentary interventions on foreign affairs have suggested. These interventions have sometimes been con-demned as anti-British, but Taylor offers some defence: "It would be wrong to suggest – as exasperated members of the establishment have often done – that the Dissenters cared nothing for the national interest" (*ibid.*: 13).

Taylor credits the Dissenters with being principled, but he also argues that principle can lead to inflexibility, dogmatism, oversimplification, and distortion: "the campaigner" rather than the "statesman". "The Dissenters were critics by definition. They were more concerned to attack an existing policy than to state their alternative" (*ibid.*: 13). Taylor demonstrates that when the Dissenters occasionally got it "right", the longer-term consequences for British foreign policy could be quite negative. Dissenters John Bright and Richard Cobden denounced the Crimean War, and Crimea turned out to be a disaster. This led British foreign policy-makers from the mid-1860s up to the 1900s to avoid further incursions in Europe, even when it meant abandoning friendly nations like Denmark in its struggle with Prussia. Taylor observers that subsequently no British government seriously contemplated armed intervention on the continent. Nonetheless, Taylor concludes that their mistakes were made with the best of intentions and "if I had been their contemporary [...] I should not have been ashamed to have made their mistakes" (*ibid.*: 9). Another parallel can be drawn with Corbyn's dissenting foreign policy. Because Corbyn got it "right" on the invasion of Iraq, he was sure that further Middle East adventures would be equally disastrous, including acting to stop chemical weapons attacks in Syria. Iraq has served as the empirical validation and moral justification of all of Corbyn's subsequent foreign policy positions.

## Conclusion

The German politician Karl Liebknecht was a left-wing member of the Social Democratic Party (SPD) in the early twentieth century. He served as a member of the Reichstag, rebelling against his party on multiple occasions. Liebknecht was opposed to German involvement in the First World War and was the only member of parliament to vote against continued financing of the war effort in December 1914. That same month, with Rosa Luxemburg he founded the Spartacus League, named for the leader of the slave rebellion in Rome. A few months after the League's formation, while still an SPD member of parliament, Liebknecht penned the leaflet *Der Hauptfeind steht im eigenen Land*. In it, he declared, "The main enemy of the German people is in Germany: German imperialism, the German war party, German secret diplomacy [...] The main enemy is at home!" (Liebknecht 1952: 296–301).

While operating in decidedly different circumstances from the left-wing German MP, Jeremy Corbyn's worldview could be captured by these words. For Corbyn, the enemies of peace can be found within the British establishment and those of Britain's allies, especially in the United States and the European Union. On the BBC television programme *The Big Questions* in 2014, Corbyn was asked about taking action against Russia after the invasion of Ukraine. Corbyn replied, "The West has no moral authority whatsoever to lecture on this – after drone strikes, after Iraq, after so many other internal coups and conflicts around the world". He received generous applause from the audience, foreshadowing the following year's Labour leadership election.

After Corbyn's resignation as Labour leader in the wake of the 2019 general election, it was all too easy to pass judgement on the role that foreign policy had played in the thwarting of his radical alternative for Britain. From Ibrahim's perspective, Corbyn continued to display a "binary" worldview which transposed Western (i.e. US) ideas of friendly and antagonistic powers. The reality, as we have shown, is different. On becoming Labour leader, Corbyn was compelled to compromise on many of the subjects that, as a backbencher, he had felt able to appraise in binary terms; and while his position would obviously have been strengthened had Labour returned to office under his leadership, his well-publicized belief that executive power in such matters should be reduced makes it most unlikely that he could ever have resiled from these compromises. Moreover, in spite of Corbyn's obvious personal interest in foreign affairs, it was on these matters that he seemed most willing to "fudge" to buy goodwill from sceptics in the party. This is probably because there was greater consensus in the PLP on domestic policy.

As Labour leader, Corbyn "fudged" the issue of nuclear weapons, and retreated from the purist national sovereignty line he had previously taken in respect of defence cooperation. Above all, he was forced to deny that he was a pacifist, which would open a Corbyn-led government to criticism if it refused to endorse (or join) military intervention in any future crisis which (like Rwanda) involved unequivocal issues of moral principle. In short, unless they take Lansbury's view that all violence is wrong – which, by his own testimony, Corbyn does not – political leaders who maintain that their countries play a significant role in international affairs are forced to exercise political judgement when confronted with the possibility that pre-emptive force or transnational interventions will prevent avoidable human misery. Arguably Corbyn's failure to address these dilemmas, created by his change of status from backbench "Trouble Maker" to Labour leader, made little difference to his party's fortunes in 2017: but they helped to ensure that two years later he was widely regarded as an electoral liability.

### References

BBC 2013. "Miliband eyes Nordic living standards for UK". BBC News, 19 February. https://www.bbc.co.uk/news/av/uk-politics-21510493 (accessed 22 March 2021).

Benn, T. 2002. *Free at Last: Diaries 1990–2001*. London: Hutchinson.

Benn, T. 2007. *More Time for Politics: Diaries 2001–2007*. London: Hutchinson.

Benn, M. 2009. "Remembering Labour's roots". *The Guardian*, 23 February. https://www.theguardian.com/commentisfree/2009/feb/23/labour-poverty-history-george-lansbury (accessed 7 April 2021).

Bew, J. 2017. "Why Jeremy Corbyn is not part of the Clement Attlee internationalist tradition within Labour". Policy Exchange, 15 May. https://policyexchange.org.uk/why-jeremy-corbyn-is-not-part-of-the-clement-attlee-internationalist-tradition-within-labour/ (accessed 22 March 2021).

Bloomfield, S. 2018. "The world according to Corbyn". *Prospect*, 16 May. https://www.prospectmagazine.co.uk/magazine/the-world-according-to-corbyn (accessed 22 March 2021).

Bush, S. 2018. "The key to understanding Jeremy Corbyn is that he'd rather be Foreign Secretary". *New Statesman*, 15 August. https://www.newstatesman.com/politics/uk/2018/08/key-understanding-jeremy-corbyn-he-d-rather-be-foreign-secretary (accessed 17 March 2021).

Cameron, H. 2012. "British state complicity in genocide: Rwanda 1994". *State Crime Journal* 1(1): 70–87.

Clarke, H., D. Saunders & M. Stewart 2009. *Performance Politics and the British Voter*. Cambridge: Cambridge University Press.

Clinton, B. 2004. *My Life*. New York, NY: Knopf.

Corbyn, J. 2014. "Jeremy Corbyn MP: should the West go to war over Ukraine?" Stop the War, 8 March. https://www.stopwar.org.uk/article/the-history-lurking-behind-the-crisis-in-ukraine-by-jeremy-corbyn-mp/ (accessed 22 March 2021).

Corbyn, J. 2015. "Why I'm stepping down as chair of the Stop the War Coalition". https://www.stopwar.org.uk/article/jeremy-corbyn-statement-to-the-stop-the-war-conference-19-september-2015/ (accessed 7 April 2021).

Corbyn, J. 2017. "Chatham House speech", 12 May. https://labour.org.uk/press/jeremy-corbyn-speech-at-chatham-house/ (accessed 22 March 2021).

Corbyn, J. 2020. "Tweet, 6.28 pm, 11 July". https://twitter.com/jeremycorbyn/status/1282003750069116929 (accessed 22 March 2021).

Dallaire, R. 2004. *Shake Hands with the Devil*. New York, NY: Random House.

East London Mosque 2018. "Jeremy Corbyn supports commemoration of Srebrenica genocide". https://www.eastlondonmosque.org.uk/news/jeremy-corbyn-supports-commemoration-srebrenica-genocide-london-muslim-centre (accessed 7 April 2021).

*Economist* 2019. "¡Hasta la victoria Corbynista!". 2 February. https://www.economist.com/britain/2019/02/02/latin-america-provides-a-canvas-for-jeremy-corbyns-worldview (accessed 22 March 2021).

Fieldhouse, E. & C. Prosser 2017. "General election 2017: Brexit dominated voters' thoughts". BBC, 1 August. https://www.bbc.co.uk/news/uk-politics-40630242 (accessed 22 March 2021).

Garnett, M., S. Mabon & R. Smith 2017. *British Foreign Policy since 1945*. London: Routledge.

*Hansard* 1983. 47 Parl. Deb. H.C. (6th ser.) cols 312–15. https://hansard.parliament.uk/commons/1983-10-26/debates/a13d51ea-9fc0-4ce1-bb51-8693385b7d03/Grenada(Invasion)#contribution-ee56c7e2-904c-456e-97df-bc5a85146881 (accessed 22 March 2021).

*Hansard* 1994a. 246 Parl. Deb. H.C. (6th ser.) col 449. https://hansard.parliament.uk/commons/1994-07-07/debates/57b6a290-46a2-4461-8452-fe1aed58519f/UnSecurityCouncil#contribution-8d004904-10f7-4d60-a88d-d2e763c41a36 (accessed 22 March 2021).

*Hansard* 1994b. 247 Parl. Deb. H.C. (6th ser.) cols 473–5W. https://api.parliament.uk/historic-*Hansard*/written-answers/1994/jul/21/rwanda#S6CV0247P0_19940721_CWA_435 (accessed 22 March 2021).

*Hansard* 1999a. 331 Parl. Deb. H.C. (6th ser.) cols. 923–5. https://hansard.parliament.uk/Commons/1999-05-10/debates/21c168d7-8dd0-4e1a-bd84-c77d241a9d4f/Kosovo (accessed 22 March 2021).

*Hansard* 1999b. 331 Parl. Deb. H.C. (6th ser.) col 924. https://hansard.parliament.uk/commons/ 1999-05-18/debates/31da096a-240a-4848-8a31-246db78a42f6/Kosovo#contribution-b18d96ad-08d9-4d77-9656-e07d93c1c36b (accessed 22 March 2021).

*Hansard* 2000a. 351 Parl. Deb. H.C. (6th ser.) col. 23. https://www.theyworkforyou.com/ debates/?id=2000-05-15a.23.0&s=speaker%3A10035 (accessed 22 March 2021).

*Hansard* 2000b. 351 Parl. Deb. H.C. (6th ser.) cols 45–67WH. https://api.parliament.uk/ historic-*Hansard*/westminster-hall/2000/jun/07/sri-lanka#S6CV0351P0_20000607_WH_14 (accessed 22 March 2021).

*Hansard* 2001. 372 Parl. Deb. H.C. (6th ser.) cols 689–810. https://api.parliament.uk/historic-Hansard/commons/2001/oct/04/international-terrorism#S6CV0372P1_20011004_HOC_132 (accessed 22 March 2021).

*Hansard* 2013a. 563 Parl. Deb. H.C. (6th ser.) col. 1175. https://Hansard.parliament.uk/Commons/ 2013-05-21/debates/13052186000002/Syria(EURestrictiveMeasures)?highlight=Jeremy%20 corbyn%20syria (accessed 22 March 2021).

*Hansard* 2013b. 563 Parl. Deb. H.C. (6th ser.) col. 1192. https://hansard.parliament.uk/commons/ 2013-05-21/debates/13052186000002/Syria(EURestrictiveMeasures)#contribution-1305223000027 (accessed 22 March 2021).

*Hansard* 2014. 580 Parl. Deb. H.C. (6th ser.) col. 181WH. https://publications.parliament.uk/ pa/cm201314/cmhansrd/cm140513/halltext/140513h0001.htm (accessed 22 March 2021).

Hobson, J. 1902. *Imperialism: A Study*. New York, NY: James Pott & Company.

Hurd, D. 2003. *Memoirs*. London: Abacus.

Ibrahim, A. 2019a. *The Prospective Foreign Policy of a Corbyn Government and its U.S. National Security Implications*. Washington, DC: Hudson Institute.

Ibrahim, A. 2019b. "Is Jeremy Corbyn a friend of all Muslims?" *The Spectator*, 11 October. https://www.spectator.co.uk/article/is-jeremy-corbyn-a-friend-of-all-muslims-(accessed 22 March 2021).

Ipsos-Mori 2003. "Iraq, the last pre-war polls". 21 March. https://www.ipsos.com/ipsos-mori/ en-uk/iraq-last-pre-war-polls (accessed 22 March 2021).

Johnson, R. & A. Walsh 2012. *Camaraderie: One Hundred Years of the Cambridge Labour Party, 1912–2012*. Cambridge: Labour Party.

Kennard, M. 2018. "Jeremy Corbyn's views on Latin America". Latin America Bureau, 21 November. https://lab.org.uk/jeremy-corbyns-views-on-latin-america/ (accessed 22 March 2021).

Knight, S. 2016. "Enter left: will a fervent socialist reshape British politics or lead his party to irrelevance?" The New Yorker, 16 May. https://www.newyorker.com/magazine/2016/05/ 23/the-astonishing-rise-of-jeremy-corbyn (accessed 22 March 2021).

Kriner, D. & G. Wilson 2016. "The elasticity and reality of British support for the war in Afghanistan". *British Journal of International Relations* 18(3): 559–80.

LAB 2018. "Jeremy Corbyn's views on Latin America". Latin American Bureau, 21 November. https://lab.org.uk/jeremy-corbyns-views-on-latin-america/ (accessed 7 April 2021).

Labour Party 2019. *It's Time for Real Change: The Labour Party Manifesto 2019*. London: The Labour Party. https://labour.org.uk/wp-content/uploads/2019/11/Real-Change-Labour-Manifesto-2019.pdf (accessed 22 March 2021).

Liebknecht, K. 1952. *Ausgewählte Reden und Aufsätze [Selected speeches and essays]*. Berlin. Trans. by John Wagner for Marxists' Internet Archive (2002) https://www.marxists.org/ archive/liebknecht-k/works/1915/05/main-enemy-home.htm (accessed 7 April 2021).

Mullin, C. 2011. *A Walk-On Part: Diaries, 1994–1999*. London: Profile Books.

Norman, M. 2013. "An end to the emotional nonsense from Malcolm Rifkind". *The Independent*, 1 September.

Pugh, M. 2010. *Speak for Britain*. London: Vintage Books.

Ross, T. 2013. "Ed Miliband visits Denmark for anti-austerity drive". *The Telegraph*, 18 February. https://www.telegraph.co.uk/news/politics/labour/9877977/Ed-Miliband-visits-Denmark-for-anti-austerity-drive.html (accessed 17 March 2021)

Sassoon, D. 2019. "Letters: Jeremy Corbyn, Hobson's Imperialism, and antisemitism".
*The Guardian*, 2 May. https://www.theguardian.com/news/2019/may/02/jeremy-corbyn-hobsons-imperialism-and-antisemitism (accessed 22 March 2021).
Serhan, Y. 2019. "Jeremy Corbyn's Britain would reshape Western alliances". *The Atlantic*, 23 September. https://www.theatlantic.com/international/archive/2019/09/jeremy-corbyn-britain-foreign-policy/598564/ (accessed 17 March 2021).
Seymour, R. 2016. *Corbyn: The Strange Rebirth of Radical Politics*. London: Verso.
Smith, M. 2015. "Jeremy Corbyn says Tony Blair should be tried for war crimes". The Mirror, 4 August. https://www.mirror.co.uk/news/uk-news/jeremy-corbyn-says-tony-blair-6194941 (accessed 22 March 2021).
Spanner, H. n.d. "Far Sighted?" Third Way. https://www.thirdwaymagazine.co.uk/far-sighted/ (accessed 22 March 2021).
Taylor, A. 1957. *The Trouble Makers: Dissent Over Foreign Policy, 1792–1939*. London: Faber.
TeleSur 2017. "Jeremy Corbyn – a tireless campaigner for Latin America". 7 June. https://www.youtube.com/watch?v=IpsfaQIrusg (accessed 22 March 2021).
Thatcher, M. 1993. Interview with Peter Sissons, BBC, 13 April. https://www.margaretthatcher.org/document/110821 (accessed 6 April 2021).
Turner, A. 2013. *A Classless Society: Britain in the 1990s.* London: Autrum Press.
UK Parliament 1994. EDM 1129, "The Situation in Rwanda". 27 April.
https://edm.parliament.uk/early-day-motion/8851/situation-in-rwanda (accessed 8 April 2021).
Unkovski-Korica, V. 2019. "From the Cold War to the Kosovo War: Yugoslavia and the British Labour Party". *Revue d'études comparatives Est-Ouest*, 1(5): 115–45.
Whittell, G. 2019. "Jeremy Corbyn's journey". Tortoise Media, 24 September. https://www.tortoisemedia.com/2019/09/24/corbyns-foreign-policy-190924/ (accessed 22 March 2021).

# 14

# CORBYN AND ANTISEMITISM

*Andrew Barclay*

In April 2016, former London mayor and long-standing political ally of Jeremy Corbyn, Ken Livingstone was suspended from the Labour Party for bringing it into disrepute. Livingstone's suspension came days after his BBC interview in which he had claimed that Adolf Hitler supported Zionism before he "went mad and ended up killing six million Jews" (BBC 2016a). It was not apparent at the time, but this episode triggered what was to become one of the defining features of Corbyn's tenure as leader and one that ultimately led to his suspension from the Labour Party: the increasingly strained relationship between Labour and Britain's Jews.

To many observers, the idea that Labour and particularly Jeremy Corbyn's Labour should be responsible for anti-Jewish racism appeared counterintuitive to say the very least. Labour are the party that has consistently been preferred by the overwhelming majority of Britain's ethnic and religious minority voters (Martin 2019), and the received wisdom on the politics of Britain's Jews is one that tells a story of a strong and reciprocated historical affinity with the Labour Party. What is more, Jeremy Corbyn personally has a history of allying himself with a range of anti-racist causes, a point that has been made repeatedly by both Corbyn and his supporters over recent years. Nevertheless, the scale of Labour's problems by the end of his leadership reached the point that they were investigated by the Equality and Human Rights Commission (EHRC) for their treatment of Jewish members, as the only party investigated by the EHRC since the British National Party in 2010. On 29 October 2020, the EHRC published the findings of their investigation, which found that Labour broke equality law through the harassment of Jewish members and through political interference in dealing with disciplinary cases relating to anti-Jewish prejudice (EHRC 2020).

This extraordinary event followed a protracted series of controversies surrounding antisemitism within Labour throughout the period of Corbyn's leadership (for a discussion on how Corbyn sought to limit the damage to his reputation, see Heppell 2021). It also arose within the context of substantial disagreement about how to understand these controversies. Critics of the Corbyn project have linked increased prominence of anti-Jewish sentiment within the party specifically to the brand of politics adopted by Corbyn, which is suggested to be predisposed to employing conspiratorial antisemitic tropes about Jews (Rich 2019). Conversely, a good number of ideological and political allies of Corbyn spent the years leading up to the EHRC's report rejecting this notion, with some suggesting that claims of antisemitism were either exaggerated or even manufactured in an attempt to undermine Corbyn as leader (Graeber 2019). It was Corbyn's apparent support for this position in response to the EHRC's report that led to him being suspended from the party he had led into a general election less than 12 months previously.

This chapter examines some of the key episodes that were at the heart of these disagreements. The sheer number of allegations made since 2015 means it is only possible to scratch the surface of the total number of cases of antisemitism, but these are sufficient to reject entirely the notion that these complaints were simply a smear orchestrated by Corbyn's political opponents. The chapter does not overly concern itself with the question of whether Corbyn or other Labour figures are antisemites per se, but instead shows how their actions and wider political outlook "facilitated and amplified" antisemitism within the party (Lipstadt 2019). It concludes by detailing how Labour's crisis has affected British Jews themselves, who have (perhaps unsurprisingly) almost en masse moved away from the party, which was once considered their natural political home.

### The emergence of the crisis and the first inquiry

Before Jeremy Corbyn was elected leader of the party, any discussions relating to Labour and antisemitism tended to be isolated to certain media portrayals of Ed Miliband, the party's first Jewish leader (Rich 2016). This was no different in the early months of Corbyn's tenure as leader. While there was no shortage of critical voices from inside and outside the party when it came to his supposed electoral appeal, and general suitability to being leader of the opposition, there was little in the way of discussion of Labour's relationship with Jews among most observers of British politics.

This began to change in the early months of 2016, shortly prior to Ken Livingstone's televised comments. Among the first of the events that resulted in this change was a complaint made by Alex Chalmers, the former chair of Oxford University Labour Club, who claimed that members of the club were responsible for creating a poisonous atmosphere towards Jewish students at the University. Around the same time a Labour MP was also accused of anti-Jewish prejudice. A social media post from 2014 by Naz Shah, the MP for Bradford

West, emerged, which displayed an image of Israel superimposed onto a map of the United States, with the caption "Solution for [the] Israel-Palestine Conflict" (BBC 2016b). Shah herself was quick to apologize once her post came to light, but it was the initial criticism of her that then prompted Livingstone to air his comments about Hitler supporting Zionism, first on radio and latterly on the BBC's *Politics Live* programme.

Both Shah and Livingstone were temporarily suspended, but their actions were enough to spark a national conversation surrounding antisemitism in the Labour Party. As attention towards the issue grew, so too did the number of Labour councillors, officials and other members who were found to have made public statements or posts on social media that were alleged to have contained anti-Jewish prejudice. By the summer there were dozens of Labour members who were suspended from the party pending investigation into antisemitism, and there was no sign of the situation abating in the near future. Thus, the party appointed human rights lawyer Shami Chakrabarti to chair an independent inquiry into the prevalence of antisemitism within Labour, and whether recent suspensions reflected a broader problem that the party had with its treatment of Jews, albeit with "other forms of racism" included within the scope of her inquiry.

The Chakrabarti Report invited expert submissions on antisemitism and published its findings in June 2016, around two months after being commissioned. In doing so Chakrabarti concluded that Labour was not "overrun by antisemitism, Islamophobia or other forms of racism" but also that there was an "occasionally toxic atmosphere" within the party, and also that there was "too much evidence of [...] hateful or ignorant attitudes" (Chakrabarti 2016).[1] The report also made further recommendations about the use of language, particularly in discussion of Middle Eastern politics and the Israel–Palestine conflict, but these recommendations were initially lost in the report's launch, which was itself bad-tempered and brought about fresh controversies surrounding Labour's handling of antisemitism claims. First, there was the treatment of Jewish Labour MP Ruth Smeeth, who was reported to have been "verbally attacked" at the event by a Labour activist who accused her of "working hand in hand" with the right-wing press (Marshall 2016). Following this, there was the statement from Corbyn himself, who in an attempt to endorse the inquiry's findings clumsily remarked that "our Jewish friends are no more responsible for the actions of Israel or the Netanyahu government than our Muslim friends are for those various self-styled Islamic states or organisations" (Hirsh 2017). These events coupled with some

---

1. The Chakrabarti Report attracted praise from some quarters for its recommendations on language (e.g. Kahn-Harris 2016; Rich 2016), but was criticized from others who claimed that the report only superficially engaged with specifically left-wing antisemitism, and that contributors making this point were sidelined (Hirsh 2017).

of the findings of the report itself meant that Labour were unable to draw a line under antisemitism and public scrutiny of the issue continued.

A further consequence of the Chakrabarti Report is that it helped frame the terms of the argument surrounding Labour antisemitism, which would come to characterize the following years. In particular, it gave rise to the line that was consistently taken by Corbyn and many of his supporters that antisemitism existed in the party in the form of a tiny percentage of its members, but that this was no worse and no different than the antisemitism found in British society, traces of which would be expected to be present even in the ranks of an ostensibly anti-racist progressive party such as Labour. The "few bad apples" theory gave the foundation to the argument of some Corbyn supporters that not only were there nominal levels of anti-Jewish prejudice within the party, but any claim to the contrary was a part of a witch hunt or smear campaign against the leader from the disenchanted Labour right who would oppose Corbyn's leadership on whatever basis they could muster (Johnson 2019). As a result, battle lines were drawn around the question of whether there was anything distinctive about antisemitism in the Labour Party under Corbyn.

## Antisemitism among anti-racists

Left-wing antisemitism may have only become a prominent feature of British politics during Corbyn's time as Labour leader, but hostility towards Jews from the Left can be traced back almost as far as organized democratic socialism (Feldman & McGeever 2018). Even accounting for historically higher levels of antisemitism in wider society, there has existed a separate strain of left-wing antisemitism, which associates Jews with international finance and, in doing so, holds Jews responsible for the various ills and injustices that arise through the capitalist system (Lipset 1969). This view was famously dubbed the "socialism of fools" and was responsible for numerous examples of anti-Jewish prejudice within the early labour movement. Jewish workers were denied membership of some trade unions in the early twentieth century (Alderman 1983) and even the first leader of the Labour Party, Keir Hardie, evoked classic antisemitic tropes by implying that a secretive cabal of Jewish finance houses were behind the Second Boer War (Wistrich 2012).

Associating Jews with capitalism has not exclusively been a feature of left-wing antisemitism, but its existence shows the potential for a distinctive form of antisemitism to be prevalent among anti-capitalists. Yet on first inspection, there appears to be little in common between this supposed association between Jews and international finance and the cases of antisemitism during the Corbyn years. Certainly, there was no obvious connection with the controversies involving Ken Livingstone, Naz Shah and the Oxford University Labour Club, which led to the Chakrabarti Inquiry. What these episodes did have in common was a more recent feature of left antisemitism; discussing Israel and Zionism in a way that goes far beyond what would be considered typical criticism of a foreign state, often while using antisemitic stereotypes about supposed Jewish power.

Support for the Palestinians in their conflict with Israel has been commonplace on the British left for some decades, and this is especially true for the traditions most closely associated with Corbyn and many of his political allies, for whom anti-Zionism is axiomatic and a key tenet of their political identity (Rich 2019). Advocates of this position would with some justification argue that even robust criticism of Israeli policy is no more or less problematic than criticism of any other state or government (Fine & Spencer 2018). And yet it is equally true that discussions surrounding Israel have provided fertile ground for the use of more ostensibly antisemitic language (Allington 2019). Where previously Jews may have been depicted as exercising disproportionate and malevolent influence over global affairs, these conspiratorial tropes are instead made about Israel or Zionism in what has been described as a part of the "new antisemitism" (Taguieff 2004). Even when such tropes are absent, there are other ways in which anti-Zionist discourse has proven to be problematic. British Jews have diverse range of views when it comes to the present policies of the Israeli government, and yet the overwhelming majority retain some affinity with the country as a central part of their Jewish identity (Miller, Harris & Schindler 2015). Using Zionist as a pejorative term of abuse or opposing Zionism as inherently racist, while technically making no reference to Jews as a discrete group, is in effect to extend this view to the large majority of Jews who view Israel as a component of being Jewish. Similarly, using Zio or Zionist as a euphemism for Jewish even when the individual in question has no stated opinion on Middle Eastern politics was an issue cited in the Chakrabarti Report as a problem that occurred frequently enough to raise "alarm bells" in the Jewish community (Chakrabarti 2016).

It has been possible for those sympathetic to the Corbyn project to acknowledge that anti-Jewish racism can be cloaked in the language of anti-Zionism, while at the same time arguing that there is nothing antisemitic about the anti-Israel positions held by many of Corbyn's supporters. Survey evidence was regularly cited in support of this view, particularly a 2017 survey conducted by the Institute of Jewish Policy Research (JPR 2017), which showed that support for a range of antisemitic statements was significantly higher among those who identify with the political far right than respondents from the Left. When it came specifically to Corbyn's supporters within the Labour Party, a survey of "new" members who joined after the 2015 general election showed that just 1 per cent of respondents would have any objection to having a Jewish neighbour (Bale, Poletti & Webb 2016).[2]

At face value, these surveys suggest that there was no large-scale problem with antisemitism, either among Labour members generally or Corbyn supporters specifically. However, both surveys also contained evidence of the prevalence of anti-Israel positions among voters most likely to be supportive of Labour and Corbyn, and of the association between these positions and conspiracist antisemitic tropes. The JPR survey for instance also asked for respondents' views on several statements concerning Israel, several of which either contained reference to antisemitic tropes or had no relation to Israel's conflict with the Palestinians.[3] Respondents identifying as very left-wing were by some distance most likely to agree with these anti-Israel statements, and there was a strong correlation between displaying more anti-Israel sentiment with also displaying prejudice towards Jews. The issue of antisemitism within the Labour Party was also viewed with a large degree of scepticism. In the weeks leading up to the Chakrabarti Report, over 85 per cent of Labour members believed that the public controversies surrounding antisemitism were being deliberately exaggerated, either in an attempt to undermine the Labour leadership or to stifle legitimate criticism of Israel (Bale, Poletti & Webb 2016).

Determining the existence of Labour's problem became more straightforward following the Chakrabarti Report's publication, when material examples of antisemitism from Labour supporters, members or officials were becoming increasingly commonplace. This was especially true in online spaces. An investigation conducted by the *Sunday Times* found over 2,000 separate examples of antisemitic content in the largest Corbyn-supporting Facebook groups (Kerbaj *et al.* 2018) including examples of Holocaust denial and abusive posts criticizing Jewish Labour figures who had spoken out against antisemitism. The official Labour response to the exposé was to point out that there was no formal connection between these groups and the party, and while this was true, the increased media spotlight on the party ensured that there was no shortage of similar stories that emerged concerning identifiable Labour candidates who had also made antisemitic comments over social media.

Neither were incidents of antisemitism limited to these online spaces. A recurring complaint made throughout Corbyn's tenure as leader was that of Jewish members being subject to abuse and bullying on account of their Jewish identity. Certainly, the levels of abuse endured by Jewish MPs who were critical of the leadership were severe. Most emblematic of this was the prolonged harassment of Luciana Berger, the former MP for Liverpool Wavertree, who faced a varied

---

2. This form of question is commonly used when detecting prejudice among the public.
3. As an example, one statement was "Israel has too much control over global affairs".

catalogue of abuse before eventually resigning from the party in protest in 2019 (Pogrund & Maguire 2020). Berger was confronted by thousands of abusive messages as her opposition to the leadership's handling of antisemitism became more apparent, but alongside this she was also subject to several threats of physical harm, including a death threat in 2018, which Labour failed to inform either herself or the police about. She required a police escort at the 2018 Labour conference to guarantee her safety (BBC 2018) and upon leaving the party some months later had reached the conclusion that it was "institutionally antisemitic" (BBC 2020).

The complaints made by Luciana Berger were echoed not just by most of Labour's other Jewish MPs, but also by activists without their public profile. The best example of this came in the form of the BBC's *Panorama* programme in 2019, where eight former Labour employees gave testimony not just of the existence of a hostile culture towards Jews within the party, but also that the party machinery intervened in the disciplinary process to downgrade complaints made about the alleged antisemitism of certain members (*Panorama* 2019). These cases included members who had referred to Jewish Labour MPs as Zionist infiltrators, and implied that Jews were responsible for 9/11 (Lampert 2019). Labour initially contested the claims of the whistle-blowers, whom they declared to be "disaffected former officials [...] who have always opposed Jeremy Corbyn's leadership" (Walker & Elgot 2020), but latterly retracted their accusations and in 2020 apologized unreservedly for their treatment (O'Carroll & Elgot 2020).

Taking each of these episodes into consideration, it is not credible to look back at the Corbyn years and claim that Labour did not have a problem when it came to antisemitism that was different to the prejudice found in the wider population in both its scale and its character. Examples of anti-Jewish prejudice came most frequently from individuals who identified with Jeremy Corbyn's politics. In isolation, this says little about if and how Jeremy Corbyn himself contributed to this broader problem. Even many of his critics at the outset of the crisis were often at pains to stress that they were not suggesting that Corbyn personally displayed anti-Jewish prejudice, rather that he was not sufficiently able to recognize antisemitism among his political allies (Freedland 2020). This view proved to become increasingly difficult to sustain, however, as more and more stories emerged of cases of antisemitism that not only related to Labour members or even Corbyn supporters, but in fact concerned the Labour leader personally.

### Corbyn's record

More assiduous followers of debates surrounding Israel and Middle Eastern politics were well aware of Jeremy Corbyn's associations with known antisemites even prior to his election as leader. In August 2015 as the leadership election drew to a close, the *Jewish Chronicle* publicly asked Corbyn to clarify his links with a series of figures with a history of taking antisemitic positions, including Holocaust denier Paul Eisen, and more infamously his inviting representatives from both Hamas and Hezbollah to the House of Commons where he was alleged to refer to them as his "friends" (*Jewish Chronicle* 2015). However, most critics of Labour's handling of antisemitism in the early years of Corbyn's tenure as leader were often at pains to point out that they were not claiming that Corbyn himself was an antisemite (Freedland 2016). It was much more frequently suggested that a mixture of incompetence and an unwillingness to condemn ideological bedfellows was responsible for him not opposing antisemitism in sufficiently robust terms.

As time progressed, however, an increasing number of cases came to light which related specifically to Corbyn's positions and associations that made it much more difficult to somehow detach him from the wider problem which existed within Labour. Among the first of these cases concerned a mural in Islington North, Jeremy Corbyn's constituency, painted by the graffiti artist Mear One in 2012 when Corbyn was still a backbench MP. The mural depicted six men, some of whom were Jewish caricatures, playing a game of Monopoly on the backs of dark-skinned figures. In case there was any doubt about the intention of the piece, the artist himself clarified matters by saying that his work portrayed an "elite banker cartel" who profit at the expense of the oppressed majority. The Jewish stereotypes employed were condemned by local politicians of both Left and Right and were described by the historian of antisemitism Deborah Lipstadt as imagery akin to that used in *Der Stürmer* in Nazi Germany (Lipstadt 2019). The local council agreed and ordered its removal, but this was not before Jeremy Corbyn had offered his support to the artist on social media and questioned the decision to remove the mural (Pogrund & Maguire 2020).

When this came to light in early 2018, Corbyn stated that he regretted not having initially looked closer at the image. Despite the rather blatant antisemitic overtones (Bush 2020), it would have been much easier to downplay Corbyn's role in deepening Labour's problems with antisemitism had this been the only case that he had to answer. This was not the case. Shortly after the row about the mural died down, a video emerged of Corbyn speaking at a meeting in parliament, where he was recorded saying that a group of "Zionists" present in the audience had two problems: "that they don't want to study history and secondly, having lived in this country for a very long time, probably all their lives, they don't understand English irony either" (Stewart & Sparrow 2018). The statement was widely interpreted as a way of implying that Jews, euphemistically referred to as Zionists, are somehow not quite acquiring "English" characteristics despite being born in the UK (Hirsh 2018). Corbyn later denied antisemitic intent in his statement, claiming that he was using Zionist in the literal sense while acknowledging that the term is sometimes used as an antisemitic euphemism for Jews, but this episode was still regarded as a watershed for some commentators to move away from giving him the benefit of the doubt as someone who failed to identify and deal with antisemitism, rather than actively facilitating it (e.g. Freedland 2020).

Also compounding such a perception was the revelation that in 2014, Corbyn attended a memorial ceremony in Tunisia, ostensibly for the commemoration of the attack on the Palestinian Liberation Organization offices in 1985. However, photos emerged from the same trip of Jeremy Corbyn seemingly also laying a wreath on four graves including those of members of Black September, the group responsible for perpetrating the 1972 Munich massacre, in which 11 members of the Israeli Olympic team were murdered. In an attempt to distance himself from these events, Corbyn told reporters that he was indeed present at the ceremony but denied any involvement in the laying of the wreaths specifically (Sabbagh 2018). This explanation, along with those for each of these events, could plausibly have been taken at face value in isolation. Collectively however, they contributed to a sense that Corbyn not only was insufficiently robust in dealing with anti-semitism within his party, and actively contributed to the sense that the party was hostile towards Jews. Neither were these the only examples. There was the case of his interview with Press TV in 2014, where he said he suspected the influence of the "hand of Israel" in a terrorist attack on Egyptian police (Cohen 2018). There was also his sponsorship of an Early Day Motion in 2011 to rename Holocaust Memorial Day to Genocide Memorial Day (UK Parliament 2011) as well as his active membership of online groups that promoted antisemitic con-spiracy theory (although Corbyn was not responsible for such posts himself; see Allington 2018). All of this and more led Dr Dave Rich, researcher on antisem-itism and the head of policy at the Community Security Trust, to brand him as the "unluckiest anti-racist in history" (Rich 2018), and for the Simon Wiesenthal Center to name his overseeing of Labour's struggle with antisemitism at the top of their annual list of global antisemitic incidents for 2019 (Haaretz 2019).

The volume of other cases of antisemitism during the Corbyn years shows that Labour's problems were not simply about the views of one man. Nevertheless, the controversies surrounding Jeremy Corbyn personally were important in exacerbating the crisis. At the very least they signalled that the form of anti-Zionist politics that had previously been found on the fringes of the labour movement was now consolidated within the party leadership. Some of these revelations also made it much more difficult to argue that Labour's problems were just about its policy towards Israel, as they had little, if anything at all, to do with the country. More than just this however, they also perfectly encapsu-lated the paramount importance of anti-Zionism to his overall political outlook. This mattered a great deal when it came to the practical handling of Labour's antisemitism crisis, as Corbyn and his office were notably unwilling to make compromises over this part of their politics, even when there were obvious political incentives to be more flexible. This was at its most obvious in the row over the definition of antisemitism in 2018.

## The IHRA definition of antisemitism and the response of British Jews

Following the protracted levels of attention that both Corbyn and Labour were receiving for their records on antisemitism, the party adopted a new code of conduct on antisemitism in the summer of 2018. Reinforcing the rules regarding antisemitism may have presented an opportunity to begin a process of reconciliation with Britain's Jews, but Labour's proposed changes instead acted as a catalyst for the party's crisis to reach new depths. They also provided the clearest example of how anti-Zionist politics were of such importance to many figures on Labour's Corbynite wing that they took precedence over measures to address at least the salience of antisemitism that was damaging the party, if not antisemitism itself.

The point of contention surrounded Labour's reluctance to adopt the International Holocaust Remembrance Alliance (IHRA) definition of antisemitism as a part of their disciplinary procedure. The IHRA definition is the one presently adopted by the UK government, and provides a list of 11 illustrative examples of antisemitic practices (IHRA 2020). Many of these examples, such as Holocaust denial, are self-evidently antisemitic, and there was unsurprisingly little resistance within Labour in recognizing them as such. However, some within the party did (at least to begin with) take issue with four of the examples, which resulted in their adopting a modified code of conduct on antisemitism in July 2018 (Rich 2018).

Each of the four examples that were either omitted or modified related to discourse surrounding Israel and were resisted largely as a result of a perception on the part of some of those on the anti-Zionist left that these illustrative examples acted to suppress criticism of Israel (Lerman 2018). Most notably, the revisions omitted the example that stated that it is antisemitic to infer that Jews are more loyal to Israel than they are to their own state. Charging Jews with disloyalty to their country of origin or residence is a trope that is not just a feature of antisemitism on the left, but has been central to the antisemitism from the right, which Labour has consistently claimed to oppose (Rich 2018).[4] The other examples

---

4. Labour's revised code of conduct did state that implying Jews' dual loyalty in this way should not be encouraged, but stopped some way short of saying that this insensitive language should be considered antisemitic.

initially rejected by Labour related more specifically to language used to describe the state of Israel. The IHRA examples deem it antisemitic to compare the actions of Israel to those of the Nazis, to imply that the existence of the state of Israel is an inherently racist endeavour, or to otherwise hold Israel to a standard of behaviour that would not be expected of any other democratic nation (IHRA 2020). According to Labour's proposed definition, such statements would only be considered as prejudiced towards Jews if there was evidence of "antisemitic intent" (Sugarman 2018).

A small number of advocates of these changes defended their stance on the grounds that the new code of conduct in fact represented a more robust definition of antisemitism than the one provided by the IHRA. Jon Lansman, founder of Momentum and himself Jewish, described the changes as representing a "gold standard" for other parties to follow (Lansman 2018). Others, including researchers of antisemitism, pointed to some imprecise language in the IHRA definition (Feldman 2016) but it was much more common to find critics of the IHRA's examples on the basis that they would impede supporting the Palestinian cause (Burden 2018).

The response from large swathes of the Jewish community was hostile. At the heart of the criticism was that decisions were being taken on what constitutes anti-Jewish racism without consulting Jews themselves. The Board of Deputies and the Jewish Leadership Council (JLC), two of the largest representative bodies of Anglo-Jewry, released a joint statement stating that it is "for Jews to determine what antisemitism is", before pointing out the wide range of Jewish communal organizations, as well as governmental bodies and states across the world, which had adopted the IHRA definition (JLC 2018). A large number of Corbyn-sceptic Labour MPs were happy to publicly support the JLC and Board of Deputies in their criticism of their party (BBC 2018), with the MP for Barking, Margaret Hodge, subject to disciplinary action for calling Corbyn a "racist and antisemite" although the action was later dropped (Crerar & Stewart 2018). The three newspapers which cater for Britain's Jews, the *Jewish Chronicle*, the *Jewish Telegraph* and the *Jewish Times*, ran a joint front page for the first time in their history, describing the prospect of a Corbyn-led government as an existential threat to British Jews and citing the failure to adopt the IHRA definition as the final straw which led to their decision (*Jewish Chronicle* 2018). Perhaps even more extraordinary was an open letter, this time signed by 68 rabbis from across the denominational spectrum, condemning the Labour Party for not adopting the IHRA definition in full. Indirectly evoking the so-called MacPherson principle of allowing minorities to define the prejudice they face (Katz & Langleben 2018), the rabbis' letter claimed that it was "not the Labour party's place to rewrite a definition of antisemitism" (Harpin 2018a).

In the face of intense and sustained pressure to do so, the NEC eventually adopted the IHRA definition with each of its illustrative examples, although even this olive branch was accompanied by Jeremy Corbyn making a statement reaffirming that free speech on Israel would not be restricted (Rodgers 2018). This caveat is a good illustration of how Labour's antisemitism crisis was allowed to reach the scale that it did. In a purely pragmatic sense, there was little to be gained for Labour to instigate another bitter and public row over antisemitism some two years after it had first become a national political story. Many of those close to the Labour leadership (reportedly including the shadow chancellor, John McDonnell; Pogrund & Maguire 2020) were desperate to take the necessary measures to take the heat out of a highly damaging issue for the Labour Party, and yet Corbyn, alongside some close allies, remained highly resistant to making any compromise on their stance on what was and remains a key tenet of their politics. It was this lack of flexibility that caused the rabbis to make their intervention into the debate, and that also led to other strong reactions from within the Jewish community.

Further embarrassment for Labour arrived in the weeks prior to adopting the IHRA definition. Long-standing NEC member Peter Willsman was recorded referring to many within the Jewish community as "Trump fanatics",[5] before stating that claims of antisemitism had been falsified on social media (Harpin 2018b). The fallout from these comments involved strong criticism from the JLM and several Labour MPs, as well as calls for Willsman's expulsion from the Board of Deputies (Schofield 2018). He was even dropped from the slate of candidates representing the Corbyn-supporting Momentum group in the upcoming elections to the NEC. In spite of this, and to the dismay of his critics, Willsman was re-elected to the NEC and faced no further action for his comments.

The public criticism that Corbyn and his allies received from Jewish public figures, be they religious, political or cultural, unsurprisingly attracted a good deal of attention. Less attention has been paid to how the community as a whole viewed Labour, and this was the more dramatic response in some respects. Even as early as 2016, a representative sample of British Jews showed that a comfortable majority thought Labour were performing badly on antisemitism (Dysch 2017), as did a plurality of respondents who had voted Labour in 2015 (Barclay 2019). As the crisis continued, so too did the poor esteem in which Labour was held among most Jews. A series of polls conducted by Survation showed an ever-decreasing number of Jewish voters declaring their support for the party at the ballot box, with only 6 per cent of Jews being estimated to still be supporting Labour at the time of the 2019 general election (Survation 2019).

---

5. An especially curious statement given that American Jews were among the Democrats' strongest supporters in the elections of 2016 and 2020 (Wald 2019).

The ironic context to this is that there were many similarities between British Jews and the sorts of voters the Corbyn project was otherwise successful in attracting. Most Jews live within Britain's major cities, particularly London and Manchester, and were considerably more likely to have voted Remain than the national average (Bush 2020). There is little doubt that antisemitism was the key reason why Labour was unable to replicate the success they had among these groups with Jewish voters. A survey conducted by the European Union Agency for Fundamental Rights (FRA 2018) showed that more than half of British Jews believed that antisemitism had increased a lot in the UK over the previous five years, and that the most common manifestation of anti-Jewish racism was within political life. While the survey made no reference to antisemitism within the Labour Party specifically, it is reasonable to assume that this is the case given other surveys conducted during Corbyn's leadership. Marginally fewer than nine out of ten Jewish voters believed Jeremy Corbyn to be personally antisemitic (Sugarman 2018) and almost half even reported considering leaving the country in the event of a Corbyn premiership (*Jewish Chronicle* 2019).

## The EHRC report and Jeremy Corbyn's suspension

The depth of feeling felt by many Jews and others within the Labour Party was reflected in the increasing number of formal complaints to the EHRC. By the summer of 2019, the number and severity of the complaints had reached such a severe stage that the EHRC felt the need to launch a formal investigation into Labour for its treatment of Jews, specifically whether the party had unlawfully discriminated against, harassed or victimized people because they were Jewish (BBC 2019). The EHRC's purview was to explore the specific complaints that were referred to them while adjudicating on whether Labour had broken equalities legislation, and therefore it did not attempt to conduct a broader review of the existence of an antisemitic culture within the party.

October 2020 saw the publication of the EHRC's findings, which despite the rather narrow scope of the investigation, were damning for both party and leader. Labour were found to have broken the Equality Act in three respects: by not providing adequate training to those handling antisemitism complaints, political interference from the leader's office in dealing with disciplinary cases including complaints made against Corbyn himself, and even harassment of Jewish members, which at various times included the use of antisemitic tropes and suggesting that complaints of anti-Jewish prejudice were a political smear intended to undermine the party leadership (EHRC 2020). On this last point, the report specifically referenced the behaviour of Ken Livingstone and Pam Bromley, a councillor in Lancashire, as the clearest examples of harassment.

Far from being the only perpetrators, however, the report is clear in stating that they were the "tip of the iceberg" of antisemitic conduct even within the limited sample of cases on which EHRC based its judgement. According to the report, it was not credible to sustain the view that Labour antisemitism did not exist bar the activity of a "few bad apples".

An important difference between the EHRC report and the various other investigations into Labour during this period, including the Chakrabarti Report (other than its political independence), is that they had the statutory powers to make legally binding recommendations. More optimistic followers of Labour's antisemitism crisis could therefore have been forgiven for expecting the report's publication to at least provide a degree of closure to the issue, if not even to signal the start of healing relationships inside and outside of the party (Freeman 2020). However, such hopes of drawing a line under these disputes appeared to be dashed less than an hour of the report having first come to light. While Keir Starmer was telling the country's media outlets that Labour would seek to begin to regain the trust of British Jews by accepting and implementing the EHRC report in full, Jeremy Corbyn released a statement that directly contradicted the new leader's stance. Despite the legal authority granted to the EHRC, Corbyn not only wrote on his Facebook page that he did not agree with each of the report's findings, but also reiterated his long-held stance that the scale of antisemitism within Labour on his watch had been "dramatically" exaggerated by his political opponents, both inside and outside of the party as well as within the media (Walker & Elgot 2020).

Implying that complaints of antisemitism are smears or exaggerated for political ends was specifically referred to by the EHRC as an example of the harassment faced by Jewish members, and it was therefore this statement that led the party hierarchy to take the decision to suspend Jeremy Corbyn from the party he used to lead for bringing it into disrepute. Corbyn is no longer suspended by the party at the time of writing, but he has yet to have the Labour parliamentary whip restored to him and it remains unclear how the internal factions within Labour will respond to the consequences of this development. Certainly, his closest supporters as leader showed some dissent over their former leader's suspension. Len McCluskey, the leader of the trade union and Labour's biggest donor, Unite, was by far the most critical of the decision in public, referring to the decision as "a grave injustice", before warning that it would lead to disunity within the party which would ultimately "compromise Labour's chances of a general election victory" (McCluskey 2020). McCluskey was certainly right to suggest that the episode presented Labour as more divided. A YouGov survey found that 57 per cent of British voters viewed Labour as a disunited party following Corbyn's suspension, an increase of around 20 per cent in just a few days since the publication of the EHRC report (Conner 2020). Other prominent allies of Corbyn, including former shadow cabinet members John McDonnell, Diane Abbott and Richard Burgon, also spoke out against the decision to remove the whip by promoting a petition to reinstate Corbyn. Notwithstanding this disquiet, and despite some concerns among the Socialist Campaign Group (of which Corbyn has been a long-standing member) about whether "resignations should be on the table" (Pogrund 2020), a more robust response has yet to materialize.

**Conclusion: a crisis unresolved**

Upon winning the Labour leadership in April 2020, Keir Starmer declared that he measured success in dealing with anti-Jewish prejudice in his party by the return of former Jewish members (Harpin 2020). It remains to be seen whether he will be successful in his efforts, but in the meantime it seems unlikely that the fallout from the EHRC report will be the final word on Labour's strained relationship with Britain's Jews. The present Labour leadership have attracted criticism from all directions by lifting Corbyn's suspension from the party while at the same time refusing to allow to him to sit as a Labour MP in parliament (Bush 2020b) and it is far from clear at the time of writing, if and how the controversy surrounding Corbyn will be resolved. Neither is it clear whether the wider issue of antisemitism within the party will continue to be a prominent part of the national political discussion. One of the EHRC's recommendations is to implement a fully independent process for dealing with antisemitism complaints, meaning that historical cases of antisemitism may attract the attention of the public as they are revisited.

What is more certain is that, despite protestations to the contrary, Labour under Corbyn had a very real problem with its treatment of British Jews. This chapter has shown that this problem, to use the language of Dave Rich (2019), is not simply a few bad apples within a broadly anti-racist barrel. It was the barrel itself that was the issue, which was facilitated and exacerbated by the politics of both Jeremy Corbyn himself and a number of his allies and supporters. This exposes one of the key contradictions at the heart of the Corbyn project: that a Labour leader whose appeal was almost uniquely built upon a history of supporting anti-racist causes would himself become synonymous with leading a party that was discriminatory against a minority group in Britain.

In part this was a consequence of how classically antisemitic ideas of Jewish power and influence have been allowed to permeate anti-Zionist discourse, particularly in the political traditions most closely associated with Jeremy Corbyn. In other ways this was an institutional problem, with key figures within the party being unwilling to show the necessary flexibility, self-reflection or political will to address the issue, therefore allowing it to grow worse over the course of Corbyn's tenure as leader. As for Corbyn himself, it is highly likely that many of his remaining supporters will continue to argue that his association with antisemitism in Labour is unfair. Nevertheless, anti-Jewish racism is bound to characterize the legacy of the Corbyn years, which is in equal measure a remarkable and lamentable outcome.

# References

Alderman, G. 1983. *The Jewish Community in British Politics.* Oxford: Clarendon Press.
Allington, D. 2018. "'Hitler had a valid argument against some Jews': repertoires for the denial of antisemitism in online responses to a survey of attitudes to Jews and Israel". *Discourse, Context & Media* 24: 29–136.
Allington, D. 2019. "The politics of antisemitism: analysis of survey findings". *Antisemitism Barometer 2019.* https://antisemitism.org/wp-content/uploads/2019/12/Analysis-of-Antisemitism-Barometer-Survey-Findings-Allington-2019.pdf (accessed 23 March 2021).
Bale, T., M. Poletti & P. Webb 2016. "Submission to the Chakrabarti Inquiry on behalf of the ESRC Party Members Project". https://esrcpartymembersprojectorg.files.wordpress.com/2015/09/balewebbpolettisubmission4chakrabarti3rdjune2016-1.pdf (accessed 23 March 2021).
Barclay, A. 2019. "Labour and Jewish voters: a deteriorating relationship". *Political Insight* 10(2): 30–33.
BBC 2016a. "Ken Livingstone stands by Hitler comments". BBC News, 30 April. https://www.bbc.co.uk/news/uk-politics-36177333 (accessed 23 March 2021).
BBC 2016b. "Naz Shah MP quits role over Israel post on Facebook". BBC News, 26 April. https://www.bbc.co.uk/news/uk-politics-36142529 (accessed 23 March 2021).
BBC 2018. "MPs join criticism of Labour's antisemitism code". BBC News, 5 July. https://www.bbc.co.uk/news/uk-politics-44732720 (accessed 23 March 2021).
BBC 2019a. "No-confidence vote in Labour MP Luciana Berger pulled". BBC News, 8 February. https://www.bbc.co.uk/news/uk-politics-47178203 (accessed 23 March 2021).
BBC 2019b. "Equality watchdog launches Labour antisemitism probe". BBC News, 28 May. https://www.bbc.co.uk/news/uk-48433964 (accessed 23 March 2021).
BBC 2020. "A guide to Labour Party antisemitism claims". BBC News, 18 November. https://www.bbc.co.uk/news/uk-politics-45030552 (accessed 23 March 2021).
Burden, R. 2018. "Why I'm concerned about the IHRA definition of antisemitism". LabourList, 18 July. https://labourlist.org/2018/07/richard-burden-why-im-concerned-about-the-ihra-definition-of-antisemitism/ (accessed 23 March 2021).
Bush, S. 2020a. "There are 45,000 reasons for Jeremy Corbyn's suspension: one for each Jewish voter to abandon Labour". *New Statesman*, 4 November. https://www.newstatesman.com/politics/uk/2020/11/there-are-45000-reasons-jeremy-corbyn-s-suspension-one-each-jewish-voter-abandon (accessed 23 March 2021).
Bush, S. 2020b. "Jeremy Corbyn's readmittance is a blow to Keir Starmer – and to his allies' judgement". *New Statesman*, 17 November. https://www.newstatesman.com/politics/uk/2020/11/jeremy-corbyn-s-readmittance-blow-keir-starmer-and-his-allies-judgement (accessed 23 March 2021).

Chakrabarti, S. 2016. "The Shami Chakrabarti Inquiry". https://labour.org.uk/wp-content/uploads/2017/10/Chakrabarti-Inquiry-Report-30June16.pdf (accessed 23 March 2021).

Cohen, J. 2018. "Corbyn 'suspected hand of Israel' in Egypt bombing during Press TV interview". *Jewish News*, 29 July. https://jewishnews.timesofisrael.com/corbyn-suspected-hand-of-israel-in-egypt-bombing-during-press-tv-interview/ (accessed 23 March 2021).

Conner, J. 2020. "Almost six in ten think the Labour party is divided". YouGov, 9 November. https://yougov.co.uk/topics/politics/articles-reports/2020/11/09/almost-six-ten-think-labour-party-divided (accessed 23 March 2021).

Crerar, P. & H. Stewart. 2018 "Labour acts against Margaret Hodge for calling Corbyn racist" *The Guardian*, 18 July. https://www.theguardian.com/politics/2018/jul/18/labour-party-to-take-action-against-mp-who-called-corbyn-a-racist (accessed 23 March 2021).

Dysch, M. 2017. "Labour support just 13 per cent among UK Jews". *Jewish Chronicle*, 30 May. https://www.thejc.com/news/uk/labour-support-just-13-per-cent-among-uk-jews-1.439325 (accessed 23 March 2021).

EHRC 2020. "Investigation into antisemitism in the Labour Party". https://www.equalityhumanrights.com/sites/default/files/investigation-into-antisemitism-in-the-labour-party.pdf (accessed 23 March 2021).

Feldman, D. 2016. "Will Britain's new definition of antisemitism help Jewish people? I'm sceptical". *The Guardian*, 28 December. https://www.theguardian.com/commentisfree/2016/dec/28/britain-definition-antisemitism-british-jews-jewish-people (accessed 23 March 2021).

Feldman, D. & B. McGeever 2018. "British Left's antisemitism problem didn't start with Corbyn. It's been festering for a century". *Haaretz*, 9 April. https://www.haaretz.com/opinion/labour-s-festering-anti-semitism-problem-didn-t-start-with-corbyn-1.5980426 (accessed 23 March 2021).

Fine, R. & P. Spencer 2018. *Antisemitism and the Left: On the Return of the Jewish Question.* Manchester: Manchester University Press.

FRA 2018. "Experiences and perceptions of antisemitism: second survey on discrimination and hate crime against Jews in the EU". European Union Agency for Fundamental Rights. https://fra.europa.eu/sites/default/files/fra_uploads/fra-2018-experiences-and-perceptions-of-antisemitism-survey_en.pdf (accessed 23 March 2021).

Freedland, J. 2016. "Labour and the left have an antisemitism problem". *The Guardian*, 18 March. https://www.theguardian.com/commentisfree/2016/mar/18/labour-antisemitism-jews-jeremy-corbyn (accessed 23 March 2021).

Freedland, J. 2020. "Labour's institutional antisemitism crisis". *Corbynism: The Post-Mortem* Podcast. https://podcasts.apple.com/gb/podcast/corbynism-the-post-mortem/id1494568978 (accessed 23 March 2021).

Freeman, H. 2020. "After Wiley, I didn't have a fight on my hands for once. Why did that feel so weird?" The Guardian, 8 August. https://www.theguardian.com/music/commentisfree/2020/aug/08/after-wiley-didnt-have-a-fight-on-my-hands-for-once (accessed 8 April 2021).

Graeber, D. 2019. "For the first time in my life, I'm frightened to be Jewish: and non-Jews attacking the Labour Party aren't helping". Open Democracy, 6 September. https://www.opendemocracy.net/en/opendemocracyuk/first-time-my-life-im-frightened-be-jewish/ (accessed 23 March 2021).

Haaretz 2019. "Corbyn's Labour 'worst global antisemitic incident,' Simon Wiesenthal Center says". *Haaretz*, 9 December. https://www.haaretz.com/world-news/europe/corbyn-s-labour-worst-global-anti-semitic-incident-simon-wiesenthal-center-says-1.8234437 (accessed 23 March 2021).

Harpin, L. 2018a. "68 rabbis from across UK Judaism sign unprecedented letter condemning Labour antisemitism". *Jewish Chronicle*, 16 July. https://www.thejc.com/news/uk/rabbis-letter-labour-antisemitism-1.467264 (accessed 23 March 2021).

Harpin, L. 2018b. "Bombshell tape shows Jeremy Corbyn ally blamed 'Jewish Trump fanatics' for inventing Labour antisemitism". *Jewish Chronicle*, 30 July. https://www.thejc.com/news/uk/bombshell-recording-proves-corbyn-ally-blamed-jewish-trump-fantatics-for-false-antisemitism-clai-1.467802 (accessed 23 March 2021).

Harpin, L. 2020. "Sir Keir Starmer: I will judge my success at tackling Labour antisemitism by the return of Jewish members". *Jewish Chronicle*, 4 April. https://www.thejc.com/news/uk/sir-keir-starmer-i-will-judge-my-success-as-labour-leader-by-the-return-of-jewish-members-1.498781 (accessed 23 March 2021).

Heppell, T. 2021. "The British Labour Party and the Antisemitism Crisis: Jeremy Corbyn and Image Repair Theory". *British Journal of Politics and International Relations*.

Hirsh, D. 2017. *Contemporary Left Antisemitism*. London: Routledge.

Hirsh, D. 2018. "Corbyn to Zionists: even if you've lived here all your life, you don't get the English". *Jewish News*, 23 August. https://blogs.timesofisrael.com/corbyn-to-zionists-even-if-you-lived-here-all-your-life-you-dont-get-the-english/ (accessed 23 March 2021).

IHRA 2020. "Working definition of antisemitism". International Holocaust Remembrance Alliance. https://www.holocaustremembrance.com/resources/working-definitions-charters/working-definition-antisemitism (accessed 23 March 2021).

*Jewish Chronicle* 2015. "The key questions Jeremy Corbyn must answer". *Jewish Chronicle*, 12 August. https://www.thejc.com/news/uk/the-key-questions-jeremy-corbyn-must-answer-1.68097 (accessed 23 March 2021).

*Jewish Chronicle* 2018. "Three Jewish papers take the unprecedented step of publishing the same page on Labour antisemitism". *Jewish Chronicle*, 25 July. https://www.thejc.com/comment/leaders/three-jewish-papers-take-the-unprecedented-step-of-publishing-the-same-page-on-labour-antisemitism-1.467641 (accessed 23 March 2021).

*Jewish Chronicle* 2019. "To all our fellow British citizens". *Jewish Chronicle*, 7 November. https://www.thejc.com/comment/leaders/to-all-our-fellow-british-citizens-1.491812 (accessed 23 March 2021).

JLC 2018. "JLC and Board of Deputies Statement on Meeting with Jeremy Corbyn". Jewish Leadership Council, 24 April. https://www.thejlc.org/jlc_and_board_of_deputies_statement_on_meeting_with_jeremy_corbyn (accessed 23 March 2021).

Johnson, A. 2019. "Institutionally antisemitic: contemporary left antisemitism and the crisis in the British Labour Party". *Fathom* 19. https://fathomjournal.org/wp-content/uploads/2019/03/Institutionally-Antisemitic-Report-FINAL-6.pdf (accessed 23 March 2021).

JPR 2017. "Antisemitism in contemporary Great Britain". Institute of Jewish Policy Research. https://jpr.org.uk/documents/JPR.2017.Antisemitism_in_contemporary_Great_Britain.pdf (accessed 23 March 2021).

Katz, M. & A. Langleben 2018. "The Jewish labour movement did not approve Labour's antisemitism guidelines. Here's why". *New Statesman*, 6 July. https://www.newstatesman.com/politics/religion/2018/07/jewish-labour-movement-did-not-approve-labour-s-anti-semitism-guidelines (accessed 23 March 2021).

Kahn-Harris, K. 2016. "This antisemitism report deserves Labour's calm, close attention: no chance". *The Guardian*, 30 June. https://www.theguardian.com/commentisfree/2016/jun/30/labour-antisemitism-report-shami-chakrabarti-jeremy-corbyn (accessed 23 March 2021).

Kerbaj, R. *et al.* 2018. "Exposed: Jeremy Corbyn's hate factory". *Sunday Times*, 1 April. https://www.thetimes.co.uk/article/exposed-jeremy-corbyns-hate-factory-kkh55kpgx. (accessed 23 March 2021).

Lampert, N. 2019. "What is the Labour antisemitism row about?" Medium, 27 February. https://medium.com/@nicoletalampert/what-is-the-labour-antisemitism-row-about-f2c9022286e (accessed 23 March 2021).

Lansman, J. 2018. "Labour's antisemitism code is the gold standard for political parties". *The Guardian*, 12 July. https://www.theguardian.com/commentisfree/2018/jul/12/labour-antisemitism-code-gold-standard-political-parties (accessed 23 March 2021).

Lerman, A. 2018. "Labour should ditch the IHRA working definition of antisemitism altogether". Open Democracy, 4 September. https://www.opendemocracy.net/en/opendemocracyuk/labour-should-ditch-ihra-working-definition-of-antisemitism-altogether/ (accessed 23 March 2021).

Lipset, S. 1969. " 'The socialism of fools': The Left, the Jews and Israel". In M.S. Chertoff (ed), *The New Left and the Jews*, 103–31. New York, NY: Pitman.

Lipstadt, D. 2019. *Antisemitism, Here and Now.* New York, NY: Schocken.

Marshall, T. 2016. "Labour MP Ruth Smeeth storms out of antisemitism report launch 'in tears'". *Evening Standard*, 30 June. https://www.standard.co.uk/news/politics/labour-mp-ruth-smeeth-storms-out-of-antisemitism-report-launch-a3285106.html (accessed 23 March 2021).

Martin, N. 2019. "Ethnic minority voters in the UK 2015 general election: a breakthrough for the Conservative Party?" *Electoral Studies* 57: 174–85.

Massey, C. 2020. "Jeremy Corbyn's suspension from the Labour Party: a move with few historical precedents". LSE Politics and Policy blog, 30 October. https://blogs.lse.ac.uk/politicsandpolicy/corbyn-suspension-precedent/ (accessed 23 March 2021).

McCluskey, L. 2020. "McCluskey: Corbyn suspension could cause chaos, find a unifying way forward". Unite: The Union, 29 October. https://unitetheunion.org/news-events/news/2020/october/mccluskey-corbyn-suspension-could-cause-chaos-find-a-unifying-way-forward/ (accessed 23 March 2021).

Miller, S., M. Harris & C. Schindler 2015. "The attitudes of British Jews towards Israel". Yachad. http://yachad.org.uk/wp-content/uploads/2015/11/British-Jewish-Attitudes-Towards-Israel-Yachad-Ipsos-Mori-Nov-2015.pdf (accessed 23 March 2021).

O'Carroll, L. & J. Elgot 2020. "Labour pays out six-figure sum and apologises in antisemitism row". *The Guardian*, 22 July. https://www.theguardian.com/politics/2020/jul/22/labour-pays-out-six-figure-sum-and-apologises-in-antisemitism-row (accessed 23 March 2021).

*Panorama* 2019. "Is Labour antisemitic?" BBC 2, 15 July.

Pogrund, G. & P. Maguire 2020. *What's Left? The Inside Story of Labour Under Corbyn.* London: Bodley Head.

Rich, D. 2016. "The left's Jewish problem" Interview with Fathom Forum. https://www.youtube.com/watch?v=S9TTXGlkdno (accessed 23 March 2021).

Rich, D. 2018. "The etiology of antisemitism in Corbyn's Labour Party". *Israel Journal of Foreign Affairs* 12(3): 357–65.

Rich, D. 2019. *The Left's Jewish Problem: Jeremy Corbyn, Israel and Anti-Semitism.* London: Biteback.

Rodgers, S. 2018. "NEC adopts full IHRA antisemitism definition plus 'statement'". LabourList, 4 September. https://labourlist.org/2018/09/nec-adopts-full-ihra-antisemitism-definition-plus-statement/ (accessed 23 March 2021).

Sabbagh, D. 2018. "Jeremy Corbyn: I was present at wreath-laying but don't think I was involved". *The Guardian*, 14 August. https://www.theguardian.com/politics/2018/aug/13/jeremy-corbyn-not-involved-munich-olympics-massacre-wreath-laying (accessed 23 March 2021).

Schofield, K. 2018. "The Labour leadership are standing by Peter Willsman for now". PoliticsHome, 31 July. https://www.politicshome.com/news/article/analysis-the-labour-leadership-are-standing-by-peter-willsman-for-now (accessed 23 March 2021).

Stewart, H. & A. Sparrow 2018. "Jeremy Corbyn: I used the term 'Zionist' in accurate political sense". *The Guardian*, 24 August. https://www.theguardian.com/politics/2018/aug/24/corbyn-english-irony-video-reignites-antisemitism-row-labour (accessed 23 March 2021).

Sugarman, D. 2018. "More than 85 per cent of British Jews think Jeremy Corbyn is antisemitic". *Jewish Chronicle*, 13 September. https://www.thejc.com/news/uk/more-than-85-per-cent-of-british-jews-think-jeremy-corbyn-is-antisemitic-1.469654 (accessed 23 March 2021).

Survation 2019. Jewish Community Poll. https://www.survation.com/wp-content/uploads/2019/10/Jewish-Leadership-Council-Tables-2019-For-Website.xlsx (accessed 8 April 2021).

Taguieff, P.-A. 2004. *Rising from the Muck: The New Anti-Semitism in Europe.* Chicago, IL: Ivan R. Dee.

UK Parliament 2011. EDM 1360, "Never Again for Anyone Initiative". https://edm.parliament.uk/early-day-motion/42381/never-again-for-anyone-initiative (accessed 23 March 2021).

Wald, K. 2019. *The Foundations of American Jewish Liberalism.* Cambridge: Cambridge University Press.

Walker, P. & J. Elgot 2020. "Labour responsible for harassment and discrimination, EHRC antisemitism inquiry finds". *The Guardian,* 29 October. https://www.theguardian.com/politics/2020/oct/29/labour-accused-of-harassment-and-discrimination-in-antisemitism-inquiry (accessed 23 March 2021).

Wistrich, R. 2012. *From Ambivalence to Betrayal: The Left, the Jews, and Israel.* Lincoln, NE: University of Nebraska Press.

## 15

# FAN WARS: JEREMY CORBYN, FANS AND THE "ANTIS"

*Phoenix C. S. Andrews*

This chapter examines Jeremy Corbyn's supporters and detractors in the context of fandom. I use the concepts of politics fandom and anti-fandom, common in fan studies, as a framework for understanding how Corbyn interacted with his base and how the public interacted with him and others connected to his politics. There are three parts to the Corbyn fandom: emotional and defensive attachments to the man, the project and the Left itself. These elements are also those that are rejected by the anti-fandom, who similarly gained identity, community and a sense of purpose through their activities attacking Corbyn and anyone who expressed support for him. This chapter will conclude that Corbyn himself and his key critics have a limited understanding of fandom logics, but some of the younger employees of Momentum and his "outriders" in the media and online enabled Corbynism to harness the positive aspects of fandom and fannish behaviour while struggling to curb its worst tendencies. Broadsheet columnists inflamed the anti-fandom and encouraged their behaviour by contrasting the "cult" of Corbynism with the "sensible" politics of the technocratic era it replaced and to which Keir Starmer has returned.

A fandom is a community of enthusiasts or supporters formed around a cultural property, such as a sports team, a music group or an actor. Joining a fandom, an intentional act, gives the fan an identity, community and direction that is weak or missing when they enjoy the property alone as an individual fan. They are able to find people who understand and will discuss their interest, a social network and a sense of being part of something bigger than themselves. Anti-fans ("antis") get a similar sense of purpose, identity and even joy to that experienced by fans from despising a cultural property (Alters 2007; Gray & Murray 2016; Hill 2015). It is emotionally intense. When they join with others, they experience the power of community as an anti-fandom. Fandoms and anti-fandoms pit themselves in battles against each other, not merely for or against the object of their passions. In politics, fans and fandoms can be attached to politics as a whole, political parties, campaigns and individual politicians or activists

(Andrews 2019; 2017). Between 2015 and 2020 Jeremy Corbyn was able to ignite not only a fandom on a scale not seen in the UK since Tony Blair, but also its equal and opposite reaction, an anti-fandom.

The identity of "fan" outside sports and teenage years is one often attached to gendered criticism, stigma, shame and mockery (Yodovich 2016). While fandom as a whole has been mainstreamed somewhat in recent years, with the popularity of previously niche genre films and activities such as the Marvel Cinematic Universe and Comic-Con events, areas of interest remain where to be a fan is to be emotional, irrational and easily discarded. Politics is one of those areas. Social and legacy media alike are often awash with anti-fan critique. It is "cringeworthy" to "stan" (be an intense fan of) a politician. Interestingly, a lot of the people making these criticisms are also fans of politics or a political party. They follow it so keenly that it is clearly a strong interest for them. They read articles, watch television and collect books and merchandise related to politics and discuss politics with friends they have made through their shared interest. For any other cultural property, this behaviour would be quickly read as fandom and not, as it is, denied and disparaged and put onto other people as an identity rather than the fans themselves (Stanfill 2013). It is therefore perhaps understandable that all early references to fans of Jeremy Corbyn were derogatory. Commentators were embarrassed at the outpouring of interest in and defence of the man and saw the existence of this fandom as both exceptional and against the nature of British politics (it was not, as I will go on to discuss). Only later was the identity of "Jeremy Corbyn fan" and an associated community or fandom positively claimed by his supporters. Momentum, the left-wing faction emerging from Corbyn's leadership campaign, veered between voice of the grassroots left and Jeremy/ Spirit of Jeremy fan club during his tenure and beyond. Unlike Progress, the faction of Tony Blair supporters, they have never been able to move beyond an organization that regularly holds rallies for Corbyn himself.

Fandom and anti-fandom are not new in British politics or even the Labour Party, despite their portrayal in the media. You can find the photographs and video clips of autograph hunters and screaming crowds for politicians yourself, as they date back as far as these technologies. Harold Wilson strode through crowds of fans, celebrity Tony Blair fans still pose for selfies in the US (where his image is less tainted) and Margaret Thatcher drew fans to party conferences with banners and homemade t-shirts and jumpers bearing her image, for all the world like boy band screamers. Tony Benn frequently wrote (Benn 2020), spoke in interviews (Hobsbawm 1980) and gave speeches about the dangers of the NEC and parliament itself becoming a fan club for the Labour leader – while the right wing dominated the party. He had enough fans of his own, as referred to in his own diaries and even by those sympathetic to him on the left (Hallas 1985). People made effigies of Thatcher to set on fire when she died, and the range of merchandise for her fans and antis in the 1980s was astounding. However, the intensity of and opposition to Corbyn fandom is probably without parallel in the UK, because of the role of social media in its amplification.

More important than rushing to delegitimize Corbyn fans is to understand *why* the fandom happened and continues to burn so brightly for its remaining members. After years of technocratic apathy, many people – young and old alike – were seeking emotional engagement in politics and campaigns. Corbyn as a leadership candidate offered change; finally there was someone new to the challenge rather than the "all the same" of the rest of the line-up. Even his detractors claimed that he was a decent person, and his record inside and outside parliament was consistent. The early frontrunner in the contest, Andy Burnham, was doing well with the public, and has since as mayor of Greater Manchester, but it is not for nothing that his ever-changing political position led him to be nicknamed "Flip Flop". Corbyn's relative unfamiliarity to most members and new joiners to the Labour Party – a surge accompanies every leadership contest for eligibility in the vote – enabled people to project possibility onto him. He became all things to all people who wanted to give him a try (Flinders 2018). Added to that, the Left had been resurging for a while following the Occupy and student protest movements, and younger people were more open to electoral politics. The rallies and personal engagement of Corbyn's leadership campaign were a world away from the New Labour-style detachment of other candidates. The fandom was welcoming, something people could be part of and do good within. The level of mass membership (Bale, Webb & Poletti 2018; Webb, Poletti & Bale 2017; Whiteley *et al.* 2018) was initially seen as good for both party coffers and for democratizing politics (Watts 2016, 2018), even if these members were seen by more traditional Labour supporters as entryists, who did not do enough of the hard work of canvassing outside election periods.

All factions behave the same when trying to seize power and do as they were done unto in the past. Much of what drew attacks in Corbyn's early leadership campaign echoed the proclamations and actions of early New Labour, as outlined in *The Blair Revolution* by Peter Mandelson and Roger Liddle. The party must have a mass membership, the levers of power throughout the party must be controlled by supporters of the leader and so on. However, Corbyn had to contend with fulsome opposition from most of the PLP and the mainstream media. The perception, in most cases correct, that Corbyn was being treated unfairly even for a Labour leader (who is rarely given an easy ride in the press) served to galvanize the burgeoning fan community.

The Corbyn fandom developed beyond the leadership election, which is unusual. Leadership contests in the Labour, Conservative and Liberal Democrat parties have traditionally driven growth in membership both before and after the elections, in order to support candidates, and short-term fandoms have often sprung up around the campaigns. The Standies, the Lisa Nandy fandom in the 2020 Labour contest, or the Layla Moran fans from the Liberal Democrat contest, spawned fan-generated tweets, Instagram posts, memes and fancams (short videos focusing on an individual) galore but these simmered back down after the campaigns ended. The reaction of those on the right of the Labour Party, of anti-Corbyn journalists and of celebrities supporting Corbyn's win pushed the fan activities further into 2015. The attempted "chicken" coup of 2016 (Mason & Asthana 2016), in which frontbenchers resigned their posts and Owen Smith eventually stood against Corbyn and lost in another leadership contest, only solidified the need to support the beleaguered leader. He was their guy, and he was under attack. The coup and the Labour left's reaction to it, on the other hand, drove the growth in Corbyn anti-fandom, as did Corbyn's lack of enthusiasm in campaigning for Remain in the 2016 Brexit referendum.

In 2015 and 2016, criticism from the centre and right of politics and the media concentrated on the legitimacy of both Corbyn himself as Labour leader and his supporters (Kuper 2017; Maiguashca & Dean 2019). This theme continued throughout his leadership, even once it became apparent after the 2017 general election that forcing either or both out of the party in the short term was impossible. Although Corbyn fandom was described as a cult of personality, those who study fandom as well as those who supported the leader could see that this was far from the case – support for Corbynism was driven from the grassroots (Bunce 2017), rather than imposed from the top, and came from the same rational attachments to values and ideologies from which any leading politician garners fervent support. It certainly was not the case that Corbyn was a particularly physically attractive or charismatic person around which to form a cult. Unlike his friend and hero Tony Benn, Corbyn had not previously enjoyed fannish support and was not a witty and urbane speaker on the arts centre and festival circuit. Instead, his consistency and humanity appealed and the distinct personality of Corbynism came from the fans rather than the man.

The main rival tendencies within Corbyn fandom, which spilled over into the Labour Party, were described well by Bolton and Pitts (much loathed by the fans) as "the Bennite left and the postcapitalist utopians" (Bolton & Pitts 2018: 8), which generally (but not entirely) split generationally between those old enough to remember Benn and those who became politically active in the dying days of New Labour or early days of the coalition government of 2010–15. However, the message of "hope" and "change" cut through to a large number of people beyond these groups, often on the soft left, who proudly supported Corbyn until well into 2018 and then were dissuaded by the antisemitism crisis and other issues that challenged their moral attachment to the project. The scarves, t-shirts and colouring books that formed the physical merchandise expression of Corbyn fandom sold well to this group, who formed the bulk of the Labour membership and were neither "moderate" nor "hard left" (Whiteley *et al.* 2018).

The glorious summer of 2017, when Labour did much better than expected in the election and calls for Corbyn to resign were momentarily quelled, made fans of all groups hopeful (Barnett 2017), and the antis furious. The memes, videos and fan accounts that sprang up from April to October that year were equalled only by those produced by Bernie Sanders' supporters in the US (Penney 2017). A whole new language of Corbyn fandom, from "melts" and "slugs" to disparage their enemies to celebration of "the absolute boy" (Chakelian 2017) helped forge a sense of identity and community in the fandom and drive in-group status, along with the chant of "Oh Jeremy Corbyn" heard at Pride marches, football matches and festivals as well as Labour rallies (Middleton 2018). Intermediary groups of fans, such as Grime4Corbyn (using high-profile musicians to solidify support among young people, especially from BAME communities), Acid Corbynism (Sheil 2017) and Mums For Corbyn (who used education and childcare as key campaigning issues) provided targeted resources beyond Momentum and the party's official communications. Satellite campaigns, those beyond party structures and control, were able to draw on support from these groups (Dommett & Temple 2018) to provide information, drive voter registration and turn out the vote.

Smartphone ubiquity means more and more people no longer simply talk to friends and family online anymore. They are happy to add strangers, who share their interests, to their networks. Thanks to political and technological changes across the world, older people who did not previously engage with politics online were joining and increasing their activity on social media platforms during the period of Corbyn's leadership. Brexit, Trump, Boris Johnson and Extinction Rebellion all managed to push users onto platforms they had previously avoided (Booth & Hern 2017; Dean 2018; Vaccari & Valeriani 2016) or only used for following news and topics of special interest to them. The lurkers became posters, emotionally reacting for or against topics in the news. The Brexit vote's effect on UK politics fandom was astounding. New political alignments were created for Remain and Leave and voter turnout and interest in party politics rose. Many of these people had very strong views on Jeremy Corbyn and joined one politics fandom or another online (Clarke 2019) – emotion in politics being normalized (rather than a topic to be politely avoided) by events.

Notionally left and centrist media as well as the right wingers wrote about Corbynism and the Left as a temporary aberration, focusing on accounts from internal opponents and dedicating regular column after column to disparaging the man and his followers (Chadwick, Vaccari & O'Loughlin 2018). This only forced the fandom into defending the indefensible (people, policies, actions) and made an alternative to rather than replacement for Corbyn impossible. Stephen

Bush, a self-defined centrist liberal with Blairite tendencies, was the only non-activist journalist to accurately report on the movement and try to understand its appeal and the ideas that underpinned it. Even then he was accused by the right of the Labour Party of being a Corbyn fan, despite it being clear since before Starmer's installation that he was anything but. *The Guardian* is a liberal newspaper with some leftist content, but the constant Corbyn critique in reporting and comment pieces, exacerbated by the harder line of sister paper *The Observer* and its ex-left commentators, exhausted supporters who felt betrayed. This "line" was broken up only by left-wing commentary from Owen Jones, Dawn Foster, Gary Younge and others, without the same balance applied to reporting. Some of Corbyn fans' frustrations with the media also applied to the Labour Party, at least in England, which became more apparent after his resignation. Former members criticize it and say they want it to go away or to start something new, but it cannot be replaced and its capacity to be rebuilt is limited. It has to be worked with and shaped as it is, not as how it is dreamed of being.

Following the 2017 general election, previous distrust led to more or less a declaration of war between the mainstream media and Corbyn fans and between Corbyn antis and any media platform that was anything other than highly critical of the Left. *The New Statesman* is, nominally at least, a left-wing magazine – even if it is mostly staffed by those on the right of the Labour Party. In 2017, its editor Jason Cowley called *The Guardian* "Corbynite Pravda" (Cowley 2017), because a minority of its columnists supported Labour in the election. This was not an isolated incident, and Corbyn fans "ratioed" (negatively replied to, screenshot and commented on in large numbers) the tweet and went on to treat other Corbyn-obsessed hostile journalists in the same manner. This media rejection as much as Corbyn enthusiasm drove the new media practices of fans. During the election campaign and beyond, bloggers and Facebook and Twitter accounts created and shared memes and videos in support of Corbyn that exploited the social media algorithms of the time (since changed, especially at Facebook) to get high levels of engagement compared with official Labour Party sources or traditional media. The years 2017 and early 2018 were the high point for left-wing "shitposters" (posting aggressively and often abstractly for their own entertainment), makers of fan videos and graphic designers.

Fan-owned media platforms proved to be more problematic. New sites like The Canary and Skwawkbox were fed content from Corbyn's office and funds from friendly trade unions, while defending antisemitism and bad behaviour, while anti-Corbyn blog The Red Roar took a Guido Fawkes (less than ethical) approach to hunting out gossip and leaks and attacked and smeared young left-wing women in particular. Anyone was fair game if they were a Corbyn fan or ally.

Later in 2018, the atmosphere became much more unpleasant amidst the growing Labour Party antisemitism crisis. It was clear to them that he did not live up to their initial hopes, even if some quieter members were still happy to embrace his policy positions and enjoy "Corbynism without Corbyn". His leadership was no longer working for a majority of the public and his poll ratings tanked. Defensive and toxic fandom (Andrews 2020a) became more of a problem because of the brittle attitude of Corbyn and the people around him when he made mistakes and the aggressive behaviour of his detractors. Defensive fans will attack anyone who attacks the object of their fandom as well as posting online and speaking regularly in support of them. Toxic fans put people off the object of their fandom by acting obnoxiously and loudly and even bullying minorities. The older conspiracist element of the Left engaged in denial of antisemitism within Labour and Corbyn's tolerance for antisemitic people and actions. High-profile members, some of whom identified as Jewish, were thrown out of the Labour Party for antisemitic language and behaviour, and supporting Corbyn politically became associated with being an antisemite. As Gidley, McGeever & Feldman (2020) explain, the focus on individuals rather than on the proliferation of antisemitic tropes made it hard to demonstrate to doubters that the culture of Labour itself was a problem and that it was not just a case of fixing it by getting rid of certain people (the Right) or Corbyn opponents inflating a problem for factional reasons so that members could not make legitimate criticisms of Israel (the Left).

Noisy celebrities, some of whom muddied the waters intentionally by arguing with Corbyn supporters unprovoked and by lying about the Left while being victims of trolling attacks from across the political spectrum, made anti-fandom of Corbyn an identity. This was often tied up with peak Brexit tensions and threats to MPs and journalists from extremists. The conflation of the left of the Labour Party with the often-derogatory "hard-left" and "Corbynite" made it difficult for many to distinguish between policy support and fandom.

Defending Corbyn became about more than the man, and was instead defending the Left itself from complete delegitimization. Corbyn anti-fans posed themselves as sensible, in contrast to the "mad" Corbyn fans, even though they both appeared to be obsessive and distraught.

Television producers stoked the unrest by booking polarized commentators for panel debates and paper reviews. As with other political factions past and present, Corbyn's Labour had its media outriders – sympathizers who could articulate the messages of the campaign without the constraints of an elected role or shadow ministry. They had far fewer of these than the libertarian wing of the Tories, Brexiteers or the right of the Labour Party – and less funding – but these big-name fans had big social media followings and their mistakes and arguments drew much more attention from supporters and those who despised them alike. Owen Jones, Ash Sarkar and Dawn Foster appear to receive as much fan mail and hate mail as actual politicians. New pro-Corbyn groups (e.g. Jewish Voice for Labour and Labour Against the Witch Hunt) sprang up as more members were suspended for antisemitism and bringing the party into disrepute, and even those banned or attached to other parties identified as Corbyn supporters. All of this did the Corbyn brand even more harm in the eyes of fans losing faith in his leadership and the fandom.

After the rout of the December 2019 general election, it became clear that Corbyn would resign and that would be the end not just of his leadership, but probably any real influence for the Left in the UK for some years. Those who had previously been fans of Tony Benn knew the story well – they would be cast out into the wilderness and struggle to regain the levers of power within the Labour Party or the country. The Corbyn fandom fragmented surprisingly quickly, with less committed fans quickly falling away and voting for Keir Starmer in the leadership election. Many leftists vocally resigned their membership of the Labour Party (Barnfield & Bale 2020) and some were so depressed that they even deleted their social media accounts. Fan media engagement on Twitter and Facebook dropped and pro-Corbyn accounts pivoted to posting mostly anti-Starmer material even while the leadership election was ongoing, with Rebecca Long-Bailey the presumptive heir to Corbyn. Changes to the Facebook algorithm showed how siloed pro-Corbyn social media was, with its messages rarely being exposed to anyone who was not still a committed fan. Some of this social media took on a more and more anti-Labour angle, as Starmer's leadership pledges – calculated to appeal to the membership who had voted in 2015 and 2016 for Jeremy Corbyn – began to fall.

Corbyn's fans were right that he was monstered by the media and treated unfairly, but he was not the gentle, lovely, always on-the-right-side of history guy of legend. Some of the Corbyn anti-fans are also Starmer-critical, whereas others have turned to Starmer fandom in the hope that he will become prime minister. This number is fairly low and mostly belongs to the Labour-To-Win faction, formed from the ashes of Blairite group Progress and old left organizers Labour First. Corbyn's biggest anti-fan, Tony Blair, has never gone away, making regular proclamations on various topics in the media, and his position as the only Labour leader to have won a general election in recent history is unassailable. The failure of the Corbyn project and (to them, extremely depressing) assumption that you have to have the politics of a Blair to actually succeed, has led many of his fans to declare their dissatisfaction with the limitations of electoral politics and some have already returned to dedicating their attention to campaigns outside the party. A proportion of the fandom desires a new left-wing political party led by Corbyn, but more battle-weary supporters warn that previous experiments in this vein – in the form of Respect, TUSC and other micro-parties – have failed. The consistent work of Keir Starmer to detoxify the Labour Party brand and dissociate it from the failures of Corbyn further drives civil war and intensifies both fandom and anti-sentiment in the media and beyond. Far from bringing the party or country together in unity, he appears to disappoint everyone. This is not helped by the fantasy version of Corbyn and his Labour Party that exists for both his fans and his anti-fans when they argue online and in the media. Was the man who did not restore welfare spending in his manifesto and wanted more police and less immigration really the pro-people hero his fans are selling? Were the hyperbolic statements that Corbyn was a Marxist dictator who would start new concentration camps for his enemies helpful to the discourse? Absolutely not. Emotion in politics is good (Marcus 2002; Wahl-Jorgensen 2012); misinformation is not.

The final section of this chapter must deal with Jeremy Corbyn's suspension from the Labour Party by General Secretary David Evans in October 2020. In the run-up to the release of the EHRC report into antisemitism in the Labour Party and the leak of a report from the former leader of the opposition's staff, many comments were made in the press that made fans defend Corbyn and his allies harder, however indefensible the things they were defending, and made antis unpleasantly smug and determined to prove that they had their party back. On Times Radio, Jewish columnist Giles Coren directly compared Corbyn with Hitler, part of a lineage that made outrageous claims in December 2019 that Corbyn would start a new Holocaust and make Britain hostile to Jewish people. This frightened Jews and upset fans who liked Corbyn for being gentle and good. It is not acceptable that fans defended things that were terrible and true, but that radicalization of fans was inextricably linked with inaccurate attacks on both their character and that of their hero. As with other radicalized fandoms, such as that of Tommy Robinson (Andrews 2020b) or anti-trans defenders of J. K. Rowling, their reaction to attack is to double down, and they receive support from conspiracists with genuinely abhorrent views that now make sense to them as part of the same "package". To be a radicalized Corbyn fan is to minimize antisemitism and the behaviour of suspended antisemitic members, call criticism "hysterical", defend Julian Assange without caveat, be pro-Assad and spread misinformation about MPs and activists in other factions. To be a radicalized Rowling fan is to defend groups that demand the repeal of equality laws and the mocking of individuals. Handling these fandoms requires proportionate responses and responsible accuracy from opponents and impartial reporters as well as condemnation of actual offences.

The EHRC report condemned the Labour Party for the hostile environment it created for Jews. However, it was also apparent from the report that complaints were suppressed and mishandled by Labour Party staff who were anti-Corbyn, for factional reasons as well as the antisemitic culture of the party extending back before 2015. Again, responses from both pro- and anti-Corbyn commentators sought to maximize the findings that made their position look good and min-imize those which condemned them. A 100+ page report became short and inaccurate graphics in the hands of the most intense fans and antis, hoping to simplify the story and create a clean narrative with goodies and baddies. Jewish MPs were constantly asked if Jeremy Corbyn should be kicked out of the Labour Party, again bringing a problem of culture down to that of an individual. Corbyn released his own statement and gave interviews that were inflammatory to many people and, whether it was proportional or not, he was suspended, and the Labour whip was removed from him as an MP. A crowdfunder for poten-tial legal action against Corbyn, started when whistle-blowers spoke out against Corbyn and his allies on the BBC's *Panorama* programme (Starmer settled out of court once he took the leadership), saw a surge in contributions from fans. Once again, he was standing in as a proxy for the hurt of the Left. The JLM made it clear that they did not want culture change or responses to the EHRC report to be about Jeremy Corbyn, but his anti-fans were calling for his suspension long before it happened and were furious that it was overturned.

Nuanced accounts such as those of current youngest MP Nadia Whittome continue to be seen as fan apologism, even when they clearly state that Corbyn's statement was wrong. Everything in this political and media environment must be couched as unconditional support for Corbyn's worst behaviour or total con-demnation of Corbyn, the Left and any policy position he may ever have held. Those invited onto television and radio to discuss the issue are chosen for their extreme level of partisanship in one direction or the other, for example pitting Jewish Voice for Labour member Naomi Wimborne-Idrissi, a Jew known for denying antisemitism and defending Corbyn on the podium at party conference in an emotional and strident style, against self-confessed Tony Blair fan and journalist from the right wing of the party John Rentoul, who speaks in a more measured tone. This invites the audience to pick a side between two unreason-able people rather than understand why most of the left of the party and main-stream Jews alike feel sad and conflicted about the situation, whether or not they instinctively supported Corbyn in the past.

Most people even in the Labour Party membership care more about winning than factions. Controlling the party was the problem for the right/centre of the party and also for the soft/hard left. Starmer won in part by not calling any of the party names, but being conciliatory to all. A lot of members backed Corbyn because he was different and also because he did not engage in *ad hominem* attacks. Many stopped backing him because he lost and became a liability on the doorstep, not because he was on the left. Any account of the rise and fall of Corbynism must understand that the fandom and the Left are not inseparable. The mistakes Keir Starmer made in repeating the tactics of the right of the party in the 1980s and 1990s did not help him to be seen as a sensible and unifying figure. His actions resulted in making Corbyn even more of a totem for the Left than Tony Benn, and the focus solely on antisemitism on the left rather than changing the culture of Labour has led to crushing dissent and "purging" members rather than properly discussing why high-profile leftists were suspended and why the EHRC's recommendations could not be ignored. Starmer supporters called for pluralism, but their defence of Starmerism (Thompson, Pitts & Ingold 2020) was built wholly from opposition to Corbynism and its fans. This made unity all but impossible.

The fantasy versions of Corbyn peddled by fans and anti-fans alike make discussion of his legacy impossible. He was neither as terrible nor as brilliant as either group portrays him, and both constantly emit misinformation and bad faith attacks in order to defend their own position. To not oppose Corbyn's suspension is to fail as a socialist and decent person. To include a single line of support or regret for Corbyn in any communication is to fail as an anti-racist who cares about Jewish people. The anti-fandom is every bit as irrational and noisy as the fandom and is not the normative position it assumes itself to be. However, the civil war is what really upsets the voters and not fandom itself. Understanding fandom means understanding and being able to communicate effectively with activists and voters. After all, it is not just much maligned "populists" (Dean & Maiguashca 2017) like Corbyn, Farage, Trump and Johnson who are willing and able to harness it, or up-and-coming stars like Alexandria Ocasio-Cortez, but also those "sensible, centrist" politicians much loved by their detractors: Tony Blair, Barack Obama, Jacinda Ardern and Emmanuel Macron. They know how to stoke their base and upset their antis. Fandom is not going away.

## References

Alters, D. 2007. "The other side of fandom: anti-fans, non-fans, and the hurts of history". In J. Gray, C. Sandvoss & C. Harrington (eds), *Fandom: Identities and Communities in a Mediated World*, 344–56. New York, NY: New York University Press.

Andrews, P. 2017. "Every day can be Ed Balls day in UK politics fandom". *Discover Society*, Social Research Publications 46(July). http://discoversociety.org/2017/07/05/every-day-can-be-ed-balls-day-in-uk-politics-fandom/ (accessed 23 March 2021).

Andrews, P. 2019. "Can I have a selfie, minister?" Tortoise, 10 September. https://www.tortoisemedia.com/2019/09/10/political-fandom-190910/ (accessed 23 March 2021).

Andrews, P. 2020a. "Receipts, radicalisation, reactionaries, and repentance: the digital dissensus, fandom, and the COVID-19 pandemic". *Feminist Media Studies* 20(6): 902–7.

Andrews, P. 2020b. "Choose your fighter: loyalty and fandom in the free speech culture wars". In C. Riley (ed.), *Free Speech Wars*, 251–60. Manchester: Manchester University Press.

Bale, T., P. Webb & M. Poletti 2018. *Britain's Party Members: Who They Are, What They Think, and What They Do*. https://www.qmul.ac.uk/media/qmul/media/publications/Grassroots,-Britain%27s-Party-Members.pdf (accessed 23 March 2021).

Barnett, A. 2017. "With victory in sight, how can the British Left gain hegemony?". Compass. https://www.compassonline.org.uk/wp-content/uploads/2017/10/TP-91-Hegemony-of-the-British-Left.pdf (accessed 23 March 2021).

Barnfield, M. & T. Bale 2020. "'Leaving the red Tories': ideology, leaders, and why party members quit". *Party Politics*, September. https://doi.org/10.1177/1354068820962035.

Benn, T. 2020. "My last real conference?" *The Guardian*, 20 September. https://www.theguardian.com/commentisfree/2007/sep/20/comment.politics (accessed 23 March 2021).

Bolton, M. & F. Pitts 2018. "Corbynism and blue Labour: post-liberalism and national populism in the British Labour Party". *British Politics* 15(1): 88–109. https://doi.org/10.1057/s41293-018-00099-9.

Booth, R. & A. Hern 2017. "Labour won social media election, digital strategists say". *The Guardian*, 9 June. https://www.theguardian.com/politics/2017/jun/09/digital-strategists-give-victory-to-labour-in-social-media-election-facebook-twitter (accessed 23 March 2021).

Bunce, R. 2017. "Corbyn supporters are not a cult". Politics.co.uk, 3 July. http://www.politics.co.uk/comment-analysis/2017/07/03/corbyn-supporters-are-not-a-cult- (accessed 23 March 2021).

Chadwick, A., C. Vaccari & B. O'Loughlin 2018. "Do tabloids poison the well of social media? Explaining democratically dysfunctional news sharing". *New Media & Society* 20(11): 4255–74.

Chakelian, A. 2017. "The absolute boy and the melts: how Corbynism created a new political language". *New Statesman.* https://www.newstatesman.com/politics/uk/2017/10/absolute-boy-and-melts-how-corbynism-created-new-political-language (accessed 23 March 2021).

Clarke, C. 2019. *Warring Fictions*. London: Rowman & Littlefield.

Cowley, J. 2017. "Dawn, come back to me". Twitter. https://twitter.com/JasonCowleyNS/status/871831880471113728?s=20 (accessed 23 March 2021).

Dean, J. 2018. "Sorted for memes and gifs: visual media and everyday digital politics". *Political Studies Review* 17(3): 255–66.

Dean, J. & B. Maiguashca 2017. "Corbyn's Labour and the populism question". *Renewal* 25(3/4): 56–65.

Dommett, K. & L. Temple 2018. "Digital campaigning: the rise of Facebook and satellite campaigns". *Parliamentary Affairs* 71(1): 189–202.

Flinders, M. 2018. "The (anti-)politics of Brexit". In P. Diamond (ed.), *The Routledge Handbook of the Politics of Brexit*, 179–93. Abingdon: Routledge.

Gidley, B., B. McGeever & D. Feldman 2020. "Labour and antisemitism: a crisis misunderstood". *Political Quarterly* 91(2): 413–21.

Gray, J. & S. Murray 2016. "Hidden: studying media dislike and its meaning". *International Journal of Cultural Studies* 19(4): 357–72.

Hallas, D. 1985. "The Labour Party: myth and reality". Socialist Workers' Party pamphlet.

Hill, A. 2015. "Spectacle of excess: the passion work of professional wrestlers, fans and anti-fans". *European Journal of Cultural Studies* 18(2): 174–89.

Hobsbawm, E. 1980. "Eric Hobsbawm interviews Tony Benn". *Marxism Today* (October): 5–13.

Kuper, S. 2017. "Trumpsters, Corbynistas and the rise of the political fan". *Financial Times*, 20 July.

Maiguashca, B. & J. Dean 2019. "'Lovely people but utterly deluded': British political science's trouble with Corbynism". *British Politics* 15(1): 48–68.

Marcus, G. 2002. *The Sentimental Citizen: Emotion in Democratic Politics*. University Park, PA: Penn State University Press.

Mason, R. & A. Asthana 2016. "Labour crisis: how the coup against Jeremy Corbyn gathered pace". *The Guardian*, 26 June. https://www.theguardian.com/politics/2016/jun/26/labour-crisis-how-coup-plot-jeremy-corbyn-gathered-pace (accessed 23 March 2021).

Middleton, A. 2018. "'For the many, not the few': strategising the campaign trail at the 2017 UK general election". *Parliamentary Affairs* 72(3): 501–21.

Penney, J. 2017. *The Citizen Marketer*. Oxford: Oxford University Press.

Sheil, J. 2017. "How memes are spreading 'acid Corbynism'". Novara Media, 5 October. http://novaramedia.com/2017/10/05/how-memes-are-spreading-acid-corbynism/ (accessed 23 March 2021).

Stanfill, M. 2013. "'They're losers, but I know better': intra-fandom stereotyping and the normalization of the fan subject". *Critical Studies in Media Communication* 30(2): 117–34.

Thompson, P., F. Pitts & J. Ingold 2020. "A strategic left? Starmerism, pluralism and the soft left". *Political Quarterly* . https://doi.org/10.1111/1467-923X.12940.

Vaccari, C. & A. Valeriani 2016. "Party campaigners or citizen campaigners? How social media deepen and broaden party-related engagement". *International Journal of Press/Politics* 21(3): 294–312.

Wahl-Jorgensen, K. 2012. "Future directions for political communication scholarship: considering emotion in mediated public participation". In A. Valdivia (ed.), *The International Encyclopedia of Media Studies*, 455–78. Oxford: Wiley-Blackwell.

Watts, J. 2016. "Reorganising Labour: constructing a new politics". *Renewal* 24(4): 52–9.

Watts, J. 2018. "The lost world of the British Labour Party? Community, infiltration and disunity". *British Politics* 13: 505–23. https://doi.org/10.1057/s41293-017-0057-5.

Webb, P., M. Poletti & T. Bale 2017. "So who really does the donkey work in 'multi-speed membership parties'? Comparing the election campaign activity of party members and party supporters". *Electoral Studies* 46: 64–74.

Whiteley, P. *et al.* 2018. "Oh Jeremy Corbyn! Why did Labour Party membership soar after the 2015 general election?" *British Journal of Politics and International Relations* 21(1): 80–98.

Yodovich, N. 2016. "'A little costumed girl at a sci-fi convention': boundary work as a main destigmatization strategy among women fans". *Women's Studies in Communication* 39(3): 289–307.

## 16

# CORBYN AND LEADERSHIP SATISFACTION RATINGS

*Timothy Heppell and Thomas McMeeking*

The rationale for this chapter stems from the fact that Jeremy Corbyn is the latest leader in a growing line of leaders of the opposition in recent decades who failed to secure their objective of getting out of opposition and back into government. Since the general election of May 1979, in which the Labour Party, led by Prime Minister James Callaghan, lost to the opposition Conservatives under Margaret Thatcher, there have been only two governing transitions: at the general election of May 1997 when the John Major-led Conservatives were defeated by New Labour and Tony Blair; and at the general election of May 2010 when the Gordon Brown-led Labour administration was replaced by the Conservative-led coalition with the Liberal Democrats under new Prime Minister David Cameron (and Deputy Prime Minister Nick Clegg) (Butler & Kavanagh 1980, 1997; Kavanagh & Cowley 2010).

Between October 1980 – when Michael Foot replaced Callaghan as leader of the Labour Party and leader of the opposition – and the general election of December 2019 – when Corbyn failed to move from leader of the opposition to prime minister – there have been a total of ten leaders of the opposition. As mentioned above, only Blair and Cameron have been successful in terms of recovering power and making that transition. Electoral defeats have been the experience of the following: Foot for Labour at the general election of 1983; Neil Kinnock for Labour at the general elections of 1987 and 1992; William Hague and Michael Howard for the Conservatives at the general elections of 2001 and 2005 respectively; Ed Miliband led Labour to defeat at the general election of 2015; and Corbyn did likewise at the general elections of 2017 and 2019. Alongside these six leaders of the opposition who failed to become prime minister were two others who did not contest general elections – John Smith led the Labour Party for two years between 1992 and 1994 (until his death); while Iain Duncan Smith led the Conservatives for two years between 2001 and 2003 before his removal via a confidence motion (for discussions on opposition politics and the role of leader of the opposition; see Punnett 1973; Johnson

1997; Ball 2005; Norton 2008; Fletcher 2011; Heppell 2012; Bale 2015; Heppell, Theakston & Seawright 2015).

Is there an argument to suggest that Corbyn can be differentiated from the other leaders of the opposition since 1980 who failed to go onto win the next general election? Maiguashca and Dean (2020), Allen (2020) and Allen and Moon (2020) imply that political commentary on Corbyn's leadership by political journalists (for a sample of negative media appraisals see Bartlett 2020; Harris 2020; Peck 2020) and political scientists (see Bale 2016; Diamond 2016; Dorey & Denham 2016) have been disproportionately critical. However, Maiguashca and Dean consider the leadership of Corbyn in isolation. They do not attempt to consider how his leadership performance compares to other leaders of the opposition – so, for example, although Maiguashca and Dean (2020: 55) argue that Corbyn was not an electoral liability to the Labour Party, they do not consider whether other leaders of the opposition, either Labour or Conservatives, were or were not electoral liabilities.

This chapter compares the performance of Corbyn against those leaders of the opposition since 1980 who have gone on to contest a general election, drawing on opinion polling evidence as a means of measuring perceptions of their (in)effectiveness. In justifying our use of opinion polling as a means of assessing Corbyn, relative to other leaders of the opposition, we note the following. Exploiting opinion polling data, as descriptive statistics, Pierce argues, enables us to summarize, compress and resolve complex issues, from which we can present an "accurate impression" of events to readers (Pierce 2008: 183; albeit these are "unprocessed facts [...] selected, organized [and] packaged to make a point"; Haskins & Jeffery 1990: 11).

In tracking the satisfaction ratings of different leaders of the opposition it is acknowledged that this could be a symbiotic relationship. A popular and effective leader of the opposition may aid the overall standing of their party in the opinion polls, or the popularity of the party may aid the ratings for their leader; and an unpopular and ineffective leader of the opposition may undermine the standing of their party in the opinion polls, or poor party image may depress their personal ratings. Moreover, we acknowledge that perceptions of both the leader of the opposition and the opposition party are conditioned by the performance (competence) of the prime minister and the governing party: for example, it was easier to oppose the Major government in the mid-1990s than to have to oppose Blair in the 1997 to 2001 period (on the leaders' and parties' reputation dynamics, see Davies & Mian 2010; Denver & Garnett 2012).

We also acknowledge that leaders of the opposition can be subjected to relentless press criticism, and that historically the biases within the print media have ensured that their treatment of Labour leaders of the opposition has been particularly hostile (Thomas 2005). However, while the print media criticism to which Corbyn was subjected to was particularly intense (Cammaerts, DeCillia & Magalhaes 2020), we counter this with the following observations.

The decline in print media sales, and thereby readership, means that many voters might no longer be subjected to the negative propaganda spewed out by the print media.[1] Running parallel to this, parties can attempt to circumnavigate (or minimize) print media influence[2] by the direct communications with voters that they can secure via social media outlets. On the one hand, the print media bias in favour of Boris Johnson and the Conservatives was pronounced in the general election of 2019; as Wring and Deacon note, 72.5 per cent of newspaper sales in the campaign were for papers endorsing the Conservatives (*The Sun, Daily Express, Daily Mail, Daily Telegraph, The Times*), as compared to 12.8 per cent endorsing Labour (*The Daily Mirror, The Guardian*). On the other hand, with a 25 per cent decline in newspaper sales and readership between the general elections of 2017 and 2019 (Wring & Deacon 2019), voters were increasingly acquiring their political information by alternative means, with social media outlets the new source for political knowledge for younger voters. Walsh notes that at the time of the 2019 general election campaign, over 23 million voters had Instagram accounts (surpassing the combined sales of all newspapers at 4.5 million) and in terms of video views on that platform, 3,973,708 were identifiable as pro-Labour and 1,293,743 were pro-Conservative. Moreover, the ten most watched videos were all Corbyn videos, and Corbyn was being followed by 443,661 users as compared to Johnson on 292,771 users (Walsh 2019). With Instagram being just one such outlet, it is clear the very real disadvantage that Corbyn and Labour had with the print media (ditto Miliband, Kinnock and Foot, but also Hague and Howard when leading the Conservatives into the 2001 and 2005 elections when a pro-Labour bias was briefly evident), was being partly offset by the fact that online media skews to the left (McDowell-Naylor & Thomas 2019).

---

1. *The Sun* has repeatedly produced the most contentious general election coverage and advanced the most significant claims regarding their influence – from "it's the Sun wot won it" in relation to their endorsement for the Conservatives in the general election of 1992, to "it's the Sun wot swung it" after they switched their endorsement to Labour in the general election of 1997. In the years of those two general elections their sales were 3,570,562 (1992) and 3,877,097 (1997). Their sales remained high by the time they switched their allegiance back to the Conservatives for the general election of 2010 (at 3,006,565) but by the time of their backing for the "get Brexit done" Conservative campaign for the general election their sales were averaging 1,206,595 (Reid 2020).

2. Although the diet of relentless negativity that characterizes print media coverage, and its personalized attacks are distasteful, the extent to which print media endorsements influence voter opinion or preference has been demonstrated to have its limits (see Reeves, McKee & Stuckler 2016).

Therefore, although a myriad of factors contribute to the framing of how political elites are presented to voters, and that framing process raises questions, we still believe comparing the leadership satisfaction ratings can be illuminating. As a consequence, this chapter tracks the leadership satisfaction ratings for Corbyn and his predecessors since 1980, and then compares these to the following: (a) the projected vote of their party, to determine the extent to which they were an asset or a liability to their party; and (b) the leadership satisfaction ratings of the incumbent prime minister, to determine whether they are deemed to be more (or less) competent. Using these measures of (in)effectiveness, the chapter will then compare the performance of Corbyn to that of "effective" leaders of the opposition (Blair and Cameron) and "ineffective" leaders of the opposition (Foot, Kinnock, Hague, Howard and Miliband).

## Why party leaders matter

Before assessing public opinion on Corbyn – relative to his predecessors in relation to the projected party vote and prime-ministerial satisfaction ratings – the chapter will briefly consider the importance of analysing why leadership satisfaction ratings matter.

Our understanding of electoral competition in postwar British politics has evolved since the era of positional politics and class and partisan alignment. As the class cleavage, an explanation of voter choice, has been challenged and as partisanship has eroded, so voter choice has been increasingly shaped by perceptions of competence vis-à-vis the two main parties (Clarke *et al.* 2004, 2009; Denver 2005; Green 2007; Green & Jennings 2011, 2012, 2018; see also Evans & Tilley 2012). This shift towards valance politics has coincided with the personalization of politics and personality-driven campaigning, both in terms of how the media cover politics, but also how parties project and market themselves (Smith 2009; French & Smith 2010; Langer 2011; Smith & French 2011). The consequence has been that the charisma and performative abilities of leaders have increased in importance: they have come to represent an "informational short cut" for voters, helping those with less interest in politics and policy to make their democratic choice (Smith 2009: 212). That trend has been reinforced by the increasing dominance in general election campaigns since 2010 of prime-ministerial or leadership debates (see e.g. Wring & Ward 2010; Chadwick 2011; Pattie & Johnston 2011; Shepherd & Johns 2012; Allen, Bara & Bartle 2013, 2017). Academics have argued that these trends have had consequences; numerous studies demonstrate that parties can be aided, or undermined, by the apparent competence, charisma or likeability of their respective leaders (see e.g. Stewart & Clarke 1992; Crewe & King 1994; Clarke & Stewart

1995; Clarke, Ho & Stewart 2000; Stevens, Karp & Hodgson 2011; Whiteley *et al.* 2013; Clarke *et al.* 2016; Milazzo & Hammond 2017).[3]

Running parallel to these trends we have seen a reduced tolerance of failure with regard to party leaders. Since 1979 resignations have become more commonplace, especially after suffering an electoral defeat, than used to be the norm in the period between 1945 and 1979. The following Conservative and Labour party leaders led their parties to an electoral defeat and continued to either the next general election or lasted a further 18 months in their position: Winston Churchill (after 1945 and 1950), Clement Attlee (after 1951), Hugh Gaitskell (after 1959), Edward Heath (after 1966) and Harold Wilson (after 1970). Only three resigned or were challenged shortly after their electoral rejection: Attlee (after 1955), Alec Douglas-Home (1965) and Edward Heath (1975). When we compare these figures to the period after 1979 the following emerges. Only two party leaders have survived after leading their parties to defeat: Corbyn after 2017 and Kinnock after 1987. The following have resigned within 18 months of defeat: Callaghan in 1980, Foot in 1983, Kinnock in 1992, Major in 1997, Hague in 2001, Howard in 2005, Brown in 2010, Miliband in 2015 and then Corbyn in 2020 (see Stark 1996; Heppell 2008, 2010; McAnulla 2010; Quinn 2012; Denham, Dorey & Roe-Crines 2020).

Not only is there a reduced tolerance of electoral failure in the age of valance politics (Andrews & Jackman 2008), but there is academic research to suggest that changing the party leader – which occurs most often after an electoral defeat – can be beneficial to parties. For example, Stark has demonstrated that by tracking public opinion of parties (pre- and post-leadership change) in relation to their projected vote, leadership satisfaction and internal unity, parties can improve their overall image and popularity (Stark 1996: 142, 161–2; see also Punnett 1992; Brown 1992; Heppell & McMeeking 2021). And the comparative political leadership literature emphasizes that a new party leader can increase voter understanding on where a party stands on policy, which can aid their electoral prospects by improving their credibility (Somer-Topcu 2017; Fernandez-Vasquez & Somer-Topcu 2019; on leadership transitions, see Bynander & 't Hart 2006, 2008).

Where does Corbyn fit into these debates? His leadership was subjected to such widespread criticism by leading political scientists (see e.g. Bale 2016;

---

3. For a more sceptical interpretation of the "scale" of the impact of party leaders on voter choice, see Bartle and Crewe 2002; Denver and Garnett 2012. See, from the comparative academic literature, King 2002; Bittner 2012; and Costa-Lobo and Curtice 2015. For a discussion of the damaging consequences of personality-driven campaigning, for example, the narrowing of the political agenda, demanding conformity in behaviour and message, and its links to political disengagement, see Scammell 1999; Lilleker and Negrine 2003; and Needham 2005.

Diamond 2016; Dorey & Denham 2016) that it led to a backlash from Corbyn-sympathizing academics (Allen 2020; Allen & Moon 2020; Maiguashca & Dean 2020). Writing before the general election of 2019 (in a paper published in 2020), Maiguashca and Dean identified what they saw as a "Corbyn problem" within political science, in which academics were promoting "politicised scholarship" in which "normative opposition all too often spills over into un-reflexive and un-rigorous scholarship" (2020: 56, 63). Specifically, Maiguashca and Dean identified three key ways in which Corbyn was being unjustifiably criticized (*ibid.*: 55). First, his leadership had intellectually reenergized the Left. Second, his leadership had coincided with a massive growth in the membership of the Labour Party (from 198,000 to 552,000 between 2015 and 2017; Whiteley *et al.* 2019: 81). And finally, they argued that the negativity that political scientists had demonstrated with respect to Corbyn's leadership had been disproved by the performance of the Labour Party in the general election of 2017 (where their vote relative to the general election of 2015 went up from 9,347,273 votes, or 30.4 per cent to 12,877,860 votes, or 40 per cent; Dorey 2017).

As a consequence, Maiguashca and Dean concluded that Corbyn was neither a "liability" electorally to the Labour Party, nor a "bad" leader (2020: 55). Tracking the leadership satisfaction ratings for Corbyn relative to the projected Labour Party vote and relative to the prime minister's leadership satisfaction ratings, and then comparing his leadership satisfaction ratings to his predecessors enables us to place the leadership performance of Corbyn in context.

## Measuring and comparing satisfaction ratings and projected voters

We have used opinion polling data from the archive of polls conducted by Ipsos-Mori.[4] These date back to the late 1970s and they have the advantage of posing similar questions, by similar methods, enabling us to track trends in a transparent way.

In terms of what we decided to measure we acknowledge that opinion polling on leadership satisfaction covers three issues: (1) voters who are satisfied with the performance of the leader of the opposition; (2) voters who are not satisfied with the performance of the leader of the opposition; and (3) those that fall into the category of "don't know". We also acknowledge that from this we can construct a net satisfaction rate based on subtracting those who are dissatisfied from those who are satisfied. However, we decided to focus on the percentage of voters who were satisfied with the leader of the opposition, as this provides the clearest basis for one of our comparisons: the projected vote

---

4. Listed at https://www.ipsos.com/ipsos-mori/en-uk/political-monitor-archive.

for the party that the leader of the opposition represents. We also wanted to see which leaders of the opposition have had satisfaction ratings which were ahead, level with, or behind their party's projected vote, and we also want to see the scale of the gap and the timing of it – that is, near the beginning of a leadership tenure and that start of a general election campaign. We also wanted to compare the leader of the opposition to the incumbent prime minister in terms of satisfaction ratings.

In summary, we wanted to track the relationship between eventual political success and regaining power – the evidence of "effectiveness" as leader of the opposition – and being (a) an asset to your party because your personal ratings outrun the party's projected vote; and (b) a greater asset to your party than your primary opponent, the prime minister, is to theirs. We selected these two comparisons as they speak to the aforementioned academic debates within valance politics on perceptions of leadership competence (and the debates on personalization).

Figures 16.1–16.8 provide the individual details of the performance of each leader of the opposition in terms of their leadership satisfaction ratings as compared to (1) their party's projected vote; and (2) the leadership satisfaction rate of the incumbent prime minister. This is presented across their leadership tenures at three-month intervals.

Opposition leadership satisfaction and the projected party vote

The relationship between the satisfaction ratings of respective leaders of the opposition, the projected vote of their parties and their subsequent general election performance produces some clear trends in relation to those party leaders that become prime minister and those that do not.

Let us start by considering the two leaders of the opposition – Blair and Cameron – who went on to become prime minister. Blair had a satisfaction rating of 51 per cent and the projected Labour vote was at 50 per cent at the onset of the 1997 general election campaign; Cameron had a satisfaction rating of 42 per cent and the projected Conservative vote was 32 per cent at the onset of the 2010 general election campaign. However, we should caveat this by noting that when we track the opinion polling across the Blair tenure, his satisfaction rating was lower than the projected Labour vote for most of the 1994 to 1997 period, although the projected Labour vote was remarkably high (oscillating between 50 and 61 per cent) and Blair had satisfaction ratings that exceeded those of all other leaders of the opposition (with the exception of a low initial rating of 33 per cent in September 1994 his ratings were between 42 and 53 per cent throughout the opposition era) (on the Blair era in opposition, see McAnulla 2012). In the first

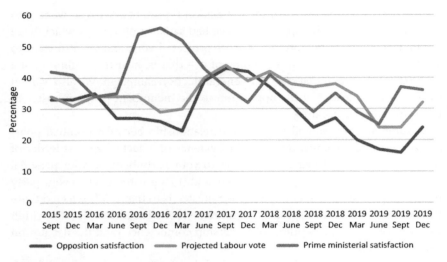

**Figure 16.1** Leadership satisfaction in Jeremy Corbyn
*Source*: Ipsos-Mori 2021a, 2021b

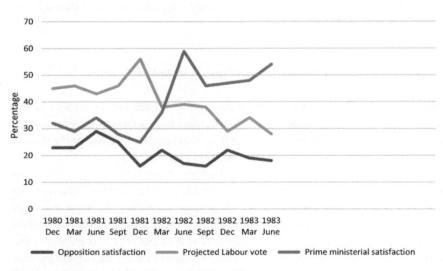

**Figure 16.2** Leadership satisfaction in Michael Foot
*Source*: Ipsos-Mori 2021c, 2021d

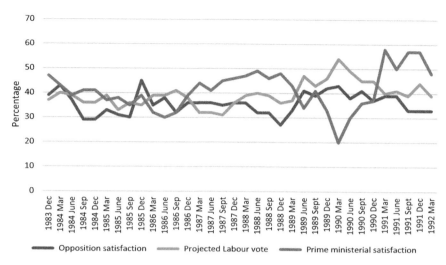

**Figure 16.3** Leadership satisfaction in Neil Kinnock
*Source*: Ipsos-Mori 2021c, 2021d, 2021e, 2021f

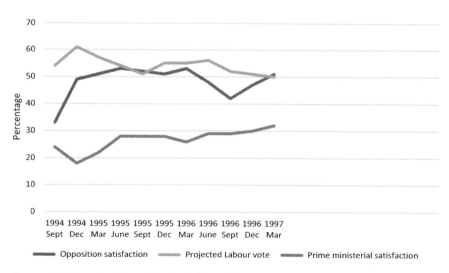

**Figure 16.4** Leadership satisfaction in Tony Blair
*Source*: Ipsos-Mori 2021e, 2021f

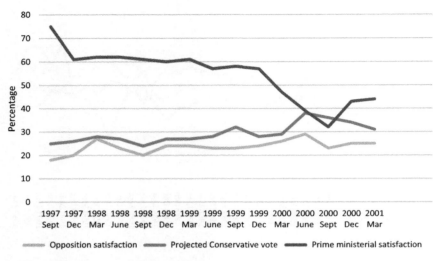

**Figure 16.5** Leadership satisfaction in William Hague
*Source*: Ipsos-Mori 2021b, 2021g

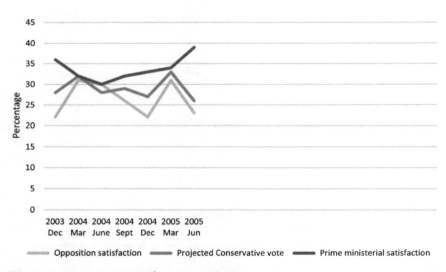

**Figure 16.6** Leadership satisfaction in Michael Howard
*Source*: Ipsos-Mori 2021a, 2021b

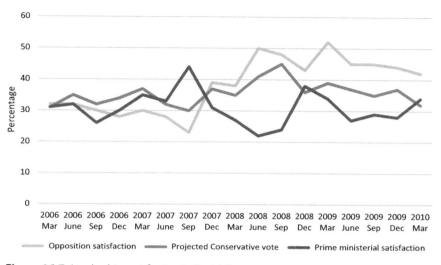

**Figure 16.7** Leadership satisfaction in David Cameron
*Source*: Ipsos-Mori 2021a, 2021b

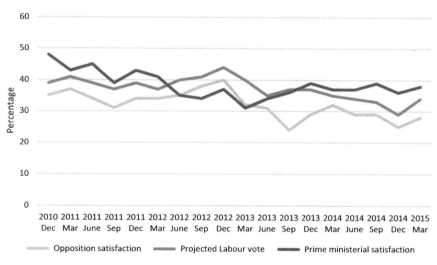

**Figure 16.8** Leadership satisfaction in Ed Miliband
Source: Ipsos-Mori 2021a, 2021b

two years of his leadership tenure (2006 and 2007) Cameron had satisfaction ratings hovering around the projected Conservative vote in a pattern of trendless fluctuation, but after March 2008 he consistently out-scored the projected Conservative vote, peaking at March 2009 when the gap between his satisfaction rating (at 52 per cent) and the projected Conservative vote (at 39 per cent) was 13 per cent (for a discussion on the Cameron era in opposition, see Dorey, Garnett & Denham 2011: 57–91; Heppell 2019: 11–33).

Of those leaders of the opposition who failed to become prime minister, and were defeated at the subsequent general election, we can detect the following in relation to their satisfaction ratings and projected party vote at the onset of general election campaigning. All of them, bar one, had satisfaction ratings that were lower than their own party's projected vote as the campaigning period commenced. The exception was Kinnock entering the 1992 general election campaign, in which he had a marginal lead of 2 per cent (41 per cent satisfaction as opposed to a 39 per cent projected Labour vote; on the Labour Party defeat that year, see Heffernan & Marqusee 1992). At the onset of the 1987 general election campaign, Kinnock was behind the projected Labour vote by 4 per cent (28 per cent satisfaction; 32 per cent projected Labour vote); and small gaps existed for Hague (24 to 28 per cent), Howard (31 to 33 per cent) and Miliband (28 to 34 per cent) (for a discussion of the Labour Party leading up to the 1987 and 2015 campaigns, see Butler & Kavanagh 1984: 47–73 and Fielding 2015; and for a discussion of the Conservative Party leading up to the 2001 and 2005 campaigns, see Collings & Seldon 2001; Seldon & Snowdon 2005). The largest gaps were for Corbyn at the general elections of 2017 (23 to 30 per cent) and 2019 (16 to 24 per cent, see Goes 2018) and Foot at the general election of 1983 (18 to 26 per cent, see Butler & Kavanagh 1984).

These ratings were reflective of patterns that had been established throughout their leadership tenures. For Conservative leaders we can note that Hague remained behind the projected Conservative vote throughout peaking at a gap of 13 per cent in September 2000 (23 to 36 per cent); and Howard was behind the projected vote of the Conservatives in all but one poll. For Labour leaders, the figures for Foot and Miliband were uniformly poor. Despite the potential unpopularity of the Cameron–Clegg coalition government's austerity programme (see Beech & Lee 2015), Miliband remained behind the projected Labour vote throughout peaking at a gap of 13 per cent in September 2013 (24 to 37 per cent); but Foot was even worse in terms of the gap, with his worst returns creating a gap of 33 per cent, when the Labour Party was projected at 56 per cent of vote in December 1980, but Foot had a satisfaction rating of 23 per cent. The travails of the Labour Party throughout 1981 – the splintering off of parts of the social democratic right to form the Social Democratic Party (SDP) and the infighting associated with the deputy leadership election between Denis Healey and Tony Benn – would see their projected vote halve by December 1981 (to 29 per cent) and the gap to Foot on satisfaction would shrink to 13 per cent, with Foot securing a lamentable return of 16 per cent of voters being satisfied with his leadership (Shaw 1994; and on the formation of the SDP, see Crewe & King 1995). Kinnock was able to secure far better satisfaction ratings. Throughout his eight-and-a-half-year leadership tenure his personal ratings and the projected Labour vote were more closely aligned: Kinnock's satisfaction ratings went from a low of 27 per cent in late 1988 (coinciding with the challenge to his leadership by Benn) to a high of 45 per cent in December 1985 (Heppell 2010: 117–32). The projected Labour vote throughout this period remained relatively stable: it was consistently in the 30s and 40s throughout, peaking at 54 per cent in March 1990.

Where does Corbyn fit in? He was behind the projected Labour vote at the onset of both the general election campaigns of 2017 and 2019. However, it is important to stress that his satisfaction ratings across his leadership tenure, relative to the projected party vote, were stronger than some of the other leaders of the opposition who went on to be defeated at a general election. For example, when compared to Foot, Hague and even Miliband, there are periods when his satisfaction ratings were reasonably strong. However, his polling showed a degree of volatility relative to other leaders of the opposition. He secured satisfaction ratings in the aftermath of defeat at the general election of 2017 that were comparable to some of the findings for Blair or Cameron: for example, in December 2017 he had a satisfaction rating at 42 per cent that outstripped the projected Labour vote (39 per cent) by 3 per cent. However, Corbyn would also secure some of the worst satisfaction ratings, and he reached his nadir (at 16 per cent satisfaction) just as the general election campaign of 2019 was about to commence (Goes 2020).

## Opposition leadership satisfaction and prime-ministerial satisfaction

When it comes to the relationship between the satisfaction ratings of respective leaders of the opposition as compared to the incumbent prime minister, and subsequent general election performance, clear trends are also evident.

Let us begin with Blair and Cameron, the two leaders of the opposition who won general elections. In the straight head-to-head with Major on satisfaction ratings, Blair was ahead and by a considerable margin for much of the 1994 to 1997 period. At the onset of the general election campaign of 1997 he had a lead of 19 per cent: 51 per cent of voters were satisfied with the opposition leadership of Blair as compared to the prime ministership of Major. The picture was more complex with regard to Cameron. At the onset of the general election campaign of 2010 he did have higher satisfaction ratings than Brown (42 to 34 per cent) and this was part of a trend throughout the 2008 to 2010 period, with Cameron peaking at 50 per cent against Brown on 22 per cent in June 2008 (on leadership effects in the general election of 2010, see Stevens, Karp & Hodgson 2011). However, even when he was newly elected as leader of the Conservative Party in the 2006–07 period, and when opposing Blair, whose appeal was in decline by this stage (post-Iraq), his satisfaction ratings were very similar to Blair's, and briefly, when Brown replaced Blair in June 2007, Cameron would fall a long way behind Brown (44 to 23 per cent in September 2007) (on the decline and fall of the Brown premiership, see Heppell 2013; Gaffney 2017: 64–8).

For those leaders of the opposition who went on to lose the subsequent general election a link is evident between electoral rejection and their satisfaction ratings relative to the prime minister. For example, those who went on to suffer heavy electoral defeats had experienced a large gap in their leadership satisfaction ratings. Foot was behind Thatcher throughout, initially by a small margin (23 to 32 per cent in December 1980) but the gap was significantly larger by June 1982 (17 to 59 per cent, capturing the impact of the Falklands factor) and this gap remained until the start of the general election campaign of 1983 (18 to 54 per cent) (on the electoral impact of the Falklands War, see Sanders *et al.* 1987). When compared to Blair, Hague started off remarkably badly (18 to 75 per cent in September 1997) and although the gap gradually shrunk throughout the 1997 to 2001 parliament, the gap remained large at the start of the general election campaign of 2001 (at 25 to 44 per cent). Howard secured lower satisfaction ratings than Blair, but his performance was stronger than that of Hague (trailing 31 to 34 per cent at the onset of the general election campaign of 2005) (on the leadership limitations of the Conservatives between 1997 and 2001, see Cowley & Quayle 2002; Cowley & Green 2005).

Kinnock, Miliband and Corbyn all experienced periods when their satisfaction ratings matched or exceeded those of the prime ministers they opposed. For example, Kinnock could compete with Thatcher, as evidenced from March 1990 when his satisfaction rating was 43 per cent to her 20 per cent. However, the Conservative Party was willing to remove her from the leadership in the challenge of 1990 (see Alderman & Carter 1991; Cowley & Garry 2000) and her replacement, Major, established a clear lead over Kinnock (e.g. 57 to 33 per cent in September 1991) that he retained as they entered into the general election campaign of 1992 (Major 48 per cent; Kinnock 41 per cent). Kinnock had also been behind Thatcher at the time of the general election campaign of 1987 (Thatcher 44 per cent; Kinnock 28 per cent). Miliband was briefly able to secure stronger satisfaction ratings than Cameron, for example, holding a lead in late 2012–early 2013, but the pattern was one of Cameron securing stronger satisfaction ratings (e.g. 45 to 34 per cent in June 2011) and the gap between them was 10 per cent at the onset of the general election campaign of 2015 (38 to 28 per cent).

The misfortune for the Labour Party and Corbyn was that at the start of the general election campaigns of 2017 and 2019 (Goes 2018, 2020; Mellon *et al.* 2018) his satisfaction ratings were at their lowest: 23 per cent to May on 52 per cent as the campaigning period began and 16 per cent to Johnson on 37 per cent two years later. He did, however, experience periods when his satisfaction ratings enabled him to compete with May, notably in late 2017, but despite the governing failures of the 2018 to 2019 period, he would remain behind May and Johnson in terms of satisfaction ratings (Heppell & McMeeking 2021).

## Analysis and conclusion

The figures above demonstrate that there is a broad correlation between parties that regain power at a general election having a party leader who has satisfaction ratings higher than in (or close to) their party's projected vote and better leadership satisfaction ratings than the incumbent prime minister. It also demonstrates that there is a link between failing to regain power and having a party leader whose leadership satisfaction ratings are behind their party's projected vote and the leadership satisfaction ratings for the incumbent prime minister. When we consider these findings from a Corbyn-specific perspective, we can draw the following conclusions in terms of whether he was a "liability" for the Labour Party or was perceived to be a "bad" leader relative to the incumbent prime minister.

On the question of whether Corbyn was a liability or an asset to the Labour Party we need to note the following. Of all of those leaders of the opposition who contested a general election and lost – Foot, Kinnock (twice), Hague, Howard, Miliband and then Corbyn (twice) – not one of them had a lower leadership satisfaction rating than Corbyn had at the onset of the general election campaign of 2019, at only 16 per cent. Most of those leaders of the opposition had satisfaction ratings that were in the 20s or 30s, considerably lower than the satisfaction ratings for the two successful leaders of the opposition, Blair and Cameron, who were both polling well above 40 per cent as the campaigning period started. Only Foot comes close to Corbyn in terms of low satisfaction ratings, at 18 per cent. If Corbyn had the lowest satisfaction ratings at the time of electioneering of all of the leaders of the opposition who failed to regain power, then what about the relationship between satisfaction ratings and the party's projected vote?

By this measure, Corbyn had a rating of –7 at the general election of 2017 with his 23 per cent satisfaction entering the 2017 campaign against a 30 per cent Labour Party projected vote; and a –8 rating at the general election of 2019 (satisfaction rating of 16 to a projected Labour vote of 24 per cent). Those gaps are slightly larger, however, than for previous leaders of the opposition who went on to suffer defeat; for example, when Hague led the Conservative Party to defeat at the general election of 2001, he entered the campaigning period with his own leadership satisfaction ratings (25 per cent) behind his party's projected vote (31 per cent). Miliband, who led the Labour Party to defeat at the general election of 2015, entered the campaigning period with his own leadership satisfaction ratings (28 per cent) running close to his party's projected vote (29 per cent). On the gap between leadership satisfaction rating and the party's projected vote, Corbyn is only outnumbered by Foot, who entered the general election of 1983 with a leadership satisfaction rating of 18 per cent, which was 16 percentage points lower than the Labour Party projected vote at 34 per cent.

On the question of whether Corbyn was a "bad" leader, we can consider his leadership satisfaction ratings relative to those of the prime ministers he opposed, and then by considering former leaders of the opposition against the prime ministers that they opposed. We have already demonstrated that a link existed between regaining power and having a party leader whose satisfaction ratings outstrip those of the incumbent prime minister; see figures 16.4 and 16.7 on Blair versus Major and Cameron versus Brown, respectively. Here Blair held a lead approaching 20 percentage points over Major (Blair 51 per cent satisfied to Major 32 per cent) and Cameron held an 8 percentage-point lead over Brown (42 to 34 per cent). Of those leaders of the opposition who failed to regain power for their parties, they all trailed when comparing leadership satisfaction ratings. Kinnock trailed both Thatcher in 1987 (by 8 percentage points, 36 to 44 per cent) and Major in 1992 (by 15 percentage points, 33 to 48 per cent). For the Conservatives against Blair, both Hague and Howard trailed him; Hague by a large margin of 19 percentage points in the 2001 general election (25 to 44 per cent), and Howard by a small margin of just 3 percentage points in the 2005 general election (31 to 34 per cent). Likewise, Miliband polled lower than Cameron in the 2015 general election on leadership satisfaction: Cameron led by 10 percentage points, with Miliband on 28 per cent and Cameron on 38 per cent.

The three largest gaps were for Foot and Corbyn. At the general election of 1983 Thatcher held a 29 percentage-point lead over Foot in relation to leadership satisfaction: Foot on 19 per cent and Thatcher on 48 per cent. As Corbyn led the Labour Party into the general election of 2017 he trailed May by 29 per cent (May on 52 per cent and Corbyn on 23 per cent). As he led the Labour Party into the general election of 2019, he trailed Johnson by 21 per cent (Johnson on 37 per cent and Corbyn on 16 per cent). However, we have to acknowledge that the general election campaign exposed the limitations of May as a political communicator and campaigner, as Corbyn would go on to compete favourably with May on leadership satisfaction ratings in the period between mid-2017 and early 2018 (Atkins & Gaffney 2020).

However, this period of competitiveness in terms of leadership satisfaction does have to be placed in context. The circumstances of May versus Corbyn between June 2017 and July 2019 are complex. May was a prime minister who was leading a minority administration, pursuing a long-standing and unpopular austerity agenda, and she was simultaneously attempting to negotiate and implement a Brexit deal with the European Union within a logjammed parliament (Russell 2020; Thompson 2020). Opposition leaders have a better chance of looking comparatively effective when the prime minister is facing a confidence motion to remove her as party leader (Roe-Crines, Heppell & Jeffery 2020) and when the prime minister's political capital is diminishing because of their performative limitations and their constraining circumstances (Worthy & Bennister 2020). Conversely, Hague may have had lamentable leadership satisfaction ratings across the whole of the 1997 to 2001 parliament, but he was facing a competent, unified and well-led Labour administration, presiding over a period of economic prosperity and providing political stability (Cowley & Quayle 2002).

Alongside the two general election defeats, the opinion polling evidence suggests that Corbyn was both a "liability" and a "bad" leader, thus challenging the arguments advanced by Maiguashca and Dean (2020: 55). For example, in the aftermath of the 2019 general election reversal of the party's fortunes, voters were asked to identify their reasons for not voting Labour. When we consider those Labour voters from the general election of 2017 who could not support the Labour Party at the general election of 2019 two factors explained their defection: the Labour Party's position on Brexit and doubts about the leadership capability of Corbyn (Curtis 2019). The question of whether public opinion on party leaders in terms of perceptions of their competence *should* be an influence on voter choice is a different one from whether they are. When we consider the effectiveness of Corbyn as leader of the Labour Party and leader of the opposition, it is worth noting that Green and Jennings (2018: 11) argued that not only do perceptions of competence influence voting behaviour, but those perceptions are magnified in times of political crisis. Given that Corbyn opposed a crisis-ridden Conservative administration, it is a damning indictment on him that he was deemed to be so inferior to a series of Conservative prime ministers whose claims to competence were compromised by the convulsions created by austerity and Brexit.

# References

Alderman, K. & N. Carter 1991. "A very Tory coup: the ousting of Mrs Thatcher". *Parliamentary Affairs* 44(2): 125–39.
Allen, N., J. Bara & J. Bartle 2013. "Rules, strategies and words: the content of the 2010 prime ministerial debates". *Political Studies* 61(1): 92–113.

Allen, N., J. Bara & J. Bartle 2017. "Finding a niche? Challenger parties and issue emphasis in the 2015 televised leaders' debates". *British Journal of Politics and International Relations* 19(4): 807–23.

Allen, P. 2020. "Political science, punditry and the Corbyn problem". *British Politics* 15(1): 69–87.

Allen, P. & D. Moon 2020. "Predictions, pollification, and pol profs: the Corbyn problem beyond Corbyn". *Political Quarterly* 91(1): 80–88.

Andrews, J. & R. Jackman 2008. "If winning isn't everything, why do they keep score? Consequences of electoral performance for party leaders". *British Journal of Political Science* 38(4): 657–75.

Atkins, J. & J. Gaffney 2020. "Narrative, persona and performance: the case of Theresa May 2016–2017". *British Journal of Politics and International Relations* 22(2): 293–308.

Bale T. 2015. "If opposition is an art, is Ed Miliband an artist? A framework for evaluating leaders of the opposition". *Parliamentary Affairs* 68(1): 58–76.

Bale, T. 2016. "The loser takes it all: Labour and Jeremy Corbyn". *Political Quarterly* 87(1): 18–19.

Ball, S. 2005. "Factors in opposition performance: the Conservative experience since 1867". In S. Ball & A. Seldon (eds), *Recovering Power: The Conservatives in Opposition since 1867*, 1–27. Basingstoke: Palgrave Macmillan.

Bartle, J. & I. Crewe 2002. "The impact of party leaders in Britain: strong assumptions, weak evidence". In A. King (ed.), *Leader's Personalities and the Outcomes of Democratic Elections*, 70–95. Oxford: Oxford University Press.

Bartlett, N. 2020. "Keir Starmer admits Jeremy Corbyn's leadership was number one issue in election defeat". *Daily Mirror*, 7 May 2020. https://www.mirror.co.uk/news/politics/keir-starmer-admits-jeremy-corbyns-21988864 (accessed 24 March 2021).

Beech, M. & S. Lee (eds) 2015. *The Conservative-Liberal Coalition: Explaining the Cameron-Clegg Government*. Basingstoke: Palgrave Macmillan.

Bittner, A. 2012. *Platform or Personality? The Role of Party Leaders in Elections*. Oxford: Oxford University Press.

Brown, J. 1992. "The Major effect: changes in party leadership and party popularity". *Parliamentary Affairs* 45(4): 545–64.

Butler, D. & D. Kavanagh 1980. *The British General Election of 1979*. London: Macmillan.

Butler, D. & D. Kavanagh 1984. *The British General Election of 1983*. London: Macmillan.

Butler, D. & D. Kavanagh 1997. *The British General Election of 1997*. London: Macmillan.

Bynander, F. & P. 't Hart 2006. "When power changes hands: the political psychology of leadership succession in democracies". *Political Psychology* 27(5): 707–30.

Bynander, F. & P. 't Hart 2008. "The art of handing over: (mis)managing party leadership successions". *Government and Opposition* 43(3): 385–404.

Cammaerts, B., B. DeCillia & J.-C. Magalhaes 2020. "Journalistic transgressions in the representation of Jeremy Corbyn: from watchdog to attackdog". *Journalism* 21(1): 191–208.

Chadwick, A. 2011. "Britain's first live televised party leaders' debate: from the news cycle to the political information cycle". *Parliamentary Affairs* 64(1): 24–44.

Clarke, H. *et al.* 2004. *Political Choice in Britain*. Oxford: Oxford University Press.

Clarke, H. *et al.* 2009. *Performance Politics and the British Voter*. Cambridge: Cambridge University Press.

Clarke, H. et al. 2016. *Austerity and Political Choice in Britain*. Basingstoke: Palgrave.

Clarke, H., S. Ho & M. Stewart 2000. "Major's lesser (not minor) effects: prime ministerial approval and governing party support in Britain since 1979". *Electoral Studies* 19(2/3): 255–73.

Clarke, H. & M. Stewart 1995. "Economic evaluations, prime ministerial approval and governing party support: rival models reconsidered". *British Journal of Political Science* 25(2): 145–70.

Collings, D. & A. Seldon 2001. "Conservatives in opposition". *Parliamentary Affairs* 54(4): 624–37.

Costa-Lobo, M. & J. Curtice (eds) 2015. *Personality Politics? The Role of Leader Evaluations in Democratic Elections.* Oxford: Oxford University Press.

Cowley, P. & J. Garry 2000. "The British Conservative Party and Europe: the choosing of John Major". *British Journal of Political Science* 28(3): 473–99.

Cowley, P. & J. Green 2005. "New leaders, same problems: the Conservatives". In A. Geddes & J. Tonge (eds), *Britain Decides: The UK General Election 2005*, 46–68. Basingstoke: Palgrave Macmillan.

Cowley, P. & S. Quayle 2002. "The Conservatives: running on the spot". In A. Geddes & J. Tonge (eds), *Labour's Second Landslide: The British General Election of 2001*, 47–65. Manchester: Manchester University Press.

Crewe, I. & A. King 1994. "Did Major win? Did Kinnock lose? Leadership effects in the 1992 election". In A. Heath, R. Jowell & J. Curtice (eds), *Labour's Last Chance? The 1992 Election and Beyond*, 125–48. Aldershot: Dartmouth.

Crewe, I. & A. King 1995. *SDP: The Birth, Life and Death of the Social Democratic Party.* Oxford: Oxford University Press.

Curtis, C. 2019. "In their own words: why voters abandoned Labour". YouGov, 23 December. https://yougov.co.uk/topics/politics/articles-reports/2019/12/23/their-own-words-why-voters-abandoned-labour (accessed 24 March 2021).

Davies, G. & T. Mian 2010. "The reputation of the party leader and the party being led". *European Journal of Marketing* 44(3/4): 331–50.

Denham, A., P. Dorey & A. Roe-Crines 2020. *Choosing Party Leaders: Britain's Conservatives and Labour Compared.* Manchester: Manchester University Press.

Denver, D. 2005. "Valence politics: how Britain votes now". *British Journal of Politics and International Relations* 7(2): 292–9.

Denver, D. & M. Garnett 2012. "The popularity of British prime ministers". *British Journal of Politics and International Relations* 14(1): 57–73.

Diamond, P. 2016. "Assessing the performance of UK opposition leaders: Jeremy Corbyn's straight talking, honest politics". *Politics and Governance* 4(2): 15–24.

Dorey, P. 2017. "Jeremy Corbyn confounds his critics: explaining the Labour Party's remarkable resurgence in the 2017 Election". *British Politics* 12(3): 308–34.

Dorey, P. & A. Denham 2016. "The longest suicide vote in history: the Labour Party leadership election of 2015". *British Politics* 11(3): 259–82.

Dorey, P., M. Garnett & A. Denham 2011. *From Crisis to Coalition: The Conservative Party 1997-2010.* Basingstoke: Palgrave Macmillan.

Evans, G. & J. Tilley 2012. "How parties shape class politics: explaining the decline of the class basis of party support". *British Journal of Political Science* 42(1): 137–61.

Fernandez-Vasquez, P. & Z. Somer-Topcu 2019. "The informational role of party leader changes on voter perceptions of party positions". *British Journal of Political Science* 49(3): 977–96.

Fielding, S. 2015. "Hell, No! Labour's campaign: the correct diagnosis but the wrong doctor?". *Parliamentary Affairs* 68(S1): 54–69.

Fletcher, N. (ed.) 2011. *How to be in Opposition: Life in the Political Shadows.* London: Biteback.

French, A. & I. Smith 2010. "Measuring political brand equity: a consumer-oriented approach". *European Journal of Marketing* 44(3/4): 460–77.

Gaffney, J. 2017. *Leadership and the Labour Party: Narrative and Performance.* Basingstoke: Palgrave Macmillan.

Goes, E. 2018. "Jez, we can! Labour's campaign: defeat with a taste of victory". *Parliamentary Affairs* 71(S1): 59–71.

Goes, E. 2020. "Labour's 2019 campaign: a defeat of epic proportions". *Parliamentary Affairs* 73(S1): 84–102.

Green, J. 2007. "When voters and parties agree: valence politics and party competition". *Political Studies* 55(3): 629–55.

Green, J. & W. Jennings 2011. "Issue competence and vote choice for parties in and out of power: an analysis of valance in Britain 1979–1997". *European Journal of Political Research* 51(4): 469–503.

Green, J. & W. Jennings 2012. "Valence as macro-competence: an analysis of mood in party competence evaluations in Great Britain". *British Journal of Political Science* 42(2): 311–43.

Green, J. & W. Jennings 2018. *The Politics of Competence: Parties, Public Opinion and Voters.* Cambridge: Cambridge University Press.

Harris, K. 2020. "Jeremy Corbyn was Labour's worst leader ever – 'couldn't have been worse if he tried'". *Daily Express*, 8 April. https://www.express.co.uk/news/politics/1266775/jeremy-corbyn-labour-party-leader-poll-keir-starmer (accessed 24 March 2021).

Haskins, L. & K. Jeffrey 1990. *Understanding Quantitative History.* Cambridge, MA: MIT Press.

Heffernan, R. & M. Marqusee 1992. *Defeat from the Jaws of Victory: Inside Neil Kinnock's Labour Party.* London: Verso.

Heppell, T. 2008. *Choosing the Tory Leader: Conservative Party Leadership Elections from Heath to Cameron.* London: I. B. Tauris.

Heppell, T. 2010. *Choosing the Labour Leader: Labour Party Leadership Elections from Wilson to Brown.* London: I. B. Tauris.

Heppell, T. (ed.) 2012. *Leaders of the Opposition from Churchill to Cameron.* Basingstoke: Palgrave Macmillan.

Heppell, T. 2013. "The Fall of the Brown Government 2010". In T. Heppell & K. Theakston (eds), *How Labour Governments Fall: From Ramsay MacDonald to Gordon Brown*, 141–70. Basingstoke: Palgrave.

Heppell, T. 2019. *Cameron: The Politics of Modernisation and Manipulation.* Manchester: Manchester University Press.

Heppell, T. & T. McMeeking 2021. "The Conservative Party leadership transition from Theresa May to Boris Johnson: party popularity and leadership satisfaction". *Representation*, forthcoming.

Heppell, T., K. Theakston & D. Seawright 2015. *What Makes for an Effective Leader of the Opposition?* London: Centre for Opposition Studies.

Ipsos-Mori 2021a. 'Voting Intentions in Great Britain 2002-present' https://www.ipsos.com/ipsos-mori/en-uk/voting-intentions-great-britain-2002-present (accessed 6 April 2021).

Ipsos-Mori 2021b. 'Political Monitor: Satisfaction Ratings 1997-present' available at: https://www.ipsos.com/ipsos-mori/en-uk/political-monitor-satisfaction-ratings-1997-present (accessed 6 April 2021).

Ipsos-Mori 2021c. 'Voting Intentions in Great Britain 1976-1987' https://www.ipsos.com/ipsos-mori/en-uk/voting-intentions-great-britain-1976-1987 (accessed 6 April 2021).

Ipsos-Mori 2021d. 'Political Monitor: Satisfaction Ratings 1977-1987' https://www.ipsos.com/ipsos-mori/en-uk/political-monitor-satisfaction-ratings-1977-1987 (accessed 6 April 2021).

Ipsos-Mori 2021e. 'Political Monitor: Satisfaction Ratings 1988-1997' https://www.ipsos.com/ipsos-mori/en-uk/political-monitor-satisfaction-ratings-1988-1997 (accessed 6 April 2021).

Ipsos-Mori 2021f. 'Voting Intentions in Great Britain 1987-1997' https://www.ipsos.com/ipsos-mori/en-uk/voting-intentions-great-britain-1987-1997 (accessed 6 April 2021).

Ipsos-Mori 2021g. 'Voting Intentions in Great Britain 1997-2002', https://www.ipsos.com/ipsos-mori/en-uk/voting-intentions-great-britain-1997-2002 (accessed 6 April 2021).

Johnson, N. 1997. "Opposition in the British political system". *Government and Opposition* 32(4): 487–510.

Kavanagh, D. & P. Cowley 2010. *The British General Election of 2010.* Basingstoke: Palgrave Macmillan.

King, A. (ed.) 2002. *Leaders' Personalities and the Outcomes of Democratic Elections.* Oxford: Oxford University Press.

Langer, A. 2011. *The Personalisation of Politics in the UK: Mediated Leadership from Attlee to Cameron.* Manchester: Manchester University Press.

Lilleker, D. & R. Negrine 2003. "Not big brand names but corner shop: marketing politics to a disengaged electorate". *Journal of Political Marketing* 2(1): 55–75.

Maiguashca, B. & J. Dean 2020. "'Lovely people but utterly deluded'? British political science's trouble with Corbynism". *British Politics* 15(1): 48–68.

McAnulla, S. 2010. "Forced exits: accounting for the removal of contemporary party leaders". *Political Quarterly* 81(4): 593–601.

McAnulla, S. 2012. "Tony Blair, 1994–1997". In T. Heppell (ed.), *Leaders of the Opposition: From Winston Churchill to David Cameron*, 168–83. Basingstoke: Palgrave Macmillan.

McDowell-Naylor, D. & R. Thomas 2019. "An uncertain future for alternative online media". In D. Jackson, E. Thorsen, D. Lilleker & N. Weidhase (eds), *UK Election Analysis 2019: Media, Voters and the Campaign*, 108–9. Bournemouth: Centre for Comparative Politics and Media Research.

Mellon, J. *et al.* 2018. "Brexit or Corbyn? Campaign and inter-election vote switching in the 2017 UK general election". *Parliamentary Affairs* 71(4): 719–37.

Milazzo, C. & J. Hammond 2017. "The face of the party? Leader personalization in British campaigns". *Journal of Elections, Public Opinion and Parties* 28(3): 263–82.

Needham, C. 2005. "Brand leaders: Clinton, Blair and the limitations of the permanent campaign". *Political Studies* 53(2): 343–61.

Norton, P. 2008. "Making sense of opposition". *Journal of Legislative Studies* 14(1/2): 236–50.

Pattie, C. & R. Johnston 2011. "A tale of sound and fury, signifying something? The impact of the leaders' debates in the 2010 UK general election". *Journal of Elections, Public Opinion and Parties* 21(2): 147–77.

Peck, T. 2020. "Jeremy Corbyn just delivered a masterclass in how to be the worst party leader in political history". *The Independent*, 8 January. https://www.independent.co.uk/voices/corbyn-pmqs-boris-johnson-trump-trade-deal-brexit-commons-a9275186.html (accessed 24 March 2021).

Pierce, R. 2008. *Research Methods in Politics*. London: Sage.

Punnett, R. 1973. *Front-Bench Opposition: The Role of the Leader of the Opposition, the Shadow Cabinet and the Shadow Government in British Politics*. London: Heinemann.

Punnett, R. 1992. *Selecting the Party Leader: Britain in Comparative Perspective*. Hemel Hempstead: Harvester Wheatsheaf.

Quinn, T. 2012. *Electing and Ejecting Party Leaders in Britain*. Basingstoke: Palgrave Macmillan.

Reeves, A., M. McKee & D. Stuckler 2016. "'It's the Sun wot won it': evidence of media influence on political attitudes and voting from a UK quasi-natural experiment". *Social Science Research* 56(1): 44–57.

Reid, A. 2020. "A history of *The Sun*". https://www.historic-newspapers.co.uk/blog/sun-newspaper-history/ (accessed 24 March 2021).

Roe-Crines, A., T. Heppell & D. Jeffery 2020. "Theresa May and the Conservative Party leadership confidence motion of 2018: analysing the voting behaviour of Conservative parliamentarians". *British Politics*. https://doi.org/10.1057/s41293-020-00138-4.

Russell, M. 2020. "Brexit and Parliament: the anatomy of a perfect storm". *Parliamentary Affairs*. https://doi.org/10.1093/pa/gsaa011.

Sanders, D. *et al.* 1987. "Government popularity and the Falklands War: a reassessment". *British Journal of Political Science* 17(3): 281–313.

Scammell, M. 1999. "Political marketing: lessons for political science". *Political Studies* 47(4): 718–39.

Seldon, A. & P. Snowdon 2005. "The Conservative campaign". *Parliamentary Affairs* 58(4): 725–42.

Shaw, E. 1994. *The Labour Party since 1979: Crisis and Transformation*. London: Routledge.

Shephard, M. & R. Johns 2012. "A face for radio? How viewers and listeners reacted differently to the third leaders' debate in 2010". *British Journal of Politics and International Relations* 14(1): 1–18.

Somer-Topcu, Z. 2017. "Agree or disagree: how do party leader changes affect the distribution of voters' perceptions?". *Party Politics* 23(1): 66–75.

Smith, G. 2009. "Conceptualizing and testing brand personality in British politics". *Journal of Political Marketing* 8(3): 209–32.

Smith, G. & A. French 2011. "Measuring the changes to leader brand associations during the 2010 election campaign". *Journal of Marketing Management* 27(7/8): 718–35.

Stark, L. 1996. *Choosing a Leader: Party Leadership Contests in Britain from Macmillan to Blair*. London: Macmillan.

Stevens, D., J. Karp & R. Hodgson 2011. "Party leaders as movers and shakers in British campaigns? Results from the 2010 Election". *Journal of Elections, Public Opinion and Parties* 21(2): 125–45.

Stewart, M. & H. Clarke 1992. "The (un)importance of party leaders: leader images and party choice in the 1987 British election". *Journal of Politics* 54(2): 447–70.

Thomas, J. 2005. *Popular Newspapers, the Labour Party and British Politics*. London: Routledge.

Thompson, L. 2020. "From minority government to parliamentary stalemate: why election 2019 was needed to break the Brexit logjam". *Parliamentary Affairs* 73(S1): 48–64.

Walsh, M. 2019. "#GE2019 – Labour owns the Tories on Instagram, the latest digital battlefield". In D. Jackson *et al.* (eds), *UK Election Analysis 2019: Media, Voters and the Campaign*. www.electionanalysis.uk/ (accessed 24 March 2021).

Whiteley, P. *et al.* 2013. *Affluence, Austerity and Electoral Change in Britain*. Cambridge: Cambridge University Press.

Whiteley, P. *et al.* 2019. "Oh, Jeremy Corbyn! Why did Labour Party membership soar after the 2015 general election?". *British Journal of Politics and International Relations* 21(1): 80–98.

Worthy, B. & M. Bennister 2020. "Dominance, defence and diminishing returns? Theresa May's leadership capital, July 2016–July 2018". *British Politics*. https://doi.org/10.1057/s41293-020-00133-9.

Wring, D. & D. Deacon 2019. "The final verdict: patterns of press partisanship". In D. Jackson *et al.* (eds), *UK Election Analysis 2019: Media, Voters and the Campaign*. www.electionanalysis.uk/ (accessed 24 March 2021).

Wring, D. & S. Ward 2010. "The media and the 2010 campaign: the television election?" *Parliamentary Affairs* 63(4): 802–17.

# INDEX